REASON FOR THE HOPE WITHIN

REASON FOR THE HOPE WITHIN

Edited by

Michael J. Murray

William B. Eerdmans Publishing Company
Grand Rapids, Michigan / Cambridge, U.K.

2140 Oak Industrial Drive N.E., Grand Rapids, Michigan 49505 /
P.O. Box 163, Cambridge CB3 9PU U.K.

Printed in the United States of America

11 10 09 08 07 06   11 10 9 8 7 6 5

Library of Congress Cataloging-in-Publication Data

Reason for the hope within / edited by Michael J. Murray.
p. cm.
ISBN-10: 0-8028-4437-5 / ISBN-13: 0-8028-4437-8 (pbk. : alk. paper)
1. Christianity — Philosophy. I. Murray, Michael J.
BR100.R35 1999
239 — dc21 98-49100
CIP

www.eerdmans.com

Contents

Acknowledgments

In preparing this book, the authors gathered for two weeks in July of 1997 at Gordon College in Wenham, Massachusetts, to read through and discuss the manuscript collectively. Following this two-week period, the authors, in conjunction with the Center for Christian Studies and Gordon College, sponsored a two-day apologetics workshop for Christian leaders and laity from the New England area. During the workshop, authors presented the material from these chapters in small group settings in order to provide some "hands on" training in apologetics, as well as to "road test" the material for this volume. Both the authors' conference and the workshop were instrumental in producing this book. Without both of them, it is unlikely this work would have ever made it to completion.

So many people were involved in launching and seeing through the conference and the workshop, it is hard to acknowledge them all. Thanks must first of all go out to Tom and Lynn Shields for the enthusiasm and vision they exhibited for this project before it was even formally underway. Their encouragement, advice, and financial support in bringing about the conference and the book were critical to getting these projects through their birth pangs. All of the authors are deeply grateful to Gordon College, the Center for Christian Studies, and a few individuals who supported and financed these events. First and foremost we thank Harold Heie, Director of the Center for Christian Studies. Harold's vision for this project very early on allowed it to become something more than any of us could have dreamed. His determination and hard work were the main reason the conference and workshop happened.

In addition we would like to thank Gordon College President Jud Carlburg and Provost Mark Sargent for their support and nurture of this project. Very special thanks are due to Dwight and Deborah Anderson, Preston and Pamela Mason, Charles and Carol Purdy, Tom and Mary Morris, Alvin Plantinga, and to Millersville Bible Church (PA). They had faith in this project and in turn provided the financial and moral support that brought it to fruition.

We are also deeply indebted to Amy Kvistad, Ron Hilton, and Chris Underation of Gordon College for the untiring efforts at working out all of the million details for our summer gathering.

We are especially grateful to those who attended and participated in the workshops with us. They provided us with invaluable feedback as we "road tested" this material. Their forthrightness helped us see when the material was too difficult or not relevant to their concerns. The changes that resulted from this feedback have been nothing short of drastic. We are also grateful to Peter Kreeft and Gordon MacDonald for their support of and participation in the two-day workshop.

All of the authors would like to express their gratitude to Eleonore Stump, William Alston, Brian Leftow, William Wainwright, Laura Ekstrom, and Kelly Monroe for their participation in the conference as well. Their encouragement, mature guidance, and helpful feedback were instrumental in guiding our subsequent revisions.

All of the authors would also like to thank their spouses for their patience during that summer event. Many of them had to endure van rides to Boston from as far away as Texas and Wyoming. Since most of the authors have small children, spouses spent a number of very hot days and nights in dorm rooms running around after a dizzying blur of children and babies while we worked on this book. No expression of our appreciation could adequately measure our gratitude for their loving support. We promise air conditioning next time!

An extra measure of thanks is due to my wife, Kirsten, and my three children, Sam, Elise, and Julia. Not only did they have to endure some of the trying circumstances surrounding our summer event, but they had to put up with the many hours of planning, meetings, trips, etc., that preceded it. In addition, Kirsten willingly took on the difficult role of conference organizer during much of the year preceding the conference and was the "go to" person for many of the practical details during that summer. Her exceptional organizational talents made so much of this seem effortless. Without her many hours of time on the phone, on e-mail, writing letters, etc., I would surely have made a mess of things.

Finally, I would like to thank the three senior pastors under whom I have sat during my Christian life. Rich Ainsworth, Craig Clapper, and Steve Butts not only ignited and sustained in me a hunger for a knowledge of and a relationship with God, but, through their teaching, fed me more richly than I could have hoped for. I have been truly blessed to have been instructed by them. But beyond being good teachers and expositors of the Scriptures, they were and are men who have modeled the godly Christian life *in excelsis*. It is to them that this book is dedicated.

Michael J. Murray

Foreword

Reason for the Hope Within is a wonderful idea, splendidly executed. Further, its presence and execution is a greatly encouraging sign. When I began teaching philosophy forty years ago, the conventional wisdom was that Christianity was doomed; it might persist in a few culturally isolated pockets — the deep south, perhaps, and maybe western Michigan — but its future was continued marginalization, irrelevance, and diminution to museum status. This process was particularly clear in academia, where the process was already far advanced.

Of course this wasn't the first time for such predictions: one thinks of Voltaire's and Thomas Jefferson's expression of similar sentiments in the eighteenth century, and of Nietzsche's strident declarations in the nineteenth. Like them, this one turned out decidedly premature.[2] Christian belief is doing much better than predicted. This is true even in academia and even in philosophy, which has not traditionally been thought a bastion in defense of the faith. Indeed, this is true especially in philosophy; a fairly sizeable proportion of this country's philosophers are prepared to identify themselves as Christians by way of membership in the Society of Christian Philosophers or the American Catholic Philosophical Association. The fact is plain even if the reasons are obscure: there is now more serious involvement with Christian thought in philosophy than there has been for a very long time.

Now one presumes that being a Christian will make a difference to one's philosophy. Centrally important here is this: a Christian philosopher will take seriously her responsibility to the broader Christian community.

She will see herself as in the presence of the Lord and her work in the light of Christian faith. But that can cast a decidedly different slant on things. What is philosophy for, and why should a Christian work at it? Not just because (like Mt. Everest) it is there, not just as a career (and certainly not because it is a way of raising oneself above one's untutored fellows); and not even just because it is supremely interesting and absorbing. Rather, working at philosophy is one way, even if a humble way, of serving the Lord.

How does one do that, in philosophy? One way, no doubt, is by producing beautiful philosophical work: by rolling back the frontiers of knowledge, by penetrating further into a given area than has been done before, by putting various elements together into a powerful picture. But this is not something Christian philosophers need to be invited or advised to do; they are already invited, nay, urged to do this by the whole structure of the profession. They are brought up, as philosophers, to think that their main allegiance is to the philosophical community at large, and that real success consists in winning the plaudits and exciting the admiration (and envy) of other philosophers. And that means that what one writes can ordinarily be read only by other philosophers.

Work of this kind is indeed imperative, and part of the Christian philosopher's service to the Lord. But there is another way of serving the Lord that is at least as important. This involves serving his children, the Christian community. That community needs to know how to think about a thousand things. For example, we are currently bombarded by claims to the effect that we must understand ourselves in terms of our evolutionary origin; and the kind of evolution in question is not to be thought of as guided or orchestrated by the hand of God. Nearly every issue of the *New York Review of Books* contains a review of another volume in which someone, a scientist or perhaps scientist wannabe, proposes to explain some important element of our human life — morality, religion, humor, music, aggression, science itself — in terms of our animal origins. These vary from the serious to the trivial: according to Michael Ruse and Edmond Wilson, morality is a trick played on us by our genes; according to Steven Pinker, we human beings like lawns because we evolved on the grassy plains of Africa. (I suppose a corresponding Christian just-so story would be that we human beings like gardens because of our origin in the garden of Eden.) The Christian community needs to know how to think about these things, and how to think more generally about science and its relation to the Christian faith. And of course this is just one example out of many. Contemporary Christians face many issues: perennial questions of pain and suffering and evil, questions about religious pluralism and other religions, wild and woolly postmodern claims about truth, questions about the nature of faith, about how to live and raise one's children in a pluralist society, about divine providence and human freedom, about miracles, heaven and hell, the future life, the nature of biblical authority. All of these issues and others are often baffling, perplexing, and troubling. The Christian community needs clarity and leadership in thinking about them. Christians want and need to know about these matters, and do not necessarily want to be obliged first to get a Ph.D. in philosophy.

And that brings us to this book. What we have here is an effort to address some of these questions and topics — an effort that is serious, but also couched in language that is available to the Christian community at large, not just other philosophers or other academics. These philosophers recognize the very sort of responsibility I was just mentioning, and have gone out and done something about it. And what is particularly interesting and heartening about this particular venture is that nearly all of the contributors are *young* philosophers. This is not your typical scenario, where some senior scientist, having made his mark in his field, steps back in later life to offer some valedictory reflections on the human condition (in a book reviewed in the *New York Review of Books*). These are people who take time out from their struggle to get tenure and from ordinary academic pursuits to do something that doesn't contribute much to academic success or getting tenure. (Indeed, it sometimes counts against it.) But what they have done is something of real importance for the Christian community.

So this book is an occasion for thanksgiving. It is of course a mere beginning; we have an extraordinarily long way to go. But it *is* a beginning, and an auspicious beginning. I say Bravo!

Alvin Plantinga

Introduction

Michael J. Murray

"But why do you think *that?*" It was a question that rang in the ears of the fellow who witnessed to me throughout the summer of 1980. It was during that summer that the two of us shared a monotonous job that afforded us plenty of time for conversation. The job? Repotting fifteen thousand Mountain Laurel plants at a local nursery. Let me tell you, this wasn't brain surgery. And so we filled the time talking about baseball, the Beatles (in *1980?*), college plans, and, along the way, his Christian belief.

Being a fairly vigorous atheist I was not about to be persuaded. But since conversation was the only merit to the job, we talked . . . and talked and talked and talked. . . . It was in September of that year when the Holy Spirit moved my heart and led me to repentance and surrender. But the questioning spirit that I had during the summer didn't go away. And when I arrived on the campus of Franklin and Marshall College in the fall of '81, I found plenty more people who were asking the same questions I had been asking. With all the enthusiasm of a typical young Christian I spent a great deal of time talking to folks on my hall and in my classes about the gospel. And as I did, I was challenged to think hard about my own faith. This in turn prompted me to drop most of my semester allowance at the local Christian bookstore where I feasted for the first time on the writings of Norman Geisler, R. C. Sproul, Gordon Lewis, Clark Pinnock, Cornelius van Til, B. B. Warfield, Wilbur Smith, John Warwick Montgomery, Francis Schaeffer, F. F. Bruce, and on and on.

It wasn't long before I realized that my interest in these matters was, well, extraordinarily strong. So, at the end of the summer following my freshman year, I returned to campus, canceled all my preregistered courses, and signed up for a philosophy major (the most reasonable home for a budding Christian apologist). As I spent more time with my admittedly unsympathetic professors, I tried out some of the moves I was learning from the Christian reading I had been doing. I was disappointed that I was meeting with less than complete success. They just seemed to be able to come up with very effective counterpunches to the arguments I was raising.

As I reached the end of my college career I went through a long struggle trying to decide whether I should continue my schooling in an apologetics program in seminary or at a graduate school in philosophy. I ended up following the latter course and with no regrets. I entered graduate school at the University of Notre Dame fully realizing that it was considered to be the central think-tank for Christian philosophy. But what I found as I began my study there was nothing at all like those things I had been learning from the apologetics literature. The aim was the same, but the material was altogether different. These folks were addressing many of the same questions addressed in the traditional apologetics literature, but in doing so they were taking advantage of the most recent resources and information that the academic world had to offer.

As you might imagine, I was a bit surprised at this dichotomy of approaches. Why was it that the folks teaching apologetics at evangelical seminaries were accessing one pool of information, while those in graduate programs with an emphasis in Christian philosophy were accessing an entirely different pool? I am still not sure of the answer. In part, it appears that it is the same phenomenon that suppresses interdisciplinary research in other areas. It is the sort of partisanship that keeps psychologists and neurochemists (or psychiatrists for that matter!) apart, not to mention anthropologists and religious studies specialists, sociologists and ethicists, and so on. There is plenty of room for cross-fertilization in all of these areas, but it happens only in fits and starts.

Part of the reason for the divide is surely that contemporary Christian philosophy is a Johnny-come-lately. In the half-century prior to 1970, there was almost no work done on Christian philosophy in mainstream academic philosophy. In fact, identifying oneself as a Christian or even a theist before that time was often to put oneself at risk of considerable derision. But the tide has turned dramatically over the last twenty-five years. In that period of time, the work of philosophers such as Alvin Plantinga, Robert and Marilyn Adams, William Alston, Eleonore Stump, Peter van Inwagen, Richard Swinburne, and numerous others has brought uniquely

Christian philosophical work back into the center of the contemporary philosophical scene. Now there are numerous journals devoted to philosophy of religion and Christian philosophy, sundry annual Christian philosophy conferences held at major colleges and universities around the country, a vast number of books from major university presses on topics in Christian philosophy (topics as centrally Christian as the nature of atonement, the Incarnation, the Trinity, miracles, hell, etc.). And in the midst of all this, there is a thriving Society of Christian Philosophers, founded in 1978, which has since grown to become the largest special interest group in the American Philosophical Association.

The gap between the work being done in Christian philosophy and in seminary apologetics is totally inexcusable. And it is a gap that divides in both directions. Christian philosophy students at Notre Dame don't read Montgomery, Bruce, or Warfield. Seminary apologetics students don't read Plantinga, Stump, or van Inwagen. And since most of our pastors are taught by the partisans of seminary apologetics, the work of Christian philosophers just has not trickled down out of the ivory tower and into the pews. That is a sad state of affairs. It is sad not only because a significant body of very high-quality work on apologetics has not made it to the laity, but also (and now I am afraid I will have to tip my own hand a bit) because this work is oftentimes of better quality.

Since that last remark is likely to upset a few people, I need to qualify it a bit. The work that has been done by seminary apologists (or at least the work which has made it into the Christian bookstores) is pitched at a certain level. It presupposes no particular background in theology or philosophy, and usually it does not presuppose any prior academic preparation. As a result it can only take the reader so far into the relevant issues. The work being done in Christian philosophy circles has no such restrictions. In fact, most of it is written in such a way that it is utterly inaccessible to those without a significant measure of background in theology and philosophy. As a result, the work being done in those circles goes on at a deeper level. But the depth of the work simultaneously precludes that work from having much of an impact on the church at large.

I recall having a number of talks with fellow graduate students about this gap in the Christian literature. We would lament together the fact that no one had taken the time to put the work of recent Christian philosophy into a format that would make it accessible to the lay person. At one point I remember sitting with a group of them over lunch, making a pact that if we survived graduate school and made it through tenure, we would produce such a book, if no one beat us to it. I received tenure in 1996. And since no such book has yet appeared, what you hold in your hands is the fulfillment of the pact.

Our aim here is not to present what philosophers whimsically call "beach reading." While this book is a condensation of recent work in Christian philosophy, and while it presupposes no special background in philosophy, we aim to make you work a bit here. There just aren't many books of this sort that force you to stretch intellectually. We want you to stretch here. As a result, this is a book that is to be read with pencil in hand, in a quiet place, alone, a full chapter at a time. Don't try to read three paragraphs per day. Don't read it with the Walkman on (much less the TV!). Don't try to read a page per minute. While we have done our best to fill the text with pointed illustrations and helpful examples, the topics under discussion here are deep and hard. And Christians who want to have a good grasp of their faith, a grasp that will allow them to share confidently with others, will want to get a good intellectual workout in preparation. It is worth adding here as well that this is not a book for everyone. It is for those who have a deep intellectual curiosity about their faith and who are willing to invest a bit of time in satisfying that curiosity. In this way, cultivating a thoughtful Christian faith is analogous to gourmet cooking. While one can slog through the world securing nutrition from ready-made microwaveable food, there is a gustatory pleasure to be had from food well-prepared that just can't be had without a significant investment of time (or, alternatively, money). Likewise, one can't come to a deep and reflective view of one's faith without a sincere and concerted effort. The sort of effort that will be required, and richly rewarded, by those who take some time with the pages of this book.

1

Reason for Hope (in the Postmodern World)

Michael J. Murray

As indicated in the Introduction, this book is an attempt to present a broad-reaching Christian apologetic or defense of the Christain faith. Before we begin, however, it is of the utmost importance that we pause briefly to discuss exactly what it is that a "defense of the Christian faith" is supposed to do. Is it supposed to present us with arguments that will bring all non-Christians to their intellectual knees? Is it supposed to show without question that the Christian worldview is more compelling than any other worldview? In order to understand how this book should be used, we need to answer these questions first.

Defenses of the Christian faith of the sort we are offering in this book have two aims. The first, and I think primary, aim of such a defense is that it builds up the believer by helping him or her to understand the deep, puzzling, seemingly paradoxical riches of the Christian faith. Such building up helps believers better understand their faith and, more importantly, to appreciate in more profound fashion the glory of the Creator they love and serve. In addition, this deeper understanding helps them to share their faith with others. It can do this because the more intimately we understand what it is we are sharing the more intelligently and convincingly we can do so.

Ambassadorial Apologetics

The biblical notion of the Christian as ambassador for the kingdom of God is particularly instructive in helping to sort out the relationship between these two aims of apologetics. Imagine that you are the leader of a small island nation that is economically dependent on tourism. For you and your nation, it is very important to have ambassadorial representatives who will go to other nations in order to represent your interests and to portray your land in a positive light. Whom would you choose? I, at any rate, would choose someone who was both head over heels in love with their nation and who knew how to generate that sort of enthusiasm in others who had never before visited. Part of what is required to have those abilities is a very thorough knowledge of the land. You would need to be able to tell people all about the place and why they would love it as much as you do. The Christian ambassador in a way has similar aims. God wants believers to love their "homeland" and to know enough about it to be able to tell others about it effectively. And to do this we need to have a detailed understanding of the "lay of the land."

Notice, however, that in both cases, we would want someone whose love for the homeland is primary; love which in turn motivates their wanting to know it inside and out. In other words, the president searching for his ambassador doesn't want someone who simply sounds like he swallowed the almanac. Having the facts down is important, but the job can't be effectively carried off if one is just a proficient reciter of facts. (Imagine a travel brochure that consisted of a photocopy of the relevant page from the world almanac. That, we can all agree, would not be effective advertising!) It is odd, then, that we often think of Christian apologetics in just this way. When I have taught adult Sunday school classes on apologetics I find many people who simply want to memorize all the relevant facts so they can go out in the world and recite them in just the right order. Their aim is noble, but the procedure is wrong. Like the ambassador, we need to become people who want to understand our "homeland" simply because we love the Lord and want to know him better. When we have gotten this far, we are ready to absorb the depths of the Christian faith which in turn makes us ready to share it with others.

I fear that putting it as I have above will make some readers think that evangelism is only for the experts. Far from it! While the Christian faith is as deep, puzzling, and unfathomable as any aspect of theoretical physics, the fundamental message of the gospel is straightforward. And as believers it is this simple message that we are compelled to share with the world. Nonetheless, we have all encountered people whose doubts about the Christian faith run deep. And although it is oftentimes difficult to know what to say to such skeptics, we are obliged to do what we can to honestly address their doubts. What follows in this book is an attempt to provide some assistance with this task.

As mentioned in the Introduction, our aim is to give the late twentieth-century church a chance to look in on the discussion of these matters that has been unfolding in the arena of academic Christian philosophy. In doing this, we hope that this book will act as a primer for an apologetic for the church as it enters the third millennium.

Recent Challenges to the Apologetic Enterprise

But before we turn to this task, let's consider some recent challenges that the late twentieth century is offering to the project of "defending the Christian faith" or religious belief of any sort. These recently raised challenges come as much from within the Church as from without. As I discussed this project with a number of folks over the last few years, I often met with a remark that went something like this: no one will read a book like that because people just don't ask those sorts of questions anymore. To this I responded "why not?" And the answer that came back (when there was an answer at all) would almost always point to one of the three "bogeymen" of our so-called postmodern age. These three bogeymen have as their task to scare people away from doing apologetics or even raising apologetic-type questions. And so, before we get down to business, it is only appropriate to pause long enough to say something about the bogeymen in order to allay our fears about them and give us confidence to press on.

The three bogeymen are skepticism, relativism, and antirealism. Christians are often at least acquainted with the first two; few have met up with the third (at least as far as they know). Below I will give a brief description of each and how each can be seen as undermining the project of Christian apologetics. After this I will take a look at each of these three challenges and say a few words about how the Christian should respond to them.

One more word before I go on. The aim of this book is to take what has been happening in the halls of academic Christian philosophy and make it accessible and useful to church leaders and laity. I am aware of the fact that no small number of professional Christian academics will have a look at this book, and no doubt at this chapter. My aim here is not to resolve all the intramural academic disputes about "presuppositionalism," "deconstruction," "metanarratives," "paradigms," "incommensurability," "plausibility structures," the "autonomy of human reason," and the long list of other technical jargon-filled topics. I think the things I say here will carve out what I take to be a new position in much of the literature that worries about apologetics. But my aim is not to make heavy weather over that fact. My aim is simply to present what I take to be the very best and most current philosophical thinking about the epistemology of "worldviews," presented in an accessible manner.

Bogeyman Number One: Skepticism

In general, a skeptic is someone who thinks that people are duty bound to refrain from coming to hold beliefs on some matter or other. Skepticism comes in a wide variety of flavors. Some think that the scope of our skepticism should extend farther than others. *Mitigated skeptics* think that we should refrain from coming to settled beliefs only about certain areas of knowledge; *global skeptics,* on the other hand, think that we ought to withhold belief on *all* matters (or at least all matters except one: that we should withhold belief on everything except the skeptical injunction). Some skeptics are more humble in their skepticism than others. That is, some skeptics think that we should withhold belief because, for example, we have not yet collected enough evidence about a certain matter to know the right answers with confidence (so, one might be "skeptical," for example, about whether or not physicists have now identified the true fundamental particles in nature); others, however, might think that there is something about our human powers of inquiry that simply make knowledge about certain things *absolutely impossible,* no matter how much data we gather. Knowledge of some things, they argue, is just beyond the human intellectual capacities.

It should be clear, then, how at least some versions of skepticism might serve to undermine apologetics. If one thinks that religious or theological claims are ones that are simply beyond the reach of human intellectual powers or that the evidence available to us simply can't settle the matter, then one will think that apologetics is simply doomed to failure. This is one issue that comes up semester after semester in my discussions with college students. Students are usually convinced up front, without ever having examined the matter, that these subjects are just not fit for resolution by us meager-minded humans. And so, a Christian who wants to defend his or her faith will need to say something about why skepticism does not undermine this project.

Bogeyman Number Two: Relativism

Relativism is a bit more insidious doctrine. A relativist holds that the truth cannot be known about some subject matter or other. In this way the relativist is like the skeptic. But the skeptic thinks that the problem is that we, for some reason or other, can't (yet) get to the truth. The relativist on the other hand thinks that we can't get to the truth because there simply is *no truth to be known*. Even this characterization oversimplifies matters a bit. An example will help us to sort out exactly what the relativist has in mind. Imagine that someone stops you on the street and says the following "I am with the ABC market research firm and we are doing a survey trying to determine which tastes better: vanilla or chocolate. Could you tell us?" You reply, "Well, I am not sure what you mean. Are you asking me what flavor *I* think is better?" "No," the inquirer replies, "We want to know which is *actually* better, not just which one *you think* is better." It is pretty clear that the person asking the question here is confused. They think that there is a single right answer to the question of which tastes better. But of course, which flavor tastes better depends on whom you ask. To me, chocolate is better, to another vanilla is better. The claim, "Chocolate tastes better than vanilla," is neither true for everyone nor false for everyone. Whether it is true or false depends on whom you ask. And, in this sense, the claim is *relative*.

Put this way, you can see that what I said above is strictly speaking false. The relativist doesn't think that there is *no truth* to be known. There is a truth to be known, but the truth in question is not *intersubjective*. That is, the same claim might be true for some folks and at the very same time be false for others. Most of us think that claims concerning *manners* or *matters of taste* are relative in this way. Whether putting your napkin in your lap at mealtime is good or bad is dependent upon the customs or beliefs in a given culture. Similarly, whether "Vanilla tastes better than chocolate" is true or false depends on whom you ask. Most of my students believe (at least initially) that all ethical claims are likewise relative or subjective. But some want to claim that religious claims are like this as well. If they are right, of course, then the project of apologetics, the project of trying to convince the unbeliever of the rational superiority of the

Christian worldview, looks as silly as trying to convince the vanilla lover that chocolate *really is* better.

Bogeyman Number Three: Antirealism

Antirealism and relativism are not unrelated doctrines. But let me try to separate them as completely as possible here. A "realist" as I am using the term here is someone who thinks that there is an *objective, mind-independent reality* to be known, and that the beliefs that we come to hold about the world represent (or fail to represent) the world "as it is." An "antirealist" on the other hand is one who thinks that the description of the world that we carry around with us is one that might be thoroughly *adequate for our purposes,* but they deny that this description maps onto "the way the world really is."

A brief example will help us to get a grip on what the antirealist has in mind. Most of us are aware of a bit of physics, at least enough physics to know that perceiving the color of an object is something that happens when light reflects off an object with a certain wavelength. Visible light with short wavelengths appears purple, whereas visible light with long wavelengths appears red. Wavelength in both cases is a measure of the energy level of the light which is reflected. Short wavelength equals higher energy, long wavelength equals lower energy. To summarize our brief physics lesson, what happens when you see color is that light of a certain energy level bounces off some object and hits you in the eye!

Now let's say that you are admiring your friend's blue dress one day. What is it exactly that you are admiring here? "Well, the color," you say. But imagine that I am a physicist, a physicist who then responds to you in the following way:

> "You say that you are admiring the color, and I agree. But what this really means is that you are admiring the *sensation of blue* that you find inside your mind when you perceive that dress. You may think that is an odd way of putting it since you may think that the blue color you are admiring is not 'in your mind' but is a feature, property, or characteristic of the dress. But of course, you can't be right about that. All that this dress does is reflect light of a certain energy. That light then cause nerves in your eye to fire in a certain way, and those patterns of firing generate a sensation in your mind, a *sensation of the color blue.* But this means that the color blue isn't *really out there* in *the dress.* The

dress is just a bunch of molecules reflecting energetic light. It is *your mind* that converts stimuli produced by the energetic light into a 'picture,' and in doing so it makes different wavelengths of light result in colored sensations of a certain sort in your mind. As a result, it is not that the *dress* is blue, it is just that the dress reflects wavelengths of light which your mind *converts* into a sensation of blue.

"If the point is still eluding you, think of it this way. There is no reason in principle why those wavelengths of light that you perceive as blue might not instead have been perceived as red. And the wavelengths you now perceive as red, might have instead given rise to sensations of blue in you."

This physicist is explaining why it is that we should think that color is not really a feature of objects (or, you might say "in" the objects), but is instead a result of how we "digest" certain sorts of external stimuli.

This is not an easy point to see. But once one sees it one realizes how compelling this picture is. The same point seems to hold for other qualitative components of our experience. There is no "salty taste" out there *in the world,* there is just sodium chloride which gives rise to a certain sensation (a "salty" one) *in me*. Further, there is no hot or cold "out there in the world." There are simply objects with molecules of varying energy levels. Energetic ones give rise to a sensation of "hot" *in us* whereas ones with less energy give rise to sensations of "cold" *in us.* The famous seventeenth-century philosopher René Descartes made this point by noting how odd it is that we think that boiling water really does have heat *in it* since it feels hot when we put our hand nearby, but that we do not think that pain is *in* the water, even though that is the sensation we get when we put our hand *in* the boiling water! Why do we think heat is in the water but not pain? Descartes' solution is to say, as our imaginary physicist has above, that neither the heat nor the pain are *in* the fire. Both are merely sensations *in us.*

What does all of this have to do with antirealism and apologetics? Notice that our common practice is to think of the world as having objects that are *really colored* or *really hot or cold* even after we recognize the points made above. Our operating picture of the world puts these characteristics *out there* even though in our more reflective moments we realize that they really are not. I talk about the "blue dress" though I don't literally mean "the dress which itself is blue." In this way, you might say, I am an *antirealist* about color. While the view of the world that I carry around inside and work with every day attributes properties of color *to things in the world,* in reality, I think there is no color *in the world.* And this fits nicely with the definition of antirealism I gave above according to which "an antirealist . . . is one who thinks that the description of the world that we carry around with us is one that might be thoroughly adequate for our purposes, but they deny that this picture maps onto 'the way the world really is.'"

Now as with skepticism, antirealism comes in different varieties. Some are antirealists about color and heat; others might be antirealist about the fundamental particles that physics proposes (quarks, etc.). Some might be antirealists about the existence of a material world;[1] others might be antirealists about anything "nonscientific"; and, increasingly commonly, some are antirealists about "everything." It is not hard to see how an antirealism with broad scope might undercut the project of apologetics. If one were an antirealist with respect to religious matters, or with respect to everything (the view that is characteristic of most species of so-called "postmodern" philosophy), then apologetics would be tantamount to arguing with someone about whether or not the water in the swimming pool is really cold or not. For some it will feel cold (those who just jumped out of the spa, for example), whereas for others, it really does feel warm. Each view is right and "works" for those situated in that way.

Handling the Bogeymen: A Christian Reflection

What then should the Christian say about these three challenges to the project of apologetics? Most Christians, upon considering the threat posed here, are tempted simply to dismiss all three challenges. If we deny skepticism, relativism, and antirealism, then there is no foe to worry about. But this would be a mistake. While certain forms of these positions might undermine attempts to defend the Christian faith, this is no cause to reject them entirely. So let's take a more careful look at these three positions, finding what we can in them that a Christian can agree with.

On Skepticism

Let's begin with skepticism. Above I noted that skepticism comes in a variety of flavors. Some are mitigated skeptics, others global skeptics. As ev-

1. As even some Christian thinkers have been, such as the Irish philosopher George Berkeley in the eighteenth century.

eryone knows, the most global form of skepticism, the one that says "doubt everything," is incoherent. The reason it is incoherent is that it is self-refuting: believing in it would require that you not believe in it, and that is an impossible trick to pull off! So, coherent global skeptics instead argue that our mental faculties are so weak or their resources so limited, etc. that the best we can do is to withhold judgment on all of our beliefs except those few that explain how beliefs should be governed. Seen in this way, the difference between global skepticism and mitigated skepticism is merely one of degree. Mitigated skeptics might carve out certain areas of knowledge as beyond our grasp; global skeptics might argue that all areas are beyond our reach.

But it is worth noting to start out that Christians themselves are obliged to be skeptics in certain respects. That is, like the mitigated skeptic, we too think that there are facts about reality which are simply beyond the grasp of our finite intellectual powers. Scripture itself tells us that "God's ways are not our ways" and that "His thoughts are not our thoughts." Most Christians take this to mean that there are some things known to the mind of God that just are not knowable to us (notice, I did not say there are some things known to God which are not *known* to us; rather, the claim is that there are some things that are known to God that are not *knowable* to us). The nature of the Trinity or the way in which God brings about creation out of nothing might be two things which are simply beyond our comprehension. But it might turn out that even much more mundane things are beyond the grasp of the human mind. For example, we might think that the ultimate makeup of physical reality is beyond our grasp.

But if we are going to count a certain area of inquiry as beyond our grasp, we need to have some good reason for doing so. So, the person who is skeptical about our ability to discover the ultimate makeup of physical reality might be skeptical about such matters because they think that such knowledge could only come, say, from building particle accelerators that are bigger than any that we can build. When it comes to the topics discussed in this book, then, the obvious question to ask is: does the skeptic have any *good reason* for thinking the sorts of things discussed under the heading of apologetics are beyond our grasp? While any answer to this question would be controversial, I think we can safely answer "no." Without a doubt, there are some philosophers who think that we must be skeptical about the things discussed in apologetics. But their reasons for thinking so are not at all widely accepted. I will discuss some of these below, since some think that relativism and antirealism themselves are good reasons to be skeptical when it comes to matters of religion. But aside from these, I think that the skeptical arguments raised as a challenge to the project of apologetics are not compelling.

But if the sorts of things discussed in this book are not beyond our grasp, and if we have arguments to offer in favor of the Christian perspective on them, then, if the arguments really are good ones, we should be able to win the unbeliever over to our side, right? Not exactly. And it is a question like this that leads us straight to the heart of the issues raised by relativism and antirealism.

On Relativism and Antirealism

When someone who is not a Christian comes to you and asks you why you believe in the Christian faith, what do you say to them? The answers Christians have given me when I have asked them this question vary widely. Some say things such as "I believe in Jesus because he changed my life" or "I believe in God because I have felt the power of his presence in prayer or in the Word." These are, to my mind, perfectly satisfactory answers. But they don't really answer the question that the unbeliever meant to ask: why should I believe the things that you believe about the Christian faith? Why should I think that the Christian story or the Christian worldview is true? This is a harder question to answer because while it might be true that I believe in God because I have experienced him working in *my* life, the unbeliever has no such experience to draw on. So, why should *they* believe?

"Sledgehammer Apologetics" and Its Discontents

The official line taken by most Christian apologists is this: they should believe because it turns out that certain claims they accept entail distinctive parts of the Christian worldview. For example, the official line says, the unbeliever thinks that *order does not arise out of chance* but instead occurs by design. In addition, the unbeliever thinks that *the universe exhibits a significant amount of order.* Thus, the unbeliever is obliged to think that the universe arose not *out of chance* but *by design.* And, the official line continues, we can continue this exercise for other distinctive areas of the Christian worldview. In this way, we show the unbeliever that they are rationally compelled to believe in the central features of the Christian view and that failure to do so leaves them *irrational* in this respect.

This is what one might call "sledgehammer apologetics." The sledgehammer apologist thinks that apologetic arguments deliver the intellectual equivalent of knockout punches by making it impossible for unbelievers to rationally continue in their unbelief. But there is a serious problem with sledgehammer apologetics. Let me explain what it is by way of an example.

Consider Fred, a city apartment dweller who returns home from work one day to find his window smashed and his television missing. Fred takes note of these facts and asks himself what the explanation for the facts is. He thinks that it is likely that he was robbed. But, unsure, he invites over two of his friends, Charity and Kirk, to help him figure out what has happened. Charity is a warm, kind person who thinks that other people in the world are essentially warm and kind as well. Whenever something bad happens, she always prefers to think that the parties involved had good motives driving their behaviors. Kirk is an odd character. Having spent his childhood buried in science fiction comic books and now hooked on the series "The X-Files," he often favors fantastic and otherworldly explanations for things.

Charity looks over the situation and says this: "It is clear to me what has happened here, Fred. Some kids were playing with a ball and accidentally threw it through your window. They must have then climbed in and removed the ball. Then your neighbor, seeing the broken window, climbed in and removed your TV in order to keep it safe until you returned."

Kirk, on the other hand, draws a quite different conclusion. He looks over the scene nervously and says, "Oh no. Oh no. *That's* not what happened! I've seen this sort of thing before! I've heard that every once in a while, monitors on alien spaceships need to be replaced. Rather than going back to their home planet, the aliens swoop in on a nearby planet with an advanced society and beam up working television sets. When they do this the tractor beam can create a great deal of heat which causes the air in the room to expand and BOOM!, the windows in the room where the television is located shatter. That's what's going on here. Yep. I'm sure of it."

Fred considers these explanations and asks himself what to make of them. What is most reasonable to believe here? Is it more reasonable to believe the crook story, the neighbor story, or the alien story? Notice that each theory gives an explanation for all the facts. Fred decides that he needs to collect more evidence in order to sort through the explanations, and so he begins with a visit to his neighbor. He knocks on the door and politely asks the neighbor if he knows anything about the broken window.

The neighbor shrugs his shoulder and offers no help. "Well," Fred says to Charity, "so much for your 'friendly neighbor' theory."

"Not so fast," Charity replies. "This doesn't necessarily refute my explanation. I stick by my original theory, and I think I have an explanation for what just happened here. The explanation is this: your neighbor believes that an impostor would be coming to his door trying to get hold of the television that he is protecting. When you knocked, he believed that you were the impostor and so he denied having the television set."

Fred has provided evidence that seemed to refute Charity's hypothesis. But Charity revised her view so that it now accommodates that new evidence. She could have simply caved in and given up on her theory altogether. But maybe, as far as she is concerned, the next best theory to hers is Fred's, and she is very reluctant to accept any theory which includes people doing bad things (like being crooks).

And we could perform the same exercise in Kirk's case. If a check at the local airport revealed no UFO's on the radar screens that day, Kirk might conveniently reply: "What's the matter with you? Don't you know that aliens have the most sophisticated radar jamming equipment available?"

In both cases, new evidence which seems to count against a theory is instead *incorporated into* the theory. And the lesson we learn here can be generalized: no matter how much further data we gather, we can never *decisively refute* any theory. Philosophers sometimes call this issue "the underdetermination of theory by data." That is a fancy way of saying that any given set of data admits a large variety of explanations, and that no amount of data can decisively select for one theory or explanation over all of the competitors.

A Lesson for Christian Apologetics

But what does all of this have to do with apologetics? Earlier I said that the standard line on apologetics holds that the Christian can show the unbeliever that certain beliefs the unbeliever holds entail the truth of certain features of Christianity. So, using the example I employed earlier, one might try to show the unbeliever that her belief that order requires a designer should lead her to believe in a cosmic designer. But the problem for the Christian in this case is the same as the problem for Fred. As soon as the Christian makes the argument for his order-explaining "theory" the atheist can always add some other feature to *her own view* which accommodates the new bit of evidence or argument. So if the Christian says:

1) Order arises from design, not chance
2) The universe is ordered
3) Thus, the universe arises by design, not chance,

the atheist, upon recognizing the consequences of the two beliefs she holds (1 and 2), can either retain those beliefs and accept the conclusion, *or* backtrack and deny one of the beliefs. She might say, "Well, I used to think that order arises from design, but I now think that while order rarely arises by chance, it does sometimes happen, and the order in the universe represents one of those rare occurrences."

Most theists would look at this as an unreasonable attempt to patch up a sinking ship. But it might not be all that bad. Consider a case in which *the believer* is put on the defensive by the unbeliever. Now the atheist goes on the attack and tells the Christian that he cannot possibly believe that God exists in light of all the evil in the universe. She argues:

1) If God existed, there would be no evil except those that were necessary for bringing about greater goods or preventing lesser evils.
2) But there are evils which don't bring about any greater good or prevent a lesser evil.
3) So, God does not exist.

The Christian will likely deny premise 2. But when it comes to giving an explanation for why this or that specific evil actually occurred, the Christian will usually be at a loss to do so. Still, the Christian will say: "I know there is some reason, I just can't say what it is." And can't the atheist look at this as just as much an attempt to patch up a sinking ship as her response to the design argument?

One lesson to be learned from this is just that there is no seldgehammer apologetics. There are no arguments for the truth of Christianity which force the atheist or non-Christian to their intellectual knees. The unbeliever can always backtrack and give up some other belief instead.

But if someone can always backtrack and patch up their worldview to accommodate any sort of evidence or argument whatsoever, then it looks like the project of apologetics is, in the end, unrealistic. If no argument or bit of evidence can rationally persuade someone to change their views, then what is the point of trying to do so? These are good questions, and they take us back to our discussion of the other two bogeymen: relativism and antirealism. One might think that what I have just shown here is that worldviews, like ice cream flavor preferences, are subjective. What beliefs I choose to preserve and give up in the face of arguments and evidence is determined more by which beliefs I *want* to retain than it is by the evidence. So, why bother to offer any evidence at all? Doesn't all of this just show that people will believe what they want to believe and that arguments will never change anyone's mind?

What Christian Apologetics *Can* Do

Not exactly. To see why, let's go back to the case of Charity above. Let's say that after Charity tries to explain the neighbor's behavior, Fred goes back to the neighbor's house with her and searches it from top to bottom. "Now," says Fred, "will you agree that the neighbor did not take the set?" Again, Charity *can* backtrack and say that the neighbor has surely moved the TV to a secure location outside the house. But after a couple of rounds of such maneuvering, even Charity will begin to feel that her theory is getting too cumbersome to sustain. When we are forced to add so many twists and turns to maintain the theory, we start to see it as less and less plausible. The now-cumbersome theory might still account for all the data. But the accounting begins to look so forced and ungainly, that even Charity has a hard time continuing to believe it. And so, eventually, she gives up and admits that her hypothesis is not a good one. Why does she make such an admission? Is it because her theory no longer explains all the evidence? No. The theory still accounts for all the evidence, but it does so in an unsatisfactory or unsavory way. And thus, after a time, she begins to think that there must be a better way to keep intellectual order.

When we offer the unbeliever arguments for the Christian faith, we are trying to do for them what Fred tries to do for Charity in the above example. We can't sledgehammer unbelievers into belief. At best, we can show them how the beliefs that they hold, or that they ought to hold, lead to or support the Christian view. They can continue to backtrack and readjust to avoid these conclusions. And so the best we can hope for is to show them that their worldview, like Charity's view in the TV case, becomes so ungainly and cumbersome in accounting for things, that it is more reasonable to give a different intellectual accounting of the world.

This is one half of the apologist's task. We can call it the project of "positive apologetics." That is, this is the project of trying to point out the uncomfortable fit unbelievers experience in their belief structure, a belief structure which includes the denial of Christianity. This is the sort of approach that is found in the chapters in this book on theistic arguments, fine-tuning, ethics, religious pluralism, etc. But there is another half to the apologist's task. This other half amounts to an attempt to resolve the uncomfortable fit that unbelievers claim *exists within the Christian view.* Just as Fred points out the troubling evidence to Charity, Charity might produce some troubling data for Fred. She might point out, for example, that there is a very low crime rate in Fred's neighborhood, or that his burglar alarm never sounded. And Fred, in maintaining his view, must explain how it is that his view can accommodate these difficulties. Likewise the Christian is obliged to be able to give some explanation to the unbeliever of how puzzling and paradoxical features of the Christian faith can be understood and reasonably maintained. We can call this the project of "negative apologetics" (the rebuffing of attacks) and this is the task we will undertake in, for example, the chapters on the problem of evil, the Trinity and the Incarnation, and heaven and hell. It is in these corners of our own worldview that we feel pressures, and so we must concentrate some of our efforts in trying to ease those pressures.

What Is Right about Relativism and Antirealism

Notice then, that the Christian apologist is obliged to acknowledge some measure of relativism and antirealism in the apologetic project. Why? If for no other reason than because we are forced to recognize that there is more than one worldview that can fully and completely accommodate the facts.[2] Charity values explanations that maintain the goodness of people, Kirk values explanations that keep central the activity of extraterrestrials. Both of these are adequate explanatory frameworks. One might prefer one sort of framework to another. But which framework one adopts is not a matter that can be settled by the data or the facts

2. This is where the apologetic system of Francis Schaeffer and his followers goes astray. Schaeffer is convinced that unbelievers eventually run into an insurmountable intellectual roadblock at some point in working out their worldview. What I have shown here is that this need not be the case. For a useful critique of Schaeffer's apologetics see Thomas V. Morris, *Francis Schaeffer's Apologetics: A Critique* (Grand Rapids: Baker Book House, 1987).

alone (just as which theory one adopts about the missing TV isn't settled by the facts alone). So, we might be relativists about "frameworks." This doesn't mean, though, that we will be relativists about "the facts" (or at least some facts). One can think that different frameworks can all agree on a wide range of facts, and admit that these facts are objective: that there are TVs, that one is missing, that burglars exist, that balls can break windows, that rapid expansions of air in a room could break windows, and so on. But one might be a relativist about what the "best way" to explain the facts is.

One thing that the Christian cannot accept however, is that the facts themselves are relative. The claim that God exists is either true or it is not. Its truth does not depend on the person asserting it in the way the claim "Vanilla tastes better than chocolate" does. My undergraduate students are almost without exception utterly confused about this point. They will often say, "You think that God exists, I don't. It all just depends on what you believe." To this I reply, "Well, I am not sure what you mean by 'It all just depends on what you believe.' No doubt, we believe different things. But there is also no doubt that one of us is wrong. Either there is a being that is God or there isn't. If there is, I am right. If there is not, you are right. Now figuring out the right answer to our question might be very hard to do. But that doesn't mean there is no right answer. It just means that the answer will be hard to find."

Thus relativism has a certain place in Christian apologetics. We need to be aware of the fact that which worldview one selects depends on the assumptions one makes in inferring the best explanation. And which assumptions one adopts are sometimes a matter of mere preference. This is why people are able to "suppress the truth in unrighteousness." Stubborn refusal to rightly understand the truths that God has made clear to us in creation (Romans 1) is something we are fully capable of because we can continue, like Charity and Kirk, stubbornly to refuse to see things "as they are." But let me be clear about one thing here. What is relative is only the perceived "bestness" of a theoretical explanation. "Which worldview is best," we might ask, "Christian theism or atheism?" The Christian and the atheist will likely give us different answers to this questions, just as Fred and Charity are likely to give us different answers to the question, "Which explanation is better, the 'robbery theory' or the 'neighbor theory'?" Given what each thinks a "good explanation" looks like, they will each favor their own theory because, given the beliefs that each wants to preserve, their own theory is the best for them. That is, for each of them, their own theory best satisfies the conditions for what a good theory looks like. But this does *not* mean that none of them is *wrong* in the end. Even if the "bestness" of the explanation is relative, we need not think that the "truth" is. Which explanation is *preferable* depends on certain facts about the person doing the explaining, which one is *true* does not.[3]

Likewise, it seems that antirealism also has a place in Christian apologetics. Without a doubt, there are certain forms of antirealism that the Christian is obliged to reject. The most extreme versions of contemporary postmodernism which say that, at rock bottom, the only reality that there is, is one constructed by our minds, is a view that must be rejected out of hand. There is just no good reason to find this sort of antirealism compelling and, what is worse, the view borders on the incoherent. (If you don't see this, consider for a moment what it would mean to say that there is no reality at all except that which the mind constructs. Does this mean that there are no minds unless there are minds around to construct them? One wonders how these nonexistent minds pull off the task of constructing themselves!)

Furthermore, the Christian is obliged to reject the sort of theological antirealism that would require us to think of the resurrection story or the creation story as "mere stories," that is, merely provocative ways of thinking about the past that don't describe how the past really went. This doesn't mean that the Christian must reject all forms of theological antirealism, however. To take one simple example, consider the responses that Christians give to the problem of evil. When the Christian is challenged to explain why it is that God allows evil, the humble truth is: we

3. I have to add here that this is where many Christians just misunderstand what is valuable in so-called postmodern philosophy. Almost without exception evangelical theologians who accept the deliverances of postmodernism do so because they confuse these two points. They think that being a relativist about best-ness of theoretical explanation commits one to relativism about truth. But this is just mistaken. So, there is a lesson to be learned from postmodernism, but it is not the lesson they think. Let me further add here that it is at junctures like this that we can see just where so-called "presuppositionalists" have apologetics right. That is, it is right that both Christian and unbeliever have certain presuppositions in place when they begin to engage each other intellectually. And it is right that there is no way to decisively argue unbelievers out of their unbelief because of these very presuppositions. In this way, one might think, the insights of Cornelius Van Til are quite useful for apologetics, and what he has to say already embodies anything useful postmodernism has to teach us. It is unfortunate, however, just how poorly contemporary defenders of presuppositionalism do in making its insights clear. In part, the trouble is that they themselves are just not clear about which of the insights are valuable and which are not.

don't know. We may know the reason that God allowed some evils (such as the death of his Son). But it would be absurd to think that we do or even could know the reason that God allows all of the variety of evil the world contains. Nonetheless, we might offer some suggestions or *models* which we think show how it *might be* that an all-good God allows evils of the sort that we see in the world. Likewise, when we discuss the Trinity, we might not know how it is that there can be a single being with one divine nature which is yet composed of three persons. Still, we might be able to offer coherent *models* as to how this *might* be understood. If it turns out that our models are wrong, so be it. But at least we can offer a model to the critic which shows that the whole notion isn't incoherent, since there is at least one way that it could be worked out (and, of course, there might be other ways as well). And so, when one reads the chapters on evil or on the Trinity and the Incarnation, one might think of them not as attempts to explain how it is, but as attempts to provide useful models that can help us get an intellectual grip on how things might be. In this way, we can be antirealist about these explanations for evil or the Trinity. They provide good models for thinking about the Christian faith, even if the models themselves turn out to be incorrect.

Notice that we need to make a distinction here that is similar to the one made before. We can be antirealist about our models, but not antirealist about that which our models are trying to explain. Even if I fail to construct a model to make coherent sense of the Trinity, the Christian is still obliged to stand by the objective truth of the claim that God is three-persons-while-yet-one-nature.

Conclusion

This then is the aim of the apologetic task we are undertaking. Some of us are aiming to do positive apologetics, that is, we are aiming to show that certain views the unbeliever holds make a very uncomfortable fit with her atheism or disbelief in Christianity. In doing this we will try to take a look at the most recent resources that Christian philosophy offers us for sizing up and criticizing the various worldviews of the unbeliever. Can the unbeliever evade these arguments? Yes. But they nonetheless raise troubles that the unbeliever will have to accommodate, and usually the accommodation will make for a more or less uncomfortable fit.

Others will be engaged in negative apologetics. For the most part, doing this will mean providing models that attempt to make sense of the deep, puzzling, and seemingly paradoxical components of the faith. Again, much has gone on in recent years in Christian philosophy that helps us construct effective models; and we will try, in these pages, to make these new and innovative ideas clear and engaging. Our hope is that all of this will not only help you answer questions that unbelievers might raise when you are discussing your faith, but that it will help you to develop a richer appreciation for the glory of God and his creation and that this in turn will lead you to a deeper, more intimate relationship with him.

2

Theistic Arguments

William C. Davis

As a seminarian with more time than money, I rode the bus from San Diego to Dallas in December of 1982. In the middle of the night, somewhere in New Mexico, another earnest young man took the seat next to me; and despite the hour, we began to talk. When he learned that I was studying theology, he asked if I could prove that God exists.[1] Over the next four hours, I tried. I had studied many of the classical proofs both as an undergraduate and in seminary, but this was my first skirmish with live ammunition, and I fired off every weapon I could remember. I opened by asking why there is something rather than nothing, insisting that even if

1. Whether my companion intended it or not, I understood this as a request for a proof of the existence of the God of the Bible: the self-necessary, immaterial, omniscient, omnipotent, and wholly good creator and sustainer of all things who has acted in history to redeem a people for himself. Had I known a bit more philosophy I would have known this was a patently unrealizable goal: at most a demonstrative proof could only hope to establish the existence of a being with God's necessary attributes (self-necessity, omniscience, omnipotence, and moral perfection), and this because the conclusions of demonstrations must be, like their premises, necessary truths. Since God was not obliged to create, sustain, or redeem (he chose to do those things as a matter of will), no *a priori* demonstration could hope to establish the existence of the God of the Bible. This does not mean that there couldn't be *arguments* for the existence of the God of the Bible, only that they won't be demonstrations in the strictest sense.

For help in rendering this chapter intelligible I am especially indebted to my wife, Lynda, and to my friends at Cornerstone Presbyterian Church (PCA) in Boardman, Ohio, in particular Dean Brown, Carina Krautter, and David James.

everything could be traced back to the big bang, God had to exist as the source of the stuff that banged and the one who lit the fuse. He countered by asking what made God, and we deadlocked over whether God or the physical universe made a better unexplained brute fact. The discussion was not going the way I had expected.

I shifted my attack, asking him whether he was sure that the bus on which we were riding existed. He said that he was, so I asked him why he was sure. When he said that he trusted his senses I suggested that I trusted my sense of God's presence, and I asked him what the difference was. Even though he couldn't point out a relevant difference, he insisted that my line of reasoning made his unbelief reasonable until God revealed himself to him personally. He was willing to grant that my experience made my belief reasonable, but that reasonable beliefs could be false. By this time frustrated, I attempted to get my seatmate to admit that the complexity of the world — its orderliness and the presence of morality and consciousness — cried out for an intelligent creator as its cause. But for each feature of the world that I brought up, he insisted that even if God's existence made a neat explanation for it, there must be godless explanations that worked nearly as well; and that the many ugly and evil things in the world surely counted against the existence of a perfect God. My ammunition spent, I happily accepted an offer to discuss baseball. My first attempt to prove God's existence seemed a miserable failure.

Had I done something wrong? I would love to report that since that juvenile effort I have refined my arguments and that I have successfully argued unbelievers into belief. Sadly, I cannot; and I'm now persuaded that even knowing the arguments perfectly would not guarantee that I would be able to muscle honest unbelievers into admitting that God exists. While I could have presented the arguments more skillfully, the problem had as much to do with the nature of belief as it did with my argumentative ability. Belief in God, like *any* belief,[2] is rationally avoidable, and a determined skeptic will always be able to find a reason — even if somewhat implausible — for persisting in unbelief. This should not be surprising: no one expects to argue anyone into the kingdom. But this does not mean that there is no point in reading the rest of this chapter.

Arguments for God's existence are useful, but it is important to be clear about *how* they are useful. Ultimately, arguments are never more than tools used by the Holy Spirit. Good arguments — those that firmly connect

2. The rational resistibility of any belief is considered in detail in Michael Murray's chapter, "Reason for Hope (in the Postmodern World)" (pp. 1-19 in this volume).

the belief that God exists with other beliefs that are something like obviously true — are used by the Spirit to comfort and convict. For people who already believe, good arguments are used to strengthen their confidence; for those who do not already believe, good arguments present a challenge to their faith in God's nonexistence, but there is no argument which can force the unbeliever to choose between belief and irrationality. The primary purpose of this chapter is to show that good arguments for God's existence are available, but that none of them are unavoidably strong. This means that although believers should find this chapter legitimately encouraging, skeptics should always be able to see a way to avoid the conclusion that God exists. The way of escape will often be implausible, but it will be there. In order to show both how strong the good arguments can be and how evasion might nonetheless be possible, I will first explain two particularly strong lines of argumentation. Summaries of these and other good arguments can be found in the inset boxes. The final section will then consider whether we *need* an argument for God's existence. I conclude that we do, but *not* in order to make our faith rational.

Arguing from the Fact That There Is Something Rather Than Nothing[3]

Something Necessary Must Explain All the Contingent Facts

Christians and other theists often say that they believe that God exists because, they claim, there must be something which explains all the contingent facts. In this section I will explain how this argument is supposed to work, why it looks promising, but why in the end Christians shouldn't exaggerate its force. And while it might be frustrating to consider an argu-

3. Arguments from the mere existence of the universe (in Greek, the "cosmos") are called "cosmological" arguments. The fountainhead of this kind of argument is Thomas Aquinas's "five ways" (in his *Summa Theologicae* Ia, 2.3); but see also William Lane Craig, *The Cosmological Argument from Plato to Leibniz* (London: Macmillan, 1980), as well as his *The* Kalām *Cosmological Argument* (London: Macmillan, 1979), *The Existence of God and the Beginning of the Universe* (San Bernardino, CA: Here's Life, 1979), and *Theism, Atheism and Big Bang Cosmology* (Oxford: Clarendon, 1993). Another important formulation is given by G. W. Leibniz, in "On the Ultimate Origination of Things" reprinted in *The Philosophical Writings of Leibniz,* trans. by Mary Morris and G. H. R. Parkinson (London: Dent, 1934), 32-41.

ment that doesn't work in the way we would like, it is important to look carefully at this version of the argument because it is very similar to an argument which *does* work (which is considered in the next section).

Suppose that a tree from your front yard is uprooted and lying across the roof of your car. Why is it there? The fact that the tree damaged your car is a *contingent* fact; it didn't have to happen. And since it didn't have to happen, it is reasonable to ask: Why did it happen? In this case, the explanation is in terms of other contingent facts: the winds were unusually strong; the tree was dead; the car was parked near the tree. These contingent facts may, in turn, be explained by *other* contingent facts: for example, the car was parked near the tree because the garage was full. This inquiry after explanations can go on for quite some time, but could it go on forever? Is it plausible that *every* contingent fact is completely explained by a collection of only contingent facts?

For those already convinced that God is the ultimate cause of all contingent facts, the answer to this last question might seem to be clearly negative. But this wouldn't be correct. The complete explanation for every contingent fact might be a collection of contingent facts, the most important of which is the contingent fact that God willed the ultimate outcome. Since God isn't required to will what he wills, a complete explanation might consist only of contingent facts! For example, the ultimate cause of Jesus' resurrection might be the contingent fact that God willed it to happen. As a result, the traditional arguments for God's existence which argue from the existence of contingent *facts* to the existence of a necessary fact (God's existence) succeed only by inadvertently binding God's will. So Christians should reject *this* argument. But there is a closely related argument which is much more successful; we might call it the argument from "contingent beings."

Something Necessary Must Explain All the Contingent Beings

Consider your wrecked car again. While the contingency of the *facts* can't easily support an argument for God's existence, the contingency of *beings* involved fares much better. The car, the tree, and the wind are all contingent *beings:* they might not have existed at all. And for things that might not have existed, it is reasonable to ask what brought them into existence. For the car, the tree, and the wind, the immediate answer to this question will be in terms of other contingent beings: autoworkers, parent trees, and the earth itself. But since these beings are also contingent, we can ask what brought *them* into being, and it is this line of inquiry which strongly suggests that there must exist a *necessary* being, one which has its existence from itself and concerning which it is unnecessary to ask what brought it into being. The resulting argument for God's existence runs something like this:[4]

(a) There are contingent things (at least some things might not have existed).
(b) All contingent things are dependent (at least for their coming into existence) on something else.
(c) Not everything can be dependent on something else. (Even if the chain of dependence looped back on itself, the entire chain would still be dependent, and thus something outside the chain would be needed.)
(d) Thus, a nondependent (necessary) thing exists (which explains dependent things). (And for those already familiar with God on the basis of revelation, it is not hard to give a name to this necessary being.)

This is a good argument, but it need not *force* the unbeliever to acknowledge God's existence.

While the existence of the God of the Scriptures would easily satisfy the requirement imposed by the conclusion of this argument, all that the argument requires is the existence of a necessary being *of some kind.* And it is possible to avoid identifying God as this necessary being by insisting that the universe itself is a necessary being. This amounts to stopping the argument at the very beginning, denying the first premise (that the universe is a contingent thing). By choosing this response, the unbeliever is claiming that the correct answer to the question, "Why is there something rather than nothing?" should be, "Because there had to be something (material); it is impossible for there to be nothing (material)." And if this response isn't satisfying, another way to avoid the conclusion that there exists a necessary being external to the universe is to deny that every contingent thing is dependent upon something else for its existence. This

4. What follows is an adaptation of the argument Peter van Inwagen presents as the most promising of the cosmological arguments. See "Necessary Being: The Cosmological Argument" in *Metaphysics* (Boulder: Westview Press, 1993), especially 111ff.

An Argument from the Contingency of the Universe

The universe didn't have to be here, and even if it has always been here it didn't have to be the way it is. This means the universe is a contingent thing. But all contingent things depend for their existence upon something else. The universe may depend upon a cause which is itself contingent, but it is not possible that everything is contingent. Thus there must be a necessary (indeed, a self-necessary) being which is the ultimate cause of the universe. God is the self-necessary ultimate cause of the universe.

Greatest Strength: Pure contingency is logically untenable, so it is difficult to believe that the universe is both contingent and uncaused.

Greatest Weakness: The contingency of the universe as a whole is difficult to establish convincingly unless one is already convinced that it has a cause.

means insisting that there is at least one thing that might not have been, but nonetheless *is,* despite lacking a complete explanation.[5]

I must confess that neither of these responses is especially attractive, but then I'm not looking for a way to defend my faith in the nonexistence of God. The cosmological argument sketched here doesn't *compel* belief in God's existence, but it does force a choice about metaphysical foundations. Either the universe's existence is inexplicable (which is not an attractive conclusion), or there exists a necessary being. And this necessary being is either the universe itself (the heart of the materialist faith) or it is something distinct from the universe. A being that is nothing more than the necessarily existing cause of the universe would not be God, but God can surely fit the job description. This argument is not undeniable, but it nonetheless supplies a very good reason (from highly plausible premises) for thinking that God exists.

5. For examples of this line of response, see William Rowe, *Philosophy of Religion* (Belmont, CA: Wadsworth, 1978), 21ff., and J. L. Mackie, *The Miracle of Theism* (Oxford: Clarendon Press, 1982), 92. It is worth noting that the skeptic can admit that a personal cause of the universe is required *without* conceding that the god of standard theism exists. The finitely powerful deistic god might be thought sufficient for the narrow task of initiating the sequence of causes.

An Argument from the Definition of "God" and the Possibility That God Exists

Alvin Plantinga defines God as, together with the standard attributes, a "necessary being." A necessary being, if one existed at all, would exist no matter how the world went (it would exist in every "possible world"). If one admits that it is *possible* that God exists (as most will), then it follows that God *does* exist:

> in order for it to be possible at all, there must be at least some possible world in which it will be true that God exists (this is, philosophers argue, just what it means to say that something is "possible"); but (and here is the tricky part), if there is *some* world where it is true that god exists, then "God exists" must be true in *every* world. Why? Because the very definition of God demands that God is a necessarily existing being. Thus, we are forced to admit that if we "find" him existing in even one world, we are guaranteed (by the definition) that he must be found in every *other* possible world as well. Thus, God is found (i.e., exists) in this world.

Greatest Strength: Most opponents of theism are willing to concede that God's existence is at least possible.

Greatest Weakness: Atheists who have considered the argument can and do reject the claim that God is even possible. They argue instead that the very concept of God is incoherent since, for example, it entails paradoxes such as the paradox of the stone: Can God make a stone so big that he cannot lift it? This is supposed to show that an omnipotent being is impossible.

Arguing from the Complexity of the World

Convincing someone of the existence of something they have never experienced can be difficult. For example, it might be hard for me to convince you that I have yesterday's winning lottery ticket unless you see it with your own eyes. Unfortunately, when Christians attempt to prove God's existence, we cannot summon God as we can lottery tickets. But God is one of many things that we believe to exist even though we cannot experience them with our senses. Many of the entities at the heart of scientific theories (electrons, photons, quarks, etc.) are similarly unobservable, and yet there is near universal consensus about their existence. Now, current

An Argument from the Existence of Human Intelligence

While it is possible for complex effects to arise by accident, it is much more likely that an effect is the result of a suitably complex cause, and that specific organization in an effect depends upon at least an equal measure of organization in the cause. Human intelligence is a clear case of highly specific organization. Thus it is much more likely that the ultimate cause of human intelligence is itself at least as intelligent as the most intelligent human; and it is much less likely that the ultimate cause of human intelligence is the impersonal, unintelligent universe itself.

Greatest Strength: It is hard to believe that human intelligence is a cosmic accident; and experience tells us that organized effects result from organized (intelligent) causes.

Greatest Weakness: Many people think that Darwinian naturalism provides a mechanism for generating complex order without the need for a single, highly ordered, cause.

science could be wrong, but what matters here is the type of reasoning used to reach the conclusion that electrons exist. We are confident that electrons exist even though they've never been directly observed because the hypothesis that electrons exist contributes to an extremely successful explanation of how the world works. This is scientific reasoning: arguing from the way the observed part of the world works to what must be true about the unobserved part. And as it turns out, this same kind of reasoning also supports the conclusion that God exists. God's existence explains the complexity of the world extremely well, and certainly more completely than any alternative explanation.

But merely providing a better explanation than all known rivals is not as much as we can ask from a scientific belief. Some scientific conclusions manage to be established as *facts,* and not merely as the best explanations currently available. That the earth revolves around the sun is one such "fact"; that the earth is round is another.[6] And I will show that many people (Christians in particular) have sufficient evidence to conclude not only that the existence of God provides the best explanation for the way the world is, but also that the existence of God is a fact on a par with the fact that the earth is round.

6. Technically, of course, the earth is roughly spherical. But since it is commonly referred to as "round" it seemed less clumsy to refer to its shape in this way.

About Establishing the Best Explanation for Complex Effects

In order to see why Christians would be justified in claiming that God's existence is a fact, it is necessary to consider in some detail why it is an uncontroversial fact that the earth is round. Of course there was a time when many (maybe most) people thought that the earth was flat, and in order to appreciate the kind of scientific reasoning on display here, it is helpful to imagine that you are a sailor considering an offer to travel with Christopher Columbus as he sets sail in 1492: there are people advancing the hypothesis that the earth is round, but if they are wrong, sailing with Columbus means risking an unpleasant trip over the edge of the earth (if it is really flat). What line of reasoning might induce you to endorse the round earth hypothesis with sufficient conviction to entrust your life to it?

An Argument from the Fine-Tuning of the Universe

The physical universe is able to support life. But the ability to support life depends upon a dizzying array of physical constants being precisely what they are (the specific constants governing the fundamental forces of nature — the strong, weak, electromagnetic, and gravitational — are good examples). If *any* of these constants had been much different, life would be impossible. And while it is not impossible that all these constants had the values they did by pure chance, it is considerably more likely that they have the values they do by design. God's existence is a much better explanation for the fine-tuning of the universe than any god-free explanation.

Greatest Strength: The very narrow range of values for a large number of physical constants is highly suggestive. The closer one looks at the conditions necessary to support life, the harder it is to believe that life is a cosmic accident.

Greatest Weakness: Although it would take a very powerful being to set up a universe capable of supporting life, it wouldn't take one that was infinitely powerful. The "god" of deism would seem to be sufficient.

Showing That One Explanation Is Better Than Alternative Explanations

Thinking about the problem in the manner of twentieth-century science, you would focus your attention on the *explanatory power* of the two hypotheses.[7] Explanatory power concerns the ability of an hypothesis to account for and predict evidence. In the case of the round earth hypothesis, in 1492 it would have turned out that the evidence was somewhat mixed. Since this is similar to the case of God's existence, it is worth following how your thinking might have gone if you had been presented with the opportunity to sail with Columbus.

A reasonable way to start would have been by looking around. The earth looks flat; and the only maps that you would have ever seen (of your property, for example) would have been flat as well. If the earth really was flat, this is precisely what you would expect to happen (the earth around you looking flat and flat maps describing it well), and if the earth was actually round, you wouldn't have expected these results. So at least for this evidence, the flat earth hypothesis explains the evidence better. And if you didn't consider any other evidence, you would be foolish to risk your life sailing with Columbus towards what many expected to be the edge of the earth.

But this isn't your only evidence. While thinking about the suggestion that the earth is round, you remember that when ships return to the harbor the tops of their masts always appear first. If the earth were round rather than flat, this is what one would expect. The appearance of ships returning to harbor then, taken by itself, counts in favor of the round earth hypothesis and against the flat earth hypothesis! To this point, considering the evidence has only increased your perplexity. Fortunately, however, there is more evidence; and your hope is that further evidence will enable you to do two things: first, to decide in favor of one hypothesis over the other; and second, to suggest a way that a more complete understanding of the favored hypothesis would allow it to explain the evidence that had seemed to favor its rival. In the case of the shape of the earth, both of these hopes are realized concerning the hypothesis that the earth is round.

As you consider more evidence, the balance tilts towards thinking that the earth is round. Simply by reflecting on the matter you realize that even from the top of a hill on a clear day there seems to be a clear limit (the horizon) to how far you can see. This is what you would have expected (although you hadn't thought of it before) if you had assumed that the earth is round, especially if you assumed that it was a very large ball.

7. As Swinburne carefully explains in both *The Existence of God* (Oxford: Clarendon Press, 1979) and *Is There a God?* (Oxford: Oxford University Press, 1996), the strength of a hypothesis is a function of both its explanatory power and its simplicity. But since it is difficult to assess relative simplicity in a way which doesn't seem to beg the question, I will be assuming that the simplicity of the pairs of hypotheses considered here are roughly equal. This means that explanatory power plays the determining role.

In addition to your own observations, you might also consider the testimony of others. Here the reports are again mixed: some veterans of the seas claim that they know of ships that have sailed over the edge of the flat earth, but others report that their own determined efforts to find this edge have been unsuccessful, and that they have heard of land being sighted beyond where the edge was supposed to be. While suggestive, these results are not encouraging. Even if you are more certain of the trustworthiness of those claiming not to have found an edge, the balance only slightly favors the round earth hypothesis.

Since the evidence available to Columbus and his companions wasn't much more extensive than this, the bravery of those who went with him must have been considerable. They staked their lives on the round earth hypothesis. It was rational to go, but only barely. The success of Columbus's enterprise, however, gave important new data to those who had withheld judgment about the shape of the earth. Indeed, those waiting safely in Europe could look upon his voyage as a kind of grand scientific experiment: if he never returned, it would be evidence for the flat earth view and it would be necessary to find a way to explain away the contrary evidence; and if he returned from the east (having set out towards the west), it would be evidence for the round earth hypothesis. He returned, but from the west, having turned around. Those certain that the earth was flat could take comfort that his voyage hadn't rendered their position impossible.

An Argument from the Definition of "God" and the Superiority of Existing in Reality

Anselm defined God as that being than which no greater can be conceived, and further assumed that it is greater to exist in reality than it is to exist only in the mind (as a thought). But given these two premises, the supposition that God exists only in the mind can't possibly be true: the greatest conceivable being can't exist only in the mind because we can conceive of that same being existing in reality as well. A greatest conceivable being (God) which exists only in the mind is contradictory. Thus, God must exist in reality.

Greatest Strength: The argument requires accepting only a definition and the claim that to exist is better than not.

Greatest Weakness: It feels like a trick, even if it is hard to say why. One likely source: widespread misgivings about deriving existence from a definition.

As a matter of history, it took a great many years for the round earth hypothesis to be accepted as a matter of common knowledge. For the scientifically inclined, there were genuine experiments designed to settle the matter decisively. One particularly ingenious effort drove poles at regular intervals into a large, calm (apparently flat) lake so that the tops of the poles projected out of the water the same distance. Then the researcher looked across the tops of the poles from the top of the first to the top of the last. If the earth were flat, all of the tops should have been directly in the line of sight. But they weren't. Instead, the tops of all the intervening poles were above the line of sight, with the tops of the central poles appearing to be the tallest. This is what one would expect from the round earth hypothesis; and even more significantly, this experiment suggested a way to estimate the size of a round earth. Even in a large lake, the apparent projection of the central poles was not great, suggesting that the earth was much larger than expected, but this had the happy effect of suggesting a way to account for the evidence that seemed to favor a flat earth: flat maps worked well, and the earth appeared flat to casual observers, because the earth is so big that the curvature we experience is relatively minor. With a more complete understanding of the round earth hypothesis, it not only explained more of the evidence but it also explained the evidence that used to count against it. The evidence clearly supported the conclusion that the round earth hypothesis was superior to the flat earth hypothesis, and in time it was accepted as common knowledge.

Showing That the Best Explanation Is a Fact

As strong as this conclusion was, it is possible to ask for more. Being superior to all known rivals is significant, but it isn't sufficient to move the hypothesis beyond serious question, to show that it is a *fact.*[8] Many scientific hypotheses have been clearly superior to all known alternatives only to be surpassed later by other hypotheses. Our current confidence that it is a fact that the earth is round (and that it is more than a mere hypothesis liable to being overthrown at some point in the future) is based on evidence that wasn't available until very recently. We know that the earth is round today because people have seen the earth from space. Astronauts

8. "Fact" here is used in contrast to a mere hypothesis; the possibility the earth is *not* round is so small that it need not be taken seriously. Using Swinburne's terminology, "facts" would then be states of affairs with probabilities significantly greater than 0.5.

who have seen it with their own eyes have had direct experience that puts the matter beyond all serious question; and anyone who believes that the pictures they brought back from space are genuine and accurate must also believe that it is a fact that the earth is round. Direct experience can change a hypothesis — accepted on the basis of scientific reasoning to the best explanation — to a fact of observation.

Of course, adding the claims of astronauts and their pictures to all the other evidence for the shape of the earth isn't enough to render the flat earth hypothesis *impossible*. A skillful arguer can resist the conclusion that the earth is round by insisting that the pictures were doctored and the testimony false. The evidence, especially when taken all together, makes the belief that the earth is round obviously rational and the belief that it is not round extremely difficult to maintain; but extremely difficult is not impossible. And it is likely that unless the skeptic were to be taken into space and given the direct experience of the spherical earth, it would remain possible to insist that it is not round and remain rational — exceedingly suspicious, but rational.

This relatively lengthy discussion of scientific reasoning concerning the shape of the earth was necessary in order to explain how we might use the same kind of reasoning to support the conclusion that God exists. The world we know is enormously complex, and God's existence is at least the best available explanation for the way it is. And for those who have experienced God's presence, the evidence is sufficient to establish God's existence as a fact. As with the case of the shape of the earth, I will first show that God's existence explains the data better than the most promising alternative, which I will take to be metaphysical naturalism, the view that the physical universe, the "cosmos," is all there is (and thus that there can be no God).[9] Then I will consider the significance of the direct experience of God's presence for the conclusion that God's existence is a fact.

9. At least in the West, the chief rival to theism is some version of metaphysical naturalism. Recently, pantheistic monism has become another popular alternative to Christian theism. This is the view that all of reality is God (or some manifestation of the divine). I have two reasons for not considering this alternative here. First, pantheistic monists are typically unimpressed by arguments of any kind, and in particular arguments following scientific reasoning like inference to the best explanation. Second, it isn't clear that pantheistic monists would accept the claim that there is any "way the world is." Many, if not all, of the features I will be considering are commonly regarded by pantheistic monists as illusory anyway. For this reason, it is inappropriate to look for any explanation at all!

God as the Best Explanation for the Universe

Arguing that God provides the best explanation for the way the world is might go two different ways. On the one hand, the argument could try to show that there is one particular feature of the world for which God is clearly the best explanation. But while I think there are many such features, this way of arguing is typically unconvincing. It is all too easy for the critic to suppose that even if God was the best explanation for that one feature, there must be many other features of the world for which God isn't a plausible explanation. And even if the critic's supposition might be hard to defend successfully, the vague guess that it *could* be defended would diminish the usefulness of any argument that aimed too narrowly.

Much more convincing, but harder to present quickly, is a cumulative case argument. The goal is still to show that the existence of God provides the best explanation for the way the world is, but in a cumulative case argument the data to be explained is the whole of reality! This can't be done quickly for two reasons. First, reality is astonishingly complex. Second, for each individual feature it may be necessary to offer an argument to show how the explanation provided by God's existence stacks up against the most promising alternative explanations. And over the course of these arguments concerning individual features, it is necessary to establish two conclusions. First, that there are features of the universe which God's existence clearly explains better than the competing alternatives; and second, that there are no features of the universe clearly explained

An Argument from the Existence of Necessary Truths

Humans are capable of apprehending *necessary* truths, propositions like "2 + 2 = 4" and "No proposition can be both true and false at the same time." These truths would be true, however, even if no human existed, indeed, even if no physical thing existed at all. But no proposition could exist without a mind to entertain it, so there must be a mind (God) that necessarily exists.

Greatest Strength: The truths of logic and mathematics seem to be true in a way that is independent of both what humans think and even practical facts about the makeup of the physical universe.

Greatest Weakness: Confidence in the existence of mind-independent objective truth (let alone necessary truth) is currently declining.

better by a nontheistic alternative, especially when the details of theism are fully considered. (Remember that in the case of the shape of the earth there were features of experience that seemed to favor the flat earth position until the details of the round earth hypothesis were more completely worked out.)

In what follows I will focus on establishing the first of these conclusions (that there *are* features of the world for which God's existence is clearly the better explanation). I will not attempt to establish the second conclusion (that there are no features for which some nontheistic alternative is clearly superior). The reason for this omission is easily explained: the only feature which critics suggest might be better explained by a nontheistic alternative is the presence of evil in the world. Granted, this is an awfully important candidate, but Daniel Howard-Snyder's chapter in this volume treats the problem of evil in detail. And although this problem is challenging, I am persuaded that when the nature of evil and God's purposes in creation are carefully considered, we should conclude that while evil is deeply troubling, nontheistic explanations for the presence of evil are not clearly superior to theistic explanations.[10]

Before turning to the features of the world for which God's existence clearly provides the best explanation, I should first respond to a very common objection: that even if some kind of *being* is needed to explain the data of the world, a being much less exalted than *God* would be sufficient.[11] Many critics insist that even if, for example, an intelligent designer is the best explanation for the universe, there is no reason to think that the intelligent designer must be the omnipotent, omniscient, and

10. The problem of evil is dauntingly complex, but here the central question is whether or not evil disconfirms (makes less likely) the hypothesis of theism; and the answer to that question depends in large part on what sorts of creatures one would expect a perfectly good and free God to make. It seems at least plausible that the God of theism might be expected to make a world populated with free creatures capable of both moral good (like benevolence and worship) and moral evil, and that a world with neither would be less attractive to God. This is the conclusion reached by Swinburne in Chapter 11 of *The Existence of God*. While evil may look like defeating evidence at first blush, a more complete examination of the hypothesis suggests ways to incorporate the data of evil into it. Evil doesn't defeat theism for the same reason the apparent flatness of my neighborhood doesn't defeat the hypothesis that the earth is round: in both cases a more complete understanding of the hypothesis shows that the problematic evidence can be accommodated.

11. The classical statement of this objection is developed at length in David Hume's *Dialogues Concerning Natural Religion* (Parts II and V), and many contemporary critiques of theistic belief are indebted to it.

An Argument from the Irreducible Complexity of Living Systems

Microbiology has identified systems at work in cells which are fundamental to life and which are irreducibly complex: their function depends upon the presence and close fit of many parts. For some of these systems it appears that the only plausible explanation for their existence is that they arose all at once (since in partial form they would work against the survival of the organism). The existence of these systems is nearly inexplicable in Darwinian terms (by gradual, single steps), but is easily explained if the cause of life is an intelligent designer. The facts of microbiology are much more likely to be as they are if God exists than if God does not.

Greatest Strength: For those confident that science is close to making God unnecessary, these results present a serious challenge; and this line of argumentation may open up a consideration of the other features of reality more easily explained by God's existence.

Greatest Weakness: While it is currently difficult to see how a god-free account of these systems might work, Darwinians are convinced that such an explanation will be found.

morally perfect being Christians think God to be. But while this objection is common, it isn't a serious problem. At the heart of the objection is the claim that the Christian idea of God can't be constructed from the details of our experience. And this is clearly correct! A finite creation cannot *require* an infinite or eternal creator as its cause. But why think that we need to construct our idea of God only from the uncontroversial facts of this world? This objection is ultimately an attempt to change the subject. The issue is not whether it is possible to assemble our idea of God; rather the real issue is whether the God we know from the Scriptures provides the best explanation for the facts of the world. And there are many features of the world for which God's existence provides the best explanation.

The Kinds of Facts about the World That God's Existence Explains Best

Two features will be discussed in some detail, but there are many features of the world which are better explained by God's existence than by metaphysical naturalism (the thesis that the "cosmos" is all there is). Remember that the better explanation is the one on which the particular data would have been more likely to be the way it in fact is. For example, consider the data of useless (nonutilitarian) beauty. Is God a better explanation of that feature of the world than metaphysical naturalism? To decide, you must ask whether useless beauty is more likely to exist if God exists or if metaphysical naturalism is true. This is by no means a simple or obvious estimate; but I'm convinced that an honest evaluation leads to the conclusion that God's existence explains this and other features of the world far more successfully. Here is a list of features of the world that, it seems, are better explained by God's existence than by metaphysical naturalism:

(1) The mere existence of something rather than nothing is more likely if a personal creator exists than if one does not.[12]

(2) The universe is orderly to a remarkable degree, and in more than one way (natural laws are both simple and uniform, the capacity for reproduction is pervasive, and great complexity is produced using only a very small number of elementary particles interacting according to a small number of laws). Any one of these features suggests that it is more likely that the universe is the product of design than that it is the product of random forces impelling purposeless particles which resulted in accidental stability. Taken together, they are even more formidable as an argument for a designer.[13]

(3) Value, both moral and aesthetic, appears to be an objective feature of the world (and not merely imposed by human preferences),[14] a

12. In addition to the argument offered earlier in this chapter, see also Swinburne's reworking of the cosmological argument in *The Existence of God,* ch. 7, and Richard Taylor's explanation of the cosmological argument in *Metaphysics* (Englewood Cliffs, NJ: Prentice-Hall, 1983), 91-99.

13. All three of these versions of the "teleological" argument (from the Greek word "teleo" for "fulfilling a purpose") are developed at length by Swinburne in *The Existence of God,* ch. 8. The classic critique of this line of argumentation is found in the opening books of David Hume's *Dialogues Concerning Natural Religion.* A more contemporary argument for the plausibility of the appearance of design without a designer is given by Richard Dawkins in *The Blind Watchmaker: Why the Evidence of Evolution Reveals a Universe Without Design* (New York: W. W. Norton, 1996).

14. In the twentieth century confidence in the objectivity of moral or aesthetic truths has been on the wane; and this line of argumentation for God's existence has suffered accordingly. But even if the skeptic insists that all value judgments are expressions of private preferences, the enterprises of morality and aesthetics are nonetheless very common human activities which lack apparent survival value. So even if it is currently out of fashion to appeal to the objectivity of value, morality and aesthetics can be cited as part of argument number five on this list.

fact much more likely to have been the case if God exists than if the universe is a grand accident.[15]

(4) Human consciousness and intelligence are more likely to be the products of a conscious and intelligent creator than of a physical universe devoid of either.[16]

(5) Humans have numerous features that are more easily explained by theism than by metaphysical naturalism, if only because metaphysical naturalism currently explains all human capacities in terms of their ability to enhance survival.[17] Among these features are the possession of reliable faculties aimed at truth, the appreciation of beauty, and a sense of humor.

And this is only a partial list. To it could be added features of the universe that only a philosopher could love: the intentionality of propositions, the nature of warrant, and the coherence of mathematics.

For each of these features of the world it is possible for the determined skeptic to insist either that the feature doesn't exist at all (as with objective morality), or that the feature can be explained adequately in terms of natural forces (without God). But the best the skeptic can hope for is to show that metaphysical naturalism explains as much of what needs explaining as the existence of God explains (or, which is the same thing, showing that the features are just as likely to have arisen if God doesn't exist). In no case is it plausible that metaphysical naturalism explains the data better, and a full discussion of this line of argument would establish the superior explanatory power of God's existence for each one. I will only consider two features that have received specific attention re-

15. The classic defense of the moral argument is given by C. S. Lewis in *Mere Christianity* (New York: Macmillan, 1943), 34, but see also George Mavrodes' "Religion and the Queerness of Morality" and C. Delaney's "Moral Arguments for Theistic Belief," both in *Rationality, Religious Belief and Moral Commitment,* ed. by Robert Audi and William Wainwright (Ithaca: Cornell University Press, 1986); John Hick's *Arguments for the Existence of God* (New York: The Seabury Press, 1971), 59-67; and John Henry Newman's *A Grammar of Assent* (London: Longmans, 1870), chapter 5.

16. Swinburne develops this argument in *The Existence of God,* but the classical statement is given by John Locke in his *Essay Concerning Human Understanding,* IV.x.10.

17. This is the thrust of the last chapter of Alvin Plantinga's *Warrant and Proper Function* (Oxford: Oxford University Press, 1996), chapter 12: "Is Naturalism Irrational?" For one attempt to undermine the force of Plantinga's conclusion, see J. Wesley Robbins, "Is Naturalism Irrational?" *Faith and Philosophy* 11:2 (April 1994): 255-59.

An Argument from Religious Experience

A great many people both throughout history and throughout the world have had religious experiences. These have typically included not only an awareness of a divine presence but also a qualitative change in the behavior of the one having the experience. The existence of God explains this data much more easily than conjectures about psychological disorders, mass deceptions, or fraudulent reporting.

Greatest Strength: The pervasiveness of religious experience is well documented and accompanied by credible reports of lives being changed for the better.

Greatest Weakness: Although religious experience in general is widespread, specific experiences vary considerably.

cently: the irreducible complexity of the cell, and humanity's lust for the truth.

God's Existence as an Explanation for Biological Complexity

Especially as an explanation for the origins of life and the complexity of living beings, the dominant form of metaphysical naturalism today includes Darwinian evolution. According to this account, random mutation, natural selection (favoring traits advantageous for survival), and vast stretches of time explain the incredible complexity of every form of life. Every complex feature of living things developed by small gradual steps from simple features, with each step along the long gradual path being preserved because the slightly altered feature enhanced the chance that the organism would survive. Since nothing exists other than material things, there was (and is) no designer directing the process of development; so even if many parts of nature appear to be intentionally designed, the appearance is illusory.

Many have questioned whether there is sufficient compelling evidence for the existence of macroevolution (the development of one species out of another),[18] but Michael Behe's 1996 book *Darwin's Black*

18. See, in particular, Philip E. Johnson, *Darwin on Trial* (Washington, DC: Regnery Gateway, 1991), and Michael Denton, *Evolution: A Theory in Crisis* (Bethesda, MD: Adler & Adler, 1996).

An Argument from Objective, Nonutilitarian Value

While many human activities are pursued because of their usefulness (utility), and some are valuable only in the eyes of a few people (nonobjective), there are kinds of human activity which possess objective, nonutilitarian value. Two obvious examples of this are self-sacrificial love and artistic beauty (which may be useful, but don't need to be). If everything (including humanity) is the result of random, impersonal forces which encouraged only survival, then it seems highly unlikely that the process would yield organisms (humans) which recognized values like these which aren't survival-conducive. But values like these are what we would expect if humans (and the human environment) were created by a personal, loving, and beauty-valuing God. God's existence is a much better explanation for the existence of nonutilitarian value than any explanation without God.

Greatest Strength: Most people can be persuaded through specific examples to concede that survival is not the only objective value, and that self-sacrificial love and beauty are valuable in a way that transcends mere subjective taste.

Greatest Weakness: The late twentieth century is replete with efforts to show that the very idea of objective value of any kind is mistaken, and that all attempts to identify objective value (and especially nonutilitarian objective value) are attempts to impose subjective values on others.

Box[19] goes even further, arguing that Darwinian evolution *cannot* account for the data at the level of the cell. Cells, he argues, contain numerous systems of interrelated and interdependent parts that are irreducibly complex: if any part was missing or failed to fulfill its function, the entire system would fail to function. Behe's principal illustration is a mousetrap. If any part of a mousetrap is missing (or made of inappropriate materials, or the wrong size), the parts that are present are useless. The reason this is a serious problem for Darwinian accounts is that there is no gradual, small-step way to evolve a mousetrap *if every step must have survival advantage over the previous step.* The completed mousetrap has survival advantage over no mousetrap, but unless all the parts appear together (and with the right dimensions, etc.), the result is a pile of parts. Behe de-

19. Michael J. Behe, *Darwin's Black Box: The Biochemical Challenge to Evolution* (New York: The Free Press, 1996).

scribes numerous systems in the workings of cells that are irreducibly complex in a similar way, and argues that the only plausible explanation for these systems is that an intelligent designer directed the development of the cell.

The systems that Behe describes (including blood-clotting, cilia, immune-defense) are features of the world worthy of an explanation, and even though Behe's intelligent designer need not be omnipotent, omniscient, and wholly good to direct the construction of these irreducibly complex systems, God at least *could* account for them; whereas, it seems, the current best efforts of metaphysical naturalism cannot. If the only two alternatives were the existence of God and metaphysical naturalism, irreducible complexity at the microbiological level is powerful evidence for the existence of God: it is a clear instance of a feature of the world better explained by divine design.

For reasons already mentioned, however, this need not be the end of the story for nontheists. Since the publication of Behe's book there have been numerous attempts to provide plausible gradual, step-by-step accounts of the origins of the systems Behe finds to be irreducibly complex.[20] The responses offered so far have been sketchy, but they do not seem to be hopeless. For those determined to retain their confidence in the naturalist explanation, these efforts may provide sufficient encouragement to resist the conclusion this is a clear case where God's existence offers a superior explanation of the facts. But that is the best that the critics of theism can hope for here. The appearance of intentional design at the cellular level is considerable, and the existence of a designer is the best explanation for it.

God's Existence Explains the Reliability of Our Cognitive Powers

A second feature of the world for which God's existence proves to be a superior explanation is the reliability of our cognitive powers.[21] While a certain

20. Two recent responses are by Jerry A. Coyne, "God in the Details: The Biochemical Challenge to Evolution," *Nature* (September 19, 1996), and H. Allen Orr, "Darwin v. Intelligent Design (Again)," *Boston Review* (December/January 1996-97). The most promising Darwinian explanation for irreducible complexity appears to be the suggestion that the parts needed to construct the eventual complex system *each* had survival advantage prior to the mutation in which their interaction was found to be even more advantageous. I am indebted to Nathan Knutson for pointing out these responses to Behe's thesis.

21. The argument here is a compressed summary of Plantinga's argument in

amount of reliability would have survival value and thus would be expected on the naturalistic hypothesis, even Darwin doubted that truth-directedness in general would be favored by natural selection for its survival advantage.[22] God's existence, however, explains this feature well: truth-directed faculties are precisely the kind of equipment that an omniscient creator would be expected to give to the creatures from whom the most was expected by way of worship and service. Since it seems clear that our cognitive abilities are peculiarly focused on truth-acquisition, theism provides a better explanation for this feature of the world than does metaphysical naturalism.

It is not hard to see how this line of analysis might be developed for a wide range of features of the world, from the mere existence of conscious beings to the capacity for appreciating nonutilitarian beauty. And that is taking the features of the world one at a time. When all of the features of the world calling for explanation are taken together (even including the presence of evil), the compelling verdict is that the world is much more the way one would have expected it to be given God's existence than it would have been if metaphysical naturalism were true.[23] The same style of reasoning used to show that the belief that the earth is round is superior to the belief that the earth is flat also shows that belief in God's existence is superior to belief in metaphysical naturalism.

Direct Experience of God's Presence and the Fact of God's Existence

For those who have not experienced God's presence, this is as far as the argument can go, just as confidence that the earth is round must be lim-

---

the "Darwin's Doubt" section of the closing chapter of *Warrant and Proper Function* (New York: Oxford University Press, 1993), 219-28.

22. Plantinga cites Darwin's Letter to William Graham, July 3, 1881, from *The Life and Letters of Charles Darwin Including an Autobiographical Chapter,* ed. Francis Darwin (London: John Murray, Albermarle Street, 1887), 1:315-16. A similar misgiving is expressed by Patricia Churchland in "Epistemology in the Age of Neuroscience," *Journal of Philosophy* 84 (October, 1987): 548.

23. J. L. Mackie, in *The Miracle of Theism,* 251-53, denies this conclusion. But in his discussion of "The Balance of the Probabilities," Mackie compares the explanatory power of theism to the explanatory power of a collection of atheistic hypotheses, using the most successful alternative for each of the features of the world being considered. Even after helping himself to this maneuver his conclusion seems forced, and the maneuver dramatically weakens his thesis. Having less explanatory power than a string of alternatives each explaining only part of the evidence says very little.

ited to thinking it the best known hypothesis in the absence of direct experience or accepting the testimony of astronauts. But for those who *have* experienced God's presence, God's existence no longer has the status of a mere hypothesis; it is a fact of observation. And while our confidence in that fact is supported by arguments, it is not dependent upon them. Suppose an astronaut returning from a stay on a space station was asked to prove that the earth is round. After weeks of gazing at the earth could she provide a proof that would defeat any skeptic? No. A determined skeptic would insist on the possibility that the astronaut was either deceived or lying; and the skeptic could rationally refuse to accept the claim that the earth is round. The astronaut, on the other hand, would find the demand at least annoying (if not offensive) and frustrating, though it would not cause her to doubt her own belief on the matter. Having seen what she's seen, her confidence can't be held hostage to a demand for proof.

Had no human ever perceived God's presence, confidence about God's existence could never legitimately equal the astronaut's confidence about the shape of the earth. Because of its explanatory power, belief in God's existence would have been as rational as was the belief that the earth is round prior to space flight, but it would never have been a fact of observation. Happily, however, experience of God's presence abounds. I am aware of God's guidance when I pray; I enjoy God's comfort in times of affliction; God's presence thrills me when I worship; and I know that many other Christians have these experiences as well. These experiences do not employ one of the senses commonly called "external" (vision, hearing, smell, touch, or taste), but they are undeniably experiences.[24] For those who haven't had the experience, the testimony of those who have (together with the arguments presented in this chapter) cannot be lightly dismissed. And for those who have had the experience, the demand for proof can be both annoying and frustrating, but it shouldn't be troubling. Like the astronaut, they know what they've experienced. This leads to a final question: if experience of God's presence is really analogous to seeing the earth's shape from space, why think *any* argument is needed for God's existence?

24. That the extent of the similarity is sufficient is considered in the next section of this chapter.

Do We Need an Argument at All?

While many continue to develop good arguments for God's existence, others have labored to show that belief in God is rational without any argument at all.[25] But establishing that no argument is needed requires an argument, and the key to all efforts of this kind is the observation that a great many of our most common beliefs — that the world is more than five minutes old, that there is a physical world very much like the one reported by our senses, or that there are other minds — are accepted as rational even though all admit that there are no noncircular arguments to justify them.[26] Critics of belief in God's existence can insist that even if Christians think that they have experienced God's presence they can't *know* that God exists unless they can *prove* it. But do these critics apply this prohibition to their own beliefs? If they did, then they would have to admit that they don't know that tables and chairs exist, or that the world is more than five minutes old! These beliefs can't be proven either, but it seems strange to insist that these are not things that we know. Where there is direct experience similar to the experience of seeing tables and chairs and remembering last night, it is reasonable to conclude that the experience is reliable unless there is good reason to think otherwise. But there isn't good reason to think that our experience of God's presence is significantly different from our other (uncontroversial) experiences.

Consider the similarities between accepting what our senses tell us about the existence of external objects and the Christian practice of accepting what experience tells us about the existence of God. In both cases there are circumstances in which we reject claims supposedly based on experience. For example, no matter what he says about his experience, we don't accept as rational a psychotic person's fervent belief that his cat is

25. This effort is, of course, consistent with believing that good arguments are available. One of the most ardent proponents of the view that no argument is required, Alvin Plantinga, is also a leading contributor in the effort to develop good arguments. For a particularly forceful explanation of why we shouldn't think that an argument is necessary, see Alvin Plantinga's "Reason and Belief in God," in *Faith and Rationality,* ed. Plantinga and Wolterstorff (Notre Dame: University of Notre Dame Press, 1983), 16-93.

26. Different authors focus on different common sense beliefs. In *God and Other Minds* (Ithaca: Cornell University Press, 1967), Plantinga shows that belief in God and belief in the existence of other minds have similar justifications. William Alston makes the same argument for belief based on the senses (sight, hearing, etc.) in "Christian Experience and Christian Belief" in *Faith and Rationality,* 103-34.

speaking to him. In general, we are unwilling to trust our senses (or others' reports about their senses) when either (a) we have a strong suspicion that the senses involved are compromised by defect or ignorance, or (b) there is strong independent reason to think that what they report is false.[27] So, for example, if I am on drugs and "see" horns growing out of my friend's head, I won't expect the horns to be present when I return to my right mind. I know that drugs compromise the reliability of my senses. And if I have just seen Bill Clinton on live TV addressing a crowd in Utah, then I won't believe my eyes if I seem to see him throwing a Frisbee outside my house in Georgia.

The crucial question, then, is whether the Christian practice of trusting one's experiences of God's presence fails in either of these ways (involving a strong suspicion of compromised faculties or an independent reason to think their report false). Critics of theism (at least among philosophers) have all but given up thinking that God's existence can be disproved, so their case must depend upon showing that the experience of God's presence depends upon compromised faculties. But any attempt to define the experience of God's presence as a defect in normal functioning will end up dragging down all sorts of commonsense beliefs with it. If it is objected, for example, that the sense of God's presence is possessed only by a minority of people, this difficulty will undermine all other perceptual claims made by only a minority, such as the architect's ability to "see" that a structure is rigid or the cook's ability to "feel" that the batter is too thin. Similar considerations will apply to any attempt to disqualify only the experience of God's presence, so these experiences can be dismissed only by dismissing many other (common sense) beliefs as well.

The similarities between belief in God's existence and the beliefs of common sense are extensive, and they may be more than coincidental. Many have thought that there is good reason to believe that every normal human has a sense of God's presence as part of their standard intellectual equipment — what John Calvin called the *sensus divinitatis*[28] — which

27. For a more complete discussion of the factors which are thought to undermine perceptual claims and their implications for theistic belief, see Richard Swinburne, *The Existence of God,* chapter 13, pp. 244-76.

28. John Calvin, *Institutes of the Christian Religion* I.iii.1. "There is within the human mind, and indeed by natural instinct, an awareness of divinity (divinitatis sensum). This we take to be beyond controversy. To prevent anyone from taking refuge in the pretense of ignorance, God himself implanted in all men a certain understanding of his divine majesty" (Battles's translation). Calvin's position is based in part

tells us of God's existence in the same way that our eyes tell us about the existence of the physical things around us. Common possession of this "sense" would help explain the universality of religion, and it would make belief in God even more certainly as rational as other beliefs that arise from the senses.

The skeptic is, of course, free to attempt to disqualify testimony about experiences of God's presence on the grounds of some supposed abnormality or on the grounds that it is already known that God does not exist; but in this effort the burden of proof is on the skeptic to make the case. And to date no skeptical account has been able to establish either disqualification without taking the extreme step of disqualifying vast stretches of common knowledge along with theistic belief. Admittedly, showing that belief in God is as rational as the belief that other people exist does not *prove* God's existence. But it does show that belief in God's existence on the basis of experience is as rational as the astronaut's belief that the earth is round. And in neither case does the rationality of the belief depend upon having an argument. Good arguments for God's existence are available, but you don't need one to make your belief rational.

Conclusion

Even a relatively unsophisticated skeptic such as my bus companion can persist in unbelief, just as a determined skeptic can persist in rejecting the hypothesis that the earth is round. But someone who has seen the earth from space, who has had the hypothesis confirmed by direct experience, cannot avoid adopting the hypothesis. This is why those who have had their hearts changed by the Spirit so that they can consciously embrace their awareness of God's presence find belief in God's existence unavoidably preferable to any nontheistic alternative; while those who have not had such an experience are able to suppress the truth while maintaining what would be recognized by the world as a form of rationality.

Ultimately conviction about God's existence is dependent upon the work of the Spirit; but the Spirit may work conviction through a consideration of the evidence available in nature and in the kinds of arguments developed in this chapter. The arguments are worth knowing because each

---

on Paul's claim in Romans 1 that all people know of God's power and majesty, but that they suppress this knowledge in unrighteousness. For a contemporary echo of Calvin's position, see Alvin Plantinga's "Reason and Belief in God."

one removes an objection to theism by showing that theistic belief is on a par with those beliefs that we find most unproblematic. Studying these arguments can make us "ready to give an answer for the hope we have,"[29] answering both the doubts that assail us from time to time and the doubts of the unbeliever. No one will be argued into belief, but arguments such as these are among the ordinary tools that the Spirit uses to soften the unbeliever's heart. And while our faith is not dependent upon arguments, they may be used by the Spirit to provide comfort to us who for now must be content to see through the glass only darkly, anticipating the day when we will know as we are known, because we will see God face to face.

29. 1 Peter 3:15.

3

A Scientific Argument for the Existence of God: The Fine-Tuning Design Argument

Robin Collins

I. Introduction

The Evidence of Fine-Tuning

Suppose we went on a mission to Mars, and found a domed structure in which everything was set up just right for life to exist. The temperature, for example, was set around 70° F and the humidity was at 50 percent; moreover, there was an oxygen recycling system, an energy gathering system, and a whole system for the production of food. Put simply, the domed structure appeared to be a fully functioning biosphere. What conclusion would we draw from finding this structure? Would we draw the conclusion that it just happened to form by chance? Certainly not. Instead, we would unanimously conclude that it was designed by some intelligent being. Why would we draw this conclusion? Because an intelligent designer appears to be the only plausible explanation for the existence of the structure. That is, the only alternative explanation we can think of — that the structure was formed by some natural process — seems extremely unlikely. Of course, it is *possible* that, for example, through some volcanic eruption various metals and other compounds could have formed, and then separated out in just the right way to produce the "biosphere," but such a scenario strikes us as extraordinarily unlikely, thus making this alternative explanation unbelievable.

The universe is analogous to such a "biosphere," according to recent findings in physics. Almost everything about the basic structure of the universe — for example, the fundamental laws and parameters of physics and the initial distribution of matter and energy — is balanced on a razor's edge for life to occur. As the eminent Princeton physicist Freeman Dyson notes, "There are many . . . lucky accidents in physics. Without such accidents, water could not exist as liquid, chains of carbon atoms could not form complex organic molecules, and hydrogen atoms could not form breakable bridges between molecules"[1] — in short, life as we know it would be impossible.

Scientists call this extraordinary balancing of the parameters of physics and the initial conditions of the universe the "fine-tuning of the cosmos." It has been extensively discussed by philosophers, theologians, and scientists, especially since the early 1970s, with hundreds of articles and dozens of books written on the topic. Today, it is widely regarded as offering by far the most persuasive current argument for the existence of God. For example, theoretical physicist and popular science writer Paul Davies — whose early writings were not particularly sympathetic to theism — claims that with regard to basic structure of the universe, "the impression of design is overwhelming."[2] Similarly, in response to the life-permitting fine-tuning of the nuclear resonances responsible for the oxygen and carbon synthesis in stars, the famous astrophysicist Sir Fred Hoyle declares that

> I do not believe that any scientists who examined the evidence would fail to draw the inference that the laws of nuclear physics have been deliberately designed with regard to the consequences they produce inside stars. If this is so, then my apparently random quirks have become part of a deep-laid scheme. If not then we are back again at a monstrous sequence of accidents.[3]

1. Freeman Dyson, *Disturbing the Universe* (New York: Harper and Row, 1979), 251.

2. Paul Davies, *The Cosmic Blueprint: New Discoveries in Nature's Creative Ability to Order the Universe* (New York: Simon and Schuster, 1988), 203.

3. Fred Hoyle, in *Religion and the Scientists* (1959); quoted in *The Anthropic Cosmological Principle,* ed. John Barrow and Frank Tipler (Oxford: Oxford University Press, 1986), 22.

A few examples of this fine-tuning are listed below:

1. If the initial explosion of the big bang had differed in strength by as little as one part in 10^{60}, the universe would have either quickly collapsed back on itself, or expanded too rapidly for stars to form. In either case, life would be impossible. (As John Jefferson Davis points out, an accuracy of one part in 10^{60} can be compared to firing a bullet at a one-inch target on the other side of the observable universe, twenty billion light years away, and hitting the target.)[4]
2. Calculations indicate that if the strong nuclear force, the force that binds protons and neutrons together in an atom, had been stronger or weaker by as little as five percent, life would be impossible.[5]
3. Calculations by Brandon Carter show that if gravity had been stronger or weaker by one part in 10^{40}, then life-sustaining stars like the sun could not exist. This would most likely make life impossible.[6]
4. If the neutron were not about 1.001 times the mass of the proton, all protons would have decayed into neutrons or all neutrons would have decayed into protons, and thus life would not be possible.[7]
5. If the electromagnetic force were slightly stronger or weaker, life would be impossible, for a variety of different reasons.[8]

Imaginatively, one could think of each instance of fine-tuning as a radio dial: unless all the dials are set exactly right, life would be impossible. Or, one could think of the initial conditions of the universe and the fundamental parameters of physics as a dart board that fills the whole galaxy, and the conditions necessary for life to exist as a small one-foot wide target: unless the dart hits the target, life would be impossible. The fact that the dials are perfectly set, or that the dart has hit the target, strongly suggests that someone set the dials or aimed the dart, for it seems enor-

4. See Paul Davies, *The Accidental Universe* (Cambridge: Cambridge University Press, 1982), 90-91. John Jefferson Davis, "The Design Argument, Cosmic 'Fine-tuning,' and the Anthropic Principle," *The International Journal of Philosophy of Religion* 22 (1987): 140.

5. John Leslie, *Universes* (New York: Routledge, 1989), 4, 35; *Anthropic Cosmological Principle*, 322.

6. Paul Davies, *Superforce: The Search for a Grand Unified Theory of Nature* (New York: Simon and Schuster, 1984), 242.

7. Leslie, *Universes*, 39-40.

8. John Leslie, "How to Draw Conclusions from a Fine-Tuned Cosmos," in *Physics, Philosophy and Theology: A Common Quest for Understanding*, ed. Robert Russell et al. (Vatican City State: Vatican Observatory Press, 1988), 299.

mously improbable that such a coincidence could have happened by chance.

Although individual calculations of fine-tuning are only approximate and could be in error, the fact that the universe is fine-tuned for life is almost beyond question because of the large number of independent instances of apparent fine-tuning. As philosopher John Leslie has pointed out, "Clues heaped upon clues can constitute weighty evidence despite doubts about each element in the pile."[9] What is controversial, however, is the degree to which the fine-tuning provides evidence for the existence of God. As impressive as the argument from fine-tuning seems to be, atheists have raised several significant objections to it. Consequently, those who are aware of these objections, or have thought of them on their own, often will find the argument unconvincing. This is not only true of atheists, but also many theists. I have known, for instance, both a committed Christian Hollywood filmmaker and a committed Christian biochemist who remained unconvinced because of certain atheist objections to the argument. This is unfortunate, particularly since the fine-tuning argument is probably the most powerful current argument for the existence of God. My goal in this chapter, therefore, is to make the fine-tuning argument as strong as possible. This will involve developing the argument in as objective and rigorous a way as I can, and then answering the major atheist objections to it. Before launching into this, however, I will need to make a preliminary distinction.

A Preliminary Distinction

To develop the fine-tuning argument rigorously, it is useful to distinguish between what I shall call the *atheistic single-universe hypothesis* and the *atheistic many-universes hypothesis.* According to the atheistic single-universe hypothesis, there is only one universe, and it is ultimately an inexplicable, "brute" fact that the universe exists and is fine-tuned. Many atheists, however, advocate another hypothesis, one which attempts to explain how the seemingly improbable fine-tuning of the universe could be the result of chance. We will call this hypothesis the *atheistic many-worlds hypothesis,* or *the atheistic many-universes hypothesis.* According to this hypothesis, there exists what could be imaginatively thought of as a "universe generator" that produces a very large or infinite number of uni-

9. Leslie, "How to Draw Conclusions," 300.

verses, with each universe having a randomly selected set of initial conditions and values for the parameters of physics. Because this generator produces so many universes, just by chance it will eventually produce one that is fine-tuned for intelligent life to occur.

Plan of the Chapter

Below, we will use this distinction between the atheistic single-universe hypothesis and the atheistic many-universes hypothesis to present two separate arguments for theism based on the fine-tuning: one which argues that the fine-tuning provides strong reasons to prefer theism over the atheistic single-universe hypothesis and one which argues that we should prefer theism over the atheistic many-universes hypothesis. We will develop the argument against the atheistic single-universe hypothesis in section II below, referring to it as the *core* argument. Then we will answer objections to this core argument in section III, and finally develop the argument for preferring theism to the atheistic many-universes hypothesis in section IV. An appendix is also included that further elaborates and justifies one of the key premises of the core argument presented in section III.

II. Core Argument Rigorously Formulated

General Principle of Reasoning Used

The Principle Explained

We will formulate the fine-tuning argument against the atheistic single-universe hypothesis in terms of what I will call the *prime principle of confirmation.* The prime principle of confirmation is a general principle of reasoning which tells us when some observation counts as evidence in favor of one hypothesis over another. *Simply put, the principle says that whenever we are considering two competing hypotheses, an observation counts as evidence in favor of the hypothesis under which the observation has the highest probability (or is the least improbable).* (Or, put slightly differently, the principle says that whenever we are considering two competing hypotheses, H_1 and H_2, an observation, O, counts as evidence in favor of H_1 over H_2 if O is more probable under H_1 than it is under H_2.) Moreover, the degree to which the evidence counts in favor of one hypothesis over another is proportional to the degree to which the observation is more probable under the one hypothesis than the other.[10] For example, the fine-tuning is much, much more probable under theism than under the atheistic single-universe hypothesis, so it counts as strong evidence for theism over this atheistic hypothesis. In the next major subsection, we will present a more formal and elaborated rendition of the fine-tuning argument in terms of the prime principle. First, however, let's look at a couple of illustrations of the principle and then present some support for it.

Additional Illustrations of the Principle

For our first illustration, suppose that I went hiking in the mountains, and found underneath a certain cliff a group of rocks arranged in a formation that clearly formed the pattern "Welcome to the mountains, Robin Collins." One hypothesis is that, by chance, the rocks just happened to be arranged in that pattern — ultimately, perhaps, because of certain initial conditions of the universe. Suppose the only viable alternative hypothesis is that my brother, who was in the mountains before me, arranged the rocks in this way. Most of us would immediately take the arrangements of rocks to be strong evidence in favor of the "brother" hypothesis over the "chance" hypothesis. Why? Because it strikes us as extremely *improbable* that the rocks would be arranged that way by chance, but *not improbable* at all that my brother would place them in that configuration. Thus, by the prime principle of confirmation we would conclude that the arrangement of rocks strongly supports the "brother" hypothesis over the chance hypothesis.

Or consider another case, that of finding the defendant's fingerprints on the murder weapon. Normally, we would take such a finding as strong evidence that the defendant was guilty. Why? Because we judge that it would be *unlikely* for these fingerprints to be on the murder weapon if the defendant was innocent, but *not unlikely* if the defendant was guilty. That is, we would go through the same sort of reasoning as in the above case.

10. For those familiar with the probability calculus, a precise statement of the degree to which evidence counts in favor of one hypothesis over another can be given in terms of the odds form of Bayes's Theorem: that is, $P(H_1/E)/P(H_2/E) = [P(H_1)/P(H_2)] \times [P(E/H_1)/P(E/H_2)]$. The general version of the principle stated here, however, does not require the applicability or truth of Bayes's Theorem.

Support for the Principle

Several things can be said in favor of the prime principle of confirmation. First, many philosophers think that this principle can be derived from what is known as the *probability calculus,* the set of mathematical rules that are typically assumed to govern probability. Second, there does not appear to be any case of recognizably good reasoning that violates this principle. Finally, the principle appears to have a wide range of applicability, undergirding much of our reasoning in science and everyday life, as the examples above illustrate. Indeed, some have even claimed that a slightly more general version of this principle undergirds all scientific reasoning. Because of all these reasons in favor of the principle, we can be very confident in it.

Further Development of Argument

To further develop the core version of the fine-tuning argument, we will summarize the argument by explicitly listing its two premises and its conclusion:

- *Premise 1.* The existence of the fine-tuning is not improbable under theism.
- *Premise 2.* The existence of the fine-tuning is very improbable under the atheistic single-universe hypothesis.
- *Conclusion:* From premises (1) and (2) and the prime principle of confirmation, it follows that the fine-tuning data provide strong evidence to favor the design hypothesis over the atheistic single-universe hypothesis.

At this point, we should pause to note two features of this argument. First, the argument does not say that the fine-tuning evidence proves that the universe was designed, or even that it is likely that the universe was designed. In order to justify these sorts of claims, we would have to look at the full range of evidence both for and against the design hypothesis, something we are not doing in this chapter. Rather, the argument merely concludes that the fine-tuning strongly *supports* theism *over* the atheistic single-universe hypothesis.

In this way, the evidence of the fine-tuning argument is much like fingerprints found on the gun: although they can provide strong evidence that the defendant committed the murder, one could not conclude merely from them alone that the defendant is guilty; one would also have to look at all the other evidence offered. Perhaps, for instance, ten reliable witnesses claimed to see the defendant at a party at the time of the shooting. In this case, the fingerprints would still count as significant evidence of guilt, but this evidence would be counterbalanced by the testimony of the witnesses. Similarly the evidence of fine-tuning strongly supports theism over the atheistic single-universe hypothesis, though it does not itself show that, everything considered, theism is the most plausible explanation of the world. Nonetheless, as I argue in the conclusion of this chapter, the evidence of fine-tuning provides a much stronger and more objective argument for theism (over the atheistic single-universe hypothesis) than the strongest atheistic argument does against theism.

The second feature of the argument we should note is that, given the truth of *the prime principle of confirmation,* the conclusion of the argument follows from the premises. Specifically, if the premises of the argument are true, then we are guaranteed that the conclusion is true: that is, the argument is what philosophers call *valid.* Thus, insofar as we can show that the premises of the argument are true, we will have shown that the conclusion is true. Our next task, therefore, is to attempt to show that the premises are true, or at least that we have strong reasons to believe them.

Support for the Premises

Support for Premise (1)

Premise (1) is easy to support and fairly uncontroversial. One major argument in support of it can be simply stated as follows: *since God is an all good being, and it is good for intelligent, conscious beings to exist, it is not surprising or improbable that God would create a world that could support intelligent life.* Thus, the fine-tuning is not improbable under theism, as premise (1) asserts.

Support for Premise (2)

Upon looking at the data, many people find it very obvious that the fine-tuning is highly improbable under the atheistic single-universe hypothesis. And it is easy to see why when we think of the fine-tuning in terms of the analogies offered earlier. In the dart board analogy, for example, the initial conditions of the universe and the fundamental parameters of physics are thought of as a dart board that fills the whole galaxy, and the conditions necessary for life to exist as a small one-foot wide target. Accordingly, from this analogy it seems obvious that it would be highly improbable for the fine-tuning to occur under the atheistic single-universe hypothesis — that is, for the dart to hit the target by chance.

Typically, advocates of the fine-tuning argument are satisfied with resting the justification of premise (2), or something like it, on this sort of analogy. Many atheists and theists, however, question the legitimacy of this sort of analogy, and thus find the argument unconvincing. For these people, the appendix to this chapter offers a rigorous and objective justification of premise (2) using standard principles of probabilistic reasoning. Among other things, in the process of rigorously justifying premise (2), we effectively answer the common objection to the fine-tuning argument that because the universe is a unique, unrepeatable event, we cannot meaningfully assign a probability to its being fine-tuned.

III. Some Objections to Core Version

As powerful as the core version of the fine-tuning argument is, several major objections have been raised to it by both atheists and theists. In this section, we will consider these objections in turn.

Objection 1: More Fundamental Law Objection

One criticism of the fine-tuning argument is that, as far as we know, there could be a more fundamental law under which the parameters of physics *must* have the values they do. Thus, given such a law, it is not improbable that the known parameters of physics fall within the life-permitting range.

Besides being entirely speculative, the problem with postulating such a law is that it simply moves the improbability of the fine-tuning up one level, to that of the postulated physical law itself. Under this hypothesis, what is improbable is that of all the conceivable fundamental physical laws there could be, the universe just happens to have the one that constrains the parameters of physics in a life-permitting way. Thus, trying to explain the fine-tuning by postulating this sort of fundamental law is like trying to explain why the pattern of rocks below a cliff spell "Welcome to the mountains, Robin Collins" by postulating that an earthquake occurred and that all the rocks on the cliff face were arranged in just the right configuration to fall into the pattern in question. Clearly this explanation merely transfers the improbability up one level, since now it seems enormously improbable that of all the possible configurations the rocks could be in on the cliff face, they are in the one which results in the pattern "Welcome to the mountains, Robin Collins."

A similar sort of response can be given to the claim that the fine-tuning is not improbable because it might be *logically necessary* for the parameters of physics to have life-permitting values. That is, according to this claim, the parameters of physics must have life-permitting values in the same way 2 + 2 must equal 4, or the interior angles of a triangle must add up to 180 degrees in Euclidian geometry. Like the "more fundamental law" proposal above, however, this postulate simply transfers the improbability up one level: of all the laws and parameters of physics that conceivably could have been logically necessary, it seems highly improbable that it would be those that are life-permitting.[11]

Objection 2: Other Forms of Life Objection

Another objection people commonly raise to the fine-tuning argument is that as far as we know, other forms of life could exist even if the parameters of physics were different. So, it is claimed, the fine-tuning argument ends up presupposing that all forms of intelligent life must be like us. The answer to this objection is that most cases of fine-tuning do not make this presupposition. Consider, for instance, the case of the fine-tuning of the strong nuclear force. If it were slightly smaller, no atoms could exist other than hydrogen. Contrary to what one might see on *Star Trek,* an intelligent life-form cannot be composed merely of hydrogen gas: there is simply not enough stable complexity. So, in general the fine-tuning argument

11. Those with some training in probability theory will want to note that the kind of probability invoked here is what philosophers call *epistemic probability,* which is a measure of the rational degree of belief we should have in a proposition (see appendix, subsection iii). Since our rational degree of belief in a necessary truth can be less than 1, we can sensibly speak of it being improbable for a given law of nature to exist necessarily. For example, we can speak of an unproven mathematical hypothesis — such as Goldbach's conjecture that every even number greater than 6 is the sum of two odd primes — as being probably true or probably false given our current evidence, even though all mathematical hypotheses are either necessarily true or necessarily false.

merely presupposes that intelligent life requires some degree of stable, reproducible organized complexity. This is certainly a very reasonable assumption.

Objection 3. Anthropic Principle Objection

According to the weak version of the so-called *anthropic principle,* if the laws of nature were not fine-tuned, we would not be here to comment on the fact. Some have argued, therefore, that the fine-tuning is not really *improbable or surprising* at all under atheism, but simply follows from the fact that we exist. The response to this objection is to simply restate the argument in terms of our existence: our existence as embodied, intelligent beings is extremely unlikely under the atheistic single-universe hypothesis (since our existence requires fine-tuning), but not improbable under theism. Then, we simply apply the prime principle of confirmation to draw the conclusion that *our existence* strongly confirms theism over the atheistic single-universe hypothesis.

To further illustrate this response, consider the following "firing squad" analogy. As John Leslie points out, if fifty sharpshooters all miss me, the response "if they had not missed me I wouldn't be here to consider the fact" is not adequate. Instead, I would naturally conclude that there was some reason why they all missed, such as that they never really intended to kill me. Why would I conclude this? Because my continued existence would be very improbable under the hypothesis that they missed me by chance, but not improbable under the hypothesis that there was some reason why they missed me. Thus, by the prime principle of confirmation, my continued existence strongly confirms the latter hypothesis.[12]

Objection 4: The "Who Designed God?" Objection

Perhaps the most common objection that atheists raise to the argument from design, of which the fine-tuning argument is one instance, is that postulating the existence of God does not solve the problem of design, but merely transfers it up one level. Atheist George Smith, for example, claims that

12. Leslie, "How to Draw Conclusions," 304.

> If the universe is wonderfully designed, surely God is even more wonderfully designed. He must, therefore, have had a designer even more wonderful than He is. If *God* did not require a designer, then there is no reason why such a relatively less wonderful thing as the universe needed one.[13]

Or, as philosopher J. J. C. Smart states the objection:

> If we postulate God in addition to the created universe we increase the complexity of our hypothesis. We have all the complexity of the universe itself, and we have in addition the at least equal complexity of God. (The designer of an artifact must be at least as complex as the designed artifact). . . . *If the theist can show the atheist that postulating God actually reduces the complexity of one's total world view, then the atheist should be a theist.*[14]

The first response to the above atheist objection is to point out that the atheist claim that the designer of an artifact must be as complex as the artifact designed is certainly not obvious. But I do believe that their claim has some intuitive plausibility: for example, in the world we experience, organized complexity seems only to be produced by systems that already possess it, such as the human brain/mind, a factory, or an organism's biological parent.

The second, and better, response is to point out that, at most, the atheist objection only works against a version of the design argument that claims that all organized complexity needs an explanation, and that God is the best explanation of the organized complexity found in the world. The version of the argument I presented against the atheistic single-universe hypothesis, however, only required that the fine-tuning be more probable under theism than under the atheistic single-universe hypothesis. But this requirement is still met even if God exhibits tremendous internal complexity, far exceeding that of the universe. Thus, even if we were to grant the atheist assumption that the designer of an artifact must be as complex as the artifact, the fine-tuning would still give us strong reasons to prefer theism over the atheistic single-universe hypothesis.

To illustrate, consider the example of the "biosphere" on Mars presented at the beginning of this paper. As mentioned above, the existence

13. George Smith, "The Case Against God," reprinted in *An Anthology of Atheism and Rationalism,* ed. Gordon Stein (Buffalo: Prometheus Press, 1980), 56.

14. J. J. C. Smart, "Laws of Nature and Cosmic Coincidence," *The Philosophical Quarterly* 35 (July 1985): 275-76, italics added.

of the biosphere would be much more probable under the hypothesis that intelligent life once visited Mars than under the chance hypothesis. Thus, by the prime principle of confirmation, the existence of such a "biosphere" would constitute strong evidence that intelligent, extraterrestrial life had once been on Mars, even though this alien life would most likely have to be much more complex than the "biosphere" itself.

The final response theists can give to this objection is to show that a supermind such as God would *not* require a high degree of unexplained organized complexity to create the universe. Although I have presented this response elsewhere, presenting it here is beyond the scope of this chapter.

IV. The Atheistic Many-Universes Hypothesis

The Atheistic Many-Universes Hypothesis Explained

In response to the theistic explanation of fine-tuning of the cosmos, many atheists have offered an alternative explanation, what I will call the atheistic many-universes hypothesis. (In the literature it is more commonly referred to as the *many-worlds hypothesis,* though I believe this name is somewhat misleading.) According to this hypothesis, there are a very large — perhaps infinite — number of universes, with the fundamental parameters of physics varying from universe to universe.[15] Of course, in the vast majority of these universes the parameters of physics would not have life-permitting values. Nonetheless, in a small proportion of universes they would, and consequently it is no longer improbable that universes such as ours exist that are fine-tuned for life to occur.

Advocates of this hypothesis offer various types of models for where these universes came from. We will present what are probably the two most popular and plausible, the so-called *vacuum fluctuation* models and the *oscillating big bang* models. According to the vacuum fluctuation models, our universe, along with these other universes, were generated by quantum fluctuations in a preexisting superspace.[16] Imaginatively, one

15. I define a "universe" as any region of space-time that is disconnected from other regions in such a way that the parameters of physics in that region could differ significantly from the other regions.

16. Quentin Smith, "World Ensemble Explanations," *Pacific Philosophical Quarterly* 67 (1986): 82.

can think of this preexisting superspace as an infinitely extending ocean full of soap, and each universe generated out of this superspace as a soap bubble which spontaneously forms on the ocean.

The other model, the oscillating big bang model, is a version of the big bang theory. According to the big bang theory, the universe came into existence in an "explosion" (that is, a "bang") somewhere between ten and fifteen billion years ago. According to the *oscillating* big bang theory, our universe will eventually collapse back in on itself (what is called the "big crunch") and then from that "big crunch" will arise another "big bang," forming a new universe, which will in turn itself collapse, and so on. According to those who use this model to attempt to explain the fine-tuning, during every cycle, the parameters of physics and the initial conditions of the universe are reset at random. Since this process of collapse, explosion, collapse, and explosion has been going on for all eternity, eventually a fine-tuned universe will occur, indeed infinitely many of them.

In the next section, we will list several reasons for rejecting the atheistic many-universes hypothesis.

Reasons for Rejecting the Atheistic Many-Universes Hypothesis

First Reason

The first reason for rejecting the atheistic many-universes hypothesis, and preferring the theistic hypothesis, is the following general rule: *everything else being equal, we should prefer hypotheses for which we have independent evidence or that are natural extrapolations from what we already know.* Let's first illustrate and support this principle, and then apply it to the case of the fine-tuning.

Most of us take the existence of dinosaur bones to count as very strong evidence that dinosaurs existed in the past. But suppose a dinosaur skeptic claimed that she could explain the bones by postulating a "dinosaur-bone-producing-field" that simply materialized the bones out of thin air. Moreover, suppose further that, to avoid objections such as that there are no known physical laws that would allow for such a mechanism, the dinosaur skeptic simply postulated that we have not yet discovered these laws or detected these fields. Surely, none of us would let this skeptical hypothesis deter us from inferring the existence of dinosaurs. Why? Because although no one has directly observed dinosaurs, we do have experience of other animals leaving behind fossilized remains, and thus the dinosaur explanation is a *natural extrapolation* from our common experience. In contrast, to explain the dinosaur bones, the dinosaur skeptic has invented a set of physical laws, and a set of mechanisms that are *not* a natural extrapolation from anything we know or experience.

In the case of the fine-tuning, we already know that minds often produce fine-tuned devices, such as Swiss watches. Postulating God — a supermind — as the explanation of the fine-tuning, therefore, is a natural extrapolation from what we already observe minds to do. In contrast, it is difficult to see how the atheistic many-universes hypothesis could be considered a natural extrapolation from what we observe. Moreover, unlike the atheistic many-universes hypothesis, we have some experiential evidence for the existence of God, namely religious experience. Thus, by the above principle, we should prefer the theistic explanation of the fine-tuning over the atheistic many-universes explanation, everything else being equal.

Second Reason

A second reason for rejecting the atheistic many universes hypothesis is that the "many-universes generator" seems like it would need to be designed. For instance, in all current worked-out proposals for what this "universe generator" could be — such as the oscillating big bang and the vacuum fluctuation models explained above — the "generator" itself is governed by a complex set of physical laws that allow it to produce the universes. It stands to reason, therefore, that if these laws were slightly different the generator probably would not be able to produce any universes that could sustain life. After all, even my bread machine has to be made just right in order to work properly, and it only produces loaves of bread, not universes! Or consider a device as simple as a mousetrap: it requires that all the parts, such as the spring and hammer, be arranged just right in order to function. It is doubtful, therefore, whether the atheistic many-universe theory can entirely eliminate the problem of design the atheist faces; rather, at least to some extent, it seems simply to move the problem of design up one level.[17]

17. Moreover, the advocate of the atheistic many-universes hypothesis could not avoid this problem by hypothesizing that the many universes always existed as a "brute fact" without being produced by a universe generator. This would simply add to the problem: it would not only leave unexplained the fine-tuning or our own universe, but would leave unexplained the existence of these other universes.

Third Reason

A third reason for rejecting the atheistic many-universes hypothesis is that the universe generator must not only select the parameters of physics at random, but must actually randomly create or select the very laws of physics themselves. This makes this hypothesis seem even more far-fetched since it is difficult to see what possible physical mechanism could select or create laws.

The reason the "many-universes generator" must randomly select the laws of physics is that, just as the right values for the parameters of physics are needed for life to occur, the right set of laws is also needed. If, for instance, certain laws of physics were missing, life would be impossible. For example, without the law of inertia, which guarantees that particles do not shoot off at high speeds, life would probably not be possible.[18] Another example is the law of gravity: if masses did not attract each other, there would be no planets or stars, and once again it seems that life would be impossible. Yet another example is the *Pauli Exclusion Principle,* the principle of quantum mechanics that says that no two fermions — such as electrons or protons — can share the same quantum state. As prominent Princeton physicist Freeman Dyson points out,[19] without this principle all electrons would collapse into the nucleus and thus atoms would be impossible.

Fourth Reason

The fourth reason for rejecting the atheistic many-universes hypothesis is that it cannot explain other features of the universe that seem to exhibit apparent design, whereas theism can. For example, many physicists, such as Albert Einstein, have observed that the basic laws of physics exhibit an extraordinary degree of beauty, elegance, harmony, and ingenuity. Nobel prize-winning physicist Steven Weinberg, for instance, devotes a whole chapter of his book *Dreams of a Final Theory*[20] explaining how the criteria of beauty and elegance are commonly used to guide physicists in formulating the right laws. Indeed, one of the most prominent theoretical physicists of this century, Paul Dirac, went so far as to claim that "it is more important to have beauty in one's equations than to have them fit experiment."[21]

18. Leslie, *Universes,* 59.

19. Dyson, *Disturbing the Universe,* 251.

20. Chapter 6, "Beautiful Theories."

21. Paul Dirac, "The Evolution of the Physicist's Picture of Nature," *Scientific American* (May 1963): 47.

Now such beauty, elegance, and ingenuity make sense if the universe was designed by God. Under the atheistic many-universes hypothesis, however, there is no reason to expect the fundamental laws to be elegant or beautiful. As theoretical physicist Paul Davies writes, "If nature is so 'clever' as to exploit mechanisms that amaze us with their ingenuity, is that not persuasive evidence for the existence of intelligent design behind the universe? If the world's finest minds can unravel only with difficulty the deeper workings of nature, how could it be supposed that those workings are merely a mindless accident, a product of blind chance?"[22]

Final Reason

This brings us to the final reason for rejecting the atheistic many-universes hypothesis, which may be the most difficult to grasp: namely, neither the atheistic many-universes hypothesis (nor the atheistic single-universe hypothesis) can at present adequately account for the improbable initial arrangement of matter in the universe required by the second law of thermodynamics. To see this, note that according to the second law of thermodynamics, the entropy of the universe is constantly increasing. The standard way of understanding this entropy increase is to say that the universe is going from a state of order to disorder. We observe this entropy increase all the time around us: things, such as a child's bedroom, that start out highly organized tend to "decay" and become disorganized unless something or someone intervenes to stop it.

Now, for purposes of illustration, we could think of the universe as a scrabble-board that initially starts out in a highly ordered state in which all the letters are arranged to form words, but which keeps getting randomly shaken. Slowly, the board, like the universe, moves from a state of order to disorder. The problem for the atheist is to explain how the universe could have started out in a highly ordered state, since it is extraordinarily improbable for such states to occur by chance.[23] If, for example, one were to dump a bunch of letters at random on a scrabble-board, it would be very unlikely for most of them to form into words. At best, we would expect groups of letters to form into words in a few places on the board.

Now our question is, Could the atheistic many-universes hypothesis

22. Davies, *Superforce,* 235-36.

23. This connection between order and probability, and the second law of thermodynamics in general, is given a precise formulation in a branch of fundamental physics called *statistical mechanics,* according to which a state of high order represents a very improbable state, and a state of disorder represents a highly probable state.

explain the high degree of initial order of our universe by claiming that given enough universes, eventually one will arise that is ordered and in which intelligent life occurs, and so it is no surprise that we find ourselves in an ordered universe? The problem with this explanation is that it is overwhelmingly more likely for local patches of order to form in one or two places than for the whole universe to be ordered, just as it is overwhelmingly more likely for a few words on the scrabble-board randomly to form words than for all the letters throughout the board randomly to form words. Thus, the overwhelming majority of universes in which intelligent life occurs will be ones in which the intelligent life will be surrounded by a small patch of order necessary for its existence, but in which the rest of the universe is disordered. Consequently, even under the atheistic many-universes hypothesis, it would still be enormously improbable for intelligent beings to find themselves in a universe such as ours which is highly ordered throughout.[24]

Conclusion

Even though the above criticisms do not definitively refute the atheistic many-universes hypothesis, they do show that it has some severe disadvantages relative to theism. This means that if atheists adopt the atheistic many-universes hypothesis to defend their position, then atheism has become much less plausible than it used to be. Modifying a turn of phrase coined by philosopher Fred Dretske: these are inflationary times, and the cost of atheism has just gone up.

V. Overall Conclusion

In the above sections I showed there are good, objective reasons for claiming that the fine-tuning provides strong evidence for theism. I first presented an argument for thinking that the fine-tuning provides strong evidence for preferring theism over the atheistic single-universe hypothesis, and then presented a variety of different reasons for rejecting the

24. See Lawrence Sklar, *Physics and Chance: Philosophical Issues in the Foundation of Statistical Mechanics* (Cambridge: Cambridge University Press, 1993), chapter 8, for a review of the nontheistic explanations for the ordered arrangement of the universe and the severe difficulties they face.

atheistic many-universes hypothesis as an explanation of the fine-tuning. In order to help one appreciate the strength of the arguments presented, I would like to end by comparing the strength of the *core* version of the argument from the fine-tuning to what is widely regarded as the strongest atheist argument against theism, the argument from evil.[25]

Typically, the atheist argument against God based on evil takes a similar form to the core version of the fine-tuning argument. Essentially, the atheist argues that the existence of the kinds of evil we find in the world is very improbable under theism, but not improbable under atheism. Thus, by the prime principle of confirmation, they conclude that the existence of evil provides strong reasons for preferring atheism over theism.

What makes this argument weak in comparison to the core version of the fine-tuning argument is that, unlike in the case of the fine-tuning, the atheist does not have a significant objective basis for claiming that the existence of the kinds of evil we find in the world is highly improbable under theism. In fact, their judgment that it is improbable seems largely to rest on a mistake in reasoning. To see this, note that in order to show that it is improbable, atheists would have to show that it is *unlikely* that the types of evils we find in the world are necessary for any morally good, greater purpose, since if they are, then it is clearly not at all unlikely that an all good, all powerful being would create a world in which those evils are allowed to occur. But how could atheists show this without first surveying all possible morally good purposes such a being might have, something they have clearly not done? *Consequently, it seems, at most the atheist could argue that since no one has come up with any adequate purpose yet, it is unlikely that there is such a purpose.* This argument, however, is very weak, as I will now show.

The first problem with this atheist argument is that it assumes that the various explanations people have offered for why an all good God would create evil — such as the free will theodicy — ultimately fail. But even if we grant that these theodicies fail, the argument is still very weak. To see why, consider an analogy. Suppose someone tells me that there is a rattlesnake in my garden, and I examine a portion of the garden and do not find the snake. I would only be justified in concluding that there was probably no snake in the garden if either: i) I had searched at least half the garden; or ii) I had good reason to believe that if the snake were in the garden, it would likely be in the portion of the garden that I examined. If,

25. A more thorough discussion of the atheist argument from evil is presented in Daniel Howard-Snyder's chapter (pp. 76-115), and a discussion of other atheistic arguments is given in John O'Leary-Hawthorn's chapter (pp. 116-34).

for instance, I were randomly to pick some small segment of the garden to search and did not find the snake, I would be unjustified in concluding from my search that there was probably no snake in the garden. Similarly, if I were blindfolded and did not have any idea of how large the garden was (e.g., whether it was ten square feet or several square miles), I would be unjustified in concluding that it was unlikely that there was a rattlesnake in the garden, even if I had searched for hours with my rattlesnake-detecting dogs. Why? Because I would not have any idea of what percentage of the garden I had searched.

As with the garden example, we have no idea of how large the realm is of possible greater purposes for evil that an all good, omnipotent being could have. Hence we do not know what proportion of this realm we have actually searched. Indeed, considering the finitude of our own minds, we have good reason to believe that we have so far only searched a small proportion, and we do not have significant reason to believe that all the purposes God might have for allowing evil would be in the proportion we searched. Thus, we have little objective basis for saying that the existence of the types of evil we find in the world is highly improbable under theism.

From the above discussion, therefore, it is clear that the relevant probability estimates in the case of the fine-tuning are much more secure than those estimates in the probabilistic version of the the atheist's argument from evil, since unlike the latter, we can provide a fairly rigorous, objective basis for them based on actual calculations of the relative range of life-permitting values for the parameters of physics. (See the appendix to this chapter for a rigorous derivation of the probability of the fine-tuning under the atheistic single-universe hypothesis.) *Thus, I conclude, the core argument for preferring theism over the probabilistic version of the atheistic single-universe hypothesis is much stronger than the atheist argument from evil.*[26]

Appendix

In this appendix, I offer a rigorous support for premise (2) of the main argument: that is, the claim that the fine-tuning is very improbable under the atheistic single-universe hypothesis. Support for premise (2) will involve three major subsections. The first subsection will be devoted to explicating the fine-tuning of gravity since we will often use this to illustrate

26. This work was made possible in part by a Discovery Institute grant for the fiscal year 1997-1998.

our arguments. Then, in our second subsection, we will show how the improbability of the fine-tuning under the atheistic single-universe hypothesis can be derived from a commonly used, objective principle of probabilistic reasoning called the *principle of indifference*. Finally, in our third subsection, we will explicate what it could mean to say that the fine-tuning is improbable given that the universe is a unique, unrepeatable event as assumed by the atheistic single-universe hypothesis. The appendix will in effect answer the common atheist objection that theists can neither *justify* the claim that the fine-tuning is improbable under the atheistic single-universe hypothesis, nor can they provide an account of what it could possibly *mean* to say that the fine-tuning is improbable.

i. The Example of Gravity

The force of gravity is determined by Newton's law $F = Gm_1m_2/r^2$. Here G is what is known as the *gravitational constant,* and is basically a number that determines the force of gravity in any given circumstance. For instance, the gravitational attraction between the moon and the earth is given by first multiplying the mass of the moon (m_1) times the mass of the earth (m_2), and then dividing by the distance between them squared (r^2). Finally, one multiplies this result by the number G to obtain the total force. Clearly the force is directly proportional to G: for example, if G were to double, the force between the moon and the earth would double.

In the previous section, we reported that some calculations indicate that the force of gravity must be fine-tuned to one part in 10^{40} in order for life to occur. What does such fine-tuning mean? To understand it, imagine a radio dial, going from 0 to $2G_0$, where G_0 represents the current value of the gravitational constant. Moreover, imagine the dial being broken up into 10^{40} — that is, ten thousand, billion, billion, billion, billion — evenly spaced tick marks. To claim that the strength of gravity must be fine-tuned to one part in 10^{40} is simply to claim that, in order for life to exist, the constant of gravity cannot vary by even one tick mark along the dial from its current value of G_0.

ii. The Principle of Indifference

In the following subsections, we will use the *principle of indifference* to justify the assertion that the fine-tuning is highly improbable under the atheistic single-universe hypothesis.

a. The Principle Stated

Applied to cases in which there is a finite number of alternatives, the principle of indifference can be formulated as the claim that we should assign the same probability to what are called *equipossible alternatives,* where two or more alternatives are said to be equipossible if we have no reason to prefer one of the alternatives over any of the others. (In another version of the principle, alternatives that are relevantly symmetrical are considered equipossible and hence the ones that should be assigned equal probability.) For instance, in the case of a standard two-sided coin, we have no more reason to think that the coin will land on heads than that it will land on tails, and so we assign them each an equal probability. Since the total probability must add up to one, this means that the coin has a 0.5 chance of landing on heads and a 0.5 chance of landing on tails. Similarly, in the case of a standard six-sided die, we have no more reason to think that it will land on one number, say a 6, than any of the other numbers, such as a 4. Thus, the principle of indifference tells us to assign each possible way of landing an equal probability — namely $\frac{1}{6}$.

The above explication of the principle applies only when there are a finite number of alternatives, for example six sides on a die. In the case of the fine-tuning, however, the alternatives are not finite but form a continuous magnitude. The value of G, for instance, conceivably could have been any number between 0 and infinity. Now, continuous magnitudes are usually thought of in terms of ranges, areas, or volumes depending on whether or not we are considering one, two, three, or more dimensions. For example, the amount of water in an 8 oz. glass could fall anywhere within the *range* 0 oz. to 8 oz., such as 6.012345645 oz. Or, the exact position that a dart hits a dart board can fall anywhere within the *area* of the dart board. With some qualifications to be discussed below, the principle of indifference becomes in the continuous case the principle that *when we have no reason to prefer any one value of a parameter over another, we should assign equal probabilities to equal ranges, areas, or volumes.* So, for instance, suppose one aimlessly throws a dart at a dart board. Assuming the dart hits the board, what is the probability it will hit within the bull's eye? Since the dart is thrown aimlessly, we have no more reason to believe it will hit one part of the dart board than any other part. The principle of indifference, therefore, tells us that the probability of its hitting the bull's eye is the same as the probability of hitting any other part of the dart board of equal area. This means that the probability of its hitting the bull's eye is simply the ratio of the area of the bull's eye to the rest of the dart board. So, for instance, if the bull's eye forms only 5 percent of the total area of the board, then the probability of its hitting the bull's eye will be 5 percent.

b. Application to Fine-Tuning

In the case of the fine-tuning, we have no more reason to think that the parameters of physics will fall within the life-permitting range than within any other range, given the atheistic single-universe hypothesis. Thus according to the principle of indifference, equal ranges of these parameters should be assigned equal probabilities. As in the case of the dart board mentioned in the last section, this means that the probability of the parameters of physics falling within the life-permitting range under the atheistic single-universe hypothesis is simply the ratio of the range of life-permitting values (the "area of the bull's eye") to the total *relevant* range of possible values (the "relevant area of the dart board").

Now physicists can make rough estimates of the range of *life-permitting* values for the parameters of physics, as discussed above in the case of gravity, for instance. But what is the "total *relevant* range of possible values"? At first one might think that this range is infinite, since the values of the parameters could conceivably be anything. This, however, is not correct, for although the possible range of values could be infinite, for most of these values we have no way of estimating whether they are life-permitting or not. We do not truly know, for example, what would happen if gravity were 10^{60} times stronger than its current value: as far as we know, a new form of matter might come into existence that could sustain life. Thus, as far as we know, there could be other life-permitting ranges far removed from the actual values that the parameters have. Consequently, all we can say is that the life-permitting range is very, very small *relative* to the limited range of values for which we can make estimates, a range that we will hereafter refer to as the *"illuminated"* range.

Fortunately, however, this limitation does not effect the overall argument. The reason is that, based on the principle of indifference, we can still say that it is very improbable for the values for the parameters of physics to have fallen in the life-permitting range *instead* of some other part of the "illuminated" range.[27] And this *improbability* is all that is actu-

27. In the language of probability theory, this sort of probability is known as a conditional probability. In the case of G, calculations indicate that this conditional probability of the fine-tuning would be less than 10^{-40} since the life-permitting range is less than 10^{-40} of the range 0 to $2G_0$, the latter range being certainly smaller than the total "illuminated" range for G.

ally needed for our main argument to work. To see this, consider an analogy. Suppose a dart landed on the bull's eye at the center of a huge dart board. Further, suppose that this bull's eye is surrounded by a very large empty, bull's-eye-free, area. Even if there were many other bull's eyes on the dart board, we would still take the fact that the dart landed on the bull's eye instead of some other part of the large empty area surrounding the bull's eye as strong evidence that it was aimed. Why? Because we would reason that *given that the dart landed in the empty area,* it was very improbable for it to land in the bull's eye by chance but not improbable if it were aimed. Thus, by the prime principle of confirmation, we could conclude that the dart landing on the bull's eye strongly confirms the hypothesis that it was aimed over the chance hypothesis.

c. The Principle Qualified

Those who are familiar with the principle of indifference, and mathematics, will recognize that one important qualification needs to be made to the above account of how to apply the principle of indifference. (Those who are not mathematically adept might want to skip this and perhaps the next paragraph.) To understand the qualification, note that the ratio of ranges used in calculating the probability is dependent on how one parameterizes, or writes, the physical laws. For example, suppose for the sake of illustration that the range of life-permitting values for the gravitational constant is 0 to G_0, and the "illuminated" range of possible values for G is 0 to $2G_0$. Then, the ratio of life-permitting values to the range of "illuminated" possible values for the gravitational constant will be ½. Suppose, however, that one writes the law of gravity in the mathematically equivalent form of $F = \sqrt{U} m_1 m_2/r^2$, instead of $F=Gm_1m_2/r^2$, where $U=G^2$. (In this way of writing Newton's law, U becomes the new gravitational constant.) This means that $U_o = G_0^2$, where U_o, like G_0, represents the actual value of U in our universe. Then, the range of life-permitting values would be 0 to U_o, and the "illuminated" range of possible values would be 0 to $4U_o$ on the U scale (which is equivalent to 0 to $2G_0$ on the G scale). Hence, calculating the ratio of life-permitting values using the U scale instead of G scale yields a ratio of ¼ instead of ½. Indeed, for almost any ratio one chooses — such as one in which the life-permitting range is about the same size as the "illuminated" range — there exist mathematically equivalent forms of Newton's law that will yield that ratio. So, why choose the standard way of writing Newton's law to calculate the ratio instead of one in which the fine-tuning is not improbable at all?

The answer to this question is to require that the proportion used in calculating the probability be between *real* physical ranges, areas, or volumes, not merely mathematical representations of them. That is, the proportion given by the scale used in one's representation must directly correspond to the proportions actually existing in physical reality. As an illustration, consider how we might calculate the probability that a meteorite will fall in New York state instead of somewhere else in the northern, contiguous United States. One way of doing this is to take a standard map of the northern, contiguous United States, measure the area covered by New York on the map (say 2 square inches) and divide it by the total area of the map (say 30 square inches). If we were to do this, we would get approximately the right answer because the proportions on a standard map directly correspond to the actual proportions of land areas in the United States.[28] On the other hand, suppose we had a map made by some lover of the east coast in which, because of the scale used, the east coast took up half the map. If we used the proportions of areas as represented by this map we would get the wrong answer since the scale used would not correspond to real proportions of land areas. Applied to the fine-tuning, this means that our calculations of these proportions must be done using parameters that directly correspond to physical quantities in order to yield valid probabilities. In the case of gravity, for instance, the gravitational constant G directly corresponds to the force between two unit masses a unit distance apart, whereas U does not. (Instead, U corresponds to the square of the force.) Thus, G is the correct parameter to use in calculating the probability.[29]

28. I say "approximately right" because in this case the principle of indifference only applies to strips of land that are the same distance from the equator. The reason for this is that only strips of land equidistant from the equator are truly symmetrical with regard to the motion of the earth. Since the northern, contiguous United States are all about the same distance from the equator, equal land areas should be assigned approximately equal probabilities.

29. This solution will not always work since, as the well-known Bertrand Paradoxes illustrate (e.g., see Roy Weatherford, *Foundations of Probability Theory* [Boston: Routledge and Kegan Paul, 1982], 56), sometimes there are two equally good and conflicting parameters that directly correspond to a physical quantity and to which the principle of indifference applies. In these cases, at best we can say that the probability is somewhere between that given by the two conflicting parameters. This problem, however, typically does not seem to arise for most cases of fine-tuning. Also, it should be noted that the principle of indifference applies best to *classical* or *epistemic* probability, not other kinds of probability such as *relative frequency*. (See subsection iii below.)

d. Support for Principle

Finally, although the principle of indifference has been criticized on various grounds, several powerful reasons can be offered for its soundness if it is restricted in the ways explained in the last subsection. First, it has an extraordinarily wide range of applicability. As Roy Weatherford notes in his book, *Philosophical Foundations of Probability Theory,* "an astonishing number of extremely complex problems in probability theory have been solved, and usefully so, by calculations based entirely on the assumption of equiprobable alternatives [that is, the principle of indifference]."[30] Second, at least for the discrete case, the principle can be given a significant theoretical grounding in information theory, being derivable from Shannon's important and well-known measure of *information,* or *negative entropy.*[31] Finally, in certain everyday cases the principle of indifference seems the only justification we have for assigning probability. To illustrate, suppose that in the last ten minutes a factory produced the first fifty-sided die ever produced. Further suppose that every side of the die is (macroscopically) perfectly symmetrical with every other side, except for there being different numbers printed on each side. (The die we are imagining is like a fair six-sided die except that it has fifty sides instead of six.) Now, we all immediately know that upon being rolled the probability of the die coming up on any given side is one in fifty. Yet, we do not know this directly from experience with fifty-sided dice, since by hypothesis no one has yet rolled such dice to determine the relative frequency with which they come up on each side. Rather, it seems our only justification for assigning this probability is the principle of indifference: that is, given that every side of the die is relevantly macroscopically symmetrical with every other side, we have no reason to believe that the die will land on one side over any other side, and thus we assign them all an equal probability of one in fifty.[32]

30. Weatherford, *Probability Theory,* 35.

31. Sklar, *Physics and Chance,* 191; Bas van Fraassen, *Laws and Symmetry* (Oxford: Oxford University Press, 1989), 345.

32. Of course, one could claim that our experience with items such as coins and dice teaches us that whenever two alternatives are macroscopically symmetrical, we should assign them an equal probability, unless we have a particular reason not to. All this claim implies, however, is that we have experiential justification for the principle of indifference, and thus it does not take away from our main point that in certain practical situations we must rely on the principle of indifference to justify our assignment of probability.

iii. The Meaning of Probability

In the last section we used the principle of indifference to rigorously justify the claim that the fine-tuning is highly improbable under the atheistic single-universe hypothesis. We did not explain, however, what it could *mean* to say that it is improbable, especially given that the universe is a unique, unrepeatable event. To address this issue, we shall now show how the probability invoked in the fine-tuning argument can be straightforwardly understood either as what could be called *classical probability* or as what is known as *epistemic probability.*

Classical Probability

The *classical conception of probability* defines probability in terms of the ratio of number of "favorable cases" to the total number of equipossible cases.[33] Thus, for instance, to say the probability of a die coming up "4" is one out of six is simply to say that the number of ways a die could come up "4" is one-sixth the number of equipossible ways it could come up. Extending this definition to the continuous case, classical probability can be defined in terms of the relevant ratio of ranges, areas, or volumes over which the principle of indifference applies. Thus, under this extended definition, to say that the probability of the parameters of physics falling into the life-permitting value is very improbable simply *means* that the ratio of life-permitting values to the range of possible values is very, very small. Finally, notice that this definition of probability implies the principle of indifference, and thus we can be certain that the principle of indifference holds for classical probability.

Epistemic Probability

Epistemic probability is a widely recognized type of probability that applies to claims, statements, and hypotheses — that is, what philosophers call *propositions*.[34] (A proposition is any claim, assertion, statement, or hy-

33. See Weatherford, *Probability Theory,* ch. 2.

34. For an in-depth discussion of epistemic probability, see Richard Swinburne, *An Introduction to Confirmation Theory* (London: Methuen, 1973); Ian Hacking, *The Emergence of Probability: A Philosophical Study of Early Ideas About Probability, Induction and Statistical Inference* (Cambridge: Cambridge University Press, 1975); and Alvin Plantinga, *Warrant and Proper Function* (Oxford: Oxford University Press, 1993), chapters 8 and 9.

pothesis about the world.) Roughly, the epistemic probability of a proposition can be thought of as the degree of credence — that is, degree of confidence or belief — we rationally should have in the proposition. Put differently, epistemic probability is a measure of our rational degree of belief under a condition of ignorance concerning whether a proposition is true or false. For example, when one says that the special theory of relativity is probably true, one is making a statement of epistemic probability. After all, the theory is actually either true or false. But, we do not know for sure whether it is true or false, so we say it is probably true to indicate that we should put more confidence in its being true than in its being false. It is also commonly argued that the probability of a coin toss is best understood as a case of epistemic probability. Since the side the coin will land on is determined by the laws of physics, it is argued that our assignment of probability is simply a measure of our rational expectations concerning which side the coin will land on.

Besides epistemic probability simpliciter, philosophers also speak of what is known as the *conditional* epistemic probability of one proposition on another. The conditional epistemic probability of a proposition *R* on another proposition *S* — written as P(R/S) — can be defined as the degree to which the proposition *S of itself* should rationally lead us to expect that *R* is true. For example, there is a high conditional probability that it will rain today on the hypothesis that the weatherman has predicted a 100 percent chance of rain, whereas there is a low conditional probability that it will rain today on the hypothesis that the weatherman has predicted only a 2 percent chance of rain. That is, the hypothesis that the weatherman has predicted a 100 percent chance of rain today should strongly lead us to expect that it will rain, whereas the hypothesis that the weatherman has predicted a 2 percent chance should lead us to expect that it will not rain. Under the epistemic conception of probability, therefore, the statement that *the fine-tuning of the Cosmos is very improbable under the atheistic single-universe hypothesis* makes perfect sense: it is to be understood as making a statement about the degree to which the atheistic single-universe hypothesis would or should, *of itself,* rationally lead us to expect the cosmic fine-tuning.[35]

35. It should be noted here that this rational degree of expectation should not be confused with the degree to which one should expect the parameters of physics to fall within the life-permitting range if one believed the atheistic single-universe hypothesis. For even those who believe in this atheistic hypothesis should expect the parameters of physics to be life-permitting since this follows from the fact that we are alive. Rather,

Conclusion

The above discussion shows that we have at least two ways of understanding improbability invoked in our main argument: as classical probability or epistemic probability. This undercuts the common atheist objection that it is meaningless to speak of the probability of the fine-tuning under the atheistic single-universe hypothesis since under this hypothesis the universe is not a repeatable event.

---

the conditional epistemic probability in this case is the degree to which the atheistic single-universe hypothesis *of itself* should lead us to expect parameters of physics to be life-permitting. This means that in assessing the conditional epistemic probability in this and other similar cases, one must exclude contributions to our expectations arising from other information we have, such as that we are alive. In the case at hand, one way of doing this is by means of the following sort of thought experiment. Imagine a disembodied being with mental capacities and a knowledge of physics comparable to that of the most intelligent physicists alive today, except that the being does not know whether the parameters of physics are within the life-permitting range. Further, suppose that this disembodied being believed in the atheistic single-universe hypothesis. Then, the degree that being should rationally expect the parameters of physics to be life-permitting will be equal to our conditional epistemic probability, since its expectation is solely a result of its belief in the atheistic single-universe hypothesis, not other factors such as its awareness of its own existence.

4

God, Evil, and Suffering

Daniel Howard-Snyder

1. Evil and Suffering

Not long ago, an issue of my local paper reminded its readers of Susan Smith, the Carolinan mother who rolled her Mazda into a lake, drowning her two little sons strapped inside. It also reported the abduction and gang rape of an eleven-year-old girl by eight teenage members of Angelitos Sur 13, and the indictment on sixty-eight counts of sexual abuse of the "Frito Man", a forty-five-year-old man who handed out corn chips to neighborhood children in order to lure them to a secluded

I am grateful to the authors of this book and several others for comments on earlier drafts of this chapter, especially Terence Cuneo, William Davis, Mary Howard, Frances Howard-Snyder, Nate King, Trenton Merricks, Georgia and Tom Senor, and Michael Murray, the latter of whom exercised editorial virtues *in excelsis*. My thinking about God and evil has been shaped mostly by William Alston, Paul Draper, Alvin Plantinga, William Rowe, Peter van Inwagen, and Steve Wykstra. On this occasion, however, I want to express my deepest gratitude to Steve. His work on our topic has not only enriched my understanding of something I care about deeply, it was for me the grain of sand God used to make the unfinished pearl that is my faith. I dedicate this chapter to Steve. I would be remiss if I failed to mention that I have relied heavily on two of his papers, both of which repay careful study: "The Humean Obstacle to Evidential Arguments from Suffering: On Avoiding the Evils of 'Appearance'," *International Journal for the Philosophy of Religion* (1984), collected in *The Problem of Evil,* and "Rowe's Noseeum Arguments from Evil," in *The Evidential Argument from Evil.*

location. More recently, the headlines announced the untimely death of Ashley Jones, a twelve-year-old girl from nearby Stanwood, Washington — she was raped and bludgeoned to death while babysitting her neighbor's kids.

These are particularly disgusting, appalling cases of evil, all the more so because children are the victims. One might think that such cases occur only very rarely. I wish that were so. ABC News recently reported that in the United States a child dies from abuse by a parent or guardian every six hours. One is left with the disturbing thought: if that is how frequently a child dies from abuse in the U.S., how frequently are children *merely* abused? A sinister side effect of familial abuse is that abused children are much more likely to abuse their own children; and so the attitudes and habits of abuse pass from generation to generation, a cycle of evil and suffering from which it can be enormously difficult to extricate oneself.

Frequently, a child's suffering is unintentionally caused by those who love them most. Alvin Plantinga recalls a story about

> a man who drove a cement mixer truck. He came home one day for lunch; his three year old daughter was playing in the yard, and after lunch, when he jumped into his truck and backed out, he failed to notice that she was playing behind it; she was killed beneath the great dual wheels.[1]

And who can forget the scorching summer of 1995, when a Kentucky professor, after dropping off his wife at work, drove to school, parked, and absentmindedly left his children in the car for the day, the windows closed; they slowly baked to death.

Such suffering and evil is wrought by human hands. There are other sources, however. A visit to just about any major hospital reveals children born with grossly debilitating genetic abnormalities that impair them so severely one can't help but think that their lives are not worth living. Moreover, children are not exempt from the horrors resulting from earthquakes, tornadoes, hurricanes, famine, and the like.

Of course, adults suffer horribly and undeservedly as well, although their innocence is more frequently questionable. And the numbers are staggering: six million snuffed out in the Holocaust, thirty million in the slave trade, forty million in Stalin's purges, a third of Europe's population

1. Alvin Plantinga, "Self-Profile," in *Alvin Plantinga*, ed. Peter van Inwagen and James E. Tomberlin (Dordrecht: Reidel, 1985), 34.

during the Plague, several million starved just in my lifetime: the list goes on and on. And what about nonhuman animals? We in the enlightened West like to think we are more civilized than our predecessors in our relations to the beasts. We regard the once common practice of beating animals as barbaric, for example. Nevertheless, we don't think twice about hunting for sport, or how the livestock and poultry we don't need to eat got on our plates, or how the musk got into our perfumes. But that's nothing compared to the suffering doled out by Nature. It boggles the mind to consider the billions upon billions of animals stalked and killed or eaten alive by predators or who died slowly and painfully, decimated by disease, famine, or drought.

So it is that we must face a sobering fact: the history of our planet is a history stuffed with undeserved, horrific evil and suffering.

2. Two Problems

Evil and suffering is thought to pose a problem for Christians or, more generally, for theists, those who believe in a God who is at once all-powerful or almighty, all-knowing and perfectly good. What sort of problem is it? As it turns out, there are two problems, not one.

2.1. The Practical Problem of Evil and the Theoretical Problem of Evil

When we or our loved ones suffer horribly, we may not understand why God permits it; we may see no good it serves; we may be unable to make any sense of it. "This can be deeply perplexing," writes Plantinga, "and deeply disturbing. It can lead a believer to take towards God an attitude he himself deplores; it can tempt him to be angry with God, to mistrust God, to adopt an attitude of bitterness and rebellion."[2] In the grip of such rage, we might raise our fists toward heaven and curse God; alternatively, we might repress our feelings, become forlorn, and eventually give in to despair. A completely different stance toward evil and suffering, however, merely considers whether it is evidence that there is no God, or evidence that theistic belief is unwarranted, irrational, unreasonable, dubious, or otherwise intellectually suspect.

2. Plantinga, "Self-Profile," 35.

We have here two complex mixes of attitudes and feelings, and two corresponding problems. In the first case, the problem is how to maintain or restore a relationship with God in the face of suffering and tragedy while being true to ourselves and completely open and honest with him about how we feel. In the second case, however, the problem is to figure out whether evil and suffering is good reason to believe that the theistic God does not exist. In the first case, our relationship with God is strained; in the second, we want to know whether a certain sort of argument succeeds. The first is best conducted with the aid of a discerning pastor, priest, or mentor, on one's knees; the second requires the help of those trained to evaluate evidence and arguments, pen in hand and lots of paper nearby. The first is an intensely practical problem; the second is "merely" — as they say — theoretical.

Note two facts about these two problems. First, although we can separate them in the abstract, *they typically come together in our experience*. For example, reflecting on an impressively powerful argument from evil, I may begin to suspect that there is no God after all; my doubt may turn to fear or a sense of estrangement from God; consequently, I might become angry or forlorn. On the other hand, it is relatively easy — almost natural — for a believer to move from experienced suffering to outright disbelief. Angry at God for allowing me or my loved ones to suffer, I might lash out at him, perhaps subconsciously; and what better way to do that than to refuse him his due and to demand that he play by my rules, rules that make good sense, not just to me but to all fair-minded people. In this frame of mind, I might put God on trial for negligence and gross incompetence, and there, in the courtroom of my inner self, marshal the evidence against him. If I leave matters here — internally rehearsing my case against God, week after week, month after month — it may not be long before I wake up one morning to find the verdict delivered: what was once anger, pain, and fear is now cool, calculated disbelief.

Nevertheless — and this is the second important fact — although the theoretical and practical problems of evil come together in our experience, we must recognize that they are distinct problems and, consequently, that *a solution to one might not be a solution to the other.* The sorts of things we need to do to deal with the practical problem *might not* be relevant to solving the theoretical problem; conversely, the sorts of things we need to do to deal with the theoretical problem *might not* be relevant to solving the practical problem.

2.2. The Importance of Distinguishing the Two Problems

Now, why have I distinguished the practical and theoretical problems of evil and cautioned against our expecting a solution to the one to be a solution to the other? For two reasons. First, because in what follows I will focus on the theoretical problem, not the practical problem, and second (and more importantly), what I have to say about the theoretical problem is not intended to help with the practical problem — thus, even if what I have to say below fails with regard to the practical problem, that is no strike against it.

No doubt many readers will be dismayed by my choice of focus. I am in sympathy with them. After all, evil and suffering are too real to be dealt with on a merely theoretical level. We need practical advice and wisdom, not speculative hypotheses; we need something we can apply to our lives, something we can use, something to nourish the heart and soul, not the head. In short, we don't need a bunch of "philosophical twaddle" about God and evil, as the pastor at my mother's church put it recently.

There is an important truth lurking here; and some equally important confusions. First, the important truth. For many of us, there are times when, even if we understood completely why evil and suffering are not evidence against the existence of God, it would not matter to us. Many of us are faced with the deterioration of our bodies and minds; we are afraid and in constant, sometimes excruciating, pain; we see our loved ones crushed by cruelty or Nature's firm hand. We need solace, not syllogisms. To be offered philosophical speculation in times like these is to be offered a cold stone when only warm bread will do. So far, so good. Many people, however, go on to infer from this important truth that it is a waste of time to examine carefully whether evil is evidence against theism and to learn exactly why it is not. They infer that a deep understanding of the complexities involved in solving the theoretical problem is irrelevant to what they and others really need.

The premise here is true: for many people, there are times when "philosophical twaddle" about God and evil cannot meet their needs. But it does not follow that there is no time when such philosophical reflection would greatly benefit them; moreover, even if some people would gain nothing from such reflection, it doesn't follow that nobody would. There are two points to underscore here. First, while for many of us there are times in our lives when "philosophical twaddle" about God and evil seems nothing more than a bunch of irrelevant nonsense, for most reflective people there will come a time when almost nothing else will be more important. And, second, even if we ourselves will never benefit from knowing exactly how to solve the theoretical problem of evil, there may well be other people who will, perhaps even people we will meet. Let me illustrate both of these points briefly.

Many believers are torn up about evil and suffering precisely because it seems to be such strong evidence against their belief in a loving God. They find it difficult to love God with all their heart, soul, strength, and mind — but *especially* their minds. If such people come to understand why evil is no reason to believe that God does not love them — if they truly come to grips with the theoretical problem of evil — they may well be on their way to finding the comfort *they* need; consequently, they may gain the strength to respond aptly to the horrific evil and suffering they encounter in their own lives and in the world at large. Many unbelievers, on the other hand, doubt the credibility of basic Christian belief on account of the evil and suffering in the world. If they can be convinced that evil is not evidence against the existence of God, one of the most severe intellectual obstacles to their coming to faith may be removed.

So, from a Christian point of view, we need to take quite seriously the efforts that follow in this chapter even if they are "merely" theoretical.[3]

3. "Why Does God Permit Evil and Suffering?"

I begin with a simple observation: the theoretical "problem" of evil is often expressed in the form of a pointed question. God is able to prevent evil and suffering, and he would know about them before they happened, right? Moreover, since he is unsurpassably good, surely he would not permit them without good reason. So *why doesn't he prevent them?* Typically, however, the question is much more pointed: Why did God permit the children in the Oklahoma City bombing to suffer like that? And why did he permit my father — an honest, hard-working man — to wither away prematurely with leukemia? And even if there is a good reason for him to permit some evil and suffering, even a great deal of it, *why so much?*

3. For more on the practical problem of evil, see Nicholas Wolterstorff, *Lament for a Son* (Grand Rapids: Eerdmans, 1987); C. S. Lewis, *A Grief Observed* (New York: Bantam Books, 1961); and Harold Kushner, *When Bad Things Happen to Good People* (New York: Avon Books, 1981). Much of the insight of these authors is rooted in a resolution of the theoretical problem.

Some people readily answer such questions. They might say, for example: "God permits evil because if he didn't, we'd have no freedom; we'd be just like robots. And the same goes for the children in Oklahoma City and your father. If God had prevented the bombing, the freedom of Timothy McVeigh would have been jeopardized; and if God had prevented your father's suffering, even just a little, then he would not have been free to respond to it virtuously." Others, including devout Christians, deem such answers "tepid, shallow, and ultimately frivolous," as Plantinga puts it. We'll delve into these matters shortly; for now I want to make a different point.

Questions about why God permits evil and suffering — *when asked in a rhetorical "so there!" tone* — disguise arguments. For example, the pointed questions in the paragraph before last disguise the argument that since you can't say why God would permit evil in general or the Oklahoma City bombing or my father's painful, untimely death, there is no reason. This presupposes that you would be in a position to identify reasons that would justify God, if there were any. But isn't it perfectly sensible to ask why we should assume that? By disguising his argument in the form of a question, the questioner may be trying to evade his responsibility to defend his assumption. So, when people rhetorically ask you, "Why does God permit evil?," bring the disguised argument and its assumptions into broad daylight and assess them, as we shall in section six below.

4. The Basic Argument from Evil

A terminological note: the word "evil" can be used in many ways. An old-fashioned way uses it to refer to wickedness — "evil," strictly so called — and suffering and pain and anything else bad that happens. This use of the word has a venerable history; discussions of the theoretical problem of evil throughout history use the word "evil" in this way. In what follows, however, I will use it to refer specifically to *undeserved, intense* suffering and pain as well as *horrific* wickedness. I'm not interested here in suffering that people deserve, or in bumps and bruises or white lies and mild temper tantrums. I will focus on the stuff that turns our stomachs.

My thesis is simple: every argument from evil fails. Unfortunately, I haven't the space to consider every argument, so I will restrict myself to some popular ones and offer objections that will apply to others. I begin with the most basic argument.

4.1. The Basic Argument Stated

The most straightforward way to put the argument from evil is like this:

1. If God exists, then there is no evil.
2. There is evil.
3. So, God does not exist (from 1 & 2).

3 follows from 1 and 2, and 2 is surely true.[4] That leaves premise 1. Is it true?

J. L. Mackie famously argued for premise 1 like this:[5]

1a. A perfectly good being always prevents evil as far as he can.
1b. An omnipotent and omniscient being can do anything possible.
1c. So, if a perfectly good, omnipotent, and omniscient being exists, he prevents evil completely (from 1a & 1b).
1d. If God exists, then he is perfectly good, omnipotent, and omniscient.
1e. So, if God exists, he prevents evil completely (from 1c & 1d).

It follows from 1e that if God exists, then there is no evil — which is premise 1 of the basic argument.

Is Mackie's argument a *good* argument? That depends on whether all the premises are true. Are they?

Most theists accept 1d, but some say it is false: they say we need to give up the omnipotence and omniscience of God. Unfortunately, this tack is not as attractive as it first appears. For we would have to give up much more than omnipotence and omniscience to help out here. We would have to say God lacks power and knowledge to such an extent that he *can't* prevent evil. And there lies the trouble. For how could God have enough power and knowledge to create and sustain the physical universe

4. St. Augustine and the medieval Christian tradition generally would object that premise 2 is false. For, *strictly speaking,* there *is* no evil but only lack of good just as, *strictly speaking,* there are no holes but only lack of dirt in certain places. Unfortunately, this objection doesn't get to the heart of the matter. Premise 2 can be easily rephrased as "Sometimes sentient beings suffer intensely and undeservedly, and sometimes persons act in horrifically wicked ways," which does not imply that there *is* evil. Augustinians are invited to make the appropriate substitutions throughout the text.

5. J. L. Mackie, "Evil and Omnipotence," *Mind* (1955), collected in *The Problem of Evil,* ed. Robert and Marilyn Adams (Oxford: Oxford University Press, 1990).

if he can't even prevent evil? How could he be the providential governor of the world if he is unable to do what even *we* frequently do, namely prevent evil? So if we take this route, it seems we would have to jettison more than we bargained for. Perhaps we would do better to look elsewhere.

Consider 1a. Would a perfectly good being *always* prevent evil as far as he can? Suppose he had a reason to permit evil, a reason that was compatible with his never doing wrong and his being perfect in love, what I'll call a *justifying reason*. For example, suppose that if he prevented evil completely, then we would miss out on a greater good, a good whose goodness was so great that it far surpassed the badness of evil. In that case, he might not prevent evil as far as he can, for he would have a justifying reason to permit it. Proponents of the basic argument typically respond by modifying 1a to read: "A perfectly good being always prevents evil as far as he can *unless there is a reason that would justify him in permitting it*."

But notice that altering 1a in this way means that Mackie's argument must be altered in other ways. For if a perfectly good being might permit evil for a justifying reason, then God might do the same, in which case 1c and 1e must be similarly altered. Consequently, we must also alter the basic argument in two ways, indicated by italics below:

1. If God exists, then there is no evil, *unless there is a reason that would justify him in permitting it.*
2. There is evil.
3. *There is no reason that would justify God in permitting evil.*
4. So, God does not exist.[6]

Notice the new premise, premise 3. This modified basic argument nicely brings the main issue to the foreground, namely, whether there is a reason that would justify God in permitting evil.

4.2. The Categorical Ban on Permitting Evil

Why suppose that there is no reason that would justify God in permitting evil? One answer is that it is wrong or unloving for *anyone* to permit evil under *any* circumstances.

6. Under the influence of objections like those we will consider in section 5, Mackie reformulated his 1955 argument in *The Miracle of Theism* (Oxford: Oxford University Press, 1982), chapter 9; see especially 154-55. Something close to Mackie's reformulation is the focus of section 6.

This answer seems false. What if the only way to prevent horrible suffering is to permit less horrible but equally undeserved suffering to occur? Or, what if the only way to prevent horrible, undeserved suffering from befalling many others is to let fewer people suffer? Suppose you're a lifeguard and several swimmers are drowning. If you go after the one furthest away, you'll have to let three others nearby drown, but you can rescue the three nearby swimmers, provided you let the furthest one drown. In that case, it is neither wrong nor unloving of you to save the three and let the one drown. So it is false that it is wrong or unloving for *anyone* to permit evil under *any* circumstance.

Of course, God, unlike you, is omnipotent and omniscient. You can't get to all the swimmers; God can. One might assert, then, that the *only* reasons that justify us in permitting evil involve our impotence or ignorance. So while there may be circumstances in which it is neither wrong nor unloving for *us* to permit suffering, there can't be any for God since he is neither impotent nor ignorant. He can always bring about the greater good without permitting evil.

As plausible as this line of thought might initially appear, it fails. For even if God is omnipotent and omniscient, it does not follow that he can always bring about the greater good without permitting evil. God's power is limited to what is possible; not even an omnipotent being has the power to do what is absolutely impossible. Thus, *if* there were some greater good that *absolutely could not* occur unless evil were permitted, it might well figure in God's reason to permit evil.

Many Christians have a difficult time with sentences like "God's power is limited to what is possible." Two points might be helpful here. First, to say that God's power is limited to what is possible is not to say God's power is limited to what *we are able to do,* or to what *we think* is possible. Rather, it is to say that God's power does not permit him to do what is *absolutely impossible.* Second, very few Christian thinkers have been willing to say that it is possible for God both to exist and not exist at the very same time, or that it is possible for a man to be a bachelor and married at once, or that the number 2 can be the only whole number between 1 and 3 and be odd — and for good reason. Such things are absolutely impossible. This is the same answer Christians usually give to questions like, "Why didn't God save us without sacrificing his Son?" and "Why can't God break a promise?" It shouldn't be surprising, therefore, to countenance the same answer to questions like "Why didn't God fulfill his purposes without permitting evil?" or "Why can't God bring about every greater good while still preventing evil?" Let's return to the main thread of thought.

If there were some greater good that *could not possibly* occur unless evil were permitted, it might well figure in God's reason to permit evil. Of course, that's a big *if. Is* there a greater good that could not occur unless evil were permitted? *Is* there such a good that might figure in God's reason for permitting evil?

5. Theodicies

There are several, interrelated attempts to justify God's permission of evil, to give reasons for his permitting evil. We call them *theodicies.* I'll sketch the more popular theodicies and evaluate the standard objections.

5.1. Punishment Theodicy

God would be justified in *punishing evildoers,* and suffering is a result of his punishing them.

But What about Undeserved Suffering?

While God is justified in punishing the wicked for their wrongdoing, much of the suffering in the world is *undeserved.* And no one can sensibly say that God would be justified in punishing those who don't deserve it. But might not *all* the suffering in the world be deserved? I doubt it. Nonhuman animals, very young children and severely impaired adults suffer immensely but do not deserve it since they are not *morally* responsible for their actions. They lack the requisite capacities for moral deliberation and awareness. Moreover, although many morally responsible persons suffer to a degree that is proportionate to their sins, many more do not. (This is one of the main lessons of the book of Job.) Finally, the punishment theodicy does not even begin to explain why God permitted wickedness in the first place.

So, while *some* suffering might be accounted for by divine punishment, it cannot explain the evil with which we are mainly concerned: undeserved suffering and horrific wickedness.[7]

7. Two notes: First, if we are reincarnated, then maybe, for all we know, apparently undeserved suffering really is deserved since it is punishment for evildoing in previous lives. But the Church has always rejected the doctrine of reincarnation. Second, a Christian can affirm that there is undeserved suffering without calling into question either the doctrine of inherited sin or eternal punishment.

5.2. Counterpart Theodicy

Good and evil are like pairs of opposites or counterparts. If one exists so does the other. So, if there were no evil, its opposite — moral goodness — wouldn't exist. Thus, God would be justified in permitting evil since that's the only way there can be good.

How Can Theists Use This Theodicy?

One difficulty here is that, according to theism, God is unsurpassably morally good. Moreover, *he* could have existed without there being any evil. After all, what if he had never created anything? Then he would have existed and there would have been good — but there would have been no evil. So, according to theism, it's *false* that if there were no evil there would be no good.

Difficulties for the Opposites Exist Principle

Note that the most natural understanding of the claim that if one of a pair of "opposites" or "counterparts" exists, the other exists also is this:

> If there is something that has a certain feature, F, then there is something that has the opposite feature, not-F.

Call this the *Opposites Exist Principle*. It implies that so long as there is something that has the property of being rectangular, there is something with the property of being nonrectangular. Likewise, so long as something has the property of being morally good, there is something with the property of lacking moral goodness, being not-good, you might say.

One difficulty here is that just as there are different ways of being nonrectangular (e.g., triangular and circular), so there are different ways of being not-good. One way is to be neither morally good nor evil, just neutral between moral goodness and evil. Hydrogen atoms and mustache hairs, for example, are neutral in this way. So even if the Opposites Exist Principle is true, it does not imply that if there is something that is morally good, then there is something that is evil (rather than being neutral). Furthermore, even if the Principle did imply that there is something that is evil, it would only require a speck of evil, not a world stuffed with it like ours is. A more important difficulty is that the Principle is false. After all, it is not impossible for there to be a world in which everything was immaterial. Moreover, something has the property of being a nonunicorn, namely you. And what's the opposite of that property? Being a unicorn. So, *if* the Principle is true, then there is something that has the property of being a unicorn, which is to say that there is at least one unicorn. Of course, there are no unicorns; thus, since the Principle implies that there are unicorns, it is false.[8]

Let's now consider some theodicies that have a better chance of explaining evil.

5.3. Free Will Theodicy

God could have created us so that there was no chance of us going wrong or being bad. If he had done so the result would have been splendid, but we would have missed out on a very great good, namely, self-determination. For one to be *self-determined* is for one to be free to a significant degree with respect to the sort of person one becomes, the sort of character one has — and that requires that one have it within one's power to be both good and evil. Lacking such freedom, we could not be deeply responsible for who we are, who we will become and whether we will manifest and confirm our character through the choices we make. Since the capacity for self-determination is such a great good and it requires that we be given considerable latitude with respect to harming ourselves severely, it is a reason that would justify God in permitting evil.[9]

But Why Not Block Harm to Others?

One might object that development of my character requires only that my choices affect me, that is, that they serve to develop my character in one way or another. But couldn't God have arranged things in such a way that while my choices have an effect on me and my character, they have no effect on anyone else (or at least none of the bad ones has an effect on any-

8. Perhaps those who use the counterpart theodicy mean something very different. Perhaps they mean that we couldn't *know* one of a pair of opposites without knowing the other of the pair. Thus, we couldn't *know* good without knowing evil; and we couldn't *know* evil without there being evil; so, to know good, there has to be evil. Thus, God would be justified in permitting evil because without it we wouldn't know good. I leave as homework an evaluation of this argument.

9. See Michael Murray's chapter, "Heaven and Hell" (pp. 287-318), in this volume for a more detailed development of the line of thought here.

one else)? For example, suppose I choose freely to steal from you. My choice can contribute to my being untrustworthy without my ever actually stealing since God can arrange things in such a way that I believe I stole even though I didn't. In a nutshell, self-determination doesn't account for the bad consequences for others of evil free choices.[10]

There are several replies to this objection, foremost of which are two.

Reply 1. If God systematically prevents us from harming others yet permits us to have a significant say about the sorts of persons we become, then it will have to *look* to us as though we can harm others even though we can't. For if I know nothing I do can harm others, then I won't have the same opportunity to develop my character as I would if it seemed that I could harm others. But deception is incompatible with God's goodness, one might urge.

Unfortunately, this reply overlooks the fact that deception is not always wrong nor always unloving. (Just ask any parent.) Perhaps preventing the horrific consequences for others of our free choices is as watertight a reason for deception as there can be. Then again, perhaps not. Let's look into the matter a little more closely.

If God were to arrange things so that none of the horrific consequences for others of our choices really occurred although they appeared to, then we — each of us — would be living a massive illusion. It would seem as though we were involved in genuine relationships with others, making choices that matter for each other, when in fact nothing of the sort really occurred. Our whole lives would be a charade, a sham, a farce; and we wouldn't have a clue. While such massive deception would not result in an utterly meaningless existence (we would still be self-determining creatures), it isn't obvious that such massive deception about matters so central to our lives would be permissible or loving.

Reply 2. A related reply agrees that self-determination does not justify God's permitting us to harm others, even if it does justify God's permitting us to harm ourselves. What other goods, then, would be lost if God were to give us the freedom only to affect ourselves? Well, as indicated in the last reply, we would have no responsibility for each other and we would not be able to enter into the most meaningful relationships; for we are deeply responsible for others and can enter into relationships of love only if we can both benefit and harm others.

10. See Steven Boer's "The Irrelevance of the Free Will Defense," *Analysis* (1975), 110-12.

This point deserves development. We are deeply responsible for others only if our choices actually make a big difference to their well-being, and that cannot happen unless we can benefit them as well as harm them. This seems obvious enough. Frequently missed, however, is the fact that a similar point applies to love *relationships,* as contrasted with loving attitudes and feelings. Two persons cannot share in the most significant relationships of love unless it is up to each of them that they are so related; this fact can be seen by considering what we want from those whose love we value most. Jean-Paul Sartre expresses the point like this:

> The man who wants to be loved does not desire the enslavement of the beloved. He is not bent on becoming the object of passion which flows forth mechanically. He does not want to possess an automaton, and if we want to humiliate him, we need only try to persuade him that the beloved's passion is the result of a psychological determinism. The lover will then feel that both his love and his being are cheapened. . . . If the beloved is transformed into an automaton, the lover finds himself alone.[11]

Since those love relationships we cherish most are those in which we are most deeply vested, in light of love's freedom they are also those from which we can suffer most. It simply is not possible, therefore, for us to be in relationships of love without (at some time) having it within our power to harm and be harmed in a serious fashion.

Something analogous might be said of our relationship with God as well. Suppose God wanted a relationship of love with some of his creatures, and so made some of them fit to be loved by him and capable of reciprocating his love. Here he faces a choice: he could guarantee that they return his love, or he could leave it up to them. If he guaranteed it, they would never have a choice about whether they loved him, in which case their love of him would be a sham and he'd know it. Clearly, then, God cannot be in a relationship of love with his creatures unless he leaves it up to them whether they reciprocate his love. And that requires that they (at some time) have it within their power to withhold their love from him. But that cannot be unless they are able to be and do evil.[12]

11. *Being and Nothingness* (New York, 1956), 367, quoted in Vincent Brummer, *The Model of Love* (Cambridge: Cambridge University Press, 1993), 160.

12. A question arises: God enters into relationships of love, and yet he is not able to be or do evil; so why can't he make us capable of relationships of love while also making us unable to be and do evil? In response, some deny that God is unable to be or do evil.

Deep responsibility for others, relationships of love with our fellows and with God: if these were worthless or even meagerly good things, God would not be justified in permitting evil in order that we might be capable of them. But these are goods of tremendous — perhaps unsurpassable — value. And they are impossible in a world where our choices only have an effect on ourselves.[13]

Why Not Create Persons Who Always Freely Choose the Good?

Another objection is that, since God knows before creating how each of his creatures will act, he can make a world in which everyone *always freely* chooses the good. He is omnipotent, after all, and so he can create any world he pleases.[14] It follows that God can create a world with the great goods of self-determination, deep responsibility for others, and love *without* there being any evil at all. Thus, these goods cannot justify God's permission of evil.

Reply. Note that this objection relies on the thought that *if God is omnipotent, then he can create any world he pleases.* This is false. For if God creates free creatures, he must leave it up to them what world results from their choices. Let's develop this point briefly.

Out of all of the possible creatures God could create, suppose he aims to create me, and suppose he considers whether to make me free with respect to planting roses along Walhout Way, a little section of my garden. If he did, he would have to place me in a situation in which it is *up to me* whether I plant roses or refrain from doing so. Now, if he placed me in such a situation, either I would freely plant or I wouldn't. For the sake of illustration, suppose I would. Now imagine that God tries to make a world in which I freely *refrain* from planting. Can he? Not if he leaves it up to me whether I plant. For, given our supposition, if he left it up to me, I would *not* refrain; rather, I would plant. So, given that I would freely plant roses along Walhout Way if it were left up to me, God — even though omnipo-

---

Others distinguish love at its best *for an essentially good divine being* from love at its best *for a creature made to enter into relationships of love,* and then argue that while the latter requires the ability to withhold love, the first does not. And there are other options as well.

13. See Richard Swinburne, *The Existence of God* (Oxford: Oxford University Press, 1979); chapter 11, "Some Major Strands of Theodicy," in *The Evidential Argument from Evil,* ed. Daniel Howard-Snyder (Bloomington: Indiana University Press, 1996), 36-42; and *Providence and the Problem of Evil* (Oxford: Oxford University Press, 1998).

14. Mackie takes this line in *The Miracle of Theism,* 164.

tent — cannot make a world in which I am in that situation and I freely refrain from planting roses. To make that world God would have to *make* me so that I refrain, in which case I would not *freely* refrain.

Therefore, the assumption made by this objection is false. If God creates free persons, he *cannot* create just any world he pleases, even though he is omnipotent. Which world results from his creative activity is, in no small part, up to his free creatures.

We can go further. For we can now see that, for all we know, it was not within God's power to create a world with persons who always freely choose the good. How could this be? Well, as we just saw, if God creates free creatures, then he can't create some worlds. In the example above, God cannot create a world in which I freely refrain from planting roses along Walhout Way. That's because I would freely plant if God left it up to me. Now, what if it were true that for *any* world that has at least as much good as ours and in which every person always freely chooses the good, no matter how God started things off, persons would freely go wrong at least as much as we (actual humans) go wrong? If that were true, then no matter how hard God tried, he simply could not create a world with persons who always freely choose good, at least not one with as much good in it as our world. And here's the rub: for all we know, maybe that's the way things are.[15]

This is a good place to observe that the free will theodicy is *not* to be confused with the cliché, "God doesn't *do* evil, we do. He just *allows* it. So he's not to blame, we are." This cliché, unlike the free will theodicy, assumes that if one does not *do* evil but only *allows* it, then one is not responsible for its happening. That's false. I may not cut off my daughter's fingers but only allow my son to do it; still, if he does it, I'm at least partially responsible.

What about Evil Resulting from Natural Disturbances?

One might object that the free will theodicy doesn't explain why God would permit *natural evil*, that is, suffering resulting from natural distur-

15. A more thorough presentation of this sort of reply is in Plantinga's *God, Freedom and Evil* (Grand Rapids: Eerdmans, 1974), 32-44. Note that both the objection and the reply I gave presuppose that an omniscient being could know before creation what uncreated (merely possible) creatures would do if they were created and left it up to them how to behave. Many theists deny this. See, e.g., Robert Adams, "Middle Knowledge and the Problem of Evil," *American Philosophical Quarterly* (1977), collected in *The Problem of Evil.*

bances like earthquakes, disease, and famine — sources of evil other than free persons.

Reply. We might try to extend the free will theodicy to explain natural evil. For example, we might say that, contrary to appearances, such evil really is a *direct* result of the activity of free *nonhuman* persons, powerful evil angels intent on destroying God's creation and harming his creatures. Satan and his cohorts crumple the earth's crust causing volcanoes and earthquakes, they twist strands of DNA into destructive forms, they get inside animals and make them eat each other, and so on. This explanation, however, has questionable apologetic value since it presupposes that there are angels, a thesis not accepted by most nonbelievers. Moreover, it flies in the face of our understanding of the natural causes of volcanoes, earthquakes, genetic mutation, predation, and other sources of natural evil. A more plausible explanation is that natural evil results *indirectly* from free *human* choices. This line of thought has been sketched most recently in the context of the "natural consequences theodicy," which is worth considering in its own right as well. Let's take a closer look.

5.4. Natural Consequences Theodicy

Suppose God created humans so that he might love them and they might return his love. In giving our ancestors the power to love him, God gave them the ability to withhold their love. And that's what they did. As a consequence, they ruined themselves. Having turned from God, they began to harm one another. Moreover, the potentially destructive forces of nature became their foe since a consequence of separating themselves from God was the loss of their special intellectual powers to predict where and when natural disturbances would occur and to protect themselves from disease and wild beasts, powers dependent upon their union with God. The result is natural evil. This condition — their wickedness and helplessness — has persisted through all the generations, being somehow hereditary.

But God has not left us to our misery. He has instituted the means for us to become reconciled with him and to undo our ruin. Each of us, however, must cooperate in the venture since the sort of regeneration required involves reorienting our deepest passions and appetites away from our own power and pleasure and directing them toward him. God could miraculously and immediately regenerate us but he doesn't because our love of him would then be a sham. Unfortunately, our deepest inclinations so thoroughly turn us away from a proper love of him that we will not fix ourselves without some sort of external impetus.

The problem God faces, then, is to get us to turn to him for help while leaving us free in the matter. We will freely turn to him, however, only if we see our wretched condition and become dissatisfied with it. There is no better way for us to come to see our condition and to grow dissatisfied with it than to permit its natural consequences, the pain and suffering and wrongdoing that our separation from him has led to, and to make it "as difficult as possible for us to delude ourselves about the kind of world we live in: a hideous world, much of whose hideousness is quite plainly traceable to the inability of human beings to govern themselves or to order their own lives."[16]

An essential part of God's plan of reconciliation, therefore, is for us to perceive that a natural consequence of our attempting to order our lives on our own is a hideous world, a world with evil, including natural evil. Were God to intervene, he would deceive us about the hideousness of our living unto ourselves and he would seriously weaken our only motivation for turning to him.

What about the Suffering of Nonhuman Animals?

While the natural consequence theodicy may well account for God's permitting natural evil to befall human beings, it provides no reason for him to permit natural evil to befall nonhuman animals.

Reply. To fill the gap, one might offer the "natural law theodicy."

5.5. Natural Law Theodicy

In order to have a world with creatures who can choose freely, the environment in which they are placed must be set up in certain well-defined ways. One of these environmental requirements is that the world be governed by regular and orderly laws of nature. Why is this a requirement? Well, imagine a world in which nature was not governed by such laws.

16. Peter van Inwagen, "The Magnitude, Duration and Distribution of Evil: A Theodicy," *Philosophical Topics* (1988), collected in his *God, Knowledge and Mystery* (Ithaca: Cornell University Press, 1995), 110. My presentation follows his closely. See also Eleonore Stump, "The Problem of Evil," *Faith and Philosophy* (1985).

What would it be like? Simply put, there would be no regular relationship between the occurrence of one sort of event and another. Let go of the ball and sometimes it drops, sometimes it flies straight up, sometimes it does a loop and crashes through the window. Things would happen haphazardly. The world would be quite chaotic.

But why would this disrupt our ability to choose freely? Because without a great deal of order and regularity in nature we could not predict the effects of our choices, even in the slightest; but we can choose freely only if we can predict the effects of our choices, specifically their most immediate effects. To see the point here, imagine a world in which, despite our best efforts, things just happened haphazardly. Suppose I chose to give you a flower and a big hug to express my affection, but my limbs behaved so erratically that it was as likely that my choice would result in what I intended as that I would poke you in the eye and crush your ribs. Or suppose you were very angry with me, but the air between us behaved so irregularly that any attempt on your part to give me a piece of your mind was about as likely to succeed as rolling a pair of sixes twice in a row. If that's how things worked, then our choices would be related to the world in the way they are related (in this world) to the results of pulling a lever on a slot machine. How things came out would be completely out of our control. They wouldn't be up to us. So we cannot be free unless we are able to predict the (immediate) effects of our choices. And that requires an environment that allows our choices to have predictable effects, that is, an environment that behaves in a lawlike, regular, constant fashion.

But now the downside. The very laws of momentum that enable you to give and receive flowers will also cause a falling boulder to crush you if you happen to be under it. The same laws of thermodynamics and fluid dynamics that allow me to talk via air causing my vocal chords to vibrate also cause hurricanes and tornadoes. In general, the sources of natural evil which afflict nonhuman animals, and us — disease, sickness, disasters, birth defects, and the like — "are all the outworking of the natural system of which we are a part. They are the byproducts made possible by that which is necessary for the greater good."[17]

17. Bruce Reichenbach, *Evil and a Good God* (New York: Fordham University Press, 1982), 101. See also Richard Swinburne, "Natural Evil," *American Philosophical Quarterly* (1978): 295-301, and *The Existence of God,* chapter 11. C. S. Lewis takes this line in *The Problem of Pain* (New York: Macmillan, 1978), 30ff.

What about Worlds with Different Natural Laws?

The most wide-ranging objection to the natural law theodicy is that there are worlds God could have created which operate according to different laws of nature, laws which do not have sources of natural evil as a by-product of their operation but which nevertheless provide a sufficiently stable environment in which we could reliably predict the effects of our free choices. Thus, God could have made free creatures without permitting natural evil, in which case we can't say that God might justifiably permit natural evil for the sake of freedom.

Reply. This objection presupposes that there are worlds with the requisite sort of natural laws, those that would provide a stable environment for freedom but which don't have natural evil as a side effect. But no one has ever specified any such laws. Furthermore, the very possibility of life in our universe hangs on "a large number of physical parameters [that] have apparently arbitrary values such that if those values had been only slightly (very, very slightly different) the universe would contain no life," and hence no free human persons.[18] For all we know, the laws that govern our world are the only possible laws; alternatively, for all we know, there are very tight constraints on what sorts of adjustments in the laws can be permitted while retaining life-sustaining capabilities. Thus, for all we know, there *couldn't* be a world of the sort the objector appeals to: one suitable for free creatures to relate to each other but governed by laws which have no source of natural evil as a by-product.

Couldn't God Prevent a Lot of Natural Evil without Undermining Freedom?

Suppose we distinguish (i) cases of natural evil where God's interference would contribute to the weakening of our ability to predict the consequences of our choices from (ii) cases of natural evil where God's interference would have no such effect at all. Clearly enough, there is a lot of natural evil where God's interference would have no ramifications for our freedom — indeed, mind-boggling much when we take into account evolutionary history or predation. Thus, the only reason given in the natural law theodicy for God's permitting natural evil fails to justify his permit-

18. Peter van Inwagen, "The Problem of Evil, the Problem of Air, and the Problem of Silence," in *The Evidential Argument from Evil,* 160. For more on the physical parameters in question, see Robin Collins's chapter (pp. 47-75 in this volume), and John Leslie, *Universes* (London: Routledge, 1989), chs. 1-3.

ting (ii)-type natural evil, cases where his interference would have had no effect on our ability to predict the consequences of our choices.[19]

Reply. One might say that justice requires evenhandedness. In that case, if God — who is perfectly just — intervenes to prevent the pain of this or that nonhuman animal in isolated circumstances, he would be obliged to act similarly in all cases of similar suffering. So, for example, if he were to prevent a squirrel deep in the Cascades from feeling pain as it hit a limb on its way down from the top of a towering Douglas fir, evenhandedness would require him to prevent me from feeling pain when the wind blew the car door shut on my thumb. But if God prevented the pain of *every* nonhuman animal in isolated circumstances, then evenhandedness would require the same intervention for humans; such massive intervention would severely undermine the regularity of the laws of nature and hence eliminate our freedom.

While some people are happy with this reply, I am less sanguine. First, the Parable of the Laborers in the Vineyard suggests that God does not always treat us evenhandedly. Of course, God is perfect in justice, and so whatever he does is consistent with justice. It follows that principles of justice do not require evenhandedness — or that if they do, they can be trumped by other considerations in some cases. Second, evenhandedness requires treating like cases alike. But the cases at hand are not alike. God's systematic prevention of natural evil in the human domain would result in a loss of human freedom and all that such a loss entails. If God systematically prevents humans from harm when, for example, they collide with solid objects, their freedom will be undermined. Similar intervention in the animal kingdom would have no such effect, *provided it didn't happen around us.* More generally, if God systematically prevented nonhuman animal suffering that occurs far from human awareness (way out in the woods, you might say), nobody's freedom would be undermined. Certainly this is a relevant difference, a difference a just God would take into account.

One final, general observation. In my reply to the objection that God could have created another world with different laws, I expressed skepticism about our ability to tell whether any such laws would result in a world that was hospitable to life. This reply is a double-edged sword. For, just as we cannot confidently affirm that there are hospitable worlds

19. See William Rowe, "William Alston on the Problem of Evil," in *The Rationality of Belief and the Plurality of Faith,* ed. Thomas Senor (Ithaca: Cornell University Press, 1995), 84-87; also see Quentin Smith, "An Atheological Argument from Evil Natural Laws," *International Journal for the Philosophy of Religion* (1991): 154-74.

with different laws that would have no source of natural evil as a by-product, so we cannot confidently deny it. My sense is that we have no idea how God would be justified in permitting the isolated suffering of nonhuman animals at Nature's hand.

5.6. Higher-Order Goods Theodicy

Certain goods require evil: "higher-order goods," they are called. These include showing sympathy, compassion, and generosity to the sick, the poor, and the marginalized. It is not merely *having* these virtues that is good. Developing, exercising, and confirming them is of immense value, especially when it is difficult to do so since, in that case, a certain sort of courage, self-sacrifice, and fortitude is displayed. Likewise, forgiving wrong done to us, making compensation for having wronged others, showing gratitude for help received, and rewarding those who have done well through serious adversity all require evil. Unless there is evil, there cannot be such higher-order goods. Since these goods are of such tremendous value and they require evil, they justify God's permission of evil.[20]

Higher Order Goods Don't Require Real Evil

True enough, we cannot respond with compassion *to the poor* unless there *are* poor people. We cannot exercise fortitude *in the face of hardship* unless we *are* going through rough times. We cannot forgive *another* unless another *has* wronged us. However, we can develop, exercise, and confirm such character traits in response to *simulated* poverty, hardship, and wrongdoing, "illusory evil," we might call it. There doesn't have to be *real* evil for that to occur. To see how this is possible, imagine a world in which persons were, unbeknownst to them, plugged into "experience machines," complex devices programmed to simulate a reality with evil (a machine as in the popular Hollywood flick, *Total Recall*). Even though the poverty, hardship, wrongdoing, etc. that they "experienced" while on the machine was only illusory evil, they would still be able to respond to it in a virtuous fashion. And we can imagine the machine's program being sen-

20. See Swinburne, "Some Major Strands of Theodicy," and *Providence and the Problem of Evil;* also see John Hick, *Evil and the God of Love*, rev. ed. (New York: Harper & Row, 1978).

sitive to their responses. In that way, they would be able to develop, exercise, and confirm their characters without there being any *real* evil to which they are responding. In general, only illusory evil is required for there to be higher-order goods; real evil is unnecessary. So God could have created a world with higher-order goods but without (real) evil.

Reply. The objection correctly states that higher-order goods only require illusory evil. However, if God were to set up a world in which there was only illusory evil to which we could respond in the formation of our character, something of immense value would be missing. No one would in fact help anybody else; and no one would be helped. No one would in fact be compassionate and sympathetic to another; and no one would receive compassion and sympathy. No one would in fact forgive another; and no one would be forgiven. No one would in fact make compensation to another; and no one would receive compensation. No one would in fact praise or admire their fellows for pursuing noble ends in the face of adversity; and no one would receive such praise and admiration. No one would in fact satisfy their admirable aims and desires; and no one would be their recipient. No one would in fact generously give of their time, their talents, or their money to the poor; and no one would receive generosity from another. In short, if every opportunity for a virtuous response were directed at illusory evils, each of us would live in our own little "world," worlds devoid of any genuine interaction and personal relationships.

It seems, then, that if God were to fit us with a capacity to develop, exercise, and confirm our characters *in the context of persons forming relationships with each other,* he must permit evil.

5.7. "The Reason"

Let's take stock of what we've done in this section so far. Premise 3 of the modified basic argument from evil (p. 84) says there is no reason that would justify God in permitting evil. This premise is false. The reasons sketched above help us to understand how God would be justified in permitting *some* evil, perhaps even a great deal of it.

Still, the reasons sketched above do not allow us to see how God would be justified in permitting all the evil in the world. It isn't at all clear that any one of those reasons would justify God in permitting *so much* evil rather than a lot less. Nor is it clear that any one of them would justify God in permitting certain *instances* of horrific evil, say, the rape and bludgeoning to death of Ashley Jones. Nor is it clear that any one of them would justify God in permitting nonhuman animals to suffer in locations far removed from human concern.

One might beg to differ with me here. Perhaps one will insist that some of the reasons sketched above clearly *do* justify God in permitting so much evil and Ashley Jones's brutal rape and bludgeoning and the suffering of isolated nonhuman animals. Alternatively, one might say that even if we cannot see how any one of these reasons would *by itself* justify God in permitting these things, they can be *combined* into a single reason that would clearly justify God. Let's look into these replies briefly, focusing on the second since in assessing it we will assess the first.

Suppose we lump together all the different reasons sketched above, and let's add any we know of that have been left out, e.g., identification with Christ's suffering.[21] Call the result *The Reason*. And let's focus on the enormous quantity of evil in the world rather than some particular horror or the suffering of isolated nonhuman animals. The question, then, is this: would The Reason justify God in permitting *so much* evil rather than *a lot less?*

Well, what would count as *a lot* less? A world without genocide would do. Or how about a world in which dementia didn't occur? Or perhaps a world in which the Ebola virus never evolved. Take your pick. An omnipotent being could have easily prevented any of them. Suppose he had. Then *a lot* less suffering would have occurred. In that case, would the goods involved in The Reason have been lost or objectionably reduced? I can't see why. Suppose he had simply prevented us from ever having genocidal thoughts. Would we then have been unable to perceive the hideousness of living unto ourselves? Would we have lacked the requisite incentive to turn to God? Presumably not: our hideousness would still have been apparent in the vast panoply of nongenocidal activities we engage in.[22] What about self-determination, deep responsibility, relation-

21. See, e.g., Marilyn McCord Adams, "Redemptive Suffering: A Christian Solution to the Problem of Evil," *Faith and Philosophy* 3 (1986), and "Horrendous Evils and the Goodness of God," *Proceedings of the Aristotelian Society* 63 (1989): 297-310, collected in *The Problem of Evil,* 209-221.

22. But wouldn't God be deceiving us about the natural consequences of our ordering our lives on our own? Perhaps. But *some* deception may be worth it. Think of it like this: Suppose that unbeknownst to us, God would not allow an all-out global nuclear war even if a natural consequence of our miserable condition included an ability to do it. Should we accuse him of wrongful deception upon learning this? Hardly. We should get on our knees and thank him for his great kindness.

ships of love, higher-order goods, punishment, identification with Christ's suffering, union with God and so on, and their combination into one colossal good? We each need to answer this question for ourselves, but for my own part, on careful reflection I can't see how any of them by themselves or in combination would have been lost or significantly diminished if God had systematically prevented genocide (or, for that matter, dementia or the Ebola virus or . . .). Thus, I can't see how The Reason *requires* God to permit so much evil rather than a lot less. That's why I can't see how The Reason would *justify* God in permitting so much evil.

No doubt, many Christians will disagree with me. But let us agree on this much: no authoritative Christian source holds forth that we should expect to be able to understand why God would permit so much evil rather than a lot less. Indeed, the biblical message is that we have no business thinking we can do anything of the sort. This is the lesson of the Book of Job and the words of the prophet (Isaiah 55:8-10):

> "For My thoughts are not your thoughts,
> Nor are your ways My ways," says the LORD.
> "For as the heavens are higher than the earth,
> So are My ways higher than your ways,
> And My thoughts than your thoughts."

We do others a grievous disservice to hold out to them in private or in the pulpit any expectation to understand why God would permit so much evil or any particular instance, expectations which we have no reason to believe will be fulfilled, expectations which when left unfulfilled can become nearly irresistible grounds for rejecting the faith. We are in the dark here. We can't see how any reason we know of, or the whole lot of them combined, would justify God in permitting so much horrific evil or any particular horror. We need to own up to that fact.

6. The Argument from Amount

Premise 3 of the modified basic argument is false. But the reflections of section 5.7 might provide grist for other, better arguments from evil. For even if there is a reason that would justify God in permitting *some* evil, even a great deal of it, there may be no reason at all that would justify his permitting *so much,* or certain *particular instances* like Ashley Jones's brutal rape and beating. Indeed, that is precisely what many proponents of the argument from evil claim.

But wouldn't any such argument be doomed from the outset? After all, if there is a reason that would justify God in permitting some evil, wouldn't that *automatically* justify his permitting all the evil there is?

Not at all. One can have a reason to permit some evil, even a great deal of it, even if one has no reason to permit just any amount of it or no reason to permit some particular instance. Just because I have a reason to permit my son to treat his sister badly sometimes, I don't thereby have a reason to permit him to treat her badly all the time; nor do I thereby have a reason to permit him to push her off a cliff on some particular occasion. We'll have to think harder than this to respond to these (allegedly) better arguments from evil. Let's look into the matter more closely.

6.1. The Argument Stated

The argument from particular instances of horrific evil will go differently depending on which instance or instances are mentioned in the premises, but a typical version would go something like this:

1. There is no reason that would justify God in permitting Ashley Jones's brutal rape and bludgeoning to death.
2. If God exists, then there must be such a reason.
3. So, God does not exist.

The argument from amount can be put like this:

1. There is no reason that would justify God in permitting so much evil rather than a lot less.
2. If God exists, then there must be such a reason.
3. So, God does not exist.

In what follows, I will focus on the argument from amount. The argument from amount is not susceptible to objections to which the argument from particular instances is susceptible.[23] It is also the argument that I

23. Specifically, I don't think we should accept premise 2 of the argument from instances. See Peter van Inwagen, "The Magnitude, Duration, and Distribution of Evil: A Theodicy," *Philosophical Topics* (1988): 167-68; "The Place of Chance in a World Sustained by God," in *Divine and Human Action,* ed. Thomas V. Morris (Ithaca: Cornell University Press, 1988), 230ff; and "The Problem of Evil, the Problem of Air, and the Problem of Silence," *Philosophical Perspectives* (1991), note 11. All three essays

have found most troubling. So in an effort to put (what I think is) the best argument forward, I'll stick to the argument from amount. What should we make of it?

Well, premise 2 is true. If there is an omnipotent and omniscient being who permits the evil in our world for no reason at all or whose purposes in permitting evil could have been achieved even if he had systematically prevented, say, all genocide or the plague, but he permitted them anyway, the enormity of his hideousness defies adequate description. Of course, the inference from 1 and 2 to 3 is impeccable. That leaves premise 1. Is it true?

Several arguments for it have been given in the literature, the best of which have come from a philosopher whom I admire very much, William Rowe. I do not have the space here to do justice to his three arguments, but the objections to the one that I will assess here can, with a little ingenuity, be extended to the other two.[24]

6.2. Rowe's Noseeum Inference

Suppose that, after rummaging around carefully in my fridge, I can't find a carton of milk. Naturally enough, I infer that there isn't one there. Or suppose that, on viewing a chess match between two novices, Kasparov says to himself, "So far as I can tell, there is no way for John to get out of check," and then infers that there is no way. These are what we might call *no-see-um* inferences: we don't see 'um, so they ain't there!

Notice four things about noseeum inferences. First, they have this basic shape: "So far as we can tell, there is no x; so, there is no x." Second, note that in each of the cases just mentioned, it is possible for the conclusion to be false even if the premise is true. Even though I rummaged through the fridge carefully and my vision is in tip-top shape, I could just simply miss the carton of milk. And even Kasparov can have an off day. Nevertheless — and this is the third point — in each case the argument is

are collected in his *God, Knowledge and Mystery.* See also my "The Argument from Inscrutable Evil," in *The Evidential Argument from Evil,* 286-89.

24. I discuss the other arguments in "The Argument from Inscrutable Evil." The one I assess here is in "The Problem of Evil and Some Varieties of Atheism," *American Philosophical Quarterly* (1979), collected in *The Evidential Argument from Evil.* The other two are in "Evil and Theodicy," *Philosophical Topics* (1988), "Ruminations About Evil," *Philosophical Perspectives* (1991), and "The Evidential Argument from Evil: A Second Look," in *The Evidential Argument from Evil.*

a strong one. Under certain conditions (about which I will say more shortly), our inability to see something makes it highly likely that there isn't anything of the sort we failed to see. Finally, it won't do to object to any particular noseeum inference that even if the premise is true the conclusion *might* be false. For *every* noseeum argument — even the strongest of them — is like that. When evaluating a particular noseeum argument, we can't just write it off with a casual, "Ah! But there *might* be an x we don't know of even if so far as we can tell there isn't one." That's true, but it's irrelevant to the strength of the inference.

Now, in effect, I claimed in section 5.7 that, upon careful reflection on various theodicies, so far as we can tell, there is no reason that would justify God in permitting so much evil.[25] We might be tempted to infer that, quite likely, there is no such reason. In fact, Rowe bids us to do just that. We can put the resulting argument most simply like this:

> Q. So far as we can tell, there is no reason that would justify God.
> So, it is very likely that
> 1. There is no such reason.

What should we make of *Rowe's Noseeum Inference,* as I will call it?

Obviously enough, many noseeum inferences are reasonable. And, just as obviously, many are *not.* For example, looking at my distant garden from my kitchen window, the fact that, so far as I can tell, there are no slugs there hardly makes it likely that there are none. Likewise, a beginner viewing a chess match between Kasparov and Deep Blue would be ill-advised to reason: "I can't see any way for Deep Blue to get out of check; so, there is none." Or imagine us listening to the best physicists in the world discussing the mathematics used to describe quantum phenomena or the theory of general relativity. Presumably it would be unreasonable for us to infer that, since we can't comprehend or grasp what they are saying, there is nothing there to be grasped. The crucial question, then, is this: what distinguishes the reasonable noseeum inferences from the lousy ones?

Consider the cases already sketched. Notice that it is quite likely that I would see a milk jug in the fridge if one were there, and it is very likely that Kasparov would see a way out of check if there were one. That's because Kasparov and I have what it takes to discern the sorts of things in

25. The attentive reader will note that I might as well have claimed here that, upon reflection on various theodicies, so far as we can tell, there *is* a reason that would justify God in permitting so much evil. Clearly understanding why that thought is relevant and devastating is the goal of the rest of section 6.

question. On the other hand, it is not very likely that I would see a slug in my garden even if there were one there, at least not from my kitchen window. Nor is it very likely that a beginner would be able to see a way out of check for Deep Blue even if there were one since strategy at the grandmaster level can be very complex. And the same goes for our comprehending exceedingly complex mathematics: even if what the physicists were talking about did make sense, it isn't very likely that we would be able to understand it.

We can distill these reflections in the following principle, which marks an important difference between reasonable and unreasonable noseeum inferences:

> A noseeum inference is reasonable only if it is reasonable to believe that we would very likely see (grasp, comprehend, understand) the item in question if it existed.

Applying this principle to Rowe's Noseeum Inference, we get the following result:

> The move from "So far as we can tell, there is no reason" to "It is very likely that there is no reason" is reasonable only if it is reasonable to believe that *we would very likely see or comprehend a reason, if there were one*.

Call the italicized portion *Rowe's Noseeum Assumption.*

Now we are in a position to raise an important question. Is it reasonable to believe Rowe's Noseeum Assumption?

6.3. Tooley's Argument on Behalf of Rowe's Noseeum Assumption

Several reasons might be given here, but the most promising is: since it is very likely that we know of all the intrinsic goods there are,[26] it is very likely that we already know of all the reasons that would justify God's permission of evil; hence, if there were a reason, we would very likely see or understand it.

26. An *intrinsic* good is good in itself, not merely because it is a means to some other good. While it is debatable which goods are intrinsic goods, the most plausible candidates include pleasure, knowledge, freedom, love, and justice, among others.

This argument hangs on the thought that "since it is very likely that we know of all the intrinsic goods there are, it is very likely that we already know of all the reasons that would justify God's permission of evil." We might well question the inference here,[27] but I will focus on the premise. Why believe that it is highly likely that we know of all the intrinsic goods there are? Michael Tooley offers this argument: very few states of affairs that human beings have discovered over the course of their history are intrinsic goods, and in the past three thousand years or so no intrinsic goods have been discovered at all; so, it is "improbable in the extreme" that there are intrinsic goods other than those we know of. Thus, we very likely know of every intrinsic good.[28]

Is this a good reason to believe it's likely that we know of all the intrinsic goods there are? I think not.

First of all, *at best* the premise that humans have discovered very few intrinsic goods and no new ones recently only shows that it is very likely that we have discovered all the intrinsic goods *we are presently capable of discovering*, just as, say, cats have discovered all the intrinsic goods they are now capable of discovering. Whether there are more intrinsic goods — specifically, ones we are presently incapable of grasping — is left wide open. Hence it is unreasonable to move from "humans have discovered very few intrinsic goods and no new ones recently" to "it is very likely that we have discovered all the intrinsic goods."

Second, this move is reasonable only if our human ancestors discovered the few intrinsic goods we know of over a short span of time. For suppose otherwise: that is, suppose that our ancestors discovered intrinsic goods over the course of tens of thousands of years with several thousands of years in between when no goods were discovered. Such a sporadic progression in our discovery of intrinsic goods would not be surprising at all given that our species' ability even to conceive of them is rooted in structures in the human brain, structures which, for all we know, evolved sporadically over the course of tens of thousands of years. (It might help you to draw a time-line correlating distinct cerebral developments with distinct capacities to conceive of and appreciate different intrinsic goods.) *If* such a sporadic progression occurred, then we should

27. The inference holds only if it is also very likely that we know of all the conditions of realization for those goods we do know of. See Alston, "Some (Temporarily) Final Thoughts on Evidential Arguments from Evil," in *The Evidential Argument from Evil,* 315ff.

28. See "The Argument from Evil," *Philosophical Perspectives* (1991), especially 114-15.

expect to have discovered no goods for several millennia *even if there are many we don't know of.* So, the fact that humans have discovered few intrinsic goods and no new ones of late makes it likely that there are no others *only if* our ancestors discovered the goods we know of over a relatively short time in the history of our species.

But why should we assume *that?* The fact of the matter is that neither Tooley nor anybody else has any reason at all to believe it. There is no reason to think that our ancestors' grasp of intrinsic goods must have come in such a tightly bound package that they could not have grasped one without grasping them all. (In this connection reflect on the development in a child's awareness and appreciation of different intrinsic goods.) Moreover, given the scant archeological and paleontological evidence we have, it would not be surprising at all if the sort of sporadic progression indicated above occurred. I am not saying that we have reason to think that such a progression *did* occur. Rather, I am saying that — contrary to what Tooley assumes — the information we presently have gives us *no* reason to think that it *didn't* occur.[29]

Tooley's argument, therefore, fails to show that it is "improbable in the extreme" that there are intrinsic goods other than the ones we know of. So we cannot use it as a basis for believing that we would very likely discern a reason for God's permitting so much evil if there were one, which is just Rowe's Noseeum Assumption.

More arguments might be given for Rowe's Noseeum Assumption, but my general objection to Tooley's argument — namely, that it relies on assumptions that we are in no position to make reasonably — applies to them as well.[30] Let us turn, then, to what might be said *against* Rowe's Noseeum Assumption.

29. Some readers might say that since we have good reason to think that the Earth is no more than ten thousand years old, we have good reason to deny the multimillennia-long gaps my speculations rely on, not to mention the evolutionary anthropology it takes for granted. If this is your view, I invite you to reflect on what your audience in the apologetic task will think about these matters. In that case, you might think of my reply to Tooley as a way to show them how, *given their own views about prehistory,* they should reject Tooley's argument.

30. I discuss some of them in "The Argument from Inscrutable Evil," 291-97. The best argument for Rowe's Noseeum Assumption can be gleaned from Rowe's "The Evidential Argument from Evil: A Second Look," 276. See also my "Argument from Inscrutable Evil," 305-7. A proper assessment of that argument is beyond the scope of this chapter but can be found in *The Hiddenness of God: New Essays,* ed. Daniel Howard-Snyder and Paul K. Moser (forthcoming).

6.4. Two Strategies

I begin by distinguishing two strategies for arguing against Rowe's Noseeum Assmption. We can get at them by way of comparing two questions.

First: Is it highly likely that I would see a slug in my garden from the kitchen window if one were there? Not at all. I know that slugs are relatively small and I know that the unaided human eye is not suited to see such small things at a hundred feet; moreover, my garden is over an acre large and, per usual, it's overgrown. So we have superb reason to think that it is *false* that I would very likely see a slug in my garden even if one were there. Now, another question: Is it highly likely that extraterrestrial life-forms would contact us if they existed? The only answer suitable here is "How should I know?" If there were extraterrestrial life-forms, how likely is it that some of them would be intelligent enough to attempt contact? And of those intelligent enough, how many would care about it? And of those who are intelligent enough and care, how likely is it that they would have the means at their disposal to try? And of those with the means, how likely is it that they would succeed? I haven't the foggiest idea how to answer these questions. I can't even begin to say with even the most minimal degree of confidence that the likelihood is low or middling or high. I just don't have enough to go on. In that case, I should be *in doubt* about how likely it is that extraterrestrial life-forms would contact us if they existed. I should be of two minds, neither for it, nor against it. I should just shrug my shoulders and say "I don't know. I'm in the dark on that score."

There are two points to see here. First, in each case it is *not reasonable to believe* that the proposition in question is highly likely to be true, although for different reasons. In the first case, it is not reasonable to believe it is highly likely that I would see a slug in the garden even if there were one there because it is reasonable to believe that the proposition is positively *false* — indeed, because the garden is large and overgrown and I am viewing it from a distance, I have good reason to believe it is very, very likely that I would *not* see a slug. In the second case, however, it is *not* reasonable to believe that the proposition in question is *false*. Rather, for the reasons mentioned, we have good reason to be *in doubt* about how likely it is that we would have been contacted by extraterrestrials if there were any. Indeed, we don't even have enough to go on to make a rough guess. As a consequence — and here is the second, absolutely crucial point — having good reason to be in doubt about the matter is good enough reason all by itself to think that it is *not* reasonable to *believe* that we would probably have been contacted. For how could it be reasonable for us to believe something about which we have good reason to think we are utterly in the dark?

Now let's apply these points to Rowe's Noseeum Assumption. To assess the reasonableness of believing that we would very likely see a reason that would justify God in permitting so much evil if there were a reason, we might consider whether Rowe's Noseeum Assumption is *false*. In that case, we might try to think of reasons to believe that it is very likely that we would *not* see a God-justifying reason. We would then be treating Rowe's Noseeum Assumption as I treated the proposition that it is very likely that I would see a slug in my garden from the kitchen window.[31] On the other hand, we might consider whether we should be *in doubt* about whether we would very likely see a God-justifying reason. This would be to treat Rowe's Noseeum Assumption as I treated the proposition that it is highly likely that extraterrestrials would contact us if there were any. The crucial point to understand here is that even if *all* we have is good reason to be *in doubt* about whether it is highly likely that we would see a God-justifying reason, that's good enough reason to deny that it is reasonable to believe Rowe's Noseeum Assumption.

In what follows, I focus on reasons to be in doubt about Rowe's Noseeum Assumption rather than reasons to think it is false. Why? Because reasons to be in doubt are easier to come by and the only reasons I can think of for believing that it is false presuppose that God has informed us that we should expect to be unable to discern his purposes in permitting evil. (That seems to be the main lesson of the Book of Job, and it is arguably an implication of the doctrine of the Fall.) While such reasons provide the believer with grounds for denying Rowe's Noseeum Assumption, they do little for the nonbeliever since he does not accept the Bible as a source of information. Of course, we might try to convince him of the veracity of the Bible and then use it to argue that Rowe's Noseeum Assumption is false. But that is a circuitous route to a goal that can be more directly achieved. In what follows, I try to appeal to reasons that should be as compelling for

31. To show that Rowe's Noseeum Assumption is false we don't have to have reason to believe that it is *highly likely* that we would *not* see a God-justifying reason. All we really need is reason to believe that it is *no more* likely that we would see a God-justifying reason than that we would *not*. For if it is no more likely that we would see a God-justifying reason than that we would not, then it is *not highly likely* that we *would* see a God-justifying reason. Our plates are full enough without pursuing this option here.

nonbelievers as for believers; and since I don't know of any compelling reason for a nonbeliever to think that Rowe's Noseeum Assumption is false, I will stick to reasons for all of us — believers and nonbelievers alike — to be in doubt about Rowe's Noseeum Assumption.

6.5. Reasons to Be in Doubt about Rowe's Noseeum Assumption

Several sorts of considerations have emerged in the literature. I'll mention three.

Alston's Analogies

Rowe's Noseeum Inference involves two aspects which should make us wary of our ability to tell whether we would very likely see justifying reasons if there were any.

First, it takes "the insights attainable by finite, fallible human beings as an adequate indication of what is available in the way of reasons to an omniscient, omnipotent being." But this is like supposing that when I am confronted with the activity or productions of a master in a field in which I have little expertise, it is reasonable for me to draw inferences about the quality of her work just because I "don't get it." I've taken a year of university physics. I'm faced with some theory about quantum phenomena and I can't make heads or tails of it. Certainly it is unreasonable for me to suppose it's likely that I'd be able to make sense of it. Similarly for other areas of expertise: painting, architectural design, chess, music, and so on.

Second, Rowe's Noseeum Inference "involves trying to determine whether there is a so-and-so in a territory the extent and composition of which is largely unknown to us." It is like someone who is culturally and geographically isolated supposing that if there were something on earth beyond this forest, they'd likely discern it. It is like a physicist supposing that if there were something beyond the temporal bounds of the universe, we'd probably know about it (where those bounds are the big bang and the final crunch). All these analogies point in the same direction: we should be in doubt about whether we would very likely discern a reason that would justify God even if one were there.[32]

32. William Alston, "Some (Temporarily) Final Thoughts on Evidential Arguments from Evil," 316-19.

The Progress Argument

Knowledge has progressed in a variety of fields of enquiry, especially the physical sciences. The periodic discovery of previously unknown aspects of reality strongly suggests that there will be further progress of a similar sort. Since future progress implies present ignorance, it is very likely that there is much we are now ignorant of. Now, what we have to go on in charting the progress of the discovery of intrinsic goods by our ancestors is meager to say the least. Indeed, given the scant archeological evidence we have, and given paleontological evidence regarding the evolutionary development of the brain in Homo sapiens, it would not be surprising at all that humans discovered various intrinsic goods over tens of thousands of years dotted by several millennia-long gaps in which nothing was discovered. (Recall the point of my second reply to Tooley's argument in section 6.3.) Hence, given what we have to go on, it would not be surprising if there has been the sort of periodic progress that strongly suggests that there remain goods to be discovered. Thus it would not be surprising if there are goods of which we are ignorant, goods of which God — in his omniscience — would not be ignorant.

The Argument from Complexity

One thing Mozart's Violin Concerto No. 4, fine coffee (notably, Starbuck's), and the best sorts of love have in common when compared to Chopsticks, Folger's, and puppy love is that each illustrates the fact that the goodness of a state of affairs is sometimes greater, in part, because it is more complex. Now, since immense, undeserved suffering and horrific wickedness is so bad, it would take correspondingly greater goods to justify God's permitting so much of it rather than a lot less. Hence, it would not be surprising if God's reasons have to do with goods whose complexity is beyond our grasp. It follows that it would not be surprising if God's reasons were outside our ken.

Of course, while complexity does not *always* adversely affect our ability to recognize value, it can and sometimes does. To defend this claim, I cannot show you a complex state of affairs whose value we recognize but whose complexity hinders such recognition. I must resort to more general considerations.

First, there is the general phenomenon of the complexity of something hindering our view of some important feature it has, e.g., the complexity of an argument hindering our ability to discern its validity, or the complexity of your opponent's strategy hindering your ability to discern that unless you move your knight to queen's side bishop 5, her next move is checkmate. But, more to the point, why can a child discern the literary merits of a comic book but not *Henry V* or *The Brothers Karamazov?* Why can a child clearly discern the aesthetic value of a toffee but not coho salmon served with a lemon-dill sauce, lightly buttered asparagus al dente, and fine coffee? Why can a child recognize the value of his friendship with his buddy next door but not the full value of his parents' love for each other? Surely because great works of literature, fine cuisine, and adult love involve much more than he is able to comprehend. And this is true of adults as well, as reflection on our progress in understanding the complexity of various things of value reveals. For example, periodically reflecting on the fabric of our relationships with those whom we most love and whose love we most cherish, we might well find strands and shades that when brought to full light permit us to see this love as more valuable than we had once thought. If the failure to grasp the more complicated aspects of our relationships can prevent a full appreciation of love's value, surely the failure to grasp the complexity of a state of affairs might well hinder us from discerning its goodness. Value is often veiled in complexity.

The three considerations presented here — Alston's Analogies, the Progress Argument, and the Argument from Complexity — *together* constitute a good reason to be in doubt about whether it is highly likely that we would see a reason that would justify God in permitting so much evil if there were a reason. This is *not* to say that these considerations jointly constitute a good reason to believe that it is highly likely that we would *not* see a God-justifying reason. We must not overstate our case. Nevertheless, they constitute good reason to think that it is unreasonable to believe Rowe's Noseeum Assumption. Thus, to the extent that the argument from amount relies on Rowe's Noseeum Inference, it fails.

6.6. On "Copping Out"

Several people I have talked to about the argument from evil have responded to my deliberations in something like the following way:

> You haven't given a reason that would justify God in permitting so much evil rather than a lot less. At any rate, you haven't given a reason that quite clearly would justify him. And you admit it. You admit to failing to state any such reason. But that's just a cop out. After all, the

> problem of evil just *is* the problem of stating a justifying reason, a reason we can *see* to be justifying. And you've given up on that project. You've thrown in the towel. Put it this way: you are a Christian. As such you believe that there is a reason that would justify God's permission of so much horrific, undeserved evil in the world. So what is it? What *is* that reason? You have no answer. Your God stands accused of being a moral monster. You are defending him, you say. According to you, he's perfect in love and power and wisdom. He could prevent each and every instance of evil and suffering with the mere thought "Be stilled." You can hardly expect us, then, not to convict, not after Buchenwald and Auschwitz, not after millions have suffered undeservedly and so horrifically. We need some answers. We need to know why he didn't stop more of it. But all you give us is a bunch of remote possibilities, a bunch of hypotheticals. "For all we know, there is a reason we're ignorant of." Well, sorry, but that's not good enough. Any defense lawyer who tried that stunt in court would be tossed out on his ear. Why should we treat you any differently?

There's a lot going on in this passionate speech, some of which I have already addressed. (See section 3.) But let me underscore three points here.

First, it is true that I have not tried to argue that there is a reason that would justify God in permitting so much evil rather than a lot less. I believe that our attempts at discerning any such reason fail. Still, I believe there *is* a reason. That's because I believe there is a God and, of course, if that's right, then there is a reason, even if I can't say what it is. But the fact that I believe that there is a reason and I can't say what it is cannot substitute for an *argument* against the existence of God — unless, of course, one assumes that I (or we) would probably be privy to such a reason if there were one, an assumption that I have argued we should be in doubt about. This leads to my second point.

The judicial analogy in the speech is importantly flawed. Crucial to our practice of trying suspected wrongdoers in a court of law is the sensible assumption that we are trying *one of us,* someone whose reasons for acting would tend to be accessible to us because they are the sorts of reasons available to humans generally. Without this assumption we'd have no grounds whatsoever for ruling out reasons we don't know of. When God is in the dock, however, we cannot presume to know quite well the sorts of reasons that *he* would be privy to. As I have argued, we are in the dark on that score.

Finally, nothing I have said in section 6 presupposes that God exists or that the Bible is divinely inspired or any such thing. If you are an atheist or an agnostic who still takes theism to be a live option, you should be able to appreciate the reasons I have given for thinking that we are in the dark about Rowe's Noseeum Assumption. If you think my arguments assume that there is a God or that the Bible is God's word, you haven't understood my arguments.

So, have I "copped out"? Well, that all depends. If the game we're playing is "Let's Make a Theodicy," then yes, I copped out. If, however, the game we're playing is "Let's Make an Argument from Evil," then it is not me who has copped out but those who make impassioned speeches like the one above.

7. The Argument from Evil and Evidence for Theism

No argument from evil I am aware of makes it likely or even reasonable to believe there is no God. Evil cannot carry that evidential load. But suppose I'm wrong. Suppose evil is evidence to think God does not exist. Does it follow that it's reasonable to believe there is no God?

Let's approach this question by way of analogy. Suppose you learn in your European Culture class today that 95 percent of the French population can't swim. That statistic is some evidence to think that Pierre, your friend from Paris, can't swim. Does it follow that you should believe Pierre can't swim? Of course not. What if you and Pierre spent last Saturday afternoon together swimming and chatting about the fine-tuning argument and Albert Camus's *The Plague?* Surely, in that case, it isn't reasonable for you to believe Pierre can't swim. Your experience with him is much better evidence to think he can swim even though the statistical evidence by itself makes it very likely that he cannot.

The same goes with evil and God. Even if evil is some evidence that there is no God, you might have much better evidence to think that God exists; in that case, it wouldn't be reasonable for you to believe there is no God.

This line of thought naturally leads to some weighty questions not the least of which are these: *Is* the evidence for God significantly better than the evidence that evil provides against God? What *sources* of evidence are there? How should we *balance* the evidence for and against theism? Some answers to these and similar questions are presented throughout this book and in other sources.[33]

33. In this connection, I recommend religious experience as a source. For detailed and sympathetic treatment of the topic, see William Alston, *Perceiving God: The*

8. Conclusion

In section 2, I distinguished the practical problem of evil from the theoretical "problem" of evil. I focused on the latter. Evil constitutes a genuine theoretical problem only if there is a good argument from evil. There is no good argument from evil. So, there is no theoretical problem of evil.

What relevance does this conclusion have for the task of apologetics? Several, but most notably this. God calls men and women to love him with all their heart, soul, strength, and mind. It is that last bit that to many inside and outside of the Church seems to be an insurmountable difficulty. Love God with all your *mind.* That's where apologetics comes in. Apologetics is largely the task of removing intellectual obstacles to the love of God. Evil and suffering have always appeared to be the most troublesome obstacle. The conclusion of this chapter is that, in reality, they are no obstacle at all to a fully intelligent love of God.

Epistemology of Religious Experience (Ithaca: Cornell University Press, 1991); Keith Yandell, *The Epistemology of Religious Experience* (Cambridge: Cambridge University Press, 1994); and Alvin Plantinga, *Warranted Christian Belief* (Oxford: Oxford University Press, forthcoming).

5

Arguments for Atheism

John O'Leary-Hawthorn

Considerations about evil in the world are the most popular basis for atheism among professional philosophers and, perhaps, also among the public at large. But there are many other reasons that have been offered by reflective atheists for their view. It is the task of this chapter to offer the reader a representative sampling of such reasons and to offer some preliminary observations concerning their cogency.

It will be useful for my purposes in what follows to group atheological arguments into two categories. The first category of argument attempts to exploit the lack of palpable evidence for the existence of the Judeo-Christian God. I shall call these "No Evidence Arguments." The second category of argument begins with some observation or theory about the nature of religion and attempts to render theism unlikely on that basis. I call such arguments "Arguments from the Character of Religion." Sections one and two will be devoted to the first category of argument, outlining some atheological arguments that are pertinent to that category and then offering some critical remarks concerning them. Sections 3 and 4 will be devoted to the second category of argument.

1. No Evidence Arguments

1.1. The Core Argument

People frequently hold irrational superstitions. Some people think that certain kinds of pendants will bring them luck. But most of us feel that such people have no good reason whatsoever to believe this. Some people form expectations in accordance with the astrological deliverances of a column in their morning newspaper. But they do not have any good reason to place confidence in astrological predictions. Many atheists have an analogous attitude towards those of us who believe in the existence of the God of the Judeo-Christian tradition. By their lights, theists and astrologists are equally reckless in their willingness to form beliefs about the world that go well beyond what is warranted by the evidence. In this and the following sections, I shall be laying out some atheistic lines of thought that proceed in this vein.

The most basic and bald variety of this kind of atheistic argument is straightforward enough. The core argument is this:

1. No one has ever had any evidence whatsoever for the existence of a Judeo-Christian God.
2. When no one has ever acquired any evidence for a certain hypothesis and has no reasonable prospect of acquiring any, we should all discount that hypothesis.
3. Therefore, we should all discount the hypothesis that a Judeo-Christian God exists.

Two main ideas come into play here: *the lack of evidence,* and *the lack of prospect of acquiring it.* Both ideas are important to the line of thought under consideration. We know that in science a hypothesis, when first advanced, may not have been tested and thus may have little to no support. That does not typically mean we discount it. For we may instead set about doing some crucial experiments that provide a means of testing it. But suppose there is no evidence for some hypothesis and, in addition, no prospect of doing tests that would provide a means of gathering evidence for it. In that case we may feel altogether disinclined to take the hypothesis seriously. An atheist who advances the core argument believes that this is the situation with the hypothesis that God exists.

There are a number of ways that an atheist might, if he wished, attempt to tone down the premises of the argument. Let me mention two.

(i) As it stands, the argument makes a universal pronouncement that *no one* has any evidence for the existence of the Judeo-Christian God. There is a stripe of atheist, however, who may be willing to concede that for all he knows, someone has some evidence, insisting only that *he* hasn't any evidence. Such an atheist will, perhaps, be more interested in justifying and rationalizing his or her own views than in providing universally valid directives to others. He may say "I haven't any evidence. And until you provide me with some I will continue to discount the hypothesis that there is a Judeo-Christian God. If you are like me and haven't any evidence then I advise you to do the same. If you are unlike me and have evidence, then I cannot speak for you." (ii) As it stands, the argument claims that there is *no* evidence for a Judeo-Christian God. Some atheists might be more generous: they may concede that there is *some* evidence but argue that there is *nowhere near enough* to warrant our taking very seriously the hypothesis that there is a Judeo-Christian God. For example, an atheist might be willing to allow that the fact that sane and generally quite reasonable and intellectually respectable people believe in God all by itself counts as a little bit of evidence for the existence of God. But he may still insist that there is still nowhere near enough evidence to warrant a person coming to the issue with an impartial mind to come to believe in God. The thrust of the core argument will be unaffected as far as such an atheist is concerned. She will say: "The evidence for a Judeo-Christian God is very thin and there is no prospect of it getting much fatter. When the evidence for a hypothesis is very thin and there is no prospect of it getting much fatter, we should discount it."

Having noted these more modest versions of the premises, I wish to return to the core argument. How can the atheist motivate each premise? Let us begin with premise 1. It is very natural to think that there are two basic ways to acquire evidence for a hypothesis P. One way is to acquire direct perceptual evidence for P. (For example, the hypothesis may be that there is a cat nearby and the evidence may be your seeing it.) Another way is to get direct perceptual evidence for some claim or hypothesis, Q, that is explanatorily connected to P. After all, we often get evidence for hypotheses about things that we cannot directly perceive, including facts about the distant past or future, facts about microscopic entities and so on. So, for example, we might use evidence we can perceive about a dinosaur's skeletal structure as evidence for the hypothesis that the dinosaur caught its prey by running and pouncing (something we obviously cannot directly perceive).

Let us call these two kinds of evidence *direct perceptual evidence* and *explanatory evidence*. There is yet another sort of evidence that fits into neither of these categories: the testimony of others. After all, much of what we know is acquired by trusting other people and not by direct observation or by explanatory conjectures on our part. According to the picture being developed here, testimony plays the role of *evidence transmission*. If someone acquires evidence for P, and you trust them and believe in P, then in a sort of way, what you believe has an evidential basis. By trusting them, you inherit the respectability of the evidential basis even if it is not in your reflective possession. But crucially, trust can only provide respectability to what you believe if somewhere down the chain of testimony and trust there is direct perceptual or explanatory evidence for the hypothesis. Testimony and trust, on this picture, can preserve the respectability of believing the hypothesis only if it was at some point respectable to believe the hypothesis *on grounds other than testimony and trust*.

With this (admittedly quite natural and plausible) picture in place we can readily see how the atheist will proceed: "There is no direct perceptual evidence for the Judeo-Christian God. And there is no explanatory evidence. So there is no evidence. Neither sacred books nor religious leaders can generate evidence out of nothing. So there is no evidence for the Judeo-Christian God."

1.2. Explanation and Theism

Why do atheists think that there is no explanatory evidence for a Judeo-Christian God? A common reason is this: Many atheists believe that fundamental physics, suitably developed, will provide a complete story about ultimate reality. They conclude that theism is superfluous, that we can explain everything that we need to explain without appeal to a God. Here a well-known contemporary philosopher, David Lewis, writes about the explanatory power of natural science:

> . . . [T]here is some unified body of scientific theories, of the sort we now accept, which together provide a true and exhaustive account of all physical phenomena (i.e. all phenomena describable in physical terms). They are unified in that they are cumulative: the theory governing any physical phenomenon is explained by theories governing phenomena out of which that phenomenon is composed and by the way it is composed out of them. The same is true of the latter phe-

> nomena, and so on all the way down to fundamental particles or fields governed by a few simple laws, more or less conceived of in present-day theoretical physics.[1]

Lewis isn't saying that all we need is physics for our explanatory purposes. For example, we need psychology, and psychology is not the same as particle physics. Rather he is saying that at the fundamental micro-level, physics is the whole story, and that macro-level explanation in the lingo of psychology, geology, economics and so on will talk about phenomena that are constituted by the phenomena described by the fundamental theory of physics. (Thus, for example, he will hold that the minds we describe in the language of psychology and the living organisms we describe in the language of biology are ultimately constituted by the particles and relations that we describe in fundamental physics.) Lewis calls this thesis "The Explanatory Adequacy of Physics."

In his *Summa Theologica* (1a, 2.2), Aquinas has an interlocutor embrace the following argument: ". . . [A]ll natural things can be reduced to one principle, which is nature; and all voluntary things can be reduced to one principle, which is human reason, or will. Therefore there is no need to suppose God's existence." Lewis, and many contemporary philosophical atheists, go further. Believing that voluntary things are themselves ultimately natural phenomena, they will say, roughly: "All things in the world we live in can be reduced to one principle, which is nature. Therefore there is no need to suppose God's existence." (Think of "nature" as shorthand for "fundamental particles or fields governed by a few simple laws.")

Assume, first, that the only facts we have direct perceptual access to are physical facts. It follows that we have no direct access to the kinds of things the Christian supposes to exist (God, angels, souls, the Devil, heaven, etc.). In addition, assume now the "Explanatory Adequacy of Physics." The kinds of things the Christian supposes to exist become *explanatorily superfluous.* Finally, assume — as the earlier sketch envisioned — that evidence for theism must be either perceptual or explanatory. The result is that we are forced to conclude that there is no evidence for theism.

1. David Lewis, "An Argument for Identity Theory," *Philosophical Papers Volume One* (Oxford: Oxford University Press, 1983), 105.

1.3. Evolution

Ask atheists on the street why they don't believe in God and many will say "Because of evolution."

One source of this reaction might be that the atheist takes evolution to be undeniably true, and also takes Christianity to deny evolution. The atheist might then think that since the Christian belief in God has the same (defective) source as their belief that evolution is false (namely, the Bible), both of the beliefs should stand or fall together.

Such sentiments deserve attention, but it is beyond my scope to do so here.[2] I wish instead to locate a different possible source of the atheistic appeal to evolution, by locating that appeal within the argument I have been pursuing above. For many centuries it seemed like physics could not be explanatorily adequate precisely because it could not explain a certain group of facts, facts which philosophers call "teleological facts." Teleological facts are facts that concern the ends-seeking or goal-directed behavior we find in nature. We are all well aware of certain teleological features of the world. It is just obvious that nature works towards certain ends. Somehow or other the atoms in our body organize themselves during fetal development into a wonderfully organized living system. Somehow or other the bits of an organism's body provide the means for that organism to be well adapted to the demands of its environment, thus allowing it to conduct and achieve goals of food, reproduction, and so on. Somehow or other the little bits of stuff in a seed unfold into a wonderfully organized and geometrically elegant tree or flower. It is hardly surprising that for centuries everyone was thoroughly convinced that the principles governing the motion of little particles (that is, the principles of physics) could not account for teleological achievements like those just cited. It thus seemed to them that we must suppose that there is some sort of "guiding hand" to account for those achievements. Some held that the "guiding hand" could be located in nature itself — on the model of Aristotelian "principles of activity" (we might think of these as "life forces") that were something over and above the fundamental matter. These principles/forces organized matter in ways over and above the dictates of the laws of matter. But there was, alternatively, a compelling motivation to invoke guiding hands driven by a supernatural mind or minds — the guiding hands being something different from the minds immanent in nature.

2. For more on the relation of Christianity and evolution, the reader should consult W. Christopher Stewart's chapter, "Religion and Science" (pp. 318-44 in this volume).

From this perspective, the most pertinent fact about the theory of evolution for the atheist is that it offers the hope to many contemporary intellectuals of explaining the facts of teleology in terms of the causal properties of bits of matter. In the language of Lewis, we may say that it offers the hope of showing how the facts of teleological explanation are constituted by the facts of fundamental physics. In this way, it makes it possible for many to believe in the explanatory adequacy of physics, and (accordingly) in the explanatory redundancy or superfluousness of positing the existence of the Judeo-Christian God.

1.4. Divine Silence

The most obvious way that a lack or paucity of evidence might tell against our believing in the existence of God has already been given: We need to have evidence in order to have reason to believe any hypothesis about the world, and in any case where there is none or next to none we are in no good position to reasonably believe. But there is another, more subtle way, that a lack or paucity of evidence might be thought by some to tell in a special way against the Judeo-Christian God. For it has been alleged that if there were a Judeo-Christian God (to whose acts of creation and grace we are beholden and to whom we are in some unnegotiable way responsible), he would be sure to provide us with palpable evidence that he exists. Thus we have:

1. If there were a Judeo-Christian God, he would provide us with palpable evidence of his existence.
2. There is no palpable evidence that he exists.
3. Therefore, there is no Judeo-Christian God.

Why "palpable evidence"? Well, proponents of this line of thought tend to think that if there were a God, he would not merely provide us with a little bit of evidence that he existed; rather, he would provide evidence that is loud and clear. As an atheist I once knew put it, "He would be calling us up on the telephone."[3]

3. Recently, J. L. Schellenberg has given an extended defense of this argument in his book, *Divine Hiddenness and Human Reason* (Ithaca: Cornell University Press, 1992). A few published responses to Schellenberg (or to arguments of the type he advances) are Michael Murray, "Coercion and the Hiddenness of God," *American Philo-*

Why think that God would make it loud and clear? I suppose the atheist looks to analogues in the world of human relationships. If I want you to love me, then I would be sure to make myself rather visible to you. If I want you to behave in accordance with my wishes, I will make my wishes as evident as possible to you, especially if I am intelligent enough to put them in their most persuasive and attractive form. And so on.

But why bother having recourse to the Divine Silence argument, when the (second) premise alone — that there is no palpable evidence — appears to tell against the rationality of theism in any case? Here are three reasons:

(I) The Divine Silence argument might be used by an atheist to try to bypass any quarrels about whether there is some moderate degree of evidence for God. He may say: "Regardless of whether there is some or no evidence, the fact remains that if there really were a God, he would make his existence known loud and clear. And no one can claim that he does that: if he did, there wouldn't be so many folks like me. Thus if I am right that if he were to exist, he would make his existence known loud and clear, we can settle the matter decisively in favor of atheism."

(II) I have thus far blurred over an important distinction, namely between "What justifies atheism?" and "What justifies agnosticism?" It might be felt that the lack of evidence for theism doesn't justify atheism but only agnosticism. After all, if you can't see over the garden fence, that doesn't make it reasonable for you to believe there is nothing growing in the garden. It only makes it reasonable to suspend judgment over whether there is anything growing in the garden. Likewise, one might argue that the unbeliever who lacks evidence concerning God's existence can at best admit that they do not know whether God exists or not.

The atheist may want to resist the analogy on a number of grounds. Here is one: Does the lack of any evidence whatever warrant only agnosticism about the existence of a world of invisible goblins? In the case of the garden, we know gardens very often have things growing in them, and this prohibits our believing that the garden is empty when confronted with the tall fence. But there is no analogous belief that requires caution in the case of invisible goblins. And similarly, the atheist who believes there is no evidence for God may contend there is no analogous belief — or reason to take theism to be prima facie reasonable — in the case of

sophical Quarterly 30:1 (1993): 27-38; Daniel Howard-Snyder, "The Argument from Divine Hiddenness," *Canadian Journal of Philosophy* 26 (1996): 433-53; and Richard Swinburne, *The Existence of God* (Oxford: Clarendon Press, 1979), 153ff.

Judeo-Christian doctrine. But here is another point of disanalogy with the garden example: Even were one to think that in general, a lack of evidence only justifies a *suspension of belief* rather than *disbelief,* one may think that owing to the Divine Silence argument, a lack of evidence positively militates in favor of disbelief rather than mere suspension of belief where the existence of God is concerned. If one thinks that a certain kind of thing would elicit our attention were it to exist, then a lack of evidence for it would seem to be especially damning to the idea that it exists. One wouldn't be surprised were flowers to exist over the fence and be hidden from view. But, says the atheist, it would be very surprising for a loving God to exist and yet be hidden from view.

(III) As we shall see, some Christians have held that believers are warranted in their belief that God exists even though they have no evidence for this belief. A proponent of the Divine Silence argument might agree that there are *some* cases in which it is reasonable to hold a belief without evidence. Still, the atheist might continue, when it comes to believing that God exists, one cannot reasonably hold this belief without evidence because one ought to see that if were there a God, he would make known his existence loud and clear.

1.5. A Priori Knowledge

The basic argument from no evidence relies on the idea that in order to rationally believe something we need evidence for it. But from the perspective of many philosophers, the latter claim represents a gross overgeneralization. *At first glance,* it appears that there are some claims that we can reasonably believe without looking for evidence for them, it being somehow intrinsically rational to believe them. Take the law of contradiction which says: No claim is both true and false. We find ourselves primitively compelled to believe this claim and would find it strange were anyone to ask us to provide evidence for it. We may well say: "If you don't believe that, I pity you. For if you don't find the law of contradiction compelling all by itself, then it is unlikely that I can find anything more compelling that might lead you to it." In brief, it seems that some propositions are self-evident, meaning roughly: Any minimally rational person with their intellectual faculties intact will, by simply understanding that proposition, come to know it is true. Call the self-evident propositions *a priori axioms.* Once we have a stock of a priori axioms that we know, we can come to know further propositions by drawing inferences that are sanctioned by the axioms to move from them to various conclusions. (Think of a rigorous mathematical proof.) Let us call a proposition *knowable a priori* if it is either a self-evident axiom or else deducible from self-evident axioms. A priori knowledge does not appear to require either perceptual evidence or explanatory evidence.

As a result, we can now see that our original atheistic argument was a little quick. For now we can see that there are, in fact, beliefs which do not require evidence of the sort described in that argument. This leads us to wonder whether or not the belief *that God exists* is one of those beliefs. And as long as we are uncertain about this, we should not find the atheistic argument at all convincing.

There is no option but to refine the argument a little. It is, however, not hard to see how this can be done, *viz.:*

1. If theism is worth taking seriously, that is either because theism is knowable a priori or else because there is good evidence for theism.
2. Theism is not knowable a priori.
3. There is no good evidence for theism.
4. Therefore theism is not worth taking seriously.

The extra wrinkle is clear enough: the atheist is obliged to claim that theism is not knowable a priori. But here the atheist is, presumably, fairly well placed. Even Aquinas was at pains to deny that theism is self-evident:

> No one can mentally admit the opposite of what is self-evident. . . . But the opposite of the proposition *God is* can be mentally admitted: The fool said in his heart, There is no God (Ps. lii. I). Therefore, that God exists is not self-evident. (Summa Theologica 1a.2.1)

Furthermore, the apparent failure of a priori arguments for the existence of a Judeo-Christian God in the history of philosophical theology (and, in particular, the apparent failure of ontological arguments) seems to tell against the claim that God's existence can be derived from self-evident premises. Thus this refinement to the core argument does not immediately make serious trouble for the atheist. Go along with the atheist's contention that there is no evidence and the atheist will say: "That leaves two options. Either theism is irrational or it is a priori knowable. But it is not a priori knowable, so it is irrational."

2. No Evidence Arguments: Some Critical Remarks

2.1. A Priori Knowledge

Let us return to the refined version of the no evidence argument which figured in section 1.5:

1. If theism is worth taking seriously, that is either because theism is knowable a priori or else because there is good evidence for theism.
2. Theism is not knowable a priori.
3. There is no good evidence for theism.
4. Therefore theism is not worth taking seriously.

The premise that most philosophers would likely agree upon is premise 2. But even here, things are not clear-cut. Recall Aquinas's argument against the self-evidence of theism — namely, that there are people who understand and yet do not believe. If self-evidence requires that everyone who understands believe, then hardly anything is self-evident. Take the law of contradiction — that nothing is both true and false. Many people on the street, a lamentable number of undergraduate collegians, and a fair smattering of philosophers understand that proposition perfectly well and yet refrain from believing it. Indeed, philosophers have found weird reasons for withholding belief from a wide variety of propositions that appear to be dead obvious — say, 2 + 2 = 4,[4] and good things are good.[5] A more interesting conception of self-evidence is this:

> A proposition is self-evident if it is such that anyone who understands it and is not cognitively deficient will find that proposition *primitively compelling.*

Yes, there are fools of sufficient delinquency who deny certain laws of logic even when they understand them. But on the latter conception of self-evidence, these propositions are still self-evident. Similarly, the mere fact that there are fools who say in their heart that there is no God does not *entail* that theism does not enjoy the status described above. Now perhaps Aquinas — in the company of most contemporary philosophers —

4. See Hartry Field's *Science Without Numbers* (Princeton: Princeton University Press, 1980).

5. Consider the noncognitivist handlings of deductive inference and apparently logical truths involving the subject matter for which they wish to be noncognitivist.

is right when he says that the nature of human reason is such that it is not disposed to find theism primitively compelling. Perhaps he would be right to deny that the failure of various humans to find theism primitively compelling is best explained as an overlay of delinquency upon the natural light of reason. But the core consideration that he offers in favor of this is hardly decisive. Perhaps Christian philosophers in this century have been a little quick to concede that theism is not knowable a priori.

2.2. Evidence, a Priori Knowability, and the Gift of Faith

Most Christians on the street, upon understanding the argument from lack of evidence would reply "But what about faith?" And most atheistic philosophers would reply:

> "Without a priori knowability and without evidence, theism is not intellectually respectable. Perhaps by 'faith' you mean 'Well I believe it anyway, even though it has nothing going for it by way of evidence or by way of a priori attraction.' In short that means 'I believe it even though it's thoroughly irrational.' But no one can reasonably insist that I be thoroughly irrational. Perhaps you don't think faith is thoroughly irrational. If so please explain to me how faith — in the absence of evidence and a priori knowability — escapes the clutches of irrationality."

In support of the Christian on the street, it might be useful to lay out a model of faith that makes vivid how faith can escape a charge of irrationality. Let us return to the conception of self-evidence just presented and note a needed refinement. What is self-evident for one species/kind of individual might well fail to be self-evident for another. Perhaps God could make a race of skeptics that, while understanding a great deal, found nothing primitively compelling, nothing flat obvious. If a member of that race failed to find "2 + 2 = 4" primitively compelling, that could not be properly explained as a result of any deficiency interfering with natural, God-given, belief-forming mechanisms. Similarly, perhaps, there could be a race that found more things primitively compelling. To take a boring example, human beings do not find complicated true sums (like 117896 + 132587 = 250483) primitively compelling — though of course they can deduce it via primitively compelling moves from primitively compelling starting points. But for all that there could be a gifted race of beings that do find it primitively and immediately compelling.

Now suppose Aquinas is right that theism is not primitively compelling for humans. The natural light — which means, roughly, the dispositions accorded to human nature to find certain things obvious — may not illuminate theism. Nevertheless, perhaps God could make a species for which theism *is* self-evident. Indeed, perhaps he has. Perhaps theism is self-evident for angels but not for humans. Thinking about things in this way, it is quite easy to think of faith as a gift of grace that confers intellectually respectable belief. Take a race for which theism is primitively compelling. I take it that theism is reasonable for that race, in just that way that it is reasonable for us to believe what is flat obvious. Assume that we as a race do not by nature find theism primitively compelling. Think now of faith as a gift by which our nature is transformed into that of the former race. We become, through the gift of faith, just like them. If their theism is respectable, and we become just like them with respect to our epistemic relation to theism, then so is ours. It thus seems relatively clear that the reasonableness of theism requires neither evidence nor accessibility by the natural light of reason accorded to human beings.

The atheist may complain at this point: "But how do I know that your faith is a gift as opposed to an illusion." That is precisely a complaint that one should expect from someone who lacks the gift of faith. Consider by analogy a race of sceptics who cannot bring themselves to believe in arithmetic or the laws of logic. They come across human beings and notice that those beings feel compelled to believe in various claims of arithmetic and logic. They then say to those human beings: "How do you know that this is not an illusion as opposed to a power of knowing how things really are?" The humans will not have much to say back. They will say: "It just seems obvious and compelling to us." But that will hardly quell the suspicions of the sceptic. Indeed, unless the sceptic acquires certain abilities, there may be nothing much directly to say to the sceptic. But our inability to pacify a race of arithmetical and logical sceptics need not oblige us to stop believing in a host of propositions of arithmetic and logic. Similarly, our inability to pacify a group of atheists who lack the gift of faith need not oblige us to become less convinced of theism.

2.3. Evidence for Theism

We now turn our attention from premise 2 of the argument to premise 3 which, you will recall, claims that there is no good evidence for theism. Many Christians will claim to have had some religious experiences and treat such experiences as reasons for their belief. Some of these experiences verge on the mystical, and some do not. Some people claim to see God at work in the world in roughly the way that we see a mind at work in a body. Now of course in the crudest sense of "observe" we do not observe God in such a case. But neither do we observe other minds in the crudest sense of "observe." In both cases, however, the perceptual experience is structured by the fact that it represents mind — in one case natural, in the other supernatural — as immanent in that with which one is confronted.

If the atheist thinks that there is no way that such experiences could provide evidence for theism, it is incumbent upon him to say why. I myself know of no principled reason for denying that such experiences could provide evidence. But we can of course still very well understand the atheist who complains:

> "Well, it is possible that others have evidence. But I don't have these experiences you speak of. And how am I to know whether, in actual fact, anyone is really getting evidence for anything? All sorts of people report conflicting experiences. I have no idea who to trust. No one stands out as particularly trustworthy. Thus I am not being presented with anything that you can properly regard as evidence for me."

What should we make of such a speech? One reaction might be to attempt to invoke our notion of explanatory evidence. That is to say, we might think it reasonable to expect people to believe the core doctrines of the Judeo-Christian religion on the basis of its explanatory power. I myself am somewhat dubious about this tack. Christians shouldn't believe in the explanatory completeness of physics. Having come to believe Christian doctrine, they should believe that God explains the structure of nature's laws, that God sometimes overrides nature by miraculous intervention, and so on. Such claims put Christian doctrine to explanatory work. But let us distinguish the question of whether Christian doctrine is explanatory from the question of whether it is reasonable to expect people to believe Christianity on the basis of explanatory considerations. Many contemporary philosophers — including Christian philosophers — are pretty convinced that one cannot reasonably expect people to come to believe Christian doctrine on the basis of its explanatory power. (It should be acknowledged, though, that some other thinkers have a great deal more confidence in the explanatory virtues of theism. I invite the reader to look at the chapter on Miracles, Theistic Arguments, and the Fine-Tuning Argument as a means of forming for herself a judgment concerning whether we can reasonably believe a segment of Christian doctrine on the basis of explanatory considerations.)

Those who agree with me that those arguments do not, on their own, make belief in Christianity reasonable will hold that if someone has no compelling religious experiences and lacks the gift of faith then he is indeed poorly placed to reasonably treat anything as evidence for theism. An analogy: If a piece of music is truly beautiful and an aesthetic dullard in a world of largely aesthetically challenged people doesn't see it, what is one to do? One can hardly argue that person into a change of mind. One might say "Well, the fact that the music is truly beautiful is the best explanation of why seventeen percent of the population says it is." But surely the dullard would be quite reasonable to balk at our trying to bully him into a change of mind with such explanatory considerations. Nor will it be of much use to say "Just listen. Just listen. Don't you see?" Only when "aesthetic vision" is something that we can take for granted among the population will such pleas make any sense. What to do? Here is the best we can do: hope that he acquires the right kind of aesthetic appreciation and do what one can to provide an environment that makes it most likely that such a gift will befall him.

2.4. Divine Silence

The reader will recall a different way that a lack of palpable evidence has been used against theism. The idea is that if God existed, he would be kind enough to make his existence obvious. Many theists I know will complain "But he did make it obvious to some of us." To sidestep this complaint, let us suppose that the atheist is one who thinks that if the Christian God existed, he would make his existence pretty much obvious to *everyone*. The Christian's response to this complaint will likely be relatively short, I suspect. According to many strands of Christianity at least, it is essential to God's plans for humanity that human beings freely choose to embrace him. It's fine that, having chosen to embrace him, his existence becomes obvious. But it does not seem that we could very well *freely* choose to embrace him if his nature and plans for us were all clearly and distinctly manifest to everyone. Just as a marriage to someone would not be freely chosen if it were made perfectly clear from the outset that the partner would destroy you should you choose not to marry, so a decision to love and serve God would not be freely chosen if it were, for example, always preceded by a full guided tour of Hell. While the spectacles of faith may render God's existence manifest, it is important to God's plans for free creatures and the love and devotion he desires that one's vision be less than perfect prior to putting those spectacles on.

3. Arguments from the Character of Religion

In myriad ways, atheists have found supposed or obvious aspects of religion to count against the respectability of religious belief. Let me briefly examine three such ways.

3.1. The Evil Done in the Name of Religion

Much evil has been done in the name of religion. Even within the history of the Judeo-Christian religion, there is little doubt that a good deal of evil has been done in the name of Christianity. Christian institutions have suffered from a fair share of corruption. Christian institutions have endured a fair share of evil people in positions of power. Christian people have expressed a fair share of hatred on grounds of religious sentiments. Christian people have done a fair share of killing on grounds of theological squabbles. Christian people have perpetrated a fair share of brutality in the name of evangelism. Christian people have supported a fair share of evil regimes on the grounds of religious interests.

I suppose that the atheist might thus argue:

1. If there were a God, he would not allow his institutions on earth to perpetrate evil in his name.
2. Christian institutions frequently perpetrate evil in the name of God.
3. Therefore, there is no God.

3.2. The Diversity of Religious Belief

Human beings exhibit wildly different religious beliefs. Some find in this fact a reason for discounting any religious belief in general and hence Judeo-Christian religious belief in particular. The tacit line of thought is not hard to understand.

Let's begin this argument by assuming, as the theist seems to do, that we human beings have some ability to perceive, figure out, or somehow know the truth about supernatural reality. If we really did have such an ability, then we should expect that human beings would come to some measure of agreement about the nature of supernatural reality. (An analogy: Human beings have an ability to perceive the truth about the spatial configuration of the material objects around them — that the bookshelf is to the right of the door, for example — and because of this there is agreement among them in their beliefs about these matters.) But there clearly is no agreement in the beliefs that humans have about supernatural reality. So it seems that human beings have no distinctive ability to perceive, figure out, or somehow know the truth about supernatural reality. Once we come to see that human beings as a species have no such ability, we must react to anyone who claims to know about supernatural reality by (a) distrusting that person, or else (b) thinking that this person is very special in having a distinctive ability most others do not have. Faced with a glittering array of conflicting religious claims, the outsider seems to have no good reason to think that any particular claimant has special powers of this sort and very good reason to think that human beings in general have no such special powers. In this situation it looks like the right thing to do is to distrust all of them.

3.3. The Psychological Origin of Religious Belief

Many atheists find extremely plausible various psychological accounts of the origin of religious belief. Feuerbach thought that religious belief is best explained as a primitive form of self-knowledge, where one projects an idealized conception of one's own nature as if it belonged to something outside of oneself. Bertrand Russell, more mundanely, thought that religious belief was best explained as an expression of human beings' self-importance, whereby humans think themselves too important to enjoy a mere passing place in the "flux of nature." Another theme in Russell — one that is also extremely prevalent among many atheists — is the idea that religion is a coping strategy whereby human beings come to grips with their deep fear of death.

For simplicity's sake, let us focus on the latter explanation. Suppose that human religion is best explained as a coping strategy for death anxiety. Were someone to be convinced of that, it is not hard to see why he does not take religious doctrines very seriously. In general, we think that our knowledge must somehow depend on the subject matter we claim to have knowledge about. If people have knowledge about chairs, they form and maintain beliefs because the chairs exist in such-and-such a way. If someone's belief about chairs were produced and maintained by certain *anxieties* (he believes there is a chair nearby because he is extremely anxious that he will never sit down and wants to relieve that anxiety), then one would hardly accord that belief very much respect. We know of course that a belief may initially come about for silly reasons and then acquire respectability later on. One might believe at one time that one will soon be rich on the basis of one's horoscope and later on learn that a rich uncle died. But when a belief is grounded in things which have nothing to do with the subject matter that the belief is about, it does not look like the belief is deserving of very much respect at all. Thus, religious belief grounded in "death anxiety" does not deserve very much respect at all.

4. Arguments from the Character of Religion: Some Critical Remarks

Many Christians will certainly be troubled by the evils done by religious institutions that they believe to have been established by God. But this is a special case of a more general concern: How can we make sense of God's permitting horror and corruption among objects of his creation when it was within his power to prevent this? I recommend that the reader turn to Daniel Howard-Snyder's chapter on the problem of evil for some guidance on this difficult issue. How about the remaining arguments concerning the character of religion?

4.1. Religious Diversity

No one can deny that religions are diverse. Nor should we place too much weight on responses of the sort "Well, they are all basically saying the same thing — that there is something out there." To suppose that they are all "basically saying the same thing" is to purge religious doctrine of the details that its own proponents live by and find important and compelling. I do not want to deny that the fact of such diversity merits attention from Christian believers. Nor do I pretend to have no sympathy at all with atheists like Russell, who when faced with the facts of diversity respond with such cynicism as the following: "In practice people choose the book considered sacred by the community in which they are born and out of that book choose the parts they like, ignoring the others."[6] But let us remember that atheists and theists alike hold and feel justified in holding convictions on a variety of topics where diversity abounds. Consider the diversity of moral convictions, or the diversity of convictions about economics, about politics, about philosophy, about certain aspects of civil war history, and so on. Conviction in the face of diversity is a familiar commonplace in our epistemic lives. We Christians ought thus say to the atheist: "Why do you choose to sneer at religious belief on the basis of facts about diversity, when you yourself cling tenaciously to certain convictions in the face of diversity with commonplace frequency?" Here, as elsewhere, atheological arguments are very far from being decisive. (See also Timothy O'Connor's chapter, "Religious Pluralism," pp. 165-81 in this volume.)

4.2. The Psychological Origins of Belief

Turning finally to the third category of argument: Criticisms of religion based on accounts of psychological origin hold little sway among professional philosophers. It is all too easy to come up with speculative psychologies concerning the origin of this or that belief. But the process of arriving at such speculations seems to me and many like me altogether too undisciplined to be worthy of serious respect.

We ought also to recognize that many altogether respectable beliefs had a shaky psychological origin. To discard a theory on the basis of its origin — say a scientific theory on account of the fact that it was first thought of during a dream — is to commit what is known as the "genetic fallacy." The category of arguments that we are considering run some considerable risk of committing the genetic fallacy as well.

5. Conclusion

It is no surprise to anyone to learn that atheism is widespread in the contemporary academic community. What is surprising is to see how tenuous the arguments which favor atheism are. In this chapter we have taken a brief look at some of the ones more commonly offered and shown why they are, on the whole, something far less than rationally compelling.

6. Bertrand Russell, "An Outline of Intellectual Rubbish," *Unpopular Essays* (New York: Simon and Schuster, 1950), 81.

6

Faith and Reason

Caleb Miller

An important purpose of this book is to bring reason to bear on matters of Christian faith. But there is a widespread view among both Christians and unbelievers that Christian faith and human reason are opposed to each other. A Cornell University undergraduate student put it this way:

> I think that religiousness in a person is a sure sign of ignorance. Faith is nothing but the absence of rational thought, or of serious consideration. . . . At the same time, I cannot blame anyone for "believing" because you were taught to believe. Taught so well, in fact, that you can abandon all sense in favor of Christianity. . . . There is no more reason to think that there is a god or many gods than there is to think that Smurfs once ruled the earth. Both are equally likely, the likelihood being close to zero.[1]

This student seemed to think that if anyone were even slightly guided by reason in the relevant matters, he would have nothing to do with faith. The sixteenth-century Reformer Martin Luther, on the other hand, seemed to think that the person of faith should have nothing to do with reason. He calls reason "carnal," "stupid," a "beast," a "whore," and an "enemy of God."[2] Whatever the other differences between this appar-

1. Quoted in Martin W. Bush, "Apologetics in Cyberspace: Reflections on Contact with the E-World," *Faculty Dialogue* 21 (Spring-Summer 1994): 3-4.

2. B. A. Gerrish, *Grace and Reason: A Study in the Theology of Luther* (Oxford: Oxford University Press, 1962), 1.

ently deeply anti-Christian college student and this deeply pious and enormously influential Christian theologian, they seem to agree that faith and reason are opposed to each other, that there is something wrong with trying to mix them.

Although the antipathy to reason in the Christian tradition has been deep and widespread, it has probably been a minority movement throughout most of Christian history, at least among prominent Christian leaders. The fourth and fifth-century Christian theologian Augustine said:

> [W]e are impelled toward knowledge by a two-fold force: the force of authority and the force of reason. And I am resolved never to deviate in the least from the authority of Christ, for I find none more powerful. But as to what is attainable by acute and accurate reasoning, such is my state of mind that I am impatient to grasp what truth is — to grasp it not only by belief, but also by comprehension.[3]

John Calvin, Luther's fellow reformer, said that reason, "by which man judges between good and evil, and by which he understands and judges is a natural gift [of God]. . . ." He also said that it was reason that distinguished humanity from "brute beasts."[4] Even the eighteenth-century preacher, revivalist, and theologian, John Wesley, whose followers were criticized as "enthusiasts" by his more rationalist contemporaries, said that "a rational assent to the truth of the Bible is one ingredient of Christian faith."[5] The authors of this book stand firmly in the tradition of these Christians who regard reason, properly understood, as the friend of God. That is why we have written a book seeking to use reason in the service of Christian faith.

Another important purpose of this book is to defend the Christian faith. But, it is not the aim of this chapter to advance that purpose directly. Some defenses of that sort will be a by-product of this discussion, but my main purpose is preliminary to the defense of the faith. I shall rather explore a Christian understanding of the relationship between faith and reason, a Christian understanding, that is, of faith, a Christian understanding

3. *The Essential Augustine,* ed. Vernon J. Bourke, *Against the Academics,* III, 20.43 (Indianapolis: Hackett, 1974), 25.

4. John Calvin, *Institutes of the Christian Religion,* 2.2.12, ed. John T. McNeil, trans. Ford Lewis Battles, vol. 1 (Philadelphia: Westminster, 1960), 270.

5. Quoted in Donald A. D. Thorsen, *The Wesleyan Quadrilateral: Scripture, Tradition, Reason and Experience as a Model of Evangelical Theology* (Grand Rapids: Zondervan, 1990), 175.

of reason, and a Christian understanding of their relationship to each other. My hope is that this exploration will give the Christian believer resources for defending the faith, both in the sense of defending or reaffirming his own faith and that of others, and in the sense of defending the faith to those who do not yet believe. I intend my discussion to clarify the sorts of defenses a Christian has reason to pursue, and to clarify the sorts of apologetic strategies that Christianity gives us no reason to pursue or gives us reason not to pursue. I also hope that my discussion of faith and reason will enable a deeper understanding of what Christian faith says about faith and reason, and inspire the use of reason as a means of exploring and deepening the understanding of the Christian faith in other ways.

Before I undertake a Christian exploration of faith and reason, I shall consider some common Christian objections to reason, as well as some Christian claims made on behalf of reason that seem to me extravagant. After distinguishing several common meanings of the terms "faith" and "reason," I'll offer what I shall call a "Christian epistemology." Epistemology is the branch of philosophy that studies knowledge. The term is derived from *episteme,* one of the Greek words for knowledge. Knowledge is only of the truth. One cannot *know,* for example, that Birmingham is in England unless it is *true* that Birmingham is in England. Because of this connection of knowledge to the truth, epistemology has come to be the study, not only of knowledge, but also of a whole range of what philosophers call "epistemic" issues — issues related to the standards, processes, and methods by which we come to believe the truth and avoid falsehoods. A Christian epistemology is then a Christian view of how we come to know or believe the truth and avoid falsehoods. Finally, I shall use the resources of this Christian epistemology to give an account of the relationship of faith and reason, in their various senses, that I think is defensible from a Christian point of view.

I. Is Faith Opposed to Reason?

A. Popular Objections

To some Christians it seems obvious that faith and reason are opposed to each other. After all, our faith in God should be unquestioning and unconditional, whereas reason, it might be thought, calls our beliefs into question in order to determine whether they are true and counsels us to withhold judgment until we are sure. Faith requires us to put our trust in

God, while reason requires us to trust our own faculties. Faith requires us to trust in God's Word as it is revealed in the Scriptures, whereas reason requires us to trust our own judgment. And isn't it irreverent, or even idolatrous, to consult reason in order to determine whether we should have faith in God? By doing so are we not giving reason the final word and so indicating where our deeper trust lies? Isn't that, in some important sense, to use reason to sit in judgment over God? Isn't reason, furthermore, woefully inadequate for the task of understanding matters of faith? Christian faith is primarily about God, whose nature and ways are far beyond the capacities of human reason to discover. Wouldn't it make far more sense to take God's word for it than to use reason to try to figure out God's nature and ways by ourselves? And don't miracles always go against human reason? Isn't that, in some sense, what makes them miracles? If we were able to understand or explain them through our own reason, would they still be miracles? And yet, belief in miracles is an important part of Christian faith.

Then there is the concern, expressed by the Cornell student, that faith does not measure up well to the standards of reason. While many of the people with this view are unbelievers, many believers would agree. There are a number of reasons for holding such a view. Some people are convinced that many centuries of attempting to prove the existence of God by reason have left us without anything worthy of calling a proof. But even if we were able to prove the existence of God, we would be a long way from proving all the beliefs that Christians generally think are involved in having Christian faith. Christians, after all, believe, not only that there is such a being as God, we also believe, and think it important to believe, that God is three persons but only one being, that Jesus Christ is God incarnate, that salvation from our sins is possible only through Christ, etc. And here the problem might be worse than simple lack of proof. Both believers and unbelievers have insisted that some of the core beliefs of Christianity are, according to the canons of reason, positively absurd. Christians believe, for example, that Jesus Christ is both fully human and fully divine. We also believe that there is one God, but three persons, each of whom is God. Both of these doctrines have seemed to some people to be logically absurd. The lesson of all this, according to unbelievers who advance such claims, is that central Christian doctrines are not worthy of our acceptance. For Christians who advance the same claims, the lesson is usually thought to be that we should never submit the beliefs of faith to the evaluation of reason. To do so would be to jeopardize what should be the most important priority of anyone: the cultivation of Christian faith.

Thomas Senor addresses the objection that central Christian beliefs are logically incoherent in his chapter, "Incarnation and the Trinity" (pp. 238-60). Jan Cover addresses the objection that believing in miracles is a violation of reason in his chapter, "Miracles and Christian Theism" (pp. 345-74). Most of the remaining objections mentioned above will be addressed directly or indirectly in the remainder of this chapter. I shall now, however, deal briefly with the concern that reason is somehow opposed to faith in that it involves our trusting ourselves rather than God and God's revelation, even perhaps that it involves our sitting in judgment over God. These objections involve a confusion. Trusting our own judgment and trusting God need not be opposed to each other. Trusting in our judgment might lead us to trust God. There is, of course, a sense in which we trust our own judgment whenever we exercise reason in the consideration of a belief or commitment. But in that sense, we cannot avoid trusting our own judgment. If *we* are to come to believe the claims of Christian faith or trust in God, *we* must somehow come to recognize the truth of these claims and the trustworthiness of God. Even if this involves taking God's word for it, as it must if it is to be the adoption of *Christian* faith, such trust is still a means by which *we* come to see the truth. It would be unfaithful to think something like this: God says I should do X, but that doesn't make any sense to me, therefore I'm not going to do X. But that would not be to trust reason over God. Indeed, the person in such a situation would do well to consult reason. It is irrational to recognize a course of action as God's will while nevertheless regarding it as somehow inferior to a course of action opposed to God's will. Its being God's will entails that it is a better course of action than any course of action incompatible with it.

B. Søren Kierkegaard

Chief among those who have defended the views that reason undermines faith, and that Christian faith should spurn reason, is surely the nineteenth-century Danish philosopher, Søren Kierkegaard. While it is unwise to conclude with much confidence what Kierkegaard thought about much of anything,[6] I will focus on one argument that I think was ad-

6. This is true both because the various things he wrote are often hard to reconcile with each other and because he wrote most of his books under various pseudonyms, which, he says, express thoughts from perspectives different from each other and different from his own.

vanced in Kierkegaard's book, *Concluding Unscientific Postscript,*[7] against what he called "objective" reasoning.[8] Following Robert Adams, I shall call this argument the *approximation* argument. Objective reasoning in support of a claim, in the sense relevant for these arguments, is reasoning which would be taken by virtually all rational persons who understand it, to confirm the claim in question. Objective reasoning in support of Christian faith would include such things as cogent theistic arguments, evidence for the resurrection of Christ, evidence of miracles done in the name of Christ, etc. I shall argue that this argument fails to support Kierkegaard's conclusion. The approximation argument goes something like this. The Christian faith essentially involves certain historical beliefs (e.g., the death and resurrection of Jesus). Furthermore, the objective evidence for historical beliefs can, at best, only approximate certainty. ". . . [T]he greatest attainable certainty with respect to anything historical is merely an approximation."[9] That is, the best evidence there could be for any historical claim leaves some room for doubt. But "an approximation," he says, "is essentially incommensurable with an infinite personal interest in an eternal happiness."[10] The Christian believer has so much at stake (her eternal welfare) in her commitment to the truth of Christianity, including its historical claims, that her commitment must be unreserved. Yet, the sort of support we can get from historical evidence is less than certain. So the support of objective reasoning cannot overcome all reservations. Therefore, the only kind of commitment supported by objective reasoning must be less than unreservedly absolute. But the genuinely Christian commitment that is demanded by the eternal significance of Christian faith must be unreservedly absolute. Therefore we should not have a faith that is based on, or supported by, objective reasoning.

Much of what Kierkegaard claims here seems right to me. We do have an infinite personal stake in the truth of Christianity. Because of that

7. Søren Kierkegaard [Johannes Climacus], *Concluding Unscientific Postscript,* trans. David F. Swenson and Walter Lowrie (Princeton: Princeton University Press, 1941).

8. I am heavily indebted to Adams for this way of understanding Kierkegaard's views. See his "Kierkegaard's Arguments Against Objective Reasoning in Religion" in Robert M. Adams, *The Virtue of Faith and Other Essays in Philosophical Theology* (New York: Oxford University Press, 1987), 25-41. I recognize that Kierkegaard would probably object to my attributing arguments to him. But, with Adams, I think that the objection to objective reasoning in *Concluding Unscientific Postscript,* is defended in that book with arguments.

9. Kierkegaard, *Postscript,* 25.

10. Kierkegaard, *Postscript,* 26.

(in part), our commitment to Christ should be total and all-encompassing; we should stake everything on the truth of Christianity. Furthermore, the best support that could come from objective reasoning (the sort that should convince any rational person) cannot rule out the possibility that Christianity is false. Where Kierkegaard goes wrong is in inferring that we should therefore not support our commitment with objective reasoning. Kierkegaard seems to assume that the only degree of commitment that can be supported by objective reasoning is exactly equal to the degree of support from objective reasoning, for the truth of the belief. So, for example, evidence that makes the probability of a belief only fifty percent, supports only indifference; evidence that makes a belief ninety-nine percent probable, still supports only a commitment with some reservations. But here Kierkegaard is surely mistaken. Relatively low probabilities can rationally support very high degrees of commitment and very high probabilities can rationally support very low degrees of commitment. Suppose that I saw my daughter about to cross a busy street with speeding cars. Let us also suppose that the evidence makes the following claim only eighty percent likely to be true:

(1) If my daughter continues to walk into the street, she will be struck by a car and killed.

I have an interest in the well-being of my daughter. So any evidence for (1) supports my committing myself to prevent her walking into the street. While eighty percent probability is far short of certainty, such evidence would nevertheless justify me in making a far stronger commitment to prevent her from entering the street. Indeed, it would justify my ignoring any doubts I have about the truth of (1) and committing myself unreservedly to doing everything within my power to prevent her from walking into the street. Even far lower degrees of evidence for (1) would justify me in making such a strong commitment to its truth. If the evidence for (1) were only ten percent or one percent, it would still rationally support my making something like a one hundred percent commitment to the course of action indicated by the truth of (1).

On the other hand, the evidence for the following surely makes it at least ninety-nine percent probable:

(2) There was a major Civil War battle, with numerous casualties, fought in the vicinity of Gettysburg, Pennsylvania, in the nineteenth century.

Yet the evidence for (2), despite its being much stronger than the evidence for (1), does not rationally support my making much of a commitment at all to any course of action that depends on its truth. The reason is obvious. (2) is much less practically significant to me than (1) is. In other words, I have much less at stake in the truth of (2) than in the truth of (1) and much less at stake in my acting on the assumption that (2) is true.

What Kierkegaard ignores is that the rational degree of commitment to a claim that is supported by evidence for it depends, not only on the degree of the evidence, but also on the practical significance of the claim. It would be a complex matter to sort out just how the degree of practical significance of a claim relates to the evidence for its truth to justify degrees of commitment to its truth, but just noting that both of them are involved in determining the degree of commitment that evidence supports, is sufficient to see that Kierkegaard's argument fails. Let us suppose that the historical evidence makes the probability seventy-five percent that the following is true:

(3) Jesus Christ bodily rose from the dead.

But as Kierkegaard reminds us, we have an infinitely significant stake in the truth of (3) and an infinite stake in our commitment to the truth of (3). Our eternal welfare depends on both of them. So any evidence for (3) supports our making an overriding commitment to (3). So, far from preventing the sort of absolute commitment to (3) that Kierkegaard thinks is essential to Christian faith, the evidential support for (3) rationally *supports* just such a commitment.

C. Kierkegaard and Reformed Epistemology

So Kierkegaard's argument has not given us good reason to think that there is anything wrong or unchristian about a faith that is supported by objective reasoning. Yet, I am inclined to think that there is something right about his suspicion of objective reasoning in Christian faith. Objective reasoning, as I understand Kierkegaard, is the sort of reasoning that should convince virtually anyone who is competent, adequately informed, and intellectually honest. It is a form of argument with premises that should be accepted by all parties to the dispute, from which, all parties should agree, the conclusion follows. A number of influential contemporary philosophers,[11] most notably Alvin Plantinga,[12] have defended the claim that belief in God is or can be rational without being the conclusion of such reasoning. They have, in fact, defended the claim that it is rational to believe that there is such a being as God, without basing that belief on *any* argument. They argue instead that the Christian faith gives us good reason to think that the belief in God is properly grounded in the right sort of experiences — experiences in which we encounter God's love, forgiveness, disapproval, guidance, etc. That is, such experiences tend to produce in us the belief that there is a God, and it is rational for us to believe in God under those circumstances. Plantinga has further argued that, not only the theistic belief in God, but also the more specific beliefs of the Christian faith are, according to Christian faith, revealed to us by the Holy Spirit and are properly grounded in the experiences of such revelation.[13] This approach to the epistemology of religious belief is commonly known among philosophers as "Reformed epistemology" because it is taken to be characteristic of the Reformed or Calvinist theological tradition.

To ground religious belief in religious experience, in the way suggested by the defenders of Reformed epistemology, is not to support it with objective reasoning of the sort to which Kierkegaard objects. The grounding of one's belief in one's own experience is not the sort of support for religious belief that would be accepted by virtually anyone who is competent, adequately informed, and intellectually honest. Experience directly grounds the beliefs only of the person who has the relevant experience. My seeing a car in the parking lot makes it rational for *me* to believe that there is a car in the parking lot. My seeing it is not, however, a rational ground of anyone else's belief that there is a car in the parking lot. His seeing a car in the parking lot, or hearing me report that there is a car in the parking lot could be a ground of his belief that there is a car in the parking lot. Similarly, if I have experienced what I take to be God's forgiveness or guidance, my experience makes it rational, according to defenders of Reformed epistemology, to believe that there is a God, but it does not make it rational for anyone else to believe in God.

There are, from a Christian point of view, several advantages of hav-

11. For a good collection of the writings of such philosophers, see Alvin Plantinga and Nicholas Wolterstorff, eds., *Faith and Rationality: Reason and Belief in God* (Notre Dame: University of Notre Dame Press, 1983).

12. See his "Reason and Belief in God," in *Faith and Rationality,* 16-93.

13. *Warranted Christian Belief* (New York: Oxford, forthcoming).

ing one's religious beliefs grounded in experience over having them grounded only in objective reasoning. There are, that is, several advantages of having beliefs grounded in the experience of divine forgiveness, the conviction, inspiration, and revelation of the Holy Spirit, etc., over having beliefs that depend only on the support of such considerations as compelling historical evidence of the resurrection, theistic arguments, etc. The first advantage is just that there is not, as I see it, nearly as much rational support for theistic beliefs, especially for distinctively Christian beliefs, in objective reasoning as there is in experience. There are, I suspect, no beliefs which virtually every rational person would accept and from which virtually every rational person would infer the truth of the Christian faith. I shall not defend this claim here since that is the subject of other chapters of this book. If I am right, then our beliefs would not be rational, if we depended only on objective reasoning. There are perhaps beliefs which virtually every rational person would accept, and which she would agree provide support for Christian beliefs. There are perhaps even beliefs, other than those grounded in experience, upon which it is rational for some of us to base Christian beliefs. But even if there are, they would surely not make the beliefs of most Christians rational for them, since most Christians do not have the knowledge or sophistication rationally to base their beliefs on such reasoning.

Another advantage of experience-based Christian belief is that it is a more secure ground of Christian belief. Such a ground is more secure in two ways, psychologically and epistemically. It is psychologically more secure in that the person who accepts Christian beliefs because he takes himself to be in a personal relationship with God in which he has numerous experiences of God in his life, is much more likely to remain confident of those beliefs than he would be if he accepted them only on the basis of some argument that should convince even rational unbelievers. Whether there are such arguments that would make it rational to accept Christian faith is, at best, a very uncertain matter, not the stuff of which settled confidence is made.

It is epistemically more secure because in general it is rational to accept what experience indicates unless there is some good reason to doubt the reliability of our experience or to doubt the truth of what we take our experience to show. Thus for example since it now seems to me that there is a computer monitor on my desk, it is rational to believe that there *is* a computer monitor on my desk. For it not to be rational for me to accept the way that it seems to me, there would have to be some really compelling reason to think, either that I am suffering from a vivid illusion of some sort, or some really compelling reason, independent of my experience, to think that there is not a computer monitor on my desk. Reasons of this sort are known by epistemologists as *defeaters* of the rationality of our beliefs. Reasons of the first type are "undercutting defeaters" while reasons of the second type are "overriding defeaters." There is thus a rational presumption in favor of what experience indicates. The "burden of proof" is on the denial of what experience seems to show us. If, apart from my direct experience, the evidence for and against the claim that there is a computer on my desk is about equal, the rational thing for me to do would obviously be to accept the belief that there is a monitor on my desk. Indeed, given the clarity of my experience, the balance of the evidential weight would have to be overwhelmingly against there being a computer on my desk in order to defeat the rational presumption in its favor.

There is a similar rational presumption in favor of the deliverances of religious experience.[14] Thus, if it seems to me that God has spoken to me or forgiven me, that the Holy Spirit has revealed to me the truth of the Trinity or of the Incarnation, that God has strengthened me in a time of temptation, etc., it is rational for me to accept the corresponding beliefs unless there is an undercutting or overriding defeater of those beliefs, i.e., unless there is some good reason for thinking that my experience is illusory or that the beliefs are false. Just how strong the rational presumption is in the case of such experiences remains a matter of controversy, but that there is some such presumption is obvious. To be rational then in holding Christian beliefs that are grounded in experience requires only that the evidence seem on balance not to count against the truth of the beliefs as strongly as the experience seems to count in favor of it.

Perhaps, since he aimed his fire at objective reasoning, Kierkegaard really held a view much like that of the Reformed epistemologists. Perhaps he thought, as they did, that our Christian beliefs are better grounded in experience than in arguments. If that is the case, Kierkegaard's argument "proved too much." After all, experience does not make our Christian beliefs certain either. Like objective reasoning, the epistemic support of Christian belief can at best only approximate certainty.

But even if Kierkegaard would have been willing to give credit to experience as a ground of Christian beliefs, his antipathy toward reason

14. William P. Alston explores this analogy masterfully in "Christian Experience and Christian Belief" in *Faith and Rationality,* 103-34, and in *Perceiving God: The Epistemology of Religious Experience* (Ithaca: Cornell, 1993)

would still have been misplaced. Even if experience is typically a better ground of belief than arguments, there remain some important roles for reasoning and arguments in the Christian faith. First of all, even if our beliefs are quite securely grounded in our experience of God, they can nevertheless benefit from the support of arguments. If there are compelling arguments for the existence of God, or for the historicity of the resurrection, they can only make the believer's faith more secure, both epistemically and psychologically. Alvin Plantinga, for example, has published an argument that he takes to provide a compelling reason to accept belief in God,[15] and written an unpublished paper entitled "Two Dozen or so Good Arguments for the Existence of God." So, even if arguments are typically not necessary for the justification of Christian faith, there is no reason to spurn whatever support they might offer.

There is also an important Christian role for rational arguments in reasoning on the basis of Christian beliefs. We can deepen our understanding of God and enrich our relationship with him by means of arguments that take Christian beliefs as their premises. It is this use of reason to which Augustine was referring when he spoke of "acute and accurate reasoning," by means of which we are able "to grasp [the truth] not only by belief, but also by comprehension."

D. Reason as the Proof of Faith: Evidentialist Apologetics

Whereas Kierkegaard had an extremely negative view of human reason and thought it wrongheaded to argue for the existence of God, some Christian apologists, typically labeled "evidentialists," have claimed that reason can be used to *prove* the truth of theism or of the Christian faith by way of rational arguments based on incontrovertible evidence. Norman Geisler claims that he has proven the existence of a God who is "infinite, unchanging, all-powerful, all-knowing, and all-perfect."[16] He also claimed that "[b]oth the *authenticity* and the historicity of the New Testament documents are firmly established today."[17] Henry Morris, in a book titled *Many Infallible Proofs*, claims that one can prove (infallibly, no

15. Alvin Plantinga, "An Evolutionary Argument Against Naturalism," *Logos* (1992).

16. Norman Geisler, *Christian Apologetics* (Grand Rapids: Baker, 1976), 247-49.

17. Geisler, *Christian Apologetics*, 327.

doubt) the existence of "an infinite, eternal, omnipotent, omniscient, personal, emotional, volitional, moral, spiritual, aesthetic, holy, just, loving, living Being. And this, of course, is nothing less than a character description of the God of the Bible."[18] R. C. Sproul, John Gerstner, and Arthur Lindsley, the authors of *Classical Apologetics: A Rational Defense of the Christian Faith and a Critique of Presuppositional Apologetics,* claim that "[a]t their best, the theistic proofs are not merely probable but demonstrative."[19] "If proofs do not prove," they argue, "it is unreasonable to believe them as arguments. To do so is to say with the mind, that they do not prove and with the will that they do prove."[20]

While I remain skeptical that any of these claims are really made good by their authors, I shall leave the examination of particular theistic arguments to other authors in this book. I shall instead consider briefly the question of whether Christian faith gives us reason to think that their claims are true, i.e., reason to think that we should expect to be able to prove the existence of God so incontrovertibly. Let us dispose first of the suggestion that belief on the basis of anything short of a proof is to involve the mind and the will in a contradiction. This claim appears to depend on Kierkegaard's mistaken assumption that rationality requires the degree of our commitment to a belief to be no greater than the degree of rational support for the belief. But as we saw then, if it is rational to think that it is even probable that God exists and that our eternal welfare depends on a total commitment to God, then rationality requires, all else being equal, that we commit ourselves totally to God.

The scriptural passage most often cited in support of the claim that the existence of God is provable — the one which the authors of *Classical Apologetics* call "the text of texts to establish the biblical basis for . . . natural theology"[21] — is Romans 1:18-20:

> The wrath of God is being revealed from heaven against all the godlessness and wickedness of men who suppress the truth by their wickedness, since what may be known about God is plain to them, because God has made it plain to them. For since the creation of the world

18. Henry Madison Morris, *Many Infallible Proofs* (Green Forest, Arkansas: Master Books, 1974), 103-4.

19. R. C. Sproul, John Gerstner, and Arthur Lindsley, *Classical Apologetics: A Rational Defense of the Christian Faith and a Critique of Presuppositional Apologetics* (Grand Rapids: Zondervan, 1984), 101.

20. Sproul et al., *Classical Apologetics,* 122-23.

21. Sproul et al., *Classical Apologetics,* 43.

> God's invisible qualities — his eternal power and divine nature — have been clearly seen, being understood from what has been made, so that men are without excuse. (NIV)

This passage does seem to say that God's existence and nature would, but for sin, be obvious to everyone. What is not clear from this passage is what the above authors claim, viz., that God's existence and nature *are* obvious by way of *argument.* This passage is quite compatible with Reformed epistemology, according to which, *but for sin,* the experience of everyone would make it obvious that there is such a person as God. I am inclined to think that the best way to understand the Apostle Paul here is as saying that we would all experience this world as God's world, were it not for the obscuring effects of sin, i.e., the direct and indirect effects of the sinful suppression of our awareness of God. I see no evidence that Paul intends to assure us that there is actually some shared set of obvious beliefs from which it obviously follows that there is a God, let alone that God has the very specific nature the Christian faith attributes to him.

The authors of *Classical Apologetics* seem to be aware of this issue. They admit that there is legitimate controversy over whether this passage endorses "mediate" or "immediate" revelation. "That is, is the revelation gleaned by reasoning from the evidence for God in the medium of creation, or is the revelation a kind of a priori knowledge immediately (i.e., without means) impressed by God upon human consciousness?"[22] But there is a confusion in this way of putting the alternatives. It improperly assumes that if the acquisition of this knowledge is not by *reasoning from the evidence,* it must be *a priori* (not based in experience) and not by means of creation. But there is much a priori knowledge (e.g., complex mathematics) that is produced by a priori *reasoning.* And most of our perceptual beliefs are directly produced by *experience,* without *reasoning.* My present perceptual experience, for example, directly produces in me the belief that there is a very disorderly stack of books on the desk to my left. It is not produced by "reasoning from the evidence" but is directly produced in me upon my consideration of it in my present experience. I could, no doubt, offer an argument for that belief if I were challenged on the matter, but the actual basis of my belief is not any such argument. It is just my experience. And so it might be with belief in God. God might, as far as Romans 1:18-20 is concerned, have created our faculties and the world in such a way that when we experience the starry heavens, the or-

22. Sproul et al., *Classical Apologetics,* 43-44.

der of biological life, or the birth of a child, we are induced to think that this is a world created by God.

In the end the authors of *Classical Apologetics* conclude:

> The revelation of God in nature is mediate, but it is so manifest and so clear that it does not necessitate a complex theoretical reasoning process that could be achieved only by a group of geniuses. . . . In this sense, it may be said that if we but open our eyes, the revelation of God in nature is "immediate" with respect to time.

But because people repress their knowledge of God, complex philosophical arguments are required as "part of the unmasking process of those who refuse to acknowledge their natural knowledge of God." The refusal of the church to undertake such a project of defending the faith amounts to "capitulating to a position that is clearly antithetical to the teaching of the New Testament."[23]

Not so fast. The Romans passage contains no prescription for the church to defend the existence of God with arguments and provides us with no reason to think that any such arguments will demonstrate with certainty that there is such a God. Arguments have premises. To prove something to someone by way of argument requires that it follow from premises accepted by that person. If sin has left people without a belief in God, why should we assume that they have retained beliefs which they regard as certain and from which it obviously follows that there is a God? They may hold such beliefs, but nothing in this passage assures us that they do.

II. Understanding Faith and Reason

We have seen representative arguments for the views that reason is the enemy of faith and that the Christian faith requires that there be thoroughly compelling proofs of God's existence in the form of rational arguments. I have offered reasons to reject all of those arguments. While I have rejected arguments for some views on faith and reason that seem wrongheaded to me, I have yet to offer a positive alternative view of faith and reason. Before we proceed to look more carefully at a Christian view of faith and reason, it will be helpful to get clearer about what "faith" and "reason" are in the various uses we make of those terms.

23. Sproul et al., *Classical Apologetics,* 46-47.

A. Faith — Three Different Meanings

1. The Christian Faith

One meaning of the term "faith" is found in such expressions as: "the faith of our fathers," or "the Christian faith holds that. . . ." "The faith" or "the Christian faith" in these expressions refers to a set of beliefs that Christian have typically held to be true and central to Christianity. Among these beliefs are the beliefs that there is such a being as God, that God is three persons but only one God, that God is incarnate in Jesus Christ, that human beings are created in the image of God and fallen by sin, etc. An important project of this chapter is to explore what the Christian faith, in this sense, implies or suggests about reason and its relationship to faith.

2. Faith — The Proper Human Response to God

Virtually all Christians agree that faith is extremely important. It is the one thing that virtually all Christian traditions agree is an essential part of our response to God. But what is faith, or alternatively, what is it to have faith of the relevant sort? Christians have typically claimed that genuinely Christian faith includes both a cognitive and a noncognitive part. The cognitive part consists of believing that some important set of claims or doctrines is true. Typically the beliefs involved in having the cognitive part of faith include the belief that there is such a person as God, that Jesus Christ is God incarnate, that salvation is possible only through Christ, etc. The noncognitive element of genuinely Christian faith is usually thought to involve having some sort of personal relationship with God. This relationship is variously thought to be one of love, commitment, trust, obedience, etc. For our purposes, it is less important what exactly the noncognitive aspect of faith includes, than the idea that there is a noncognitive aspect. Since this is a chapter on faith and reason, I will focus mostly on the cognitive part of faith.

3. Faith as a Source of Belief

Philosophers, theologians, and believers have long identified some of their beliefs as truths of faith; and speak often of what we know by faith or what we believe by faith. When we talk that way we are talking about a specific way of acquiring knowledge and justifying beliefs. The truths of faith are those that can be known or justifiedly believed because of divine revelation, and are justified on the basis of their having been revealed by God. Included in the truths of faith are those revealed in the Scriptures and those revealed to the individual believer or community of believers by the illumination or guidance of the Holy Spirit. The expression "truths of faith" is perhaps misleading here since it is not the truth of these propositions that is grounded in revelation, but our knowledge of them, and our belief in their truth that is grounded in revelation. Theologians sometimes refer to these truths of faith as beliefs we know by special revelation. This is perhaps a more accurate way of describing them, since presumably all of our knowledge is revealed to us by God. Most of it, however, is revealed to us by means of nature and our natural capacities, both of which he has created. The truths of faith, however, are revealed to us by special, extraordinary, supernatural means.

B. Reason — Three Different Meanings

1. Reason as the Proper Use of Our Cognitive Faculties

Human reason, in its broadest sense, involves use of the various human faculties by which we aim to discover truth and avoid error. Let us call these faculties "cognitive" faculties. Whether beliefs are actually produced by reason — whether, that is, they are reasonable or rational — depends on whether we have used our cognitive faculties well. It depends, at least in part, on whether the use of these faculties is well-suited to believing truths and avoiding falsehoods. Thus it is typically by the exercise of reason that we form such beliefs as that there is a really noisy piece of machinery operating just outside my office window, that I had orange juice for breakfast, that $2 + 2 = 4$, that moral responsibility presupposes free will, and that falling objects in a vacuum accelerate at 9.8 m/sec^2. But if I believed that the Dodgers will lead the Western Division of the National League by five games within two weeks, given that they are currently struggling and five games behind the leader, my belief would be unreasonable, or irrational. It would not be a deliverance of reason at all but rather a piece of wishful thinking. If I formed the belief that Martians regularly visit Partridge, Kansas because I read it in the *National Enquirer,* my belief would be due to a fascination with the sensational, not to reason.

One way to consider the relationship of faith and reason is to ask whether the beliefs of the Christian faith are reasonable or rational. It is to ask alternatively whether Christian beliefs measure up to the standards of reason; whether the use of our cognitive faculties that produce Christian beliefs is well-suited to producing true beliefs and avoiding false beliefs.[24]

2. Reason as the Proper Use of Natural Human Faculties

Christians sometimes distinguish truths of reason from truths of faith. This sense of "reason" is a narrower one which refers only to the *natural* use of our cognitive faculties in our interaction with the natural world. What we know by reason is what we can know by means only of such natural human cognitive faculties as perception, reasoning, and memory, without depending essentially on any special supernatural revelation of God. Thus for example, I know by reason and not by faith, that 2 + 3 = 5, that penicillin is an antibiotic, that I am less than six feet tall, etc. I shall later turn to the question of what the Christian should do if there are apparent conflicts between the truths of faith and the truths of reason.

3. The Faculty of Reason

There is also a different, yet narrower meaning that is often attached to our use of the term "reason." One of the faculties by which we aim to discover truth and avoid error is logical *reasoning.* That is, one of the ways we have of trying to align our beliefs with the truth is to think carefully about what is implied by our beliefs, or by beliefs we are considering. Reason, in this sense, is often contrasted with experience, or intuition, as sources of belief. Another way, then, to consider the relationship of faith and reason is to examine what the Christian faith has to say about the use of this cognitive faculty — to examine, in other words, what the Christian faith has to say about reasoning. I have already suggested that such reasoning is part of our cognitive design and that it can be an important part of the faithful Christian's pursuit of the truth.

24. Alvin Plantinga has done much to help contemporary epistemologists understand the significance of properly functioning cognitive faculties. Plantinga's insights in this matter were inspired by considering the epistemological significance of his Christian belief that human cognition has been purposefully created by God. See his *Warrant and Proper Function* (New York: Oxford, 1993).

III. A Christian Epistemology

The Christian story has three major parts: creation, sin, and redemption. On a Christian view of the world, all three of those parts of the story are important for understanding human life. Human cognition is no exception to this. In what follows, I will try to examine the implications of creation, fall, and redemption for cognition, and so defend a Christian epistemology, i.e., a Christian view of what we can know, and rationally believe to be true.

A. Cognitive Creation

God, according to Christian faith, created humanity. Furthermore, he created us for a purpose, or set of purposes. He therefore created us as he did, with the nature and capacities he gave us, so that we could accomplish the purposes for which he created us. Among the more important capacities with which he endowed humanity is the capacity for forming beliefs. He did that by giving us a set of cognitive faculties, faculties for forming beliefs. Among these are perception, memory, testimony, reasoning, intuition, etc. A divinely intended function or purpose for which God intended these faculties was the production of knowledge (or at least true beliefs) and the avoidance of falsehood. Thus, for example, he gave us the capacity to see, so that we could know the truth about our environment. He gave us memory so that our beliefs about the past would reflect the way things actually were. He gave us the disposition to accept testimony so that we could benefit from the cognitive activities of others. He gave us the capacity to reason logically so that we would know what truths are implied by the truths we already believe and perhaps also to recognize falsehoods among our beliefs by understanding their more obviously false implications. And when these faculties function properly, they function reliably, i.e., the beliefs they produce are likely to be true.

The Christian does not, however, have good reason to think that such a design would make even our honest truth-seeking infallible. Given the finitude of our cognitive resources, there is an inevitable tradeoff, in an optimal cognitive design for operation in this world, between the value of believing the truth and the value of avoiding error or falsehood. An overemphasis on avoiding falsehood would make our honest truth-seeking overly skeptical and make us run the unacceptable risk of missing out on truths it is important to believe. On the other hand, an overemphasis on believing the truth would make us overly credulous and make us unacceptably prone to believe falsehoods it is important to avoid. An optimal design would make us so that, in the environment for which we are designed, our honest truth-seeking will tend to lead us to believe important truths while avoiding even more important errors, and to avoid important errors without precluding us from believing even more important truths. Christian faith gives us reason, then, to think that a reliance on reason, or an honest pursuit of the truth, will enhance rather than diminish the likelihood that we believe the truth, and avoid error, although it does not give us reason to think that even the optimal use of reason would make us infallible.

There are two features of our cognitive design that are especially important to a Christian epistemology. I take it is as evident that our faculties are designed to benefit epistemically from our social relationships. Our ability to communicate enables us to tap into the resources of other cognizers, to benefit from the experience of others, and from the learning of those who have benefited from the experience of others, and so forth. We also benefit similarly from the correction of others, who understand some matters more clearly than we do. In order to realize these social benefits, our design includes a strong inclination to accept the views of others. This is just as we should expect it to be from a Christian perspective. According to Christianity, a central purpose of human beings is the love of our fellow human beings, which includes the commitment to contribute to each other's well-being. It is not surprising, then, that we are so designed that in knowing, as in all of life, our flourishing depends crucially on what we receive from others.

A second feature of our cognitive design that Christianity gives us good reason to emphasize is a capacity for the knowledge of God. I am assuming that human cognitive faculties were designed to be able to recognize the presence of God in the environment for which we were created. John Calvin thought that God gave us a special faculty, in addition to our other cognitive faculties — a *sensus divinitatis*[25] or sense of God — designed expressly to be able to recognize God in the environment for which we were created. This is obvious from a Christian perspective, given that God designed us, that the purpose of human beings is most basically to serve God and that serving God in the relevant sense requires the knowledge of God. In section I.C, I offered some reasons for thinking that this awareness is a direct product of experience.

25. Calvin, 1.3.1, vol. 1, p. 43.

B. Cognitive Fallenness

But, of course, the Christian faith gives us reason to think that the function of our cognitive faculties is, like everything else in human life, also affected by sin, and is therefore less than optimal. Theologians sometime refer to these effects on our knowing as the "noetic" effects of sin. The noetic effects of sin are the effects, on human cognition, of the sinful nature and of the sins human beings commit. But some aspects of our cognitive life are affected by sin more than others. It is no accident that our awareness of God is particularly subject to impairment. The truth about God is such that awareness of it tends to interfere with sinful purposes. If sin inclines us to live in opposition to the purposes of God, we are, under its influence, likely to be understandably uncomfortable with the awareness that there is a morally perfect and all-powerful God who is opposed to our sinful purposes. We are accordingly inclined, under the influence of sin, to suppress our awareness of this uncomfortable truth. Our sinful projects are much less threatened by the awareness of the truth about the rate of acceleration of falling objects, the distance between Grantham and Harrisburg, or the shape of a football. The reliability of our judgments about such matters is therefore much less affected by sin. In general we should expect the noetic effects of sin to be most pronounced in moral and religious matters since the truth about such matters is more difficult to reconcile with sinful purposes. However, they are not limited to those matters. The central significance of beliefs about God in a worldview is such that unreliability in that area tends to distort our judgments about other matters. We also suffer from the tendency of *others* to suppress the truth in sin. Since God designed us to be influenced by others, we tend to be influenced, not just by their insights, but also by their sinful distortions of the truth. Again, we should expect this distortion to be most pronounced in religious and moral matters.

C. Cognitive Redemption

Just as there are, according to the Christian faith, cognitive aspects of creation and fallenness there are also cognitive aspects of redemption. Part of the redemption of the believer is sanctification, the cleansing or our hearts or the improvement of our character. Such cleansing reduces our sinful inclination to suppress the truth. In Christian community we also benefit indirectly from the Holy Spirit's sanctification since we benefit from the influence of others whose hearts have also been cleansed.

It is also a familiar claim of Christianity that the Holy Spirit is a revealer, and that included in this ministry is the work of revealing the truth of certain propositions to us. These revelations come in at least two broad categories. There is first of all the Holy Spirit's revealing to us the truth of those propositions that are involved in having Christian faith, i.e., revealing to us that God "speaks" in the Scriptures, that we are sinners in need of salvation from our sins, that faith is the divinely mandated response to God in our situation, that salvation is by the grace of God through the life, death, and resurrection of Jesus Christ, that Christ is both human and divine, that God is triune, etc. Secondly, there is the work of the Holy Spirit in individuals and groups to reveal to them particular truths that it is important for them to know, especially as a form of guidance for their lives.

These claims about the Holy Spirit's revelations are familiar Christian beliefs. But how does this really work? What reason is there really for thinking that these "revelations" are true or that they are revelations of the Holy Spirit? The answer is, I think, that these beliefs are grounded in a certain kind of experience. Just as the belief that there is a pile of books on my desk is grounded in my present perceptual experience, and as I have suggested, belief in God is grounded in our experience of certain features of the world, so the more particular claims of the Christian faith and matters of personal significance are grounded in certain religious experiences. It is often suggested, for example, that when we read the Scriptures, the Holy Spirit reveals to us the truth of what we read. How exactly does that work? The specific phenomena of such an experience, no doubt, vary a great deal from person to person and experience to experience. But the phenomena include something analogous to perceptual experience. When I have the visual perception that I am now experiencing, it just seems clear or obvious to me that there is a pile of books on my desk. Similarly when we read the Scriptures in the relevant situations, it seems clear or obvious to us that what we read is true. When we seek God's guidance in prayer, we sometimes come away with a clear sense that we should undertake a particular course of action.

But in the case of the beliefs of the Christian faith, I think the phenomena are not quite as simple as I have presented them here. It isn't as though the Holy Spirit reveals to us the truth of the Trinity, and then in another experience, or separately in the same experience, also reveals the truth of the full deity and humanity of Christ. In my own case, at any rate, it is rather more of a "package deal" than that. It would come closer to describing my experience to say that I acquire a profound sense of confidence in the Scriptures. But the more fundamental confidence I have is that God is at work in a very special sort of way in the Christian community or the Christian church. This confidence involves an interconnected web of beliefs about the epistemic grounding of Christian faith. It includes the beliefs that God has spoken through Jesus Christ, that Jesus Christ founded the church, a community of believers through whom God would work and through whom God would reveal himself, his ways, and his will to the world, and that the Holy Spirit inspired important early members of the church to write the Scriptures in order to reveal what God wanted people to know. It also includes the belief that the Holy Spirit works in the church to insure that she knows the truth about those matters it is important to know in order to relate properly to God, first by leading the church to recognize the Scriptures as God's Word, and secondly by leading the church to the right interpretations of the Scriptures on those matters most important for Christian faith and faithfulness.[26] This description is, so far, mostly autobiographical. But I am convinced that the epistemic significance of the work of the Holy Spirit is mostly a matter of aligning our discernment and belief with those of the Christian tradition. This happens, typically, not by revealing separate beliefs to us, one at a time, but rather by illuminating the Christian community or tradition as the locus of God's activity in the world, and most importantly for epistemic purposes, the locus of God's revealing activity. My suggestion then is that our confidence in the fact that the Christian community is the locus of God's revealing activity is directly grounded in experience. The other beliefs of the Christian faith are based on that confidence.

If this description of the revealing ministry of the Holy Spirit is on the right track, it underlines the extent to which revelation is a social or community matter. The individual's experience with the Holy Spirit is only one very small part of the process by which the truths of the Christian faith are revealed, even to that individual. His confidence in the truth of the relevant beliefs involves the implicit confidence that the Holy Spirit

26. Given the many differences among Christians and Christian traditions in the beliefs they hold, it is obvious that the Holy Spirit's influence does not insure an absolute infallibility in the beliefs Christians hold as constituents of their faith. My confidence is rather that the Holy Spirit is active and influential in the church's discernment and more influential on matters God deems more important for faithfulness to him.

has been active, revealing important truths to the Christian community for a very long time.

But there are other respects in which the revelation of the Holy Spirit is more communal than is often recognized. As I suggested earlier, on a Christian view, our purpose is primarily to love God, and secondarily to love our fellow human beings, and the latter love is a very significant expression of the former. Our purpose very importantly involves a concern for, commitment to, and contribution to each other's welfare. And the fulfillment of our purpose is so tied to that value that our flourishing depends crucially on what we receive from others. Accordingly, I suggest, a very important purpose of the church is to be a community that exemplifies mutual love, and mutual contribution to human flourishing — the sort of human life that glorifies God. This interdependence should affect the experiences that trigger the sense of illumination typical of the Holy Spirit's work. When we think of the circumstances in which people are moved by the Holy Spirit to accept the truths of the Christian faith, those experiences most often mentioned, at least among Protestants, are prayer, Bible reading, and listening to preaching. But it is at least as likely, I think, that the experience of Christian community is what triggers the relevant beliefs under the inspiration of the Holy Spirit. If Christian community is what it is intended to be, i.e., if people are together serving God, and under God's direction, and with God's power, serving each other and others, then the Holy Spirit often prompts the conviction that God is at work in this community. It is perhaps this sort of experience that Jesus had in mind when he said, "By this all men will know that you are my disciples, if you love one another."[27] It is the belief that God is at work in the community of Christian faith that prompts such people to accept Christian sources of authority, Christ, the Scriptures, the witness of the Holy Spirit in the Christian tradition, etc. To give it a more spiritual description, the Holy Spirit often gives us the conviction that God has *spoken* through the Church by showing us that the church is the community in whom and through whom God does his work in the world.

IV. A Christian Theology of Faith and Reason

It is now time to turn our attention to the central issues of this chapter. What is a Christian view of the relationship of faith and reason? Or more

27. John 13:35 (NIV).

accurately, what are the relationships between faith and reason in the various related senses of those terms? There are I think, broadly two different faith-reason relationships to consider. The first one is the relationship between reason in its broadest sense, as rationality, or as excellent truth-seeking, to the beliefs involved in having Christian faith. Are those beliefs reasonable in that broad sense? The second faith-reason relationship to consider is that between what we believe by faith and what we believe by reason. Christians have reasons to trust both sources of belief, but what if there appears to be a conflict between them? How should a Christian resolve them? With all of these questions, I will primarily be interested in the Christian answer to the questions.

A. Is Faith Reasonable?

Does Christian faith, by its own lights, measure up to the standards of reason? Are the beliefs involved in having Christian faith rational? There are really two questions in the neighborhood here. The first is: Is Christian faith rational for those who accept it? The second related question is: Is there a basis of persuading others rationally to accept Christian faith? Let us take these questions in order.

1. Is the Faith of Christians Rational?

Are the beliefs involved in having Christian faith rational? Are they a product of our cognitive faculties functioning properly? The Christian answer must, I think, be yes. If the Christian story is true, then when we form Christian beliefs in the circumstances described above, our faculties are functioning just as they were intended to function by their designer, which, according to Christianity, must be to function properly. The Christian has obvious reasons then to think that forming beliefs in this way is conducive to her goal of believing truths and avoiding falsehoods.

This conclusion might seem obvious, even trivial. It should not be surprising, perhaps, that the claims of Christian faith will turn out to be rational by its own standards of rationality. But it is worth noting in part because it helps us to see what is wrong with those Christians who see their faith as somehow opposed to reason. There is a second reason that this conclusion is significant. Since the Enlightenment, secular philosophers have, under the influence of the eighteenth-century philosophers

David Hume and Immanuel Kant,[28] claimed that even if the Christian faith is true, it could never be rational to believe that it is. Since the eighteenth century, this has probably been the most influential philosophic objection to Christian faith. We can now see that this objection fails.[29] The objection is based on the claim that since belief in God could not be based on sensory experience, it could never be rational to believe that there is a God. It was not, on this view, rational to believe there isn't a God either. Human beings just had nothing to guide them rationally with respect to the existence of God, or most of the other beliefs that are important to Christian faith. So, even if our beliefs were true, according to this objection, it couldn't be rational to think that they are true. But we have seen that that claim is false. If the Christian faith is true, then its claims about how we acquire our beliefs are true. According to those claims, as we have seen, we are rational in believing that the Christian faith is true.

The objector's only recourse for repairing the objection seems to be to argue that it is irrational to believe in the existence of God because it is obviously false that there is such a being. But this kind of objector can't very well make that argument, since, according to him, we have nothing to guide us rationally with respect to the existence of God, and so we, in principle, could not have a good reason for thinking that there is not a God.

2. Apologetics: Reason in Defense of Faith

So Christians have good reason to think that their own beliefs are rational, but what of others who are not believers? Do we have good reason to think that Christian beliefs are, or would be, rational for them? This book is after all a book of apologetics. Is there reason in the Christian faith for thinking that others can be persuaded rationally to accept the truth of Christian faith? The Christian epistemology that I have been defending gives us ample grounds for optimism about the enterprise of defending the faith by means of reason, much cause to think that the proper use of our cognitive faculties is likely to be supportive of Christian faith. Ac-

28. There are important differences between Hume and Kant, and Kant, in the end, offered a practical justification for theism. But it is far from clear that even Kant thought that his justification made theism epistemically rational. In any case, whatever Kant's personal motivations might have been, his legacy in philosophy has been a tradition of insisting that beliefs about God cannot be epistemically rational.

29. Plantinga offers such an argument in *Warranted Christian Belief.*

cording to Christian faith, our cognitive faculties were designed by God to be epistemically reliable. They were well designed to lead us to the truth and to avoid falsehood in the world for which he created us. Since Christian beliefs are also, according to the Christian faith, the truths about which it is most important to be right, we should not fear that the reliance on reason, or on the proper use of our cognitive faculties, would lead us away from the truth of Christianity.

Christians also have some grounds for pessimism about such a project. We believe our cognitive function has been impaired by sin. That impairment raises the likelihood that the exercise of our faculties will lead us to believe falsehoods and fail to believe truths. It leaves us without assurance that reason will tend to be effective in convincing everyone of the truth of Christianity. Rebellion against God may preclude the experience that would make the truth of Christian belief evident. Sinful suppression of the truth, and the social effects on one's epistemic situation of such suppression by others, might leave one without the beliefs that could otherwise serve as the premises of sound arguments for Christian belief. It would, in light of this, be a serious mistake to insist that the Christian faith is defensible by arguments that would convince any intelligent person. To accept such a standard for the rationality of Christian faith is to accept a burden of proof for which there is no reasonable ground, and to make the opponent the judge of when it is discharged. The Christian faith, moreover, does not give us any reason to think that there are any such arguments. In fact, it gives us reason to think that there are no such arguments precisely because of the truth of Christian beliefs about the direct and indirect noetic effects of sin, even on intelligent people.

B. Conflicts Between Faith and Reason

It might seem from what I have said that, according to Christian faith, reason, in principle, cannot ever come into conflict with faith. But that would be, at best, misleading. There is nothing in Christian belief to rule out the possibility of a conflict between what we believe by faith and what we believe by reason. There may be a conflict between what seems to be revealed in the Scriptures, for example, and what the proper use of our epistemic faculties seems otherwise to tell us. As I pointed out earlier, an optimal cognitive design for both believing truths and avoiding falsehoods will leave any finite cognitive system liable to error, at least in this world. So, even if we used our cognitive resources the way God intended us to, we might still occasionally make mistakes. So it should not surprise us if there are occasional discrepancies between the deliverances of reason and the deliverances of faith.

It might initially seem obvious that on Christian grounds we should always resolve such conflicts in favor of what we believe by faith. After all, whatever God reveals is guaranteed to be correct. True enough. But the problem is that it is not enough for God to have done his part flawlessly. In order for us to know what God has revealed, we must correctly identify it as revealed by God. Unfortunately, as in other judgments we make, we are fallible in our identifications of what God has revealed. We can make even honest mistakes in our interpretations of Scripture, our understanding of the Holy Spirit's leading, etc. So, although as Christians we should always operate on the assumption that whatever God reveals is correct, we should retain an appreciation of our fallibility in making judgments about what he has revealed. So, what should we do if there appears to be a conflict between the truth as indicated by reason, and the truth as indicated by faith? The best advice I can offer is to compare honestly the strength of the competing considerations. When it seems to us that faith tells us that something is true while reason tells us it is false, we should ask ourselves honestly, Does it seem more likely that reason is telling me that it is false or more likely that God has revealed that it is true? If it is more obvious, on Christian grounds, that God has revealed that it is true, then it is rational for the Christian to believe that it is. If it is more obvious that reason tells us it is false than that God has revealed that it is true, then we should accept the stronger support of reason for its falsehood over the weaker epistemic support for the claim that God has revealed that it is true. This is, of course, not a matter of trusting our judgments over God's. It is a matter of favoring a judgment about one matter (e.g., that science confirms a heliocentric universe) over another one about what God has revealed (e.g., that God has made the astronomical revelation through Scripture that the earth cannot be in motion).[30] In either case we are making the best judgment we can about the truth, on the assumption that Christianity is true.

But a second, more serious, kind of conflict in our epistemic judgments might also occur. In the sort of conflict discussed in the preceding paragraphs, we assumed that the Christian faith is true, that the Christian community is the locus of God's revealing activity, etc. But should a Christian believer be open to the possibility that the Christian faith itself

30. "The world is firmly established; cannot be moved" (Psalm 93:1, NIV).

is not true? Doing our best to follow the dictates of reason is really just a matter of honest truth-seeking. Are there proper Christian limits to honest truth-seeking? What if, in our honest judgment, it should ever come to seem plausible, all things honestly considered, that the Christian faith itself is not true? It might be objected that such a situation could never occur. If a person comes not to believe that the Christian faith is true, it might be argued, he must either be suppressing his awareness of its truth, or suppressing his awareness of evidence supporting it. On the other hand, there surely are people who honestly do not believe in the Christian faith. The person who is unaware of the claims of Christianity certainly cannot believe them. Such a person's failure to believe is obviously not disingenuous. If there is no guarantee that such persons do not honestly fail to believe in the truth of Christianity, on what Christian grounds can we be sure that no one who has believed could ever come, by honest truth-seeking, not to believe?

My tentative suggestion on this matter is that, regardless of whether it is possible honestly to come not to believe, there are no Christian reasons to rein in our honest truth-seeking. The suggestion is tentative because, as a Christian, I believe that it is of the highest importance to believe the truth of Christianity, since it is a necessary condition of Christian faith. So it seems that we should guard our faith very carefully. There is an obvious sense in which we should avoid the occasion of unbelief. If we have Christian reason to think that a certain sort of activity is likely to mislead us or distort our judgments, then surely we ought to avoid it. There are Christian reasons for thinking that sin, neglecting our relationship with God, and the forsaking of Christian community are likely to deprive us of the sort of experiences that make the reality of God and of God's activity in Christian community apparent. We therefore have good Christian reasons for scrupulously avoiding such directions in our lives. A Christian believer might also recognize that, on general epistemological grounds, if one exposes oneself to sophisticated objections to Christian belief without availing oneself of the sophisticated Christian responses to such objections, the experience is likely to make Christianity appear less plausible than it should. In that case, the believer would be well-advised to avail herself of such Christian resources whenever she contemplates such objections. But these are not cases of reining in honest truth-seeking, they are rather forms of honest truth-seeking. They are ways of conducting our lives that we have good reason to believe to be truth-conducive.

My suggestion is, however, that we not avoid conduct or inquiry that we have reason to believe is truth-conducive. We should not, in other words, rein in our honest truth-seeking. Even if we have no Christian guarantee that we can never, by such means, lose our faith, we do have, as I pointed out earlier, good Christian reasons to believe that honest truth-seeking is well-suited to believing the truth, especially about Christian faith. According to Christianity, I argued, we have reason to think that we have been cognitively designed by God so that when we honestly seek the truth, our cognitive faculties are reliable and that God has graciously intervened in human life to compensate for the noetic effects of sin. A Christian, then, has good reason to believe that her worldview has the most to gain and the least to lose by following reason wherever it properly leads. A Christian has good reason to believe that the chances of losing her Christian beliefs are *diminished* by endeavoring, through honest truth-seeking, to follow reason wherever it properly leads, regardless of whether Christianity offers an ironclad guarantee that honest truth-seeking makes the loss of her beliefs *impossible*.

7

Religious Pluralism

Timothy O'Connor

I. Introduction: Tolerance, Relativism, and Pluralism

For many people, the diversity of religious practices and beliefs is a fact of everyday life. When I was an undergraduate, I shared an apartment, at various times, with two Muslims and a Buddhist, among others. In addition, I have had and continue to have friendships with many more people of various religious faiths (as well as those of no faith at all). And such experience is certainly not unusual.

While we have become increasingly exposed to the diversity of religious beliefs that surround us, our culture has at the same time begun to place less emphasis on these very differences. A number of factors have led us in this direction: dismay and regret over religious persecution and cultural imperialism, to name two. But, however exactly we got here, "relativist" and "pluralist" views about religion are all the rage these days, in the academy as well as on the street. Usually, those who hold such "pluralist" views have not thought them through very carefully. Defenders of pluralism will often describe their views with slogans, such as "all religions are true," or "there are many roads to God." (Many appeal to the well-worn Hindu parable of the blind men who touch different parts of the elephant, each mistaking a different part for the whole.) Put in these simplistic terms, it's easy to show that these views are just indefensible. In fact, I'll show later on that there are powerful reasons to reject even the most sophisticated versions of pluralism.

But this offensive strategy is not my main aim here. The reason it is not is this: people today are far less committed to pluralism than they are to the belief that traditional, "absolutist," or "exclusivist" understandings of religious claims are arrogant or irrational or in some other sense unacceptable. According to this way of thinking, it's fine, e.g., to believe that Jesus Christ is *a* way to God, but improper to hold that he is *the* way to God. More radically, it's okay to believe that one has experienced the love of God the Heavenly Father, as long as one doesn't conclude from this that ultimate reality is, "absolutely speaking," a personal being. (For this would imply, e.g., that the Zen Buddhist view of *nirvana,* the pure "suchness" or ego-less being of ever-changing reality, is false.) One should instead say something more qualified, such as "in my experience, ultimate reality has taken on the appearance of a transcendent, personal being." We are thus admonished not to throw out our Christian beliefs altogether, but to hold them in a way that doesn't "delegitimize" the truths of other religions. Thus, current fashion would urge us to hold our religious beliefs in a way quite different from the way we hold our beliefs about, for example, the physical world. We all think that it is simply true that there are birds and buildings and baseballs. Anyone so mentally impaired as to deny these things is simply wrong. With respect to birds, we might say, we're all exclusivists.

For many people, then, there is a general "air of plausibility" to pluralism in matters of religion, though they don't have any worked-out view on the matter. So, if we were to proceed by arguing against one particular version of pluralism, many would likely think that, while *that* version fails, there is likely some other view that would successfully and coherently describe what they believe. A more promising tack that some contemporary Christian philosophers have taken, and that I will take here, is to root out the fundamental assumptions that lie behind appeals to pluralist doctrines. When this is done, we will see that the reasonableness of the pluralist view vanishes.

I will proceed in two stages. First, in section II, I will show that the main pluralist argument *against* exclusivist Christian belief fail. Second, in section III, I will show that the main arguments *in favor* of the most promising version of pluralism also fails. With that, the critique of pluralism will be complete.

II. Pluralist Objections to "Exclusivist" Christian Belief

Pluralists reject traditional Christianity (where this involves holding beliefs exclusively) in a number of ways. I will take up the three most common of these objections.

A. The 'No Difference in Spiritual Fruits' Objection

Unlike many atheists or naturalists, pluralists are not skeptical about religious experience (at least much of it). They're generally happy to admit that a person's religious experiences make it reasonable for him to have the beliefs he does concerning the Ultimate. Let's take me for an example. I have had experiences in which it has seemed to me that my Heavenly Father was in some manner enveloping me, communicating his love for me, and calling me to draw near to him. These are experiences of a kind typical in the Christian tradition, and they have prompted renewal of my commitments to seek deeper and more regular communion with God and to follow the example of Christ in my life. Accordingly, they give me at least some reason to believe that "the Ultimate" is manifested in the Christian tradition as the all-powerful, all-knowing, and loving Creator of all. If *everyone's* experiences were compatible with mine in the sense that they, too, depicted ultimate reality as having the character ascribed to God in the Christian Scriptures, then the reasonable conclusion would be that *that is what ultimate reality is like in itself.*

But, the pluralist points out, there is no such uniformity among religious experiences. And they cannot *all* truthfully represent ultimate reality *in itself,* for they ascribe *incompatible* attributes to it. (It makes no sense to say that ultimate reality, in itself, is both personal and impersonal.) If I conclude instead that *my* experiences are veridical — God really was present to me, communicating his love, and so forth — while the experiences of Hindus, for example, indicating that ultimate reality is "the blissful universal consciousness of Brahman," are illusory, then I am being *arbitrary.* For there is no objective basis for deciding between these two. In particular, all religions appear to be roughly equal with respect to what the pluralist holds is the common goal of religion: moving from self-centeredness to "Ultimate-Reality-centeredness." This movement is the "spiritual fruit" that comes from sincerely practicing one's faith. We don't all get as far as we'd like, of course. In all traditions, there are few "saints," others in whom there is no discernible change, and a great many more in between. As the pluralist philosopher John Hick has put it, we must, then, "avoid the implausibly arbitrary dogma that religious experience is all delusory with the single exception of the particular form enjoyed by the one who is speaking."[1] The only position, Hick argues, that is both not arbitrary and not completely dismissive of the authenticity of religious experience is the pluralist's.

Recall that, according to the pluralist, many kinds of religious experiences involve legitimate contact with "Ultimate Reality." How then can the pluralist make sense of the contradictory religious beliefs these experiences give rise to (that Ultimate reality is, for example, personal and nonpersonal)? The answer is that pluralists hold that Ultimate Reality *as it really is* is beyond our intellectual grasp — indeed, it utterly *transcends* the categories we apply to it. When we experience it, we conceptualize it in terms of categories that we have available to us (since human beings need to categorize their contact with the Ultimate to make sense of it and respond to it). Numerous categories have been devised for this purpose across cultures, but no particular packaging is necessary. Some forms may be more efficient than others, but there are evidently many forms that get the job done reasonably well.

It may be thought that some religious traditions are in greater agreement with the pluralist regarding the unimportance of creed than Christianity is. When I was a graduate student at Cornell University, the Dalai Lama came and delivered a lecture entitled "Overcoming Our Differences." In the lecture, he stressed themes for which he has become well-known in the U.S. — respect for cultural and religious differences and the centrality of practicing compassion, whatever one's creed. He was quoted in an interview as believing that Buddhism is not the best religion for everyone, and that sincere Christians who find that their faith leads them to act compassionately should by all means continue in it. Is that form of Buddhist teaching, at least, in agreement with Hick on the inessentiality of doctrine? In fact, it is not. According to this Tibetan tradition, it is *essential* to ultimate salvation or liberation that one realizes the truth of the doctrine of emptiness (sunyata). Roughly, on this view, our way of understanding the world around us is radically illusory. There are no individual objects such as birds and buildings and baseballs (and people!). Reality is a "void," empty of all substance. This recognition is thought to free one from attachment to things and ultimately to lead to liberation from the cycle of rebirth. But such Buddhists recognize that not everyone is ready

1. John Hick, *An Interpretation of Religion* (London: Macmillan, 1989), 235.

to understand this teaching. And as this ultimately necessary insight is inextricably bound up with practices (including works of compassion) that *reflect* the cognitive understanding of the doctrine of emptiness, and as good rebirths (which put one in better position to attain it) can be achieved by engaging in them, it may well be best, on the Buddhist scheme of things, for a given individual to set such doctrinal matters aside for a time (or a life or two) in order to cultivate the equally necessary "skillful means."[2] Thus, this form of Buddhist teaching is compatible with a very relaxed attitude about doctrinal religious differences — but only because of its commitment to specific propositions concerning the nature of reality which conflict with those of various other faiths, such as traditional Christianity, and which conflict with the pluralist's conception as well.

Thus, the pluralist's position is at odds with most if not all traditional religions, not just "exclusivist" Christianity. But how should we, as Christians, address the pluralist's no-difference-in-spiritual-fruits objection? The most basic point to make is that the pluralist poses a false choice. The traditional Christian who rejects pluralism is *not* thereby forced to the "arbitrary" claim that Christian experiences of God alone are reliable, while experiences of ultimate reality as mediated by other traditions are wholly illusory. The nature of religious experience and the extent to which its content is shaped by religious tradition are complex subjects, which I cannot explore here.[3] But clearly Christians can allow that non-Christians are capable of experiencing God in some manner, though we will, owing to the teachings of the faith, suppose that some of the very specific claims that are made about God (or the Ultimate) as a result of those experiences are false, stemming from the influence of false religious tenets.[4] For it is integral to Christian teaching that God is Lord of all creation and desires that all should come to him (2 Pet. 3:9). Human beings

2. My discussion throughout this paragraph is indebted to Jane Compson's recent article, "The Dalai Lama and the World Religions: A False Friend?" *Religious Studies* 32 (1996): 271-79.

3. For more on this subject, the reader should consult Caleb Miller's chapter, "Faith and Reason" (pp. 135-64), and Bill Davis's chapter, "Theistic Arguments" (pp. 20-46), in this volume as well as the magisterial treatment of this topic by the Christian philosopher William Alston in his *Perceiving God* (Ithaca: Cornell University Press, 1991).

4. In defending this contention, we ought not implausibly to assert as some occasionally do that Christian experiences of God are "self-authenticating" (have a distinguishing mark that guarantees that they're the genuine article) in a manner that other religious experiences are not.

were made to enjoy him; it is only through the effects of sin that we do not naturally experience his presence as vividly and continuously as one experiences the warmth of the sun on a bright summer day. But sin has not entirely eradicated this natural affinity for our Maker, nor has God abandoned those who have yet to come to understand his purposes and offer of redemption through Christ. None of us can say to what extent our supposed experiences of God are the result of self-delusion or of some unreliable source. Christians themselves are taught to look on their religious experiences with some degree of caution and to test whether any content they have (purporting to reveal something about God's nature or his purposes) are consistent with authoritative teaching. For we, too, are prone to all sorts of pride, dishonesty about our true condition, and susceptibility to social influences, and also to blameless forms of powerful unconscious influences. But as we know that God has not abandoned his people and we are explicitly taught to expect some measure of experience of his gracious presence (at times comforting and at times rebuking), we confidently suppose that much of our apparent experience of God is genuine. God really is intending and causing us to have some measure of heightened awareness of his nature and purposes for us, though there is indeed a degree of processing or "filtering" of "divine input" (which the pluralist supposes entirely shapes the experience), and this distorts, to some extent, what God wants us to understand about himself.

B. The Arrogance Objection

A second and quite common objection to exclusivist religious belief is that it involves arrogance on the part of the believer. If I, as a traditional Christian, suppose that I have come to have true beliefs in such an important matter as religion, where so many other human beings have not, I must think that I am superior to them in some important respect — intellectually or morally. For I have been able to discern the truth in a morally significant matter where so many others have failed.

But, common though this objection is, it is quite unpersuasive. Let us acknowledge at the outset that the Christian Church has not lacked for arrogant people. More particularly, our numbers have included those who have been highly arrogant in just the way the pluralist suggests: people who supposed that Christians have believed rightly where others have not because they are superior intellectually or ethically. This is clearly repugnant. Given the organic unity of the body of Christ, it is one of the many sins we should corporately confess. (Of course, the Church is in no way *special* in this respect: we see this sin in parts of the Church precisely because the Church draws its numbers from the full range of human beings. And humanity does not lack for ample instances of every kind of moral failing, arrogance included.)

But should we think that such arrogance is an inevitable consequence of exclusivist belief? Any one of us can point to exemplary (though still flawed) "exclusivist" Christian brothers and sisters who show no discernible trace of the kind of arrogance highlighted by the pluralist. It is, after all, a basic feature of Christian teaching that faith is a gift of God and that God is specially inclined to call on the poor and those who are "foolish in the eyes of the world." Granted, even this teaching can be (and in some cases, has been) embraced with a perverse kind of pride in one's lowly social or intellectual status. But this need not occur, and often enough it does not.

Furthermore, as Peter van Inwagen has remarked, the pluralist who presses this kind of objection to traditional Christian belief is likely to "find himself surrounded by a lot of broken domestic glass."[5] Why? Because the central idea behind the arrogance objection is one the pluralist is obliged to apply to nonreligious beliefs as well. Perhaps the following best captures this central idea:

> For any belief of yours, once you become aware (a) that others disagree with it and (b) that you have no argument on its behalf that is likely to convince all or most of the reasonable, good-intentioned people who disagree with you, then it would be *arrogant* of you to continue holding that belief.

Now let's think about this principle in light of the pluralist's own views. He embraces this principle while surely being aware that many others think *it* is false. (I myself disbelieve the principle, but as it would be immodest to point to myself as convincing proof, I'll point instead to the astute and eminently fair-minded editor of this book.) But then, to be consistent, the pluralist should abandon this very principle. Believing the principle in the face of informed disagreement, as the pluralist does, violates the principle. The moral here is that pluralism is no way of escape from the charge of arrogance.

5. See the final few paragraphs of his "Non Est Hick," in *The Rationality of Belief and the Plurality of Faith,* ed. T. Senor (Ithaca: Cornell University Press, 1995), also reprinted in *God, Knowledge, and Mystery* (Ithaca: Cornell University Press, 1995).

Some quick-thinking pluralist might retreat at this point and conclude that having any kind of view at all (including pluralism) in a climate of disagreement is what is arrogant. But why think that? Isn't it more sensible to suppose that the pluralist has gone overboard? He notes that some exclusivists have held their beliefs in an arrogant fashion, and wrongly concludes that arrogance is an inevitable result of exclusivist belief in the face of disagreement. In any case, the fact that one cannot, as we've just seen, *defend* this claim without falling prey to one's own principle should lead us to reject this pluralist argument.

C. The Irrationality Objection: "Where Reasonable People Differ, the Wise Man Withholds Judgment"

This brings us to a third and most fundamental objection to exclusivism, which, at a first pass, is that since there is no objective basis of *any* sort (experiential or otherwise) for reasonably selecting among religions, preferring some one of them (such as Christianity) above all the rest is irrational. Put this way, however, this argument deserves little sympathy. Following a long line of philosopher-theologians, I myself, for example, hold that a theistic worldview *is* rationally preferable to any of its rivals, such as philosophical naturalism.[6] I further believe we may reasonably accept the Christian revelation and reasonably prefer it to the going alternatives.

Not surprisingly, most pluralists disagree. But they do not try to engage the thoughtful Christian by pressing the specific grounds for disagreeing on this score — that is, engage in the usual back-and-forth philosophical/theological dialogue with the goal of persuading others of one's own way of understanding things. Instead, they contend that the very fact that relevantly informed, reasonable people of good will disagree with the thoughtful Christian provides a *compelling* basis for withdrawing his acceptance of Christianity as *uniquely* true.

What should the Christian think of this objection? Here the pluralist is perhaps arguing for a "principle of rational belief" which is akin to the principle described in the arrogance objection earlier. Possibly, something like this:

6. Some of these considerations are discussed in the chapters by Bill Davis ("Theistic Arguments," pp. 20-46) and Robin Collins ("Eastern Religions," pp. 182-216).

> For any belief of yours, once you become aware both that others disagree with it and that you have no argument on its behalf that is likely to convince all or most of those dissenters that are relevantly informed, reasonable, and of good will, it would be *irrational* of you to continue holding that belief.

But is this really so? One might try to draw an analogy here to science, where, we are often told, people refrain from belief until the facts come in so as to produce virtual unanimity. But this popular portrayal of the history of scientific practice and belief is a myth. There are numerous instances of scientists vigorously contending for a given theory in the face of highly distinguished opposition. This may take the form of large opposing factions or of even only one scientist defending a position against the rest of the relevant scientific community, a view which in some cases ultimately prevails. Must we say that in all such cases, knowledgeable people who carefully considered the evidence, weighed arguments for competing positions, and came to a particular view were irrational to do so?

Consider the following very recent example. In the 1980s, two researchers named Marshall and Warren uncovered strong evidence that a bacterium known as *H. pylori* is responsible (in most cases) for making the stomach and intestinal lining vulnerable to the formation of peptic ulcers. When they produced this evidence, the scientific community scoffed at it, in part because it contradicted firm opinion that no bacteria could survive in the half gallon of acid produced by a human stomach. (Marshall went so far as to consume a large quantity of *H. pylori*. After developing acute ulcers, he then treated himself with an antibiotic that permanently eradicated the problem.) Evidence for the bacterium theory mounted for several years before it was generally accepted. To this day, many who suffer from ulcers are not tested for *H. pylori* or given the necessary antibiotic.

I take it that this case strongly suggests that the principle of rational belief proposed above is implausible. However, a more reasonable pluralist might argue that the principle does not apply to beliefs of all sorts, but only to religious beliefs (and maybe a few other types of belief) since with these beliefs there is never a convergence of opinion, at least among "experts." This makes religious belief quite different from scientific belief where contested ideas come either to be accepted or rejected, owing to the uncovering of new evidence.

Yet even though there is such a difference between scientific and religious disputes, why exactly should we suppose that it is a *relevant* difference? No doubt, the fact that scientific theories are open to confirmation and disconfirmation in a way that usually leads to consensus, in the end, is a good thing. But why should we think that the fact that scientific theories can be confirmed and disconfirmed in this way makes rational disagreement, in the *absence* of conclusive evidence, acceptable in the scientific case, but not in the religious one?

Some have thought that the absence of decisive empirical testability of religious beliefs shows that they are "meaninglessness." But, again, why should anyone think this? While I haven't the space to explore this matter here, I'll say that I myself don't find the prospects for defending this pluralist principle at all promising. In any case, the reader will note that the argument beginning in the next paragraph applies equally to this restricted version of the irrationality argument.

I have argued that the "principle of rational belief" that seems to lie behind pluralist criticisms of traditional Christian belief is not at all clearly true. But matters get worse for the pluralist critic. One thing all pluralists believe is the thesis of pluralism itself. And this thesis is not something that has been widely agreed upon, even among those who have considered the question. (It has far fewer adherents, for example, than traditional Christianity.) Are not pluralists themselves, then, guilty again of violating their own principle, since *they* persist in their pluralist beliefs in the face of such honest dissent?[7]

As a final *coup de grace,* it may be noted that this alleged principle of rational belief is prone to turn on *anyone* who endorses it. The principle, you will recall, is this:

> For any belief of yours, once you become aware both that others disagree with it and that you have no argument on its behalf that is likely to convince all or most of those dissenters that are relevantly informed, reasonable, and of good will, it would be *irrational* of you to continue holding that belief.

Now, as with the "arrogance principle" discussed earlier, I know many reasonable people who deny this rationality principle. (I'll again tip my hat towards the distinguished, acutely intelligent editor of this book.) So it seems that anyone who endorses this principle in present intellectual cir-

7. This point and the one that follows have been made by Alvin Plantinga, in his essay, "A Defense of Religious Exclusivism," in *The Philosophy of Religion: An Anthology,* ed. L. Pojman (Belmont, CA: Wadsworth, 1987), and also reprinted in *The Rationality of Belief.*

cumstances has good reason to reject it: since reasonable and good-intentioned people disagree about the principle, the principle itself says that the honorable thing to do is not to believe it. It may for all that be *true,* but given the fact that we *don't* all accept it, none of us who are apprised of that fact can *consistently believe* it to be true. And if we cannot *consistently* believe it, we have quite a good reason not to believe it.[8]

The general moral to be drawn here is that we can't avoid making judgments as best we can even where others disagree. Pluralists themselves invariably make highly contentious assumptions about morality and rationality. They can do so, however, only by exempting themselves from their own arbitrary standard.

Clearly, the way to make progress here is not, as the pluralist holds, to pat the exclusivists on the head and declare all the beliefs of the disagreeing parties equally "correct" (though not correct in the way the disagreeing parties *think* they are).

III. Against Pluralism

It is worth noting that my remarks in the previous section, if successful, do not show that pluralism is *false;* rather, they only serve to undercut the arguments that pluralists make against exclusivists. But we may go further, I believe, and provide positive reasons for thinking that the pluralists'

8. Thought for the enthusiastic thinker: I have noted that there is no straightforward inconsistency in the circumstance that a principle is *true* even though none of us can consistently (or, therefore, reasonably) believe it. But there would be a special peculiarity to such an unhappy circumstance in its present application: for how could a true (and if true, importantly true) principle of *rationality* be such that we cannot rationally believe it? In such a case, we would be required to try to form beliefs *in accordance* with the principle — it is by hypothesis *true,* after all — but we could not rationally *reflect* on such practice and form a true belief about the nature of the underlying principle. I take such a bizarre consequence to constitute a "transcendental refutation" of the principle. Away with such intellectual deviltry! Exercise for the enthusiastic and *diligent* thinker: construct a rebuttal (similar to the one given in the text of the irrationality objection) of another pluralist claim — viz., that the fact that religious views are strongly correlated with birthplace and family religion should lead one to doubt their (literal) truth. ("You believe Christianity only because you were raised in a Christian culture and/or home. If you had been born in Saudi Arabia, you would have been a Muslim. Therefore . . .") [A good answer may be found in Alvin Plantinga's "A Defense of Religious Exclusivism." For Hick's reply to this and Plantinga's rejoinder, see their contributions to the symposium on pluralism in the July 1997 issue of *Faith and Philosophy.*]

own alternative view is defective. To do so, however, we need to have a concrete version of pluralism before us.

A. A Pluralist Picture of Things

Here's one way of telling the pluralist story.[9] Religious beliefs that have formed within major religious traditions such as Christianity are culturally conditioned responses to Ultimate Reality ("the Ultimate"). In itself, the Ultimate is beyond all the categories religious believers apply to it. Many devout persons of every established faith experience the Ultimate, but never as it *really is* (something which is unknowable), but only through one or other of its many manifestations, all of which are conditioned by religious tradition. This is an inevitable consequence of the gulf between this Ultimate Reality and our finite minds. When we come in contact with this Ultimate Reality, our minds actively (though unconsciously) *process* it in a way that makes it understandable *to us*. The result is an experience of the Ultimate by Christians as the Heavenly Father, and by Zen Buddhists as nirvana.

It is important to remember here, as I have hinted at earlier, that the pluralist does not think that the diversity of claims made about the Ultimate shows that those claims are false. This is the point of saying these diverse claims correspond to "authentic manifestations of the Ultimate." Sometimes manifestations are manifestations of deities (Yahweh, Allah, and Krishna) and sometimes of nonpersonal absolutes (the advaitic Hindu Brahman and the Buddhist nirvana). Rather than regarding these different ways of understanding the Ultimate as false, they are viewed as ways in which the Ultimate becomes an actual object of religious worship and pursuit. For we cannot worship the Ultimate "as it really is," since we are intellectually incapable of grasping it in this way. None of the distinctions which structure our religious experience can apply to it, not even as an approximation or by analogy. "As it really is," the Ultimate is neither personal nor impersonal, one nor many, good nor evil.

9. The story I tell (and some of the arguments against any contrasting, "absolutist" religious view, such as that of traditional Christianity) has been developed with greatest care by Professor John Hick, in such works as *An Interpretation of Religion; Disputed Questions in Theology and the Philosophy of Religion* (New Haven: Yale University Press, 1993); "Religious Pluralism," in *A Companion to Philosophy of Religion,* ed. P. Quinn and C. Taliaferro (Cambridge, MA: Blackwell, 1997); and "The Epistemological Challenge of Religious Pluralism," *Faith and Philosophy* (July 1997).

But though there are many and widely diverse authentic manifestations of the Ultimate, the pluralist is not bound to admit that "anything goes." It would be an embarrassment to the pluralist if, for example, he had to say that the theology of the Branch Davidians or the Aum Shin Rikyo cult is an equally authentic manifestation of the Ultimate. No, only some religious conceptions rightly relate us to the Ultimate. Which ones? Pluralists typically hold that a conception of the Ultimate is "authentic" if it moves adherents from being self-centered to being Reality-centered or to affirming the goodness of ultimate reality.[10]

B. Pluralism as an Explanatory Hypothesis

Pluralists commonly hold that their view is the *simplest hypothesis* that accounts for the diverse forms of religious experience and thought.[11] Thus, we should favor the pluralist hypothesis just as, for example, we favor the simplest available scientific theory capable of providing an account for a wide range of data in a certain domain. However, the supposed explanatory power of pluralism is only superficial. There certainly is a marked simplicity to the pluralist's scheme, but its shortcomings offset this particular virtue by a mile.

Consider, for starters, the relationship that the pluralist supposes exists between the Ultimate "as it really is" and individual human beings. There are at least two very odd features of this relationship, features which undercut the claim that the pluralist hypothesis is the *best explanation* for the diversity of human religious experience. First, *all* the content of religious experience, on this view, is provided by the human experiencer. The only contribution the Ultimate makes to the experience is as some sort of "ultimate source" or "ground" of that experience. But even this way of putting it may suggest too much. For it suggests that the Ultimate *causes* us to have the experience we do. But the pluralist cannot say even this, since putting it this way favor religious views (such as theism) that conceive of the Ultimate as an entity distinct from the physical universe. On other views, the Ultimate is *simply the physical universe itself,* understood in some special way, and the "relation" between human and the Ultimate involves merely an *insight* that the Ultimate and the universe are *one and the same* in this special way.

10. See Hick, *Disputed Questions,* 178, 174.
11. See, e.g., Hick, *An Interpretation of Religion,* 248.

Once we see, however, that the pluralist cannot make the very minimal claim that the Ultimate acts as cause of my experience, then the claim that the pluralist hypothesis is even *potentially* explanatory is questionable at best — let alone the claim that the pluralist hypothesis provides the best explanation.

Finally, because the pluralist holds that we can know nothing at all about the nature of the Ultimate "as it really is," the existence of this Ultimate can't do any *more* explanatory work than it does when we say that it is the "ground" of the different forms of religious experience and thought. If we cannot say even that it is active or purposive or even one or many, then we can hardly appeal to it to help us explain, for example, the existence of or order in the universe. So if the only support for the pluralist picture of the Ultimate — its potential to explain the fact of religious diversity — is itself quite weak, as I have argued, then the overall judgment we should make concerning this hypothesis is that it is not a good explanatory hypothesis *at all.*

C. The Incoherence of the Pluralist Picture

So far, I have ignored what, to my mind, is the gravest defect in at least many forms of pluralism, including the one sketched above. And that is that it is demonstrably incoherent. Out of their concern not to "unfairly" favor one religious tradition over another, pluralists usually say not just that we cannot *know* whether the Ultimate is personal or impersonal, active or passive, purposive or purposeless, one or many, etc., but that it is "beyond" these categories altogether. And this is a hard saying indeed. For while certain intellectual quarters encourage people to say such things, the claim is simply unintelligible. Perhaps the best way to make this plain is to proceed in two stages. First, I will give a simple argument for the claim that this sort of pluralist position is unintelligible. I will then note that this initial critique is *too* simple. This will show us that there is one (and only one) basic way of avoiding my critique. The second stage is to note that this way out is not one taken by the pluralist.

Here is the first (overly simple) argument against the intelligibility of pluralism:

> Anyone who asserts the "beyond human categories" kind of pluralism is either in a muddle or has lost the sense of the word "not." For consider the two claims, "The Ultimate is personal" and "The Ultimate is

not personal." These are not merely *contraries*, as logicians say, such that at *most* one of them can be true, though it might be that neither is true. (As is the case with the claims, "Tim O'Connor is the greatest living philosopher" and "Michael Murray is the greatest living philosopher." At most one of these is true, but it's also just possible that neither is.) They are logical *contradictories* — it must be that one of them is true and the other is false. If it is false that the Ultimate is personal, then it is true that the Ultimate is not personal. And vice versa. The pluralist wants to assert, however, that it is not true that "the Ultimate is personal" and it is not true that "the Ultimate is not personal." This is simply contradictory (inconsistent), and it is not intelligible that a contradiction be true.

The reason this argument is too simple is that it overlooks a pervasive feature of most of our concepts, which is that they are *vague*. One familiar example of this is our color concepts. Imagine a large array of adjacent color samples, such that the one on the left is clearly red, and the one on the right is clearly orange, and the shades in between constitute a slow transition from red to orange such that any adjacent two are barely perceptibly different in color. At what point do the red patches end and the orange patches begin? Clearly, if the differences between adjacent shades are subtle enough, there will be no definite answer to this question. There will be a border region such that it will not be (fully or definitely) true that a particular patch in the region is red, nor will it be (fully or definitely) false that it is red, either. Our concept of redness is simply not sharp enough to decide the matter one way or the other.

Now one could claim that personhood, like redness, is a vague concept, admitting borderline cases. And if this were correct, it does not clearly follow from its being not (definitely) true that the Ultimate is personal that it must be (definitely) false that it is personal — that it must be impersonal. And in this way, one might try to escape between the horns of the dilemma.

But the pluralist does not try to escape the simple critique in this way, for doing so would require that the pluralist make some very substantive claims about the nature of the Ultimate, staking out a position that directly competes with each of the major religious outlooks. And this is the very thing the pluralist wants to avoid. No, the typical pluralist's position is more radical than that, and this means that it is also incoherent. There simply is nothing for "being beyond personhood" to mean, if it is neither being utterly impersonal or being somewhere in between personhood and non-personhood. And inconsistency provides as strong a case against a view (in this instance, against pluralism) as one can make.

Maybe, however, there is a middle-of-the-road position available to the pluralist here. The pluralist might say that for any property we wish to ascribe to the Ultimate, it either has that property, or it lacks it, or it is somewhere in between having and lacking it (as some of the colors on the continuum I mentioned earlier might be between "being red" and "being not-red"). Since being one or many, being active or entirely passive, and being identical to or distinct from the physical world are pretty clearly sharp, not vague, divisions, we might feel pushed in one direction or another on properties such as these. (We might say, for example, that the Ultimate is a single, active being distinct from the universe.) But perhaps we're less sure about other attributes, such as personhood. Given disagreement across religious traditions, we could split the difference here. But now however exactly we come down on individual attributes using this procedure, aren't we just being arbitrary? Aren't we simply making our own judgments in at least some cases — thereby *contradicting* some religious tradition or other — and then splitting the difference in others, out of deference to the diversity of opinion, including the ones one has contradicted with respect to other claims? Of all the ways one might come to a developed opinion in religious matters, this seems the *most* arbitrary.

IV. Conclusion

Every age has its unreflectively held assumptions. For the present generation, a vaguely articulated notion of pluralism in relation to religion and morality is one of those assumptions. I hope to have shown that it has a lot less to be said on its behalf than many people suppose. I haven't considered every possible variation on the pluralist theme, but my arguments can, I believe, be generalized.

One less obvious form pluralism takes in our culture is a certain kind of agnosticism (which on its face seems rather different from pluralism). The usual variety is instanced by those who have considered evidence on behalf of various religious beliefs and judge the evidence to be inconclusive. Such people ought to be open to standard apologetical argument.[12] But nowadays, many who profess agnosticism about God or religious claims have not spent a lot of time considering the pros and

12. A sophisticated agnostic might, however, hold that any transcendent reality is necessarily beyond proof or disproof. For discussion relevant to that claim, see Robin Collins's chapter on the "fine-tuning" argument (pp. 47-75).

cons. Instead, they're content to gesture at the widespread disagreement and throw up their hands. ("Who can say?") Five will get you ten that underlying the view of such a person is the thought that one cannot reasonably have a definite opinion on such matters precisely because there is widespread disagreement. (That's why it's unnecessary to actually look at any arguments in detail.) And this position is unstable in just the way that holding our "principle of reasonable belief" above was seen to be unstable. For it is itself a controversial claim, and so (given what it claims) cannot be consistently held.

In the present climate of opinion, the first task for the contemporary Christian apologist in making the case for Christianity is precisely to convince those he engages of the untenability of this pluralist attitude.

8

Eastern Religions

Robin Collins

I. Introduction

Many people believe that the existence of other world religions somehow undermines the tenability of Christianity. In this chapter, I will only consider this apologetic challenge in light of the major Eastern religions of Hinduism and Buddhism. Moreover, I will only consider one type of challenge, namely the claim that Eastern religions offer a truly viable alternative worldview to that of Western theism. According to this challenge, we have no reason to prefer a Western theistic worldview over the Eastern alternatives. (For the purposes of this chapter, by a religion's *worldview* I simply mean the claims it makes about the ultimate nature and structure of reality, that is, what philosophers call its *metaphysics*.)

My basic approach to answering this apologetic challenge will be first to explicate the core worldview underlying each of the various major schools of Hinduism and Buddhism, and then evaluate their cogency and purported support. We will focus exclusively on the major traditional systems of Eastern religious thought as articulated by what advocates of these systems consider their leading philosophers.[1] Because of space con-

1. The actual beliefs of the masses who practice these religions, however, are often at odds with the claims made by these philosophers, indeed much more so than we find in Christianity. For example, many non-Western followers of Buddhism fully believe they have a real enduring ego or self that will eventually go to some "heavenly" place through following the prescribed devotional practices. Yet, core to both the Buddha's teaching and all schools of Buddhism is the *anatta,* or the no (endur-

straints and the apologetic purpose of this chapter, I will only focus on the core aspects of their worldview; moreover, I will mainly focus on the various weaknesses of the Eastern systems of thought that we will be considering, though I will attempt to be as fair as possible in the process. A full-scale evaluation, however, would also have to look at their strengths, and then compare their strengths and weaknesses with the strengths and weaknesses of Western theism. Clearly this would require a book-length treatment. This chapter, therefore, should be seen as providing only a first step towards assessing and responding to the apologetic challenge that these religions present.

I realize that, for a variety of good and bad reasons, the sort of enterprise I am engaging in is currently out of fashion. Instead, out of a supposed respect for other religions, we are often encouraged merely to describe but not evaluate them. I believe, however, that we demonstrate the highest respect for other religions by carefully evaluating them, for in doing this we show that we take their claims about reality seriously enough to merit careful investigation.

Before I begin, however, I should address several other objections to this sort of enterprise:

Objection 1: Any evaluation you offer will beg the question against the philosophies of the East since of necessity your evaluation will use Western forms of reasoning and logic; but, the East has its own way of thinking that is different from the West. *Response:* The idea that the East has a different way of thinking than the West is largely a myth that seriously underestimates the rigor and logic of their philosophical thinking. As philosopher Stephan Phillips shows,[2] many Eastern schools of thought developed sophisticated systems of logic and argumentation similar to those in the West to defend their views against opposing schools. For example, the theistic schools in ancient India offered arguments for the existence of God based on the apparent design of the universe and its moral order, what in the West are known as the teleological argument and the moral argument for God's existence, respectively.

Objection 2: You focus too much on the overall worldview of these

---

ing) self, doctrine. (See David Kalupahana, *A History of Buddhist Philosophy: Continuities and Discontinuities* [Honolulu: University of Hawaii Press, 1992], chapter 11, for a discussion of the disparity between popular Buddhism and philosophical Buddhism.)

2. Stephan Phillips, *Classical Indian Metaphysics: Refutations of Realism and the Emergence of the New Logic* (Chicago: Open Court Publishing, 1995).

Eastern thinkers, which is a Western concern. Eastern thinkers, on the other hand, are more concerned with practice. So, your whole project ends up doing an injustice to them. *Response:* Although it is true that Eastern thinkers tend to be more concerned with practice, our focus on overall worldview is appropriate since the practices of these other religions only present an apologetic challenge to Western theism insofar as they presuppose an alternative worldview.

II. Assumptions Shared by Hindus and Buddhists

Traditional Hindus and Buddhists, along with most philosophy in India, share a common set of assumptions about the nature of the cosmos and our place within it. Of particular importance are the following:

i. Absorption of Polytheism

Unlike the major Western religions, Hinduism, and to a lesser extent Buddhism, absorbed and then reinterpreted ancient polytheistic religious practice. For example, rather than opposing and eventually stamping out the worship and devotion to many gods as happened in ancient Judaism, the Hindu religion reinterpreted the gods as being special manifestations or representations of Brahman instead of independent entities. This means that what looks to us like the worship of many gods in Hinduism is really, from the Hindu perspective, the worship of one God through multiple manifestations.

ii. The Doctrines of Rebirth and Karma

Except for certain Westernized versions of Buddhism (and many Zen Buddhists), Hindus and Buddhists both accept the doctrines of *rebirth* (or reincarnation) and *karma*. According to the doctrine of rebirth, each of us existed in a previous life and will likely be reborn after death. And, according to the doctrine of karma, the circumstances of an individual in any given life are largely a result of the moral worth of their deeds and character in previous lives. Along with these ideas of rebirth and karma, traditional schools of Hinduism hold that our existence is without beginning, and hence that each of us has already undergone this process of rebirth, with its associated karma, an infinite number of times from eternity past. (Buddhists either follow Hindus here in claiming that our existence is without beginning, or following some sayings of the Buddha, remain agnostic on the issue.)

The two doctrines of rebirth and karma form the fundamental belief structure from which all Indian philosophies spring. As Edward Stevens writes with regard to Hinduism,

> All orthodox Hindus accept the doctrine of rebirth from life to life. The idea that one human life span is generally sufficient for self-liberation is preposterous to the ordinary Hindu. And since there is rebirth, there is a soul that gets reborn. In the West, we can find it worthwhile to discuss whether there is a soul and whether it is immortal. The immortality of the soul is a problem for us. For the Hindu, the existence of the self and its continual rebirth until ultimate liberation is a fact of life. It's something "everybody knows." There's nothing to discuss.[3]

iii. The Eternality of the Universe

Unlike Western theistic religions, traditional Hindus and many Buddhists believe that the universe has always existed, and has eternally been going through cycles of growth, stasis, and dissolution. Various accounts are then given of how selves survive the periods of cosmic dissolution. Furthermore, many Buddhists and Hindus believe in other universes and realities. Among other things, these other realities provide a way for Hindus and Buddhists to reconcile the increasing world population with their doctrine of rebirth: the extra selves needed to account for this increase can be postulated to come from these other universes or realities.

iv. Salvation as Liberation from Rebirth

Generally speaking, both Buddhists and Hindus see salvation (or enlightenment) as liberation from the cycle of rebirths and its associated karma. (Exceptions to this are certain westernized forms of Buddhism, and some adherents to Zen, which see salvation more in terms of achieving a state of enlightenment in this life.)

3. Edward Stevens, *An Introduction to Oriental Mysticism* (New York: Paulist Press, 1973), 72-73.

III. Hinduism

Introduction

Hinduism is a religious system dating back to at least 1200 B.C. The earliest Hindu scriptures were the *Vedas,* which are primarily writings concerned with the proper way of performing rituals and sacrifices to the gods. Eventually speculation arose about what lies behind the gods themselves. This led to the development of the idea of *Rita,* the eternal and immutable law of justice and order, and *Brahman,* the ultimate metaphysical reality that underlies the world, including the gods. The idea of *Rita* eventually spawned the idea of *karma,* with its associated idea of rebirth, and *moksha,* the idea that we can be liberated from the cycle of rebirths.

The nature of Brahman and its relation to the world, especially the human self, eventually became more fully articulated in the other major class of core Hindu scriptures, the *Upanishads.* These were written between about 400 B.C. and 200 B.C. and considered the culmination, or end of the *Vedas.* These are essentially the writings of "saints" and "seers" who were believed to have special insight into the nature of ultimate reality. Along with the *Upanishads* and *Vedas,* a variety of other sacred literature was developed. Unlike the *Vedas* and *Upanishads,* however, this literature has in general not been officially sanctioned as absolutely authoritative by orthodox Hindus, but rather is afforded a semi-scriptural status (in much the same way the Old Testament Apocrypha is viewed by Catholics and some Protestants). The most famous and widely studied of these additional writings is the *Bhagavad-Gita,* or Song of God, a work probably cited and studied more than the *Upanishads* or *Vedas* themselves.

Although there have been a variety of philosophical and religious systems of thought in India, according to most Indian thinkers the only truly live options within orthodox Hinduism today are elaborations and variations of three major Hindu theologies systematically formulated by *Sankara* (pronounced: shum cah ra) in the eighth century A.D., by *Ramanuja* (pronounced: Rah mah noo jah) in the eleventh century A.D., and that formulated by *Madhva* (pronounced: Mudh vah) in the twelfth century A.D. All three of these individuals attempted to develop a systematic Hindu theology based on the *Vedas,* the *Upanishads,* the short summary and systematization of the *Upanishads* called the *Brahma-sutra* or *Vedanta-sutra,* along with other texts, especially the *Bhagavad-Gita* in the case of Ramanuja and Madhva.

As Ninian Smart points out, "Sankara's metaphysics is *par excellence* the theology of modern Hinduism as presented to the West; and it is the most vigorous and dominant doctrine among Hindu intellectuals."[4] Unfortunately, because of this, popular Western presentations of Hinduism often present the Hindu view of reality as identical with Sankara's theology. This in turn gives the impression that Hindus all share the same view of reality, one which is radically at odds with Western theism. As Swami Nikhilananda[5] and others have noted, however, the majority of the Hindu population are followers of Ramanuja and Madhva, not Sankara, at least if we judge them by their practice. Unlike many popular presentations of Hinduism, therefore, this chapter will take seriously this diversity of Hindu views by looking at all three traditional schools of Hinduism. We will begin with Sankara.

Sankara School

Brief Explication of Core View

The Sankara school is often called *Avaita* (non-dualistic) *Vedanta* or simply *Vedanta.* As traditionally interpreted, the Sankara school claims that there is ultimately only one reality, *Brahman,* with which each of us is absolutely identical. Moreover, they claim that Brahman is pure consciousness, without any internal differentiation or characteristics whatsoever. (An analogy to their view of Brahman might be seen by considering what your own consciousness would be like if you were able to completely blank your mind of all internal differentiation and distinctions — that is, if through meditation you eliminated all sense impressions, feelings, and thoughts and simply experienced a state of pure awareness.)

Since Brahman comprises all of reality, and since there are no internal distinctions within Brahman, it follows that ultimately the world of separate entities, distinctions, and characteristics is an illusion. Followers of Sankara claim that this illusion, which they call *maya,* is produced by *ignorance* — that is, by our misapprehension of the true nature of Brah-

4. Ninian Smart, *Doctrine and Argument in Indian Philosophy* (London: George Allen and Unwin, 1964), 97.

5. Swami Nikhilananda, "The Realist Aspect of Indian Philosophy," in *The Indian Mind: Essentials of Indian Thought and Culture* (Honolulu: University of Hawaii Press, 1967).

man. Salvation therefore consists of experientially realizing, through intense meditation, the Truth about ourselves — namely, that each of us is already identical with Brahman. Once we realize this, ignorance will vanish and we will hence escape from the cycle of rebirths.

Although Hinduism is often considered to be pantheistic — that is, to be claiming that everything is God or an aspect of God — this understanding is false for the Sankara school, as it is for the other major schools of Hinduism. Advocates of the Sankara school, for example, do not claim that everything in this world — such as the rock on which you stub your toe — is God. Rather, they claim that everything in this world is an illusion, including the rock. Thus this view is perhaps better called *cosmic illusionism* instead of pantheism.

Of course, there are many more facets to Sankara's thought than has been presented above. But the above claims lie at the very heart of his worldview, and they are the points at which his worldview runs into severe problems. We will look at these problems in the next section, along with the major responses followers of Sankara have offered to them.

Evaluation

In this section we will: (1) critique the core worldview of Sankara's philosophy; then (2) examine how followers of Sankara might respond to the various critiques; and finally (3) attempt to draw an overall conclusion from our examination.

1. Critique of Sankara's View

a. The View Is Self-Contradictory

The first problem with the core of Sankara's philosophy is that it seems to be *self-contradictory*. As advocates of the other Hindu schools of thought have pointed out, if the only reality is Brahman, and Brahman is pure, *distinctionless* consciousness, then there cannot exist any real distinctions in reality. But the claim that this world is an illusion already presupposes that there is an actual distinction between illusion and reality, just as the claim that something is a dream already presupposes the distinction between waking consciousness and dream consciousness. Moreover, Sankara's idea of salvation — that is, enlightenment through recognition that all is Brahman — already presupposes a distinction between living in a state of unenlightenment (ignorance) and living in a state of enlightenment. So this view contradicts itself by, on the one hand, saying that reality (Brahman) is distinctionless, while on the other hand distinguishing between *maya* and the truth of Brahman, and by distinguishing between being enlightened and unenlightened.

b. The Impossibility of Maya

A second and related problem is that ignorance, which Sankara and his followers claim is the source of *maya,* could not exist. According to the Sankara school, Brahman is perfect, pure, and complete Knowledge, the opposite of ignorance. Hence, ignorance cannot exist in Brahman. But, since nothing exists apart from Brahman, ignorance cannot exist apart from Brahman either. Thus, it follows that ignorance could not exist, contrary to their assertion that our perception of a world of distinct things is a result of ignorance.

c. The Lack of Evidence

A final problem is that it seems that one could never have any satisfactory experiential basis for believing in Sankara's philosophy. Certainly, everyday experience and observation are completely in conflict with his claim, since they overwhelmingly testify to the existence of a real world of distinct things and properties. Indeed, even if we assume that the entire material world does not exist, but is merely a dream, experience would still overwhelmingly testify against Sankara's claim: for, within our dream itself there are innumerable distinct experiences, from the experience of feeling sad to that of seeing what looks like a rainbow. Thus Sankara's philosophy cannot even explain the world we experience as being an illusion or dream. As a result, it ends up providing close to the worst possible explanation of our experiences.

This last problem should put to rest the common assertion that aspects of modern physics, particularly quantum mechanics, supports this, or similar systems of Eastern thought such as Zen Buddhism (see below). The scientific method consists of performing various observations of the world, and then trying to construct hypotheses that explain these observations. We then choose the hypothesis that makes the best sense of these observations, and reject those hypotheses that significantly conflict with observation. Because Sankara's philosophy is in conflict with almost all of our observations, science by its very methodology could never give us good reason to believe it, but rather every reason to reject it.

2. Responses to First Two Critiques

Advocates of the Sankara school respond to accusations of logical incoherence raised above in several ways, all of which I believe are ultimately unsatisfactory. First, some Indian thinkers have defended Sankara by pointing out that he never claimed that *maya* exists: rather, Sankara claimed that ultimately *maya* has some form of reality between existence and nonexistence.[6] It is difficult to see, however, how this response helps. The claim that Brahman is pure, distinctionless knowledge implies that *maya* has no reality whatsoever, not even the quasi-existential status of neither existing nor nonexisting. The contradiction thus remains.

The second and more powerful response that advocates of the Sankara school have given is that human logic and reason operate from the standpoint of *ignorance* or *maya,* and thus are invalid.[7] Moreover, once the true perspective is obtained (in which we recognize that everything is Brahman), ignorance vanishes and consequently the self-contradiction resulting from the so-called existence of ignorance no longer poses a problem. With regard to our first two critiques of Sankara, those who offer this response could claim that the law of noncontradiction, the fundamental rule of logic according to which a statement cannot be both true and false at the same time, is ultimately invalid because it is based in *ignorance*. Thus, they could argue, we cannot legitimately reject their view because it is self-contradictory.

This second response, however, faces two major problems. First, it is what philosophers call "epistemically self-defeating." If human reason is invalid when it comes to the ultimate nature of reality, then Sankara himself could never offer us a valid reason — whether based on experience, testimony, or anything else — for believing in his philosophy. So why believe it? Moreover, this second response underestimates the seriousness of the charge that Sankara's view is self-contradictory. Certain Eastern philosophers, such as Garma C. C. Chang,[8] are correct in pointing out that Western philosophers have not proven that reality itself must

6. See Sarvepalli Radhakrishnan, *Indian Philosophy* (London: Allen and Unwin, 1923), I:34, and R. Puligandla, *Fundamentals of Indian Philosophy* (Nashville: Abingdon Press, 1975), 234, for examples of this sort of response.

7. For example, a response along these lines is given by Eliot Deutsch, *Advaita Vedanta: A Philosophical Reconstruction* (Honolulu: University of Hawaii Press, 1969), 85.

8. Garma Chang, *The Buddhist Teaching of Totality: The Philosophy of Hwa Yen Buddhism* (University Park, PA: Pennsylvania State University Press, 1971), 133-34.

always obey the law of non-contradiction; rather, Western philosophy assumes its truth. Even so, the law of non-contradiction nonetheless typically functions as a condition for the meaningfulness of statements within language. If, for instance, someone insists that their friend, John Doe, is a bachelor and then they turn around and assert that this very same person, John Doe, is married to a woman called Jane Doe, we would become very puzzled and begin to lose our grip on what they were trying to say. At best, we would begin to wonder whether they were using the English words "bachelor" and "married" in the normal English sense. If they agreed that they were, then we would have to admit a failure to understand what they were trying to say. The reason for this is that their statement that John is married to Jane would simply negate their statement that John is a bachelor, given the normal English meanings of the words "married" and "bachelor." Hence, we would be left with no meaningful conception of John's marital status.

A similar point can be made regarding Sankara's philosophy. When he says that he is offering a path to enlightenment, and that our problem is that we are in a state of ignorance, we understand him to be saying that we are in a certain state of ignorance now, and that through diligently following the Hindu meditative practices, we can arrive at a state of enlightenment and bliss at some point in the future. But, when Sankara goes on to say that each of us is already identical with Brahman, and that Brahman is pure, distinctionless consciousness without a trace of ignorance, he completely negates any understanding we had of his first claim, namely that each of us is in a state of ignorance. For, if we take his claim about our identity with Brahman seriously, we must conclude that each of us is actually presently in a state of pure Knowledge, not ignorance. Accordingly, the problem for Sankara, as he is standardly understood, is not merely that what he says must be false because it is self-contradictory, but rather that the self-contradictory character of his claims precludes our forming any definite conception of what he is saying in the first place. At best, we could understand him as using language not so much to describe his view of the nature of reality, but to point to a "reality" beyond language — much as poetry and art does, according to some. If all Sankara is doing is using language to point to the inexpressible, however, then what he says is not necessarily in conflict with most worldviews, even a Christian worldview — after all, the existence of a reality that is ultimately not completely expressible by language is certainly compatible with orthodox Christianity.

The final response we will consider to the objection that Sankara is inconsistent is that offered by philosopher Keith Ward. Essentially, Ward argues that Sankara has been misinterpreted. First, Ward claims that what Sankara means by reality is "that which is self-subsistent; which does not change or cease to be; which is not corruptible or dependent on other things." Thus, Ward tells us, when Sankara says that Brahman is the only existing reality, and that Brahman is distinctionless, this does not mean that the world does not exist. All it means is that the existence of the world is not self-subsistent and independent; rather, things in the world exist "only as appearances — that is, in relation to minds to which they appear. Taken out of relation to minds, they would cease to exist at all."[9]

The problem with Ward's interpretation is that if one takes these "appearances" (and human subjective experiences in general) as really existing in relation to some mind or minds, then either: (i) the mind which is having these appearances and experiences must be *Brahman;* or (ii) there must be minds other than Brahman that are having the appearances and experiences. If alternative (i) is adopted, then it follows that there are internal distinctions within Brahman's consciousness corresponding to the multitude of differing experiences we have every day, such as being sad, fearful, happy, or seeing a snowcapped mountain. Worse, however, if (i) is adopted, then Brahman would have the experience of being ignorant, of performing evil acts, of experiencing suffering, and the like. But, these are all contrary to what Sankara (and the other schools of *Vedanta*) claim about *Brahman:* namely, that Brahman is perfect, pure, and without ignorance. If Ward adopts (ii), on the other hand, then our selves or minds become distinct from God's consciousness, and hence Sankara's claim that we are in reality identical with Brahman is lost. Finally, if either of these alternatives is advocated, then Sankara's philosophy loses its distinctiveness and simply becomes a form of qualified nondualism or dualism, that is, a version of Ramanuja's or Madhva's metaphysics. If this is right, then we will be forced to adopt the implausible position that most Indian intellectuals were mistaken in thinking they were different from each other.[10]

9. Keith Ward, *Religion and Revelation: A Theology of Revelation in the World's Religions* (New York: Oxford University Press, 1994), 146.

10. Some of Sankara's philosophical heirs, such as Sriharsa, clearly did not interpret Sankara in the way Ward suggests since they argued that the real existence of distinctions — whether between things or properties — is self-contradictory. See Phillips, *Classical Indian Metaphysics,* 103-10.

3. Response to the Final Critique of Sankara

Above we argued that there are no sufficient reasons to believe Sankara's philosophy because it is in conflict with almost all of our experiences. The most immediate way advocates of the Sankara school could respond to this charge is by offering positive reasons for believing his claims. Three major sorts of reasons have been offered by Sankara and his followers for their belief system. First, Sankara himself primarily supported his belief system by appealing to the Hindu scriptures, particularly the *Upanishads.* Clearly for us Westerners who do not already presuppose the inspiration of these scriptures, this reason will not carry much weight. Moreover, other Indian thinkers — such as the philosophers Ramanuja and Madhva — offer very different interpretations of the Hindu scriptures.

Second, followers of Sankara presented skeptical attacks on human reason that attempted to show that we have no adequate basis for trusting human reason. Moreover, they attempted to argue that our ordinary view of the world, which includes the belief in the distinctness of things and properties, is inconsistent.[11] Since the practice of reason rests on making distinctions between things and properties, this latter set of arguments ultimately amounted to a further attack on human reason, namely that it is self-contradictory. Although the arguments they presented show great philosophical sophistication and insight, they ultimately cannot be used to support Sankara's philosophy. The reason for this is straightforward: if reason is ultimately invalid, then ultimately we cannot have valid reasons to believe anything, including Sankara's view. This is something that many followers of Sankara have recognized. Thus in the end many of them considered these arguments useful only as a way to help us break the grip that the ordinary view of reality has on us, thus preparing us for enlightenment.[12]

The third sort of reason that followers of Sankara have offered in support of their position is an appeal to mystical experiences in which people purport to have a powerful and direct experience of the absolute unity of all things, including their self and Brahman. Purportedly, the validity of these experiences cannot be doubted once one obtains it. In critique of this line of support, however, philosophers such as William Wainwright[13] have pointed

11. For an explication and analysis of some of these arguments, see Phillips, *Classical Indian Metaphysics.*

12. See Deutsch, *Advaita Vedanta,* 86 and 93-94.

13. William Wainwright, *Philosophy of Religion* (Belmont, CA: Wadsworth Publishing Company, 1988), 183.

out that mystics in other religious traditions — including other branches of Hinduism — interpret similar sorts of mystical experiences in a very different manner. Thus, these experiences are not self-validating as advocates of the Sankara school often claim. Second, as argued above, even if one did have a powerful mystical "experience" of the absolute oneness of everything, advocates of the Sankara school would still offer the worst possible explanation of the sum total of our experiences, as discussed above, for they cannot explain our much more extensive ordinary experience of distinctions in reality. In contrast, by assuming the real existence of the world we see around us, we are able not only to explain our ordinary experiences, but also to explain the mystical experiences to which Sankara appeals. For example, we could explain these mystical experiences as either being valid experiences whose content has been misinterpreted, or as being a delusion generated by, among other things, the practices of meditation.

In order to address the apparent conflict between their view and our ordinary experiences, followers of the Sankara school invoke an idea they call *subration.* Roughly, one set of experiences *subrates* another set of experiences by rendering them in some way invalid. Dreams, illusions, and hallucinatory experiences are key everyday illustrations of this process: dreams are subrated (that is, rendered invalid) by our waking experiences, and hallucinations and illusions are subrated by the correct perceptual experiences of the world around us. Followers of this school then go on to claim that their monistic mystical experiences of the absolute oneness of all things subrates ordinary waking experience, but itself cannot be subrated by any other experience. Consequently, they claim, ordinary waking experience can no more count against their philosophy than dream experiences can count against our waking experiences.

One problem with their response is that it never really explains why the purported mystical experiences subrate ordinary experiences, instead of vice versa. Indeed, if you look at ordinary cases of subration, a central reason that we take one set of experiences to subrate another set is that, from within the framework of the first set of experiences, we can explain away the second set of experiences, but not vice versa. From the framework of our ordinary waking experiences, for instance, we can explain away an LSD addict's experience of an elephant flying around in her room as just a delusion generated by her brain, whereas our ordinary experience that elephants do not fly cannot be adequately explained away from within the framework of the hallucination. Thus, the hallucinatory experience is rendered invalid (subrated) by ordinary experience, but not the other way around. Similar things could be said for why dreams and illusions are subrated by ordinary experience. By this criterion, however, it follows that ordinary experiences subrate these purported monistic mystical experiences, but not the reverse. For, within the framework of ordinary experience we can explain their mystical experiences as a misinterpretation or as a delusion generated by the brain, but as we saw above, from the perspective of these purported mystical experiences we cannot account for our ordinary experiences of the world, not even by considering them an illusion.[14]

Conclusion

Although our explication and analysis of Sankara's philosophy was brief, we uncovered severe logical problems with his core worldview. Moreover, as argued above, since Sankara's views conflict with almost all of our experiences, it seems that there cannot be any adequate reason to believe his system over standard Western views that assume the real existence of the world of distinct things and properties. In my judgment, none of these problems have been adequately answered by advocates of Sankara's position. Thus, I believe, we have much more reason to reject his core worldview than to accept it.

Ramanuja and Madhva Schools

1. Similarities and Differences to Christian Theism

Unlike Sankara, both Ramanuja and Madhva took a realistic attitude toward the world, claiming that there are really distinct things and selves; thus, they denied Sankara's doctrine of *maya*. Moreover, they affirmed that Brahman is a personal God who is omnipotent, omniscient, eternal, timeless, perfectly free, and perfectly good and loving. In these ways, their belief systems are similar to that of the Western theistic religions of Judaism, Christianity, and Islam. But beyond this, both of these schools have special similarities with Christianity. First, like Christianity, they believe that God has become incarnate in human history, though unlike Christians they believe that this has happened many times. For example, fol-

14. Indeed, these mystical experiences are further analogous to a dream in that one is not even aware of ordinary experiences, much as in dream consciousness one is not typically aware of the contents of waking consciousness.

lowing the teachings of the *Bhagavad-Gita*, they hold that during particularly dark periods of history, God becomes incarnate to "destroy the sin of the sinner and establish righteousness."[15] Second, both of these schools strongly emphasize salvation by grace, though without any doctrine of atonement. For instance, following an often-repeated teaching of Krishna in the *Bhagavad-Gita,* Ramanuja claims that we are saved by the grace that the Lord bestows on those who devote themselves to God in love and faith. Moreover, Ramanuja claims, this grace is so powerful that those who really devote themselves to God will achieve union with God and final liberation from the cycle of rebirths at the end of this life.

Yet, despite these similarities with Christianity, and Western theism, there are some major differences. Among these are: (i) their adoption and reinterpretation of the polytheistic practice of devotion to many gods; (ii) their belief in reincarnation and karma, along with the accompanying doctrine of the eternality of souls; (iii) their belief in an eternally existing, cyclical cosmos; and (iv) their denial of the doctrine of *creation ex nihilo,* that is, creation out of nothing.

2. Creation ex Nihilo and God's Relation to the World

Ramanuja's and Madhva's denial of *creation ex nihilo* bears some elaboration. Within the Judeo-Christian-Islamic tradition, the doctrine of *creation ex nihilo* serves on the one hand to make God solely responsible for the world's existence, while at the same time guaranteeing the distinctness of the world from God. Denying this doctrine leaves two alternatives regarding the origin of the world: (1) the position that the world in some sense emerges out of God, like a spider web from a spider, or (2) the position that the world in some sense exists independently from God. As we will see, Ramanuja chose the former alternative, whereas Madhva chose the latter.

Along with denying the doctrine of *creation ex nihilo,* each of these thinkers had to incorporate two important scriptural teachings concerning Brahman's relation to the world. First, Hindu scriptures affirm some sort of identity, or at least a deep sort of unity, between Brahman and the world, particularly human souls. In fact one famous text — called the "identity text" — seems to affirm the absolute identity of Brahman and our deepest self, what the Hindus call *Atman*. Second, Hindu scripture,

15. Swami Prabhavananda and Christopher Isherwood, trans., *The Song of the Lord: Bhagavad-Gita* (New York: Penguin Books, 1954), 133.

along with most traditional orthodox Hindu thought, affirms the absolute perfection of Brahman: for traditional orthodox Hindus, this means that Brahman does not act in evil ways, Brahman does not suffer, Brahman is not ignorant, Brahman does not change, and Brahman is not limited in any way. The world, and human beings in particular, have all these supposed imperfections. Thus the problem Ramanuja and Madhva face is this: how to assert a unity between the world and God that is compatible with Hindu scripture, without allowing the imperfections of the world to take away from Brahman's perfections. If, for example, they were to claim that Brahman and the world are absolutely identical, then either Brahman contains imperfections and limitations, or the world as we know it is an illusion, as Sankara asserted. Since neither Ramanuja or Madhva wanted to accept either of these alternatives, they each assert that Brahman's relation with the world was something less than absolute identity. Let's start by looking at Ramanuja's view first.

Ramanuja's Account of God's Relation to the World

Like Sankara, Ramanuja affirms a deep sort of unity between God and the world, since he believed that this was clearly taught by scripture. Specifically, Ramanuja takes seriously the so-called "identity text" mentioned above, along with those many scriptural images and metaphors that assert that the world somehow emerges or issues forth out of Brahman. Unlike Sankara, however, Ramanuja believed that the Hindu scriptures, and common experience, also clearly teach the real existence of the world. As noted above, the difficulty for Ramanuja was to develop an account of the identity between God and the world that did not at the same time either deny the existence of the world or compromise God's absolute perfection.

One way Ramanuja tried to develop such an account was by referring to the world as God's body. In calling the world God's body, however, Ramanuja should not be taken as saying that God is in any way limited by, or bound to, the world as we are to our bodies: Ramanuja is emphatic that God transcends the world, and is absolutely perfect and without any limitations. Rather, in saying that the world is God's body, Ramanuja simply means to affirm that the world is completely dependent on God for its very being, and that God expresses his nature and brings about his purpose through the world, much as we do through our own bodies. As Ramanuja puts it, "that which [e.g., the world], in its entirety, depends upon, is controlled by and subserves another [e.g., God] and is therefore its inseparable mode, is called the body of the latter." Insofar as

Ramanuja speaks of the world as God's body, therefore, his view of God's relation to the world seems perfectly compatible with Western theism.[16]

Elsewhere, however, Ramanuja seems to want to assert a deeper identity between the world and God, saying that the world, particularly sentient beings, are inseparable *aspects* or *modes* of God. At this point, Ramanuja's view becomes particularly hard to understand, since along with this assertion of an identity between world and God he also wants to assert that the world is really distinct from God. As we saw above, for instance, Ramanuja wants to assert that even though we suffer, God never suffers, and even though we commit evil acts, God never does. Thus, he wants to claim that we are really distinct centers of experience, will, and action from God. Indeed, one of the major schools of Ramanuja's followers held that we have true free will, and thus we, not God, are responsible for our actions. This sort of distinctness and distancing of selves from God, however, initially does not seem compatible with asserting that we are modes or aspects of God. It is therefore unclear whether in the end his view is coherent.

Attempts to provide a coherent interpretation of Ramanuja's thought in this regard nonetheless abound. My own attempt goes as follows. As far as I can tell, Ramanuja can reasonably be interpreted as saying that God is the source and locus of all *Being*. Imaginatively, this idea of *Being* could be thought of as something like a universal substance that underlies, and provides for the existence of all things; individual things are then the particular form and set of properties this "universal substance" of Being takes on. It follows, then, that if God is the locus of all Being then nothing has any being apart from God, and insofar as a thing has being, it partakes of God's Being. On the other hand, the individual properties a thing has, or the activities in which it engages, are truly distinct from God. For example, insofar as souls undergo change, are ignorant, experience suffering, or commit evil acts, they do not partake of God. In some ways, one could think of God's relation to the world as analogous to the relation between a vine and its branches, with the vine, its sap, and the branches being analogous to God, God's Being, and the

16. Ramanuja, *Vedarthasamgraha,* trans. S. S. Raghavachar (Mysore: Sri Ramakrishnan Ashrama, 1956), 76. Compare Ramanuja's claims here with the Christian claim that the Son of God sustains and upholds all things (e.g., Col. 1:17), and the Apostle Paul's repeated claim that we are "the body of Christ" (Eph. 5:30), that is, the body of *God* the Son.

world, respectively. Just as the branches only have life insofar as they partake of the sap of the vine, so the world has being or existence only insofar as it partakes of the being or existence of God. Moreover, just as a leaf on a branch can dry up without the branch drying up, so things in the world can undergo suffering, ignorance, and the like without God undergoing any of these things.

Given the above discussion, we could summarize Ramanuja's views regarding God's relation to the world as follows: (i) God freely, and beginninglessly, creates the world (and the souls it contains) out of his own being; (ii) God determines the karmic results that each soul will undergo because of its deeds in previous lives, and God beginninglessly causes our universe and other universes to undergo the cyclical process of formation, stasis, and dissolution; (iii) The world, and the souls therein, are completely subservient to God and are completely dependent on God for their existence and ultimate fulfillment; (iv) At their most fundamental level, that of their existence or Being, both the material world and souls are identical with God, though they are truly distinct from God in regards to their individual properties.

Madhva's Account of God's Relation to the World

To both protect God's perfection, and at the same time preserve the world's reality, Madhva went further than Ramanuja in distinguishing the world from God. Unlike Ramanuja, Madhva held that God is *neither* the source of the *being* of the world, nor any of the entities in the world. Rather, for Madhva, at least four kinds of things always existed as "brute givens" from all eternity: God, souls, non-intelligent substances, and the matter composing the physical world. None of these were derived from, or created by, any of the others, nor were they derived from any other being. Nonetheless, God does play a role in the development of the world and souls. In the case of the material world, God is responsible for each cycle of the cosmos. God is like a great potter who, during the formative phases of the cosmos, molds the matter into its various forms by giving it properties such as shape, size, and motion, and then destroys these forms in the dissolution phase. But like the potter's clay, the matter exists on its own apart from God, being a sort of found material that God uses. As for souls, God is the controller of the soul from within that enables the soul to fulfill its destiny, a destiny that is ultimately determined by the soul's inherent, uncreated nature. For most souls, this destiny is to escape the cycle of rebirths by achieving a union with God based on absolute love and adoration for God, but in which nonetheless the soul remains distinct from God. Unlike the rest of Hindu philosophy, however, Madhva allowed for the possibility that the inherent nature of some souls dooms them to either eternal rebirths or everlasting hell.

Evaluation of Ramanuja and Madhva

At least on the surface, Ramanuja's and Madhva's view of God and God's relation to the world, along with their belief in reincarnation and karma, seem to be internally coherent. Moreover, the main Western arguments for belief in God, such as the design argument and the moral argument, seem to work as well for their view of God as the Western theistic view of God.[17]

Despite this, a serious problem arises for Ramanuja's (though not Madhva's) worldview when we consider his doctrine of the eternality of souls. This doctrine is not only taught by the Upanishads, but by all three schools of Vedanta and most of Indian philosophy. According to this doctrine, souls in this world have always existed in a state of bondage within the cycle of rebirths, undergoing an infinite number of past lives in the process. Moreover, at least for Ramanuja, while the universe goes through cycles of creation and then dissolution, souls continue to exist from cycle to cycle, though they exist in a state of stasis during periods of cosmic dissolution. Within and through each cycle, souls carry their baggage of good or bad karma into the next life, determining the conditions into which they are born.

Stated in terms of Christian terminology, Ramanuja's view implies that every soul that has ever existed endured an eternity in "hell" (i.e., the cycle of rebirths) before it could enter "heaven" (i.e., union with God). Now unlike Madhva, Ramanuja claims that God *freely,* and beginninglessly, created the world, and all existing souls, out of his own being. This latter claim, however, presents Ramanuja with a very severe problem of evil: that of reconciling his belief that God is perfectly good and all-loving with God's ultimate responsibility for the beginningless existence of souls in a state of sin and suffering.

The problem of evil faced by Ramanuja here is much more severe than that faced by Western theists. First, unlike Western theists, Ramanuja cannot say that this evil is a necessary consequence of God's

17. The one exception to this is the traditional Western version of the cosmological argument, which fails in the case of Madhva's God.

creating creatures with free will. Although the suffering of a soul in any individual life could be blamed on the bad karma resulting from its free choices in previous lives, the fact that the suffering is beginningless — and hence infinite — cannot be blamed on free choice. The reason for this is that, no matter what free choices souls make in this life, or have made in any previous life, they cannot change the fact that they have beginninglessly endured an infinite amount of suffering; but one cannot be responsible for what one was powerless to change. Followers of Ramanuja, therefore, do not seem to have recourse to the traditional free will theodicy invoked in the West to explain evil.[18] Second, the amount of evil that needs to be explained is infinitely larger than that faced by Western versions of theism,[19] since, according to Ramanuja each soul has committed an infinite number of evil acts and endured an infinite period of suffering. Unfortunately, as Julius Lipner points out, neither Ramanuja, nor any other orthodox Hindu theologian, ever attempted to address this particular problem of evil since they took the eternality of the world and souls as an "unquestioned datum for life and thought."[20]

Unlike Ramanuja (and Western theism), however, Madhva's theology largely avoids the problem of evil. The reason for this is that in his theology God is neither responsible for the beginningless existence of souls in a state of bondage, nor for the fact that they continue to remain in bondage, this being ultimately the result of their inherent, uncreated nature.[21] Nonetheless, his system suffers from two drawbacks when compared to Ramanuja's view. First, Madhva's system leaves one with a plu-

18. For a detailed discussion of this theodicy, see Daniel Howard Snyder's chapter in this volume on the problem of evil, pp. 76-115, especially pp. 88-93.

19. The Christian doctrine of eternal hell is an exception, since the evil of hell lasts forever and thus could be said to be infinite. But this evil is usually explained as a result of human free will. Those who believe that God predestines some people to hell, however, do face a problem of evil arguably as severe as that faced by Ramanuja.

20. Julius Lipner, *The Face of Truth: A Study of Meaning and Metaphysics in the Vedantic Theology of Ramanuja* (Hong Kong: Macmillan Press, 1986), 94.

21. At first, one might wonder if this belief of his makes sense: if souls have already had an infinite number of past chances to gain release, shouldn't they have already done so by now? If one grants the coherence of Madhva's premise that souls with all kinds of inherent natures eternally exist as "brute givens," however, then his view really does appear to make sense. After all, one possible nature a soul could have is to be destined to beginninglessly (and hence for an infinite time) exist in a state of bondage, and then at some point in time gain release. So, one would expect to find these types of souls, along with other souls whose inherent nature dooms them never to attain release.

rality of ultimates — souls, matter, and God — without accounting for their existence. Although this is not a devastating criticism of Madhva, everything else being equal, views that hypothesize a single, unified source of everything (such as God), are in virtue of their simplicity, philosophically more satisfactory. Second, even though Madhva claimed to base his view on scripture, from the perspective of many orthodox Hindus his theology seems to contradict both those passages of Hindu scripture that appear to imply a deep sort of identity between God and souls and those that appear to imply that the world emerges out of God.

Conclusion

In my judgment Ramanuja's, and to a lesser extent Madhva's, worldview presents a philosophically viable alternative to that of Western theism and Christianity. Moreover, although Ramanuja's belief in the eternality of souls appears to present him with a serious problem of evil, in my judgment it is not central to the rest of his worldview. Thus, I believe, he could reject this belief without having to give up any of his other central beliefs. (He might, however, have to give up his belief in the infallibility of the Hindu scriptures, since Ramanuja claims that they teach this doctrine.) Accordingly, in my judgment it is unlikely that, solely based on general philosophical considerations, we can make a completely compelling case for preferring Christianity over Ramanuja's or Madhva's version of Hinduism. Rather, I believe, in making her case, the Christian apologist also will need to appeal to historical evidence, specifically historical evidence that Jesus really performed miracles, and really rose from the dead. In contrast, no relevantly equivalent sort of historical evidence can be found in support of Hinduism since it is not a religion founded on verifiable historical events.[22]

IV. Buddhism

Introduction

Buddhism was founded in India around 500 B.C. by Siddhartha Gautama, more commonly called the "Buddha," a term which means "the enlight-

22. For a good book on the historical evidence for the resurrection of Jesus, see William Lane Craig, *The Son Rises* (Chicago: Moody Press, 1981).

ened one." The oldest still-surviving school of Buddhism is the *Theravada* school (pronounced: tehr rah vaah dah, literally meaning "way of the elders"), which also is often called the *Hinayana* school (literally meaning "lesser vehicle"). By about 100 A.D., the second major school of Buddhism had developed, the *Mahayana* school (pronounced mah ha yah nah, meaning "greater vehicle"). Today, the Theravada school is primarily represented in Southeast Asia — Burma, Vietnam, Cambodia, Thailand, and Laos — and Ceylon (Sri Lanka). The Mahayana school is represented in Tibet, China, Korea, and Japan, and has by far the largest number of adherents. Although Buddhism originated in India, it has effectively died out there since most of its basic beliefs and practices were absorbed into Hinduism. After briefly looking at some key doctrines the Buddha taught that are common to both schools, we will specifically look at Theravada Buddhism and then at Mahayana Buddhism.

The Buddha expressed his core teachings in what are known as the Four Noble Truths. The First Noble Truth is that *life is suffering:* "The Noble truth of Suffering is this: Birth is suffering; aging is suffering; sickness is suffering; death is suffering; sorrow and lamentations, pain, grief, and despair are suffering. . . ."[23] Although Buddhists have often been accused of promoting an overly pessimistic view of life, a more accurate interpretation of the Buddhist notion of suffering is that it refers to any kind of dissatisfaction with life, not the sort of intense pain we normally associate with the word "suffering." In this sense, there is much truth to Buddha's First Noble Truth: by and large humans are dissatisfied, if not on the surface then at some deep level.

The Second Noble Truth is that the cause of this suffering is what Buddhists call *craving.* Often the Buddhist idea of craving is interpreted simply as *desire* thereby implying that Buddhists reject desires of any sort. If one interprets their doctrine more accurately, however, the heart of their doctrine seems to be that *attachment* is the cause of suffering, particularly attachment to one's own ego concerns. Consider, for instance, how much worry and dissatisfaction is the result of being attached to what other people think of us — we worry about how we look, about our status in life, about others getting ahead of us, and the like. Or, more generally, people's attachment to their own well-being in the future is an almost bottomless source of anxiety and dissatisfaction.

Given that attachment is the cause of suffering, it follows that to

23. From "Buddha's First Sermon," reprinted in Walpola Rahula, *What the Buddha Taught* (New York: Grove Press, 1959), 92-93.

eliminate suffering, we must eliminate attachment. This is the Buddha's Third Noble Truth. Once we have eliminated attachment, we will achieve a state called *nirvana,* a state of pure bliss that escapes the cycle of rebirths. This is the ultimate goal of Buddhist practice.

Finally, as his Fourth Noble Truth, the Buddha taught that the way to eliminate attachment and gain nirvana is to follow the Eightfold Path, which essentially consists of practicing ethical/nonviolent behavior and more importantly, acquiring the correct view of one's self and the world. What is this correct view? For Buddha and his followers, it is that given by the Buddha's doctrine of impermanence. According to this doctrine, everything is impermanent in the sense that nothing lasts for more than an extremely brief period of time. Everything is in an almost complete state of flux, like a river. Applied to the self, the doctrine of impermanence implies that there is no enduring self that continues to exist for more than a brief moment. This denial of the existence of an enduring self lies at the core of Buddhist belief and is called the *anatta,* or the "no self" doctrine. According to the Buddha, once we truly recognize the momentary nature of all existing things, especially the self, we lose all attachment and thus achieve the state of nirvana, either in this life or at the time of death. For the early Buddhists, this recognition could only come about through intense meditation which was entirely a matter of self-effort. We will see later, however, that a doctrine of grace developed in Mahayana Buddhism in which what are known as *Bodhisattvas* help one attain nirvana.

As explicated above, underlying the Fourth Noble Truth is the Buddhist claim that everything is impermanent, and thus that there is no enduring substantial self. These claims, however, were worked out differently in the two major schools, Theravada and Mahayana Buddhism. I will examine each of these in turn.

Theravada Buddhism

According to Theravada Buddhists, the self is like a candle flame. As we all know, a candle flame is simply a continuously flowing stream of heated molecules. Thus, if we consider the flame as nothing over and above the sum of its parts, then the candle flame is literally not the same flame from one moment to the next; rather, from moment to moment, one aggregate of molecules is replaced by a new aggregate of molecules. Nonetheless, for convenience we say that the *same* flame continues to burn from moment to moment. Another useful analogy is a highway. Interstate 35 goes through Austin, Texas and ends in Duluth, Minnesota. Yet interstate 35 in Duluth is not literally the same piece of blacktop that passes through Austin, Texas, even though they are officially designated as the same highway. The reason we consider them the same is that we find it convenient to do so, especially given that they are continuously connected with each other. Similarly, Theravada Buddhists claim that the word "I" or "self" does not designate any truly enduring thing that continues to exist through time. Rather, in analogy to the candle flame, the self merely consists of a continuously flowing stream of discrete mental and physical elements, such as those of sensation, feelings, consciousness, and various body processes. These discrete elements could be thought of as the "molecules" that compose the self. Moreover, like the candle flame, from moment to moment, one aggregate of these discrete elements is replaced by a new aggregate, and consequently, strictly speaking the "self" at one moment is being constantly replaced by a new "self" at the next moment. Under this view, therefore, what we call a person is really a succession of selves instead of a single enduring thing. As expressed by the Buddhist Monk Walpola Rahula,

> what we call 'I', or 'being', is only a combination of physical and mental aggregates, which are working together interdependently in a flux of momentary change within the law of cause and effect, and that there is nothing permanent, everlasting, unchanging and eternal in the whole of existence.[24]

According to Theravada Buddhists, through meditation and right action we can eventually come existentially to recognize the momentary nature of the self, along with that of the rest of reality. Once we do this, attachment and hence suffering ceases, and we attain *nirvana,* either in this life or at the time of death.

Evaluation

So far, the Theravada Buddhist story is at least initially plausible: the idea that suffering is (at least largely) the result of attachment, and that everything is impermanent makes tolerably good sense, at least on the surface. Indeed, as explicated so far the Theravada Buddhist's view of the self and reality is one that has been quite popular in the West among philosophers

24. Rahula, *What the Buddha Taught,* 66.

since at least the time of the famous Scottish philosopher David Hume. As we will see below, however, severe problems arise when this basic view of the self is combined with the additional traditional Buddhist doctrines of nirvana, rebirth, and karma. We will consider two of these problems.

1. Two Problems with Theravada Buddhism

The first major problem that these doctrines present for Theravada Buddhists is that they seem to generate a tension, if not contradiction, at the core of the Buddha's teaching. On the one hand, to eliminate attachment to our own ego concerns, the Buddha denied the reality of an enduring self. On the other hand, in order to affirm justice in the world, he had to affirm the doctrines of rebirth and karma, according to which we reap the consequences of our present thoughts and deeds in a future life. Rebirth and karma, however, seem to require the existence of an enduring self: how, for instance, could we reap the fruits of our past deeds unless our self continued to exist in the future? Moreover, the doctrine of nirvana also seems to require the existence of an enduring self: if your self does not continue to exist from moment to moment, why bother trying to obtain nirvana? Thus, on the one hand, Theravada Buddhists deny the existence of an enduring self, but on the other hand their doctrines of rebirth, karma, and nirvana seem to require that the self continues to exist through time.

The second major problem traditional Theravada Buddhists confront is what could be called the "karmic management" problem. Traditionally Buddhists have believed that by and large the circumstances of one's rebirth are determined by one's karma — that is, one's deeds, whether good or bad in this and previous lives. This, however, seems to require that there exist something like a "program" that arranges your genes, the family conditions you are born into, and the like to correspond to the moral worth of your past deeds. Such a program certainly would have to be highly complex and well-designed, much more so than any computer program that currently exists. The existence of such a karmic "program" would make sense if one believed in a God who created it, as Hindus do. But, traditional Theravada Buddhists do not believe in any such God. Thus, they are forced to simply assert that such a highly complex and well-organized system simply exists, and has always existed, as a "brute given." This, however, seems highly implausible: cases of such intricate apparent design, such as a watch, a computer program, or the human body, seem to require an explanation.

2. Attempts to Respond to the First Problem

The standard Buddhist solution to the apparent contradiction between the no-enduring self doctrine and the doctrines of rebirth, karma, and nirvana begins by admitting that one's present self does not literally get reborn since it does not exist for more than a moment even in this life; rather, they claim, one's "karmic energy," that is, the set of fundamental personality traits and life energy (one's "candle flame"), gets transferred to some future fetus.[25] Buddhists then go on to claim that although the future self is not strictly identical with our present self, it is not totally unrelated either. Thus, much as a candle flame which is passed from one candle to the next is neither the same candle flame nor a different candle flame, the future self can neither be said to be the same nor different from the present self.[26]

Although this response might seem initially plausible, it faces two significant problems. First, it does not really resolve the problem. To see this, note that the major point of the doctrine of rebirth and karma is that we should not be lax about our behavior in this life, since we will pay the consequences in the next life. This, however, not only requires a degree of sameness of the future self with our present self, but it also requires that we really care about what happens to that future self. But the more Theravada Buddhists affirm that our future self is the same as our present self, and hence that we should care what happens to it, the more the whole point of their practice and metaphysics is undermined: namely, to eliminate concern about what happens to our self by realizing that it does not exist for more than a moment. Thus, simply asserting that our future self is in some sense the same as our present self does not resolve the apparent contradiction between the Buddha's no-self doctrine and the doctrines of rebirth, karma, and nirvana.

Second, even if the reborn self is in some sense the same as our present self, it does not seem to be sufficiently continuous with our present self to justify claiming that we are actually reborn. To see this, consider the following analogy to the Buddhist's account of rebirth explicated above in which one's karmic energy, basic personality traits (and perhaps one's memories in an unconscious form) get transferred to some future fetus. Suppose a mother dies during pregnancy, and through some futur-

25. Rahula, *What the Buddha Taught,* 33; Carl Becker, *Breaking the Circle: Death and Afterlife in Buddhism* (Carbondale: Southern Illinois University Press, 1993), 9.

26. Becker, *Breaking the Circle,* 9; Paul Griffiths, *An Apology for Apologetics* (Maryknoll: Orbis Books, 1991), 105.

istic technology her newly discovered biological energy and her basic personality traits are transferred to her unborn child. Further suppose that her memories are transferred to the unborn child in an unconscious form that will never be consciously accessible to the child. In such a case, we certainly would not say that the mother continued to survive in the unborn child, except perhaps in some loose or figurative sense of "survive." Rather, we would say that a future successor of the mother survived that shared her life energy, personality traits, and her memories in unconscious form.

3. Attempts to Respond to the Second Problem

In response to the "karmic management" problem, some Theravada Buddhists, such as Alexandra David-Neel,[27] suggest a weakened version of the traditional doctrine of karma in which one's thoughts and deeds in this life only affect the character of one's reborn self, not its life circumstances. According to David-Neel, those who do good deeds progressively develop a non-ego-centered character that is better able to attain nirvana, and those who do evil deeds progressively develop a character addicted to their own ego-centered desires. Although this weakened version of the doctrine of karma largely avoids the "karmic management" problem raised above, it does so at a cost. First, this version of karma runs against what tradition records the Buddha as teaching: namely, that the circumstances of one's birth are largely determined by the deeds of one's past lives. Second, by weakening the doctrine of karma, it tends to undercut Buddhist ethics; for, as University of Chicago Buddhist scholar Paul Griffiths points out, the doctrine of karma provides the first-order prescriptions and proscriptions of Buddhist ethics (do not kill, do not steal, do not misbehave yourself sexually, and so forth) with their justification and sanction. If you do engage in such activities, you will suffer for them in this life or a future one, while if you fulfill your duties (giving to monks, developing compassion, and so forth), you will have a good rebirth.[28] Finally, this weakened version of karma almost completely undercuts the traditional Buddhist explanation of why people are born in varied, and often seemingly unfair, life circumstances, such as that of poverty or wealth.

27. Alexandra David-Neel, *Buddhism: Its Doctrines and Methods* (New York: Avon Books, 1977), 188-90.

28. Griffiths, *Apology for Apologetics,* 106.

Conclusion

In the above evaluation, I focused on what I consider some of the most vulnerable aspects of the core tenets of traditional Theravada Buddhism. Although the above critique has not definitively demonstrated that Theravada Buddhism is untenable, it does show that it runs into significant problems resulting from its belief in nirvana, rebirth, and karma, and thus that this form of Buddhism is less plausible than standard Western atheism. To see this, note that traditionally Theravada Buddhists have been atheists (or perhaps agnostics), since they do not believe in the existence of a creator God. Thus, unlike the theistic worldview, their worldview does not help explain the ultimate origin of the world, its apparent design, and the like. Instead, their worldview has the same drawbacks as standard Western atheism, along with the additional philosophical problems resulting from their doctrines of nirvana, rebirth, and karma, as elaborated above.

A Theravada Buddhist might respond to this conclusion by claiming that the problems that these doctrines present are compensated for by their positive merits, such as that they provide the basis for Buddhist meditational practices which in turn lead to peace and tranquility. In addition, they could argue, we have evidence that these doctrines are true both from the testimony of the Buddha and others who have achieved enlightenment, along with purported cases of memory of past lives. Personally, I find these to be fairly weak responses. The tranquility and peace that some Buddhists experience simply show that the meditational practices are often effective psychological techniques for producing these mental states, not that the doctrines of nirvana, rebirth, or karma are true. Moreover, in and of itself the appeal to testimony carries little weight considering that the founders, seers, and prophets of other religions give conflicting testimony: Why, for example, should we believe the Buddha's testimony over that of Jesus or the Apostle Paul, or some other venerated religious leader? Finally, these purported cases of past life memories at most provide evidence for the claim that some people are reborn; it does not provide evidence for the belief that everyone has gone through this cycle of rebirths for all eternity, or for the belief in karma and nirvana. But besides this, in my judgment the vast majority of reports of so-called past life memories can be easily explained without any appeal to the doctrine of rebirth.[29]

29. See Ian Wilson, *The Afterdeath Experience* (New York: William Morrow, 1987), chapters 3 and 4, for a plausible alternative explanation to reports of past life memories and a good critique of the evidence for rebirth.

Another response Theravada Buddhists could give to this critique is to reject some of these traditional doctrines, particularly that of rebirth and karma, as some Western Buddhists seem to do. Without these doctrines, however, the core Theravada Buddhist worldview has no hope to offer to us beyond this life; instead, it begins to look like a fairly common Western atheistic worldview coupled with a unique form of meditative practice that purportedly helps us live a more serene, ethical, and integrated life in this world. Although having such a meditative technique might make such a version of atheism practically more attractive, it does not add to its plausibility as a worldview. I conclude, therefore, that neither the traditional Theravada worldview, nor the above Westernized version of it, offers a significant additional apologetic challenge to Christian belief over and above that offered by typical Western versions of atheism.

Mahayana Buddhism

Explication

Mahayana Buddhism differs from Theravada Buddhism in two fundamental ways. First, Mahayana Buddhists stress that the only way to achieve nirvana for oneself is to strive to achieve it for all sentient beings. This is in contrast to Theravada Buddhists who by and large attempt to achieve nirvana for themselves. Moreover, this is why Mahayana Buddhists refer to themselves as the "greater vehicle" and to the Theravada Buddhists as *Hinayana* Buddhists, that is, "the lesser vehicle." Consequently, as a central element of their belief system, the Mahayana tradition developed the ideal of becoming a *Bodhisattva,* a fully enlightened being who has himself achieved nirvana, but because of his great love and power works to bring all other sentient beings to enlightenment.[30]

Along with this stress on love, Mahayana Buddhism developed a quite different view of reality than that of the Theravada Buddhists. Whereas Theravada Buddhists affirm the reality of the world and the real existence of many distinct things and properties, Mahayana Buddhists deny that any distinctions ultimately exist in reality. According to them,

30. Those Buddhists who have committed themselves to becoming such a fully enlightened being are also often called bodhisattvas.

the world of apparent distinctions, with its separate selves, is a false perception of reality. Because reality is ultimately distinctionless, it cannot be truly grasped by thought, which operates by making distinctions and assigning things characteristics; ultimate reality can only be experienced by some sort of direct "mystical intuition."

One of the three major schools of this form of Buddhism, the *Madhyamika* school (pronounced: mah dhyah mee kah), expresses this idea by saying that anything that can be spoken of or thought about is empty of content or substantial reality; indeed, they claim, all statements are empty of meaning. Accordingly, they refer to the nature of ultimate reality as emptiness or the void, though in referring to reality in this way they do not intend to give a positive account of its nature. Enlightenment thus consists of fully realizing and experiencing this emptiness.

One reason *Madhyamika* Buddhist philosophers give for this "position" is that it represents the logical implication of the doctrine of impermanence taught by the Buddha. If all things are completely impermanent, they argued, then nothing could exist for more than a instant. But in order for something to have any real existence, they claimed, it must exist for some finite amount of time — that is, for more than an instant. Thus, they concluded, the whole idea of real, distinct things existing is self-contradictory.[31] Another motivation for this doctrine is that it seems to provide the necessary philosophical basis for the ultimate Buddhist goal of eliminating suffering through eliminating attachment. Unlike the Theravada Buddhist's account of reality which allowed for attachment to one's own "stream of future selves," the Madhyamika's account eliminates the basis for any sort of attachment: once one fully realizes that everything is empty of substantiality or meaning — including the "doctrines" of Madhyamika Buddhism — one realizes that there is nothing to which to cling, and hence attachment ceases.

The second and third major schools of Mahayana Buddhism are the *Ashvaghosa* (pronounced: ahsh vah gho shah) and *Yogacara* (pronounced: yoh guh cha rah) schools. Like the *Madhyamika* school, these schools deny the existence of any ultimate distinctions in reality, such as the distinction between one person and another. Unlike the *Madhyamika* school, however, they do not speak of the nature of reality in terms of "emptiness" or "the void." Rather, the *Ashvaghosa* school claims that reality is ultimately an undifferentiated, indefinable "something" (which they called *suchness*), whereas the *Yogacara* school provides a more positive account,

31. Chang, *Hwa Yen Buddhism*, 71.

identifying reality with *pure, distinctionless consciousness.* So, for instance, the *Yogacara* school claimed that every sentient being is identical with this pure consciousness, and thus that enlightenment is achieved by recognizing this identity, usually through meditation.

As Buddhism penetrated deeply into China and adapted itself to Chinese thought, especially Taoism, a new school of Buddhism, *Ch'an* Buddhism emerged. This school in turn eventually gained foothold in Japan in the thirteenth century, becoming what is known as *Zen* Buddhism. Today Zen Buddhism is quite popular in the West. Like *Madhyamika* and *Yogacara* Buddhists, Zen Buddhists assert that human reason, thought, and language are ultimately invalid and indeed self-contradictory, and thus that they are a hindrance to enlightenment. After all, Zen Buddhists argue, if we are to experience the absolute oneness (or emptiness) of all things, we must get beyond language and reason, for the business of thought and language is to make distinctions and is thus directly opposed to the experience of enlightenment. (Language, for instance, distinguishes between red and green, big and small, intelligent and unintelligent, good and bad, and the like; and reason then uses these distinctions to draw conclusions.)

Despite their common belief in the inadequacy of reason, *Madhyamika* Buddhists and Zen Buddhists take different approaches to the use of reason. Even though they deny the ultimate validity of human reason and language, *Madhyamika* Buddhists nonetheless use philosophical arguments to expose the purported self-contradictory nature of reason and language, and thus break any attachment to it; these arguments are not meant to provide rational support for their position — since by their own admission reason is invalid — but are considered merely instrumentally useful tools that ultimately prove nothing. Zen Buddhists, on the other hand, reject philosophy and argumentation as a practical means to enlightenment and instead utilize a set of meditation techniques in order to break through the barrier of reason and language and achieve enlightenment. No doubt one of the most well-known of these meditational techniques is the Zen *koan,* a puzzling question or problem given to a Zen student that defies a rational solution. An often-repeated example of a *koan* is the question "What is the sound of one hand clapping in the forest?" The theory behind this practice is that, by meditating on the *koan* in an attempt to find a solution, the Zen student will be forced to break through the categories of language and reason and in so doing experience *satori,* that is, enlightenment.

Evaluation of Mahayana Buddhism

Let's begin our critique with *Madhyamika* Buddhism. An obvious objection to the *Madhyamika* worldview is that it is self-refuting: if, as they claim, all statements are empty of meaning, then the statement that all statements are empty of meaning is itself empty of meaning, and thus does not assert anything about reality. Thus the purported truth of the *Madhyamika* Buddhist thesis about reality is inconsistent with itself. When this objection was raised by his contemporaries, the *Madhyamika* school's leading philosopher, Nagarjuna (second century A.D.), responded by saying: "I have no proposition, no thesis to defend (which may lack any essence). If I had any thesis, I would have been guilty of the faults you ascribe to me. But I do not, hence I have no fault."[32] Nagarjuna's response has been typical of *Madhyamika* philosophers. On the one hand, *Madhyamika* Buddhists speak as though they are telling us what the true nature of reality is, but on the other hand, when pressed they end up denying that their philosophy is a view about reality at all. (More will be said on this below.)

More generally, because of their claim that reality is ultimately distinctionless, all schools of Mahayana Buddhism run into the same problems as the Sankara school of Hinduism. For example, if reality is ultimately characterless and distinctionless, then the distinction between being enlightened and unenlightened is ultimately an illusion, and even the distinction between illusion and reality is ultimately unreal. But their whole practice presupposes they are not. Otherwise, why bother trying to become enlightened? To respond to this critique, as some Buddhists do, by saying that we already are enlightened but just do not recognize it is not a sufficient answer. For this answer requires the existence of still another distinction: namely, that between knowing you are enlightened and not knowing you are enlightened.[33]

This inconsistency also penetrates into the Mahayana Buddhist

32. For a defense of Nagarjuna, see Bimal Matilal, *Perception: An Essay on Classical Indian Theories of Knowledge* (Oxford: Oxford University Press, 1986), chapter 2.

33. To this objection, Mahayana Buddhists, particularly the *Madhyamika* school, could reply that when they say that reality is distinctionless, they mean that it is completely indeterminate and hence all statements concerning reality are equally true. (For example, this is what many commentators, such as Chang [see 133-35], understand *Madhyamika* Buddhists to be claiming when they refer to reality as the void, or emptiness.) But if this is how they respond, then they must admit that the statement that Buddhist worldview is completely false is as true as the statement that Buddhist worldview is on the right track.

stress on universal love of all sentient beings, as embodied in their ideal of becoming a *Bodhisattva*. This is something Westerners have found particularly attractive about Tibetan Buddhism as presented to the West by the Dalai Lama and others. But, as stated in a well-known passage from the *Diamond Sutra*, ultimately the Bodhisattva loves no one, since no one exists and the Bodhisattva recognizes this:

> All beings must I lead to Nirvana, into that Realm of Nirvana which leaves nothing behind; and yet, after beings have thus been led to Nirvana, no being at all has been led to Nirvana. And why? If in a Bodhisattva the notion of a 'being' should take place, he could not be called a 'Bodhi-being'. And likewise if the notion of a soul, or a person should take place in him.

The Mahayana Buddhist's stress on loving others, therefore, is inconsistent with their overall worldview, because ultimately their worldview implies that there is no one to love.

Conclusion

Perhaps the above discussion can best be summed up by noting that since Mahayana Buddhists deny the validity of reason, they could never legitimately offer a good reason to believe their view. Even if practicing some form of Mahayana Buddhism (such as Zen) dramatically improved the quality of one's life, that could not constitute a reason in favor of its truth. Moreover, since *Madhyamika* and Zen Buddhists deny the ultimate validity of any philosophical thesis, it is probably best not to even consider them philosophies, but rather as forms of practice designed to achieve a certain inexpressible, ongoing experience (enlightenment) which radically alters one's orientation to the world. Even their seeming denial of the validity of all philosophical theses probably should not be taken as a claim about reality, but rather as a rhetorical device to get us directly to experience reality in a non-conceptual way. As one of today's most respected Zen masters and teachers, Thich Nhat Hanh, states,

> The aim of Madhyamika is to reduce all concepts to absurdity in order to open the door of non-conceptual knowledge. It is not the intention of the Madhyamika to propose a view of reality in order to set it up in opposition to other views of reality. *All views,* according to the Madhyamika, are erroneous, because the views are not a reality. The

> Madhyamika is, therefore, proposed as a method and not as a doctrine.[34]

Similarly, philosopher John M. Koller notes concerning Zen Buddhism, "rather than trying to say what kind of philosophy Zen is, we should conclude that it is a way of approaching reality that constitutes an alternative to the intellectual way. The rational and philosophical approach, so well known in the West, is one approach. The existential and meditative way of Zen is another."[35] Considered in this way, these forms of Buddhism are not necessarily in conflict with Christian claims about the world, since they are not making any claims to begin with; they are simply an interesting and strange practice. (It could, however, be in conflict with Christian practice.)

Overall Conclusion

In the above analysis, we looked at the underlying worldview of the three major schools of Hinduism and Buddhism — the Sankara, Ramanuja, and Madhva schools of Hinduism, and the Theravada and Mahayana schools of Buddhism. We can summarize our conclusions in the following three points: (i) Insofar as the Sankara school of Hinduism and the Mahayana school of Buddhism are interpreted as making positive claims about the nature of reality, their core worldview seems to be ultimately incoherent; (ii) The traditional Theravada Buddhist worldview seems less plausible than a common form of Western atheism, and thus does not offer an additional apologetic challenge to Christians over and above that offered by Western atheism; (iii) At least on the surface, the two theistic schools of Hinduism, the Ramanuja and Madhva schools, do appear to present a philosophically viable alternative to Western theism.

If these conclusions are correct, we can draw several lessons from them for the Christian apologist. First, they undermine the key assumption of those so-called religious pluralists who claim that all of the major world religions have equally valid claims to being true. (See Timothy O'Connor's chapter, "Religious Pluralism," pp. 165-81 in this volume.) Second, the above points show that of all the major Eastern schools of

34. Thich Nhat Hanh, *Zen Keys: A Guide to Zen Practice* (New York: Doubleday, 1995), 121.

35. John Koller, *Oriental Philosophies* (New York: Charles Scribner's Sons, 1970), 190.

thought we discussed, it is the two theistic schools of Hinduism that present a philosophically viable additional challenge to Christian belief. Finally, since the two other major world religions, Judaism and Islam, are theistic, the above conclusion suggests that the primary apologetic challenge the major world religions present Christianity is not that of challenging belief in a personal, omnipotent, all good God, but rather that of providing alternative conceptions of other aspects of the nature of God, along with alternative conceptions of God's relation to the world and of how God has acted in human history.

9

Divine Providence and Human Freedom

Scott A. Davison

1. Introduction

When you make important choices, do you ever worry about how your decision might fit into God's providential plan for the world? Does God always know in advance what you will decide to do, before you have made up your mind? Have you ever wondered whether or not God has providentially prearranged some parts of your life?

These questions concern the apparent tension between divine providence and human freedom. God is provident, which means that God exercises control over everything, in accordance with complete knowledge, in order to fulfill the divine plan for the world. But we human beings also do many things every day, exercising limited control over some parts of the world, in accordance with limited knowledge, in order to fulfill our limited plans for ourselves. How can both of these things be true? How can we have control over anything if God has complete control over everything? How can God know the future completely if the future is partially up to us?

I wish to express thanks to the Reverend Donald A. Klop, Thomas P. Flint, Courtney Clay, and the other contributors to this book for helpful comments concerning earlier versions of this chapter.

The Bible does not address these questions directly. However, it does affirm that people often act freely, that they are often responsible for their actions, and also that God is provident. (Sometimes all of these themes are emphasized together in the same passage: see Acts 2:11-26, for example.) Some people find this disturbing because for them, the tension between divine providence and human freedom seems so sharp that it constitutes either a serious obstacle to Christian faith or a strong reason for reworking our concepts of divine providence and human freedom.

In order to explore these issues and determine how sharp this tension is, it will be helpful first to explore exactly what God's providence involves. Then we can ask what human freedom is, and finally we can put all of this together in order to see what the possibilities are for relating divine providence to human freedom.

2. Divine Providence

In the most basic sense, a person is provident over something if and only if that person exercises control over it, based upon knowledge, for a good purpose. So God's providence involves three elements: power, knowledge, and good purposes.

According to the doctrine of omnipotence, God can do everything which can be done, and according to the doctrine of omniscience, God knows everything which can be known. Furthermore, God did not create the world on a whim; instead, there is a divine purpose for creation, a providential plan which God will carry to completion.

God's providence is complete, perfect, and as far-ranging as possible. We can see this by considering briefly the testimony of the scriptures and the doctrine of creation. The scriptures are full of powerful descriptions of God's providence. Here I will mention just one passage involving the Apostle Paul's address to the Athenians:

> The God who made the world and all things in it, since He is Lord of heaven and earth, does not dwell in temples made with hands; neither is He served by human hands, as though He needed anything, since He Himself gives to all life and breath and all things; and He made from one, every nation of mankind to live on all the face of the earth, having determined their appointed times, and the boundaries of their habitation, that they should seek God, if perhaps they might grope for Him and find Him, though He is not far from each one of us; for in

Him we live and move and exist, as even some of your own poets have said, "For we also are His offspring." (Acts 17:24-28)

Besides this scriptural testimony, the doctrine of creation illuminates the nature and extent of God's providence. Creation is typically understood as having the following three components (although not all Christians hold to this traditional understanding). First, there is *creation ex nihilo,* which refers to God's bringing the world into being from nothing at the first instant of time. According to this first aspect of creation, the world would never have existed at all if God had not brought it into being.

Second, there is *conservation,* which refers to God's sustaining the world in being from moment to moment. According to this second aspect of creation, the created world does not exist of its own accord; in fact, it would fall into nothingness if it were not sustained by God at every moment.

Third, there is *concurrence,* which refers to God's cooperating with the activities of every created thing. According to this third aspect of creation, even the basic powers of created beings (like the ability of fire to heat things, the ability of animals to move, and the ability of human beings to choose) cannot be exercised without God's involvement.

When we add these three elements of creation together, we can see that the doctrine of creation implies that God exercises providential control over the world. Now that we have explored briefly the nature of divine providence, let's consider the nature of human freedom.

3. Human Freedom

Most of the time, when we do something, we feel strongly that we have a choice about what we do. For example, have you ever looked closely at the back cover of this book? It's very interesting. Why don't you look at it now? Go ahead.

Just now, before reading this sentence, you made a choice. You chose whether to look at the back cover of this book, as I suggested, or to keep reading this chapter instead. Whether you looked or not, I'm sure you feel that it was up to you what to do. In other words, your choice to look or not to look was a free choice.

Life is filled with apparent examples of free choice. But what is the essence of freedom itself? Can this be defined? The first systematic investigation of this question was undertaken by Aristotle (384-322 B.C.), one of the great ancient Greek philosophers.

While discussing the notion of voluntary action, Aristotle noted that we praise and blame people for what they do only in certain special circumstances.[1] In general, we do not hold people responsible for what they do when they are forced or when they are ignorant of what they do in certain respects. For example, if you did not know that opening the door would wake the baby, and you feel badly about waking the baby, then we do not blame you for waking the baby. Or if you were forced by someone else to open the door, then we don't blame you for opening the door.

Putting these two observations together, Aristotle suggests that a person's action is voluntary only if (1) the origin of the action lies within the person, and (2) the person knows the circumstances of the action. Philosophers today still argue about whether or not Aristotle's conditions are satisfactory, especially the first condition about the origin of an action.

In fact, disagreement over this question since the time of Aristotle has led to the formulation of many theories about the essence of freedom. It will be helpful to consider here the two main kinds of theories. (A third main kind of view, which philosophers call "hard determinism," states that human persons never make any free choices. Since this view is inconsistent with the most natural sense of the scriptures, the traditions of the Church, and ordinary experience, I will ignore it here.)

4. Two Theories of Freedom

When you make a free choice (like deciding whether or not to look at the back cover of this book), are you determined to take a particular course of action or not? Many philosophers believe that when we make free choices, we are *determined* to make those choices. (Some people who hold this view, for example, believe that given the beliefs and desires which we have on any given occasion, we will act in a certain way and we are simply unable to do anything else.) Let's call these philosophers *compatibilists,* since they believe that freedom is compatible with being determined to act in a particular way. (I won't emphasize this point in what follows, but compatibilists also insist that only certain

1. What follows is a very rough summary of Aristotle's work *Nicomachean Ethics,* trans. Terence Irwin (Indianapolis: Hackett, 1985), sections 3.1–3.4.

kinds of determination are compatible with freedom; for instance, a person cannot choose freely when subject to irresistible force or coercion, but a person chooses freely when the choice is determined by "naturally occurring" beliefs and desires.) For example, a compatibilist might say that the outcome of your free choice to look or not to look at the back cover of this book a minute ago was determined by whatever was going on in your mind at the time, together with the state of your body and brain.

The other kind of theory of freedom should be called *incompatibilism,* since the people who hold theories of this kind believe that freedom is *incompatible* with being determined to act in a particular way. For example, an incompatibilist would say that if your choice to look or not to look at the back cover of this book was truly a free choice, then contrary to what the compatibilists say, you could not have been determined to choose that particular outcome; instead, it must have been up to you ultimately. Incompatibilists like to compare free choices to forks in a road: you can go this way or that way, and it is up to you to choose which way to go. (By the way, this is not an unbiblical "absolute power to the contrary," despite what some authors say;[2] instead, it is choice within a limited range of options.)

By way of summary, then, incompatibilists hold that in order for a choice to be free, the person choosing must face at least two possible courses of action, without being determined in advance to choose any particular option. By contrast, compatibilists claim that a choice may be free even though it is determined in advance. Which kind of theory is correct, compatibilism or incompatibilism? Here philosophers disagree very strongly.

Compatibilists like to point out that ordinarily, we assume that events in the world have causes; when a bridge fails or a plane crashes, for instance, we always want to know what the cause of that event was. Why should human actions be different? They also like to argue that if incompatibilism is right, then human free actions are very strange kinds of random events, since they cannot be explained scientifically (in terms of cause and effect) or rationally (since neither one's reasons nor anything else can cause one's free actions, according to incompatibilists). They also suggest that what we really want in making choices is that our actions be determined by our preferences, which is compatible with being caused to

2. See for example Donald Carson, *Divine Sovereignty and Human Freedom* (Atlanta: John Knox Press, 1981), 206-9.

act in a particular way. Finally, some Christians argue that the strongest conception of God's providential control points to compatibilism.[3]

On the other hand, incompatibilists like to point out that if compatibilism were true, then in one sense, our actions are never up to us, since they are determined ultimately by events which are beyond our control (including whatever events determined that we have our particular beliefs and desires at a given time). And if this were true, then how could people be morally responsible for what they do? Incompatibilists also suggest that reasons and preferences *influence* our choices without *determining* them, and that sometimes people can rise above their preferences in making a free choice. Finally, theists like to point out that at least God must be free in the incompatibilist's sense, since God's choices are not determined, and that it is hard to explain how God is not the author of sin if incompatibilism is not true.[4]

Arguments like these (plus many others) are debated by philosophers all the time, and probably this deep disagreement over compatibilism and incompatibilism will continue indefinitely. (Today there are probably more compatibilists than incompatibilists, but it is possible to cite examples of famous philosophers throughout history who have defended each view.)

So what should we say about the essence of freedom? I myself lean towards incompatibilism, because I believe that it makes more sense of moral responsibility than compatibilism, avoids the suggestion that God is the author of sin (which arises from compatibilism plus the belief that God is provident over the created world), and plays a crucial role in any plausible account of eternal punishment.[5] But we can't possibly settle this controversy once and for all, so probably the best thing to do is to consider both kinds of theories without trying to decide which one is correct.

At this point, then, we are in a position to consider together divine

3. For more by way of a philosophical defense of compatibilism, see Harry G. Frankfurt, *The Importance of What We Care About* (Cambridge: Cambridge University Press, 1988); Daniel C. Dennett, *Elbow Room: The Varieties of Free Will Worth Wanting* (Cambridge, MA: MIT Press, 1984); and John Feinberg, "God Ordains All Things," in *Predestination and Free Will: Four Views of Divine Sovereignty and Human Freedom,* ed. David Basinger and Randall Basinger (Downers Grove, IL: InterVarsity Press, 1986).

4. For more by way of a defense of incompatibilism, see Peter van Inwagen, *An Essay on Free Will* (Oxford: Oxford University Press, 1983), and Bruce Reichenbach, "God Limits His Power," in *Predestination and Free Will.*

5. For more on this last topic, see the chapter on heaven and hell by Michael Murray, pp. 287-317.

providence and our two kinds of theories about the nature of freedom. If God is provident, as we have said, then how can human persons be free?

5. The Power Question

There are two questions which should be distinguished under this heading. First of all, how can human beings have any control over anything if God has total providential control over the whole world? Since this is a question about God's power and human power, let's call it "The Power Question." Second, how can human beings have any options of choice if God has complete knowledge of the future? Since this is a question about God's knowledge, let's call it "The Knowledge Question." Let's consider these questions in turn, keeping in mind the distinction between compatibilist and incompatibilist theories of human freedom.

The Power Question raises a serious obstacle for those who want to affirm both that God is provident and that human persons are free. For if God has total providential control over the whole world, then it looks like human beings have no control over anything at all, and hence no free choices to make. What should we think about this question?

Before we approach the Power Question directly, we must consider the fact that there are different notions of control which could be used in order to describe God's providence. Let's distinguish the following kinds of control, using some of the rather technical and precise vocabulary developed by philosophers in order to be as clear as possible:

> An agent controls an event *in the strong sense* if and only if (i) the agent brings about the event (ii) without the independent contribution of any other agents, and (iii) the agent could have prevented the occurrence of the event.
>
> An agent controls an event *in the middle sense* if and only if (i) the agent cooperates with another agent in bringing about the event, and (ii) the agent could have prevented the occurrence of the event.
>
> An agent controls an event *in the weak sense* if and only if (i) the agent does not bring about the event at all, but (ii) the agent still could have prevented the occurrence of the event.

These three notions of control enable us to distinguish at least three different theories about God's providence. (Incidentally, since predestination involves some kind of control by God, these three senses of control could generate three different theories of predestination, but I won't discuss that issue here.) It will be helpful to consider each theory briefly.

6. Three Theories of Providence

One theory, which we could call the "Strong Theory of Providence," suggests that God controls every event in the strong sense. The highly influential theologian John Calvin (1509-1564) may have held something like this view:

> From furthest eternity, [God] ruled on what he should do, according to his own wisdom, and now, by his power, he carries out what he decided then. So we maintain that, by his Providence, not only heaven and earth and all inanimate things, but also the minds and wills of men are controlled in such a way that they move precisely in the course he has destined.[6]

Now if the Strong Theory of Providence is right, then a compatibilist theory of freedom would be the most natural choice, since compatibilism allows for the possibility of free human choices which are determined providentially by God and controlled in the strong sense. It is not surprising, therefore, to find Calvin defending a compatibilist theory of voluntary action:

> Since man was corrupted by the Fall, he sins voluntarily. There is no external force or coercion: he is motivated by his own passions. But such is the depravity of his nature, he can only move in the direction of evil.[7]

By contrast, an incompatibilist theory of freedom does not fit together with the Strong Theory of Providence. This is because incompatibilists insist that a free action is not determined, whereas the Strong Theory of Providence holds that everything (including human action) is determined providentially by God and controlled in the strong sense.

6. John Calvin, *The Institutes of the Christian Religion,* ed. Tony Lane and Hilary Osborne (Grand Rapids: Baker Book House, 1987), 74.

7. Calvin, *Institutes,* 97.

Of course, nothing we have said so far requires that we embrace the Strong Theory of Providence. The second notion of control leads to a second theory of providence, which we can call the "Middle Theory of Providence." According to this theory, God controls *some* events in the world directly, in the strong sense (like those events involved in creating the world), but controls *other* events (like those involving human free choices) in the middle sense. This means that God cooperates with human beings in bringing about their free choices, and that God could have prevented those choices.

The Middle Theory of Providence can accommodate both compatibilist and incompatibilist theories of human freedom, depending upon how we understand the notion of God's cooperation with human activities.

God's cooperation can be understood as either general or specific. Perhaps an analogy will help to make this more clear. Suppose that you are building a house next door, and that I volunteer to help you out. I could cooperate with your building activity in a general way by allowing you to use my electricity (for example), which would be channelled into various specific tools by you. Or I could cooperate with your building in a specific way, by helping you to raise up a wall (for example). In the same way, we can imagine God's cooperation with our action as either general not directed towards a specific action) or specific (directed towards a specific action).

Most compatibilists will wish to say that God cooperates with human free choices, and add that those free choices are themselves determined to be made in a particular way. According to this picture, God's cooperation is specifically directed towards the choice of a particular option by the human person in question. In other words, in terms of the building analogy, God's cooperation with your free choices is not like providing electricity, which is general; instead, it is specific, like helping you to raise a wall.

By contrast, incompatibilists will insist that God cooperates with the choices of free human beings who are not determined to choose a particular course of action. So most incompatibilists will view God's cooperation as general in nature, and not specifically directed towards the choice of a particular option by the human person in question.[8] In terms of the

8. For more on this question, see Alfred J. Freddoso, "Medieval Aristotelianism and the Case against Secondary Causes in Nature," in *Divine and Human Action*, ed. Thomas V. Morris (Ithaca: Cornell University Press, 1988).

building analogy, God's cooperation is more like providing electricity and allowing you to decide how it is used. Luis de Molina, an influential Jesuit theologian (1535-1600), seems to have held this kind of view of God's causal cooperation with human free choices:

> From what has been said we have it only that our morally evil actions are not attributed to God as to a positive cause who has an influence on them. This is in accord with the example of the workman who produces swords. For just as the deeds which are done by those who do not use the swords rightly are not imputed to the workman (for the swords are indifferent with respect to good or bad use), but are instead imputed to the free choice of those who use the swords badly, so too, since God's general concurrence is indifferent with respect to good and evil actions, the evil actions should not be attributed to God, but should rather be attributed to those who abuse God's general concurrence in order to do evil.[9]

Finally, the weak sense of control generates a third and final theory, the Weak Theory of Providence. This theory may be attractive to those who believe that God's concurrence (see section 1) is not necessary for the ordinary operations of the created world. This view may also be attractive to those who believe that God could not know in advance what people would freely choose to do. (This topic is discussed below as the "God Doesn't Know" view.)

According to the Weak Theory of Providence, which is based on the weak notion of control defined above, God is not involved in the actual production of human free choices, but still could prevent them by intervening in the natural world. Like the Middle Theory of Providence, this Weak Theory of Providence can accommodate both compatibilist and incompatibilist theories of human free choice. It also suggests a promising response to the problem of evil (since God does not control the actions of human beings in either the strong or middle sense, according to the Weak Theory of Providence). But since it involves such a weak notion of control (it denies that God's concurrence is necessary for human action, for instance), and most Christians have a stronger notion of providence (which has very strong scriptural support), the Weak Theory of Providence probably will not satisfy most Christians.

9. Luis de Molina, *Liberi arbitri cum gratiae donis, divine praescientia, providentia, praedestinatione et reprobatione concordia,* Part 2, Disputation 32, Number 18, trans. Alfred J. Freddoso (1989, unpublished).

By way of summary, our response to the Power Question is that God's providence might involve different kinds of control. Depending upon which kind of control is involved, different theories of human freedom might be correct. Only the strong sense of control rules out human freedom in the incompatibilist sense, but human freedom in the compatibilist sense fits well with all three kinds of divine control. The doctrine of omnipotence means that God *could* control every event in the strong sense, but it does not imply that God *must* do this. So there are several ways of responding to the Power Question which enable us to combine God's providence and human freedom.

Which view of providence is the right one? Once again, people disagree about this question quite a bit. I myself favor the Middle Theory of Providence, because it fits in naturally with a promising answer to the Knowledge Question (see the discussion of Middle Knowledge below), but there is room for disagreement here among committed Christians. So we should weigh the advantages and disadvantages of each view carefully before taking any sides. (Although we have not determined exactly which solution to the Power Question is the best one, at least we have identified several possible answers which can accommodate very diverse views of human freedom and divine providence.)

7. The Knowledge Question

The Knowledge Question raises a different set of problems: how can human beings have any options of choice if God has complete knowledge of the future? As St. Augustine (354-430 A.D.) noted, knowing something implies that a person could not be wrong, but freedom requires that a person could do something else instead:

> Surely this is the problem that is disturbing and puzzling you. How is it that these two propositions are not contradictory and inconsistent: (1) God has foreknowledge of everything in the future; and (2) We sin by the will, not by necessity? For, you say, if God foreknows that someone is going to sin, then it is necessary that he sin. But if it is necessary, the will has no choice about whether to sin; there is an inescapable and fixed necessity.[10]

10. Augustine, *On Free Choice of Will,* trans. Thomas Williams (Indianapolis: Hackett, 1993), 74.

How should we respond to the Knowledge Question?

First of all, let's consider this question in light of our distinction between compatibilist and incompatibilist theories of human freedom. According to compatibilism, it is possible for a person to choose a particular option freely and also to be determined to choose that particular option at the same time. But clearly God knows in advance which events will determine which other events will occur. So the Knowledge Question really doesn't pose any special problems for Christians who are compatibilists. They can simply say that God knows which free human choices will be determined in the future, in the same way that God knows how other events in the world will be determined in the future.

The problem for incompatibilists is much more difficult, though. Incompatibilists believe that in order for a human person to choose a particular option freely, that person must *not* be determined to choose that particular option. So incompatibilists believe that the outcome of a free choice is not set in advance, and this leads us to wonder how anyone, including God, could know in advance how a person would make a free choice.

Here is a way to make the problem more explicit. Remember when I asked you to look at the back cover of this book? Let's suppose that you decided not to look at the cover and kept reading this chapter instead, and let's also suppose (for the sake of the argument) that your choice was free in the incompatibilist's sense. Now one hundred years ago, according to a familiar way of describing the doctrine of omniscience, God knew that you would decide not to look at the back cover of this book today when you were reading this chapter. But if God knew this one hundred years ago, then how could it be up to you whether or not to look at the back cover today? God cannot be mistaken about the future, so wasn't it already determined that you would not look, since God knew this one hundred years ago?[11]

Or consider the argument from the other way around. When you face a free choice, like whether or not to look at the back cover of this book, it is up to you what to do. Before you make up your mind, things could go either way. But then how could anyone, including God, know what you will decide to do? Since you haven't made up your mind yet, there is nothing to know yet.

11. For a very detailed statement of this kind of argument, see Nelson Pike, "Divine Omniscience and Voluntary Action," in *Contemporary Philosophy of Religion*, ed. Steven M. Cahn and David Shatz (New York: Oxford University Press, 1982) or William Hasker, *God, Time, and Knowledge* (Ithaca: Cornell University Press, 1989).

This kind of argument has generated a great deal of reflection through the centuries. Let's consider the main kinds of responses which are available to those Christians who are interested in incompatibilist theories of human freedom.

8. The "God Doesn't Know" View

One way to respond to this problem would be to claim that God simply does not know what human persons will freely choose to do in the future. Let's call this the "God Doesn't Know" view. It has also been called the "Open Future" view, and it has been defended vigorously by several authors recently.[12]

One strategy for defending the God Doesn't Know view involves the idea that propositions about future free choices are neither true nor false until those choices are actually made. Since they are neither true nor false in advance of the choices they describe, it is impossible to know that they are true in advance. This idea is suggested by the following remarks from Clark Pinnock, a contemporary proponent of the God Doesn't Know view:

> God is omniscient in the sense that he knows everything which can be known, just as God is omnipotent in that he can do everything that can be done. But free actions are not entities which can be known ahead of time. They literally do not yet exist to be known. God can surmise what you will do next Friday, but cannot know it for certain because you have not done it yet.[13]

A different strategy for defending the God Doesn't Know view involves the claim that even if propositions about future free choices are true or false in advance of the choices they describe, still God could not know about them because not even God could distinguish the true propositions from the false ones in advance (and knowledge requires that a person be able to do this).[14]

12. See for example Richard Rice, *God's Foreknowledge and Man's Free Will* (Minneapolis: Bethany House Publishers, 1985); Hasker, *God, Time, and Knowledge*; and David Basinger et al., *The Openness of God* (Downers Grove: InterVarsity Press, 1994).

13. Clark Pinnock, "God Limits His Knowledge," in *Predestination and Free Will*, 157.

14. Scott A. Davison, "Foreknowledge, Middle Knowledge, and 'Nearby'

The God Doesn't Know view certainly solves the problem posed by the Knowledge Question, but it does so at a price. Scripture appears to teach (and Christians have almost always held) that God knows the future in all of its detail, and often they have held this for reasons having to do with the doctrine of providence. It is odd to suggest that God has a providential plan for the world but doesn't know how everything will actually turn out in the end. Also, defenders of the God Doesn't Know view have special difficulties in explaining how biblical prophecy works, since prophecies often concern future events which depend upon free human choices. Because of these problems, many Christians will not find the God Doesn't Know view acceptable, although it must be said that recent work on this view is worth considering carefully and none of the other ways of responding to the Knowledge Question is completely free of difficulties.[15]

9. The Timeless Eternity View

A second approach to answering the Knowledge Question involves suggesting that God exists outside of time altogether. This would mean that God does not *fore*know the future, strictly speaking, since foreknowledge is knowledge had in advance, but rather that God knows all events at all times from the perspective of timeless eternity. Many Christians have adopted this view throughout the centuries, including the highly influential theologian St. Thomas Aquinas (1225-1274). One of the earliest Christian theologians to defend this approach to answering the Knowledge Question was Boethius (480-524), who wrote *The Consolation of Philosophy* while awaiting execution in prison:

> [Since] God has a condition of ever-present eternity, His knowledge, which passes over every change of time, embracing infinite lengths of past and future, views in its own direct comprehension everything as though it were taking place in the present.[16]

Worlds," *International Journal for Philosophy of Religion* 30 (August 1991): 29-44, for this kind of argument.

15. For a defense of this view, see Rice, *God's Foreknowledge*; Pinnock, "God Limits His Knowledge"; Hasker, *God, Time, and Knowledge*; and Basinger et al., *The Openness of God.*

16. Boethius, *The Consolation of Philosophy,* trans. W. V. Cooper (Chicago: Regnery Gateway, 1981), 117.

Let's call this view the "Timelessness" view. It provides an answer to the Knowledge Question by insisting that God's perspective embraces all of eternity at once. However, it does not completely answer the argument behind the Knowledge Question described above. In that argument, we supposed that God knew one hundred years ago that you would choose not to look at the back cover of this book today. Now the Timelessness view suggests that we should redescribe that situation in terms of God's knowing from timeless eternity that you would choose not to look at the back cover of this book today. But does this redescription solve the problem? It doesn't seem to help very much, since whatever is true from eternity seems to be at least as set in stone as what is true one hundred years ago (if not more so).

Furthermore, the Timelessness view raises some new puzzles of its own. For example, some authors have argued that the Timelessness view represents an unbiblical picture of God derived largely from Greek philosophical influences.[17] And others charge that if God is timeless, then God cannot be omniscient or active in our ever-changing world in the ways described by the Bible.[18] But given the place of the Timelessness view in the Christian tradition, together with the fact that many people continue to explore and defend it, we should continue to keep an open mind about it.[19]

10. Middle Knowledge

A third possible response to the Knowledge Question starts with an observation concerning foreknowledge and providence. Why is knowledge of the future useful to God for the purposes of providence? Well, presumably knowledge of the future enables God to make decisions about how to

17. See for example Nicholas Wolterstorff, "God Everlasting," in *Contemporary Philosophy of Religion.*

18. See for example Steven T. Davis, *Logic and the Nature of God* (Grand Rapids: Eerdmans, 1983).

19. For further defense and elaboration of the Timelessness view, see Eleonore Stump and Norman Kretzmann's "Eternity," in *The Concept of God,* ed. Thomas V. Morris (New York: Oxford University Press, 1987), 219-52, and "Prophecy, Past Truth, and Eternity," in *Philosophical Perspectives 5: Philosophy of Religion,* ed. James E. Tomberlin (Atascadero, CA: Ridgeview Publishing Co., 1991), 395-424; Paul Helm, *Eternal God: A Study of God Without Time* (New York: Oxford University Press, 1988); and Brian Leftow, *Time and Eternity* (Ithaca: Cornell University Press, 1991).

exercise divine power in order to accomplish the purposes behind creation. But there is a problem here: knowledge of the future is just knowledge of what *will* happen (since the future is *by definition* whatever will happen), and once God knows that something definitely *will* happen, then it's too late to do anything about it. (This may sound like a limit on God's power, but it isn't; it's just a consequence of saying that something definitely *is* part of the future.) What God needs, for the purposes of providence, is not just knowledge about what will happen, but also knowledge about what *could* happen and what *would* happen in certain circumstances.[20]

Luis de Molina saw clearly the relationship between God's providence and the knowledge of what could happen and would happen in various circumstances. He drew a useful distinction between three kinds of knowledge which God possesses, which suggests a promising response to the Knowledge Question. So let's consider Molina's theory of divine knowledge and the theory of providence and divine foreknowledge which stems from it.[21]

The first kind of knowledge which God possesses is called *natural knowledge*. According to Molina, a true proposition is part of God's natural knowledge if and only if it is a necessary truth (a truth which could not be false under any circumstances whatever) which is beyond God's control. Examples of such true propositions would include "Two plus two equals four," "Nothing is both red all over and green all over at once," and "Every triangle has three sides," since these truths are necessary (they could not be false, under any circumstances) and they are beyond God's control (nobody, including God, could make them false).

The second kind of knowledge which God possesses is called *free knowledge* (because it is subject to God's free decision). According to Molina, a true proposition is part of God's free knowledge if and only if it

20. Incidentally, this argument shows that even if God foreknows the future by a kind of simple vision, this is not adequate for the purposes of divine providence. For a more rigorous version of this argument, see Hasker, *God, Time, and Knowledge,* and William Craig, *The Only Wise God* (Grand Rapids: Baker Book House, 1987).

21. For more complete and detailed presentations of this view, see Freddoso's introduction to Luis de Molina, *On Divine Knowledge (Liberi arbitri cum gratiae donis, divina praescientia, providentia, praedestinatione et reprobatione concordia,* Disputations 47-53), trans. Alfred J. Freddoso (Ithaca: Cornell University Press, 1988); Craig, *The Only Wise God*; and Thomas P. Flint's "Two Accounts of Providence," in *Divine and Human Action* and *Divine Providence: The Molinist Account* (Ithaca: Cornell University Press, 1998).

is a contingent truth (an actual truth which could have been false under different circumstances) which is within God's control. Examples of such true propositions would include "Michelangelo painted the ceiling of the Sistine Chapel," "There are iguanas in America" and "There is a rock on my desk," since God could have brought it about that these true propositions were false instead.

The third kind of knowledge which God possesses, according to Molina, is called *middle knowledge* (because it is "in between" God's natural knowledge and free knowledge). A true proposition is part of God's middle knowledge if and only if it is a contingent truth (like items of God's free knowledge) which is beyond God's control (like items of God's natural knowledge). The most frequently discussed items of middle knowledge are often called "counterfactuals of freedom" by philosophers, since they describe what people would freely do if placed in various possible situations.

Here is an example of a counterfactual of freedom: "If I had asked you to look at the front cover of this book at the beginning of the section on human freedom, then you would have looked at it freely (in the incompatibilist's sense of 'freely')." Now this is a *conditional proposition,* which means that it has an "if" part and a "then" part. The "if" part happens to be false in this case, since I didn't actually ask you to look at the front cover of this book. (I asked you to look at the back cover instead.) Is this counterfactual of freedom true or false? Well, that depends upon whether or not you would have looked at the front cover freely (in the incompatibilist's sense of freedom) had I asked you to do so; let's suppose for the purposes of illustration that you *would* have done so, and hence that this counterfactual of freedom is a true proposition.

Since it is true, Molina would say that God knows it, and because it is both contingent (it could have been false) and beyond God's control (it describes a free action, in the incompatibilist's sense of freedom, which does not depend upon God alone), it must be classified as an item of God's middle knowledge.

Molina claims that God's providence involves middle knowledge in a crucial way. Very briefly, here is how it is supposed to work (we will also consider an example in more detail below): through natural knowledge, God knows what is necessary and what is possible. Through middle knowledge, God knows what every possible person would do freely (in the incompatibilist's sense) in every possible situation. So God decides which kind of world to create, including those situations in which free human persons should be placed, knowing how they would respond, and this results in God's free knowledge (contingent truths which are up to God, which include foreknowledge of the actual future, including all human actions).

In order to make this more clear, let's consider the example of Jonah from the Scriptures. Suppose that God wants to teach Jonah a lesson about the value and worth of other human beings, so God tells Jonah to preach to the Ninevites, knowing that they will repent. Their repentance makes Jonah upset, though. (He did not even want to preach to them in first place: that's why he ran away by ship, got thrown overboard, and spent three days inside of a sea monster.) So Jonah leaves Nineveh and relaxes in the shade of a plant which God appointed to grow for Jonah's shelter. However, the next day, God appoints a worm to attack the plant, which causes it to wither, and Jonah complains bitterly to God because of the intense heat of the sun and asks to die. In response, God says this to Jonah:

> You had compassion on the plant for which you did not work, and which you did not cause to grow, which came up overnight and perished overnight. And should I not have compassion on Nineveh, the great city in which there are more than 120,000 persons who do not know the difference between their right and left hand, as well as many animals? (Jonah 4:10-11)

Molina's theory of providence can be used to explain how God's providence is at work in this case. According to Molina, God knew (through middle knowledge) that the Ninevites would repent in response to Jonah's preaching, that Jonah would not be happy about their repentance, and that Jonah would be even more upset about the withering of the plant. Knowing these things, God placed all of these people in this situation, allowing Jonah and the Ninevites to exercise their freedom of choice, and brought about many great things (including the reform of the Ninevites and the imparting of an important lesson to Jonah). This example illustrates the way in which Molina's theory of middle knowledge could help to explain how God's providence is at work throughout human history.[22]

Molina's theory of providence through middle knowledge also suggests an answer to the argument behind the Knowledge Question, which argument suggested that God's foreknowledge was incompatible with human freedom (in the incompatibilist's sense). Molina's answer is that al-

22. For more on this, see Flint, *Divine Providence*.

though God knew one hundred years ago that you would choose not to look at the back cover of this book when I asked you to do so, still this action was up to you. And if you had chosen to look at the back cover instead of choosing not to look, then God would have known all along that you would have done this instead. In other words, counterfactuals of freedom depend upon what people would choose to do freely if placed in certain situations, and God knew those things before the creation of the world.

Molina's theory of middle knowledge generates a powerful theory of providence which aims to combine a strong, traditional notion of God's providence with a robust incompatibilist notion of human freedom. It also appears to have some biblical support, because there are verses which seem to attribute middle knowledge to God (see 1 Samuel 23:6-13 and Matthew 11:20-24). But is Molina's theory the best one available?

Philosophers disagree very strongly on this issue. Critics of Molina object to his picture for several reasons. First, they wonder about these counterfactuals of freedom: can we really assume that these are either true or false? The quotation from Clark Pinnock reproduced above illustrated a doubt about propositions concerning future free actions, and a similar doubt is often raised about counterfactuals of freedom: how can they be true if the person in question is never in the situation and never actually makes a choice? What "grounds" them or makes them true?[23]

A second worry about Molina's picture has to do with the nature of knowledge. Even if a given counterfactual of freedom is true, *knowing* a proposition requires that a person be able to distinguish what is true from what is false. (For example, I cannot tell whether or not you would look at the back cover of this book if I asked you to do so, so I cannot have *knowledge* about what you would do.) The worry here is that perhaps not even God could distinguish true counterfactuals of freedom from false ones.[24]

A third worry is that Molina's picture attributes a strange power to human persons. Assuming that God knew from eternity (and hence one hundred years ago also) that you would choose freely (in the incompatibilist's sense) not to look at the back cover of this book when I asked you to do so, still it was up to you to choose otherwise. If you were to

23. This worry is expressed succinctly in Robert M. Adams, "Middle Knowledge and the Problem of Evil," *American Philosophical Quarterly* 14 (1977): 109-17, reprinted in *The Virtue of Faith and Other Essays* (Oxford: Oxford University Press, 1987).

24. See Davison, "Foreknowledge, Middle Knowledge, and 'Nearby' Worlds," for a discussion of this kind of argument.

choose otherwise, though, then God would have known something else one hundred years ago. This suggests that God's knowledge from eternity (and one hundred years ago) is within your control in a sense, which is surely a strange idea.

So there are several important and interesting objections which philosophers raise against Molina's theory of middle knowledge. Philosophers disagree sharply about whether or not Molina's theory has the resources to meet these objections.[25] But given the fact that only Molina's theory promises to combine a strong, traditional notion of God's providence with an incompatibilist notion of human freedom, we should consider it very carefully. (I myself lean towards thinking that Molina's view is correct, because I have more confidence in the claims that [1] we are free in the incompatibilist's sense and that [2] God is provident than I have in any of these objections.)

11. Conclusion

In conclusion, there are several ways to respond to the Knowledge Question. If we embrace a compatibilist theory of human freedom, then the problems suggested by the Knowledge Question evaporate, since it is easy to see how God could foreknow the future in all of its detail if we were caused to perform our free actions. But if we insist upon an incompatibilist theory of human freedom (as I am inclined to do), then there are three main avenues of response.

We could say simply that God doesn't know the future in all of its detail, but this would be departing from our theological tradition in important ways. Or we could say that God exists outside of time, but this generates new difficulties. Or we could say that God possesses middle knowledge, but this generates new difficulties also. In short, there is no easy way to answer the Knowledge Question if we are incompatibilists about human freedom; we must weigh the virtues and vices of each answer carefully in order to make up our minds, and there is room for disagreement among committed Christians.

Finally, since we have seen that there are several ways of reconciling divine providence and human freedom, the apparent tension between

25. For more on these objections, see Freddoso's introduction to Molina, *On Divine Knowledge*; Craig, *The Only Wise God*; Flint's "Two Accounts of Providence" and *Divine Providence*; and Hasker, *God, Time, and Knowledge*.

them should not constitute a serious obstacle to Christian faith. Philosophers throughout the ages, both Christians and non-Christians, have done us a great service by raising difficult questions about our beliefs in human freedom and divine providence and exploring the possible ways of combining these two beliefs. The result of this centuries-long inquiry is a heightened awareness of the difficult issues involved in describing both human freedom and divine providence, together with a clearer sense of what our options are in this area (and a deeper appreciation of the strengths and weaknesses of the options open to us). Probably the controversies concerning these issues will never be resolved to everyone's satisfaction because the issues are so complicated, deep, and hard to assess. This doesn't mean that we should stop thinking about these issues or that we should never make up our own minds about them, but it does mean that we should be tolerant of those who hold contrary views.

10

The Incarnation and the Trinity

Thomas D. Senor

Introduction

There is little doubt that the two most significant and distinctive metaphysical claims that Christians make are that God became incarnate in Jesus Christ and that the Godhead is triune or "three in one." This pair of claims has created a good deal of confusion, not only outside the church but within it as well.

In addition to the fact that these assertions are unique to Christianity, there is something else that unites them: they are the two doctrines most likely to be taken to create *logical* problems for the Christian faith. *Logical problems* are to be distinguished from *evidential problems.* To say that a body of doctrine has evidential problems is to say that the grounds for believing it are somehow problematic, that the evidence is lacking or shoddy or suspect. But one worries about evidential problems only when one is *not* concerned about logical problems. A body of doctrine, or any set of claims, is logically problematic if it is logically *inconsistent* or if it *entails a contradiction.*

Many have argued, for example, that the resurrection of Christ and the historicity of the Gospels have evidential problems, i.e., that there is insufficient evidence to support these extraordinary beliefs. Few would seriously argue, however, that these doctrines are logically contradictory. Yet that is exactly the objection that many level against the doctrines of the Incarnation and the Trinity.

I will begin by briefly explaining what these doctrines assert and making clear the logical problems that are said to infect them; I'll then proceed to outline some responses that Christians can make to show these difficulties can be avoided. It must be noted at the outset that the burden of this chapter is not to provide arguments or reasons for thinking that Jesus Christ is God, and still less to provide evidences for the resurrection. The task of this chapter is to make clear a particular kind of objection to the logical consistency of the Incarnation and the Trinity, and to show how one might go about defending the coherence of these central christological claims.

Section I: The Doctrine of the Incarnation

What Does the Doctrine Claim?

Let's take the doctrine of the Incarnation first. Anyone who ever attended Sunday school knows that Christians claim that Jesus Christ is God's Son. While this claim is fine as far as it goes, it can readily be seen to be inadequate as a complete statement of what we believe about the person of Jesus Christ. The problem with this initial formulation of the Incarnation is that there is a sense in which all believers (indeed, many would say all *persons*) are children of God, and so for the doctrine to be informative, more must be said.

The Deity of Christ

We begin to get closer to the traditional understanding of the doctrine of the Incarnation if we alter slightly the Sunday school formula to read *Jesus Christ is God the Son.* This is an improvement for a couple of reasons. First, it suggests Christ's uniqueness in a way that the first formulation does not. Second, it says more about who Christ is in a way that explains this uniqueness. For we believe not only that Christ was God's Son; we believe that he was God. And in whatever sense the Christian is willing to affirm that you and I are "sons and daughters of God," it is not the same sense in which we affirm that Jesus is the "only begotten Son" of God.

As mentioned above, a part of what we mean when we call Jesus "the Son of God" is that Jesus is God, that he is divine. Yet we must tread carefully here. For it turns out that the logic of the claims *Jesus Christ is*

God and *Jesus Christ is God the Son* are rather different, and different in a way that matters, particularly in regards to the doctrine of the Trinity which we will discuss later in the chapter. In order to understand the way these claims diverge, one must see that the word "is" is functioning rather differently in them. Philosophers call the "is" in the sentence *Jesus Christ is God the Son* the "'is' of predication." This means, essentially, that what is referred to on the left side of the "is" has the property being referred to on the right side of the "is." So *The sky is blue, The dog is longhaired,* and *Mary is kind* are all examples that include an "is" of predication. In each case, the grammatical subject of the sentence refers to an object in the world and the predicate picks out an attribute that the sentence then claims the subject has.

In contrast to this is the "is" of identity. As it sounds, the role of this "is" is to assert an identity, that is, to claim that there is a single person or object that can be referred to in two ways. For example, in the sentences *Batman is Bruce Wayne* and *The Morning Star is Venus* the "is" should be understood as meaning "is the same thing as." The terms "Batman" and "Bruce Wayne" refer to one and the same object as do the terms "Morning Star" and "Venus."

With this distinction in hand, let's look again at the basic christological formulae *Jesus Christ is God* and *Jesus Christ is God the Son.* These two sentences can now be seen to be making very different, though complementary, claims. In the former sentence, the word "is" should be understood as an "is" of predication. To affirm that *Jesus is God* is to affirm his deity. He was not only human, not only superhuman, but he was and is God in the flesh.

On the other hand, *Jesus Christ is the Son of God* is an identity claim. It asserts that Jesus of Nazareth, the son of Mary, is the same person as God the Son, the eternal second person of the divine Trinity. Of course, in identifying Jesus with a divine person, we are implicitly affirming his deity. So there is a sense in which *Jesus Christ is the Son of God* expresses everything that *Jesus Christ is God* expresses and then some.

The Humanity of Christ

This understanding of *Jesus Christ is the Son of God* takes us about half way to an understanding of the doctrine of the Incarnation. Yet traditional Christianity makes a further claim about Jesus. Not only was he the same person as God the Son, he is also a human being — "truly man" in the language of the Chalcedonian Council of A.D. 451. Quoting from the council's *Definition of Faith*:

> [W]e all unanimously teach that we should confess that our Lord Jesus Christ is one and the same Son; the same perfect in Godhead and the same perfect in manhood, truly God and truly man . . . like us in all things except sin; begotten of the Father before all ages as regards his Godhead and in the last days the same, for us and for our salvation, begotten of the Virgin Mary. . . .[1]

It is important to note here that "truly man" should be taken at face value. The council wanted to adopt a statement that would confirm not only God the Son's bodily existence (as against the heretical Platonic sect known as the Gnostics) but also his complete humanity (as against the equally heretical Apollinarians who claimed that while Christ was God in the flesh, he was not fully human since he didn't have a human soul).

The doctrine of the Incarnation can be summed up as follows: *Jesus Christ, a human being, is identical to God the Son.*

Section II: The Incoherence Objection to the Incarnation

As we've seen, the fundamental christological statement is an identity claim: Jesus Christ is God the Son. As intended, this identity claim entails that there is a person who is fully God and fully human.

It is no wonder or great secret that the doctrine of the Incarnation has been considered a mystery or even a paradox. Yet there are those who insist that "mystery" or "paradox" is too generous and that the doctrine is downright contradictory. While to many ears the difference between mystery, paradox, and contradiction might seem negligible or "only semantic," to a philosopher the difference is crucial. The difference is this: a paradox or mystery can be thought of as a statement that seems on the face of it, either to contradict itself or to defy a full or complete explanation. However, a contradiction is not merely something that defies complete explanation or that *seems* contradictory. Rather, a contradiction is a statement that genuinely *is* contradictory. And a contradiction, as any logician will tell you, is by definition a proposition that can't possibly be true. For example, the

1. As quoted in Gerald Bray's *Creeds, Councils, and Christ* (Downers Grove: InterVarsity Press, 1984), 162.

proposition *This triangle has exactly four interior angles* is contradictory because it makes two claims, each of which is inconsistent with the other: viz., it asserts *This is a triangle* and *This has exactly four interior angles.*

Now since "this" in both sentences refers to the same object, and since a triangle is by definition an object with exactly three interior angles, *This has exactly four interior angles* entails that the same object has exactly three interior angles and exactly four interior angles. But nothing could be like that. Necessarily, any object that has exactly four interior angles does not have exactly three interior angles. So the original statement is contradictory and cannot possibly be true.

Many critics claim that an exactly similar problem infects the doctrine of the Incarnation. Here's why, in the words of an imaginary christological critic.

> If Jesus is "fully God" then he must have any feature of God that distinguishes God from creatures. Traditional Christian theology claims, for example, that one such feature is God's being the uncreated creator of the universe; being the uncreated creator of everything other than the Godhead is thought to be one of the characteristics of divinity. So, then, *if Jesus is fully God, he must be the uncreated creator.* But Christians also claim that Jesus did not just take on a human body, but that he is "fully human." Thus, the doctrine of the Incarnation entails that Jesus has all of the properties necessary for being completely human. Now Christians believe that humans are created entities, and it is plausible to think that on the Christian view, being created is a fundamental characteristic of humanity. So, then, *if Jesus is fully human, he must be created.* Now the contradiction is clear. For the Christian claims that Jesus is both God and human, and given what is said above, if he has these two natures, then he must be created and uncreated. But that is a contradiction.
>
> As bad as all of this is, things get even worse, since the same problem arises for many of the properties that the "God-man" must have. Take, for example, the pair of properties: *being omnipotent* and *possessing only finite power.* The former is required for divinity, the latter for humanity and yet, clearly, no being could have them both. To extend this list, one needs only to consult the table of contents from a text on the traditional Christian conception of God (among those attributes you will find omniscience, atemporality, aspatiality, necessity, and so forth). Any such property is, allegedly at least, necessary for divinity but incompatible with properties necessary for being human (limited knowledge, temporality, spatiality, and contingency).

Section III: Initial Responses to the Contradiction Charge

The charge of logical inconsistency is a serious one that calls for a thoughtful response. When confronted with objections to what we believe, Christians often retreat to slogans about "divine mystery." While there is no doubt that it is hubris of the first order to suppose that human cognitive powers are sufficient to the task of knowing the divine nature in its completeness, it is also irresponsible to fail to use the gift of intellect to understand, as best we are able, the God who is our maker. So what we shall do now is tackle straight-on the important objection detailed above and see what headway can be made.

Let's begin by granting our opponent a few of her points. We shall grant that contradictions are necessarily false, that *Jesus Christ is the uncreated Creator* and *Jesus Christ is created* are contradictory and hence that if the doctrine of the Incarnation entails them, then it is false. What we need, then, is an account of the Incarnation that allows us to say, with some consistency and, one would hope, plausibility, that while Jesus Christ *is* fully God and fully human, he *is not* both created and uncreated.

A First Response

Many Christians, when confronted with this challenge, offer a line of response that goes something as follows. They begin by noting that the explanation of the Incarnation with which we've been working, and which the imaginary critic above accepts, is incomplete. In particular, orthodox treatments of the Incarnation also include the following claim: *The Incarnate God/Jesus Christ has two distinct, unmingled natures (one divine, one human) but is a single person.* Unlike us (or for that matter, God the Father) the Incarnate God has two natures. As a result, any time we affirm that Christ has a certain characteristic we must say exactly which of the natures it is, the divine one or the human one, which "has" the characteristic. So if we say, for example, *Jesus Christ was thirsty* or *Jesus Christ was preexistent* we fail to make ourselves clear. What we really mean to be asserting is *With respect to his humanity, Jesus Christ was thirsty* or *With respect to his divinity, Jesus Christ was preexistent.*

With this in mind, the defender continues, we can see that the alleged contradiction (or set of contradictions) described above are not contradictions at all. For *Jesus Christ is created* and *Jesus Christ is uncreated* are each ambiguous. What the traditional Christian really means by them is *With respect to his humanity, Jesus Christ is created* and *With respect to his divinity, Jesus Christ is uncreated.* But now we no longer have the simple contradiction. For these properties are attributed to Jesus with respect to two different natures.

Compare what the Christian says about Jesus with a more ordinary case. Consider John, as we shall call him, who is six feet four inches tall and is a professional basketball player. John is also a member of the Sierra Club. At six feet four, John is short when compared with his NBA colleagues. But, of course, he rather stands above the crowd at meetings of the Sierra Club. Thus we can say that *With respect to NBA players, John is short* while at the same time affirming *With respect to Sierra Club members, John is tall* without any fear of contradiction. Notice that if the *With respect to . . .* clauses were removed, the sentences would be contradictory. However, once clarified, the apparent contradiction vanishes. Similarly, the apparent contradiction seen in *Jesus Christ is created* and *Jesus Christ is uncreated* disappears once the impact of the two-natures aspect of the doctrine of the Incarnation is fully appreciated.

Why the First Response Is Inadequate

Despite its initial attractiveness, the success of this reply is at best dubious. While the traditional understanding of the Incarnation does distinguish the divine and human natures of God Incarnate, it also insists on the unity of the person, and what's more, on there being a *single person* who has all the attributes or characteristics of God incarnate. What this means is that even if there are properties that Christ has with respect to his being human and other properties are had with respect to his being divine, the properties nevertheless belong to a single person. For example, if in virtue of being a professor, Richard has an obligation to spend the weekend preparing for his Monday afternoon seminar, and in virtue of being a father, Richard has an obligation to go on a Boy Scout camp-out with his son, it is nevertheless true that Richard (and not just *Richard with respect to being a professor*) has an obligation to prepare for class and that Richard (and not just *Richard with respect to being a father*) has an obligation to go camping. The conflict here is real and can't be disregarded because they are had in virtue of different roles Richard has. Similarly, Christ's being uncreated with respect to his divinity and created with respect to his humanity wouldn't appear to change the fact that, on this view, he is both created and uncreated. So the problem persists.

But what about the example of John? He is a "single object of predication" and yet the sentences *With respect to NBA players, John is short* and *With respect to Sierra Club members, John is tall* both say something true about him, even though, purged of their *With respect to . . .* clauses, they would be contradictory. So what is going on here?

The answer is that terms like "short" and "tall" are *relative* terms in a way that "being created" and "being uncreated creator" are not. Whenever we assert that someone is tall, we (implicitly, at least) have in mind some group with whom we are comparing that person. When a term is relative, that term can apply to a person with respect to a particular group and the term's opposite can apply with respect to another group. But there are other attributes that are *not* relative and which, if had by a person, entail that the person does not have the "opposite" property. For example, if John is six feet four inches tall, he can't also be not six feet four inches tall since *being of a certain height* is not a relative property. Again, whether a swimming pool that is seventy-two degrees Fahrenheit is warm or cold is relative; but its *being seventy-two degrees Fahrenheit* is not. In the same way, the properties of being created and of being uncreated are not relative properties. And so the same maneuver that shows that seemingly contradictory sentences which ascribe relative properties to a person are noncontradictory cannot be used to defend the Incarnation against the incoherence charge. So it seems that this solution fails.

A Second Response

What, then, can the believer say to the objector? Well, the first thing to do when faced with an apparent contradiction is to take a close look at the relevant propositions to make sure that they are genuinely contradictory. But this is precisely what we just tried, and despite our efforts, the contradiction remains. Where does this leave us? Well, it means that we can't affirm both *Jesus Christ is created* and *Jesus Christ is uncreated* since they are in contradiction. Is this a cause for alarm?

That depends. We have big christological problems if we are forced to say that the doctrine of the Incarnation implicitly harbors a contradiction; since contradictions can't be true, we will then be forced to say that this key Christian claim is false. And we have seen a line of reasoning to the effect that the doctrine of the Incarnation entails both that Jesus Christ was created and that he was uncreated. So what we must do is reconsider that line of reasoning.

The trouble, of course, is that the line of reasoning looks to be cogent. The argument is that if Jesus Christ is fully God and fully human, then he must have all of the properties required for divinity and for humanity. But no one can be God who isn't the creator; and no one can be human who isn't created. Therefore, if Jesus Christ is fully God and fully human, then he must be created and uncreated. But that's a contradiction, and since anything that leads by sound reasoning to a contradiction is false, the doctrine of the Incarnation is false.

Two crucial claims of the above argument are: *Being divine entails being uncreated* and *Being human entails being created.* If either of these premises can be shown to be false or even dubious, then the particular objection we are now considering will have been defused. And if this strategy can be applied elsewhere (e.g., with respect to parallel claims about omnipotence/limited power), we might have the means to resolve the general logical problems thought to infect the doctrine of the Incarnation. More on this shortly.

Section IV: The Incarnation Defended

Now it is clear enough, I think, that traditional Christian theology commits the Christian to accepting that being uncreated is part of the essence of God. It is impossible that any being should be both God and yet created. For if he is created by another, then he is dependent on the creative activity of that being, and the existence of God can never depend on what another agent does. So I think we must agree with the objector that *Jesus Christ is uncreated* is a claim the Christian must accept.

What about the other half of the troublesome pair? Must a Christian affirm that *Jesus Christ is created?* I think the best argument for *Jesus Christ is created* is this: *Being created or caused to exist by another* is part of the very meaning of the term *human being.* While it is not easy to offer a complete and satisfactory definition of *human being,* we know that it will include *being created, being limited in knowledge and power, being in time and space,* etc. So the proposition *A human being is created* is what philosophers call "analytic" (meaning that the meaning of the predicate concept is contained in the meaning of the subject concept).

On the face of it, this is a strong argument. It certainly must be conceded that if a part of the meaning of being human is *being created,* then it is impossible for Jesus to be human and be uncreated. So if we are to resist this argument for Christ's being created, we must deny that *being created* is part of the meaning of *being human*. And, looking down the road a bit, we'll also have to deny that *being limited in knowledge and power*, for example, are part of its meaning.

But can the Christian accept this (seemingly radical) claim that a human being can be uncreated, unlimited in power, etc.? Two considerations might make us think not. First, she might think that Christian theology requires her to accept these definitional assertions (that is, for example, that *being created* is part of the concept of *being human*). Second, she might not think that there are theological constraints but that there are broader constraints of rationality. She might think that it is irrational for anyone, Christian or not, to deny that *being created* is part of the meaning of *being human*, just as it would be irrational to think that *possesses three interior angles* is not part of the meaning of *being triangular*.

I know of no good reason for thinking that traditional Christian theology commits one to anything at all regarding the meaning of *humanity*. As we've noted, the Christian will think that humanity was brought about and sustained by the creative power of God, and she'll undoubtedly have many other beliefs about humanity (e.g., that humans are made in the image of God, saved through the death and resurrection of Christ and that humans should treat one another as they'd like to be treated), but these won't be beliefs about the content of the concept.

An Important Distinction

At this point it will be useful to note another philosopher's distinction. Some concepts are called *cluster concepts*. A cluster concept is one that has as its content other concepts and only other concepts. For example, the concept *bachelor* includes the concept *being male*, *being adult*, and *being unmarried*. To use the language of a few paragraphs ago, the propositions *All bachelors are male*, *All bachelors are adults*, and *All bachelors are unmarried* are all analytic. Cluster concepts, then, are exhausted by the content of the concepts they contain. Any analytic proposition will be the unpacking of a part of the cluster of the concept.

Not all concepts are cluster concepts. Consider, for example, the concept *tiger*. A tiger can't be defined, for example, as a four-legged feline with black stripes and a tail indigenous to tropical climes. For a tiger missing a leg is no less a tiger. And zoologists might well discover a species of tiger that is native to deserts or that has no tail. Even if it were to turn out that all varieties of tigers ever discovered have tails, it wouldn't follow that nothing without a tail could be a tiger. In short, tigers are zoological kinds and questions about what tigers could be like while still being tigers are best left not to the linguist or philosopher but to the zoologist or biologist. The concept of a tiger is a *natural kind concept.*

Above, I argued that there was nothing in traditional doctrine that would require the Christian to say that the concept of *humanity* includes the concept of *being created.* But now we can see that not only is there nothing in Christian doctrine that requires this, but that a careful look at the concept *humanity* makes it clear that it includes nothing of the sort.

The reason is that *humanity* is best construed not as a cluster concept, like *bachelor,* but as a natural kind concept, like *tiger.* Whether or not *humanity* just is a natural kind will be a matter of controversy. Arguably, part of what it is for something to be a natural kind is for it to be the kind of thing whose nature can be understood by the natural sciences. Now if humans are purely biological creatures, then we are natural kinds. However, if mind/body dualism is true and we have immaterial souls, then there will be an important part of human nature that will be outside the domain of the empirical natural sciences.

Regardless of how this particular issue turns out, once we see that to be human is to be a member of a kind that is intrinsic to the created order and not merely a product of the way our language and concepts have developed (as would seem to be the case with cluster concepts like *bachelor* and *triangle*), we can see that the essence of human nature is not to be determined by philosophers sitting in armchairs and analyzing the meanings of words or concepts. Rather, our theory of human nature (our *philosophical anthropology,* as it is sometimes called) will have to be informed by our best science and our basic worldview with which we are working.

Applying the Distinction to the Incoherence Objection

With this in mind, we can then ask why the Christian should affirm that *Jesus Christ is created.* The doctrine of the Incarnation asserts that God the Son was preexistent and took on human nature. Jesus Christ, the human being, is God the Son. That means that Jesus Christ wasn't created. Notice that this is consistent with saying that both Christ's particular human body and the human nature he assumed were created. So there are truths in the near neighborhood but they don't logically imply that Christ was created. And once we see that one can't simply infer *X is created* from

X is human in the same way one can infer *X is trilinear* from *X is a triangle,* there is no longer an obvious reason for accepting this that *Jesus Christ is created.*

Similar moves can be made for most of the other logical problems involving the Incarnation. For example, being omnipotent, or maximally powerful, is required for divinity; and it is often thought that being limited in power is necessary for being human. But, again, the primary reason for insisting on this is the mistaken assumption that *by definition* a human is limited in power. Once we've seen that this isn't true, the primary reason for believing that this limitation property is required for being human is undercut.

This general reply to the incoherence charge is made even more plausible by noting a useful distinction between *common* and *essential* human properties. A *common* human property is a property that all or almost all humans have; an *essential* human property is a property that anything must have to be human. Consider the example of being born on Earth. Every human being, we may presume, who has ever existed has had this property. Yet it certainly isn't required for being human: even if it never happens, it is surely possible that someday a human baby will be born on a space station or on the moon. If this is even possible, then we know that having a terrestrial birth is not essential for being human. The Christian can plausibly maintain that the limitation properties that are often thought to be essential to human nature are rather only common. And it is an easy mistake to think that because a given property or characteristic is had by every human then it is *essential* for being human. But such is not the case.

The underlying idea is that while the Christian, as a Christian, is committed to the truth of certain claims about God and about what is essential for divinity, she is under no such pressure, as a Christian or as even just as a rational, educated person, to make general claims about what is essential or required for being human.

Two Pitfalls to Be Avoided

a. Pitfall One: "In Every Way Like Us . . ."

This strategy does well in getting around the logical difficulties the doctrine of the Incarnation is said to have. However, the Christian must tread carefully here. For even if the reply we've been articulating allows her to affirm an orthodox christology without the threat of logical inconsistency, she must be careful to avoid two further pitfalls: first, she might have cause to worry that the model of the Incarnation we now have is one that stresses the divinity at the expense of the humanity of Christ. The concept of humanity is the one that we found to have suitable flexibility, and so the properties that are in logical tension with the properties of divinity were compromised. The potential problem, then, is that while the malleability that we found in the concept of *humanity* might allow us to affirm the divinity and humanity of Christ, we might end up with an account of the Incarnation in which the Incarnate God's ability to share our condition, to "know it from the inside" as it were, is seriously imperiled. For example, if Jesus had the omniscient mind of God, we might wonder in what sense his humanity was anything like ours. After all, whatever exactly the divine mental life is like, it's a safe bet that it is strikingly different than ours. Besides, we must be careful not to fall into the heresy of Apollinarius, viz., that Jesus was the divine soul in a human body. To be fully human requires having not just a human body but a human mind as well. So we must affirm both that Christ was omniscient and that he had the mind of a human.

b. Pitfall Two: "I Know Not the Day or the Hour . . ."

The second pitfall to be avoided is that of incompatibility with the Gospel accounts of the life of Christ. The Gospels themselves portray Christ as claiming that he doesn't know the date of the Second Coming, that it is known only to the Father.[2] Yet omniscience, by definition, requires knowing everything there is to know. So it would seem that the strategy discussed above won't work where God the Son's knowledge is concerned.

Two Strategies for Avoiding the Pitfalls

a. Kenoticism

There are two options open to the Christian to meet these concerns. The first of these is actually a more general strategy for dealing with the incoherence charge. There is a theological tradition known as *kenoticism* that takes its name from the Greek word *kenosis,* which means "self-

2. Matthew 24:36.

emptying." The scriptural starting point for this view can be found at Philippians 2:5-11 where Christ is said to have given up his divine position in order to take on our nature. A kenotic theology would handle the tricky matters we are now considering by maintaining that the preexistent second Person of the Trinity, God the Son, gave up his position and certain features of divine existence in order to take on humanity. Among those things he emptied himself of was his omniscience. And any other characteristic that would have prevented him from living fully human life would have also been surrendered, at least for the duration of his earthly mission.

Although the kenotic strategy is attractive, it is also problematic. The chief difficulty is this: if God the Son *gives up* or *empties himself* of many of the divine attributes, how can we continue to hold that he is *fully* God? On the contrary, it appears that in giving up or emptying himself of these divine qualities *he gives up his divinity*. Remember that christological orthodoxy requires not only that we say that Jesus Christ is identical to the preexistent God the Son, but that he is *fully* God as well as fully man. The chief concern for the kenoticist is to demonstrate the consistency of her view with the claim that during his earthly ministry, Jesus was fully divine. Still, there is something initially attractive and plausible about the kenotic position and one must not underestimate its potential to answer objections such as this.[3]

b. The Two-Minds View

The second way of avoiding the aforementioned pair of pitfalls is to attribute to the Incarnate God two minds, one human and one divine. The divine mind is omniscient, while the human mind contains limited knowledge of the sort common to first-century Jews (and it might also have contained false beliefs that would have been typical of humans living in that place and time). Similarly, one might eschew talk of two distinct minds and attempt to model Christ's knowledge after his power. Presumably, the Incarnate Christ possessed the omnipotence of God but, in most instances, refrained from exercising more power than would have been exercised by an average human. In the same way, it can be suggested that

3. In his essay "Reconsidering Kenotic Christology" (in *Trinity, Incarnation and Atonement,* ed. Ronald J. Feenstra and Cornelius Plantinga, Jr. [Notre Dame: Notre Dame University Press, 1989], 128-52), Ronald J. Feenstra considers objections such as this and tries to show that kenoticism has the resources to answer them.

his taking on humanity, including a human mind, required the masking of his divine knowledge. Just as contemporary psychology suggests that much of what goes on in the human mind goes on below the conscious surface, one might suppose that taking on humanity required Christ's consciousness to be similar to ours but that below the conscious surface there existed the omniscient mind of God. Of course, this wouldn't mean that Jesus was limited to only the contents of his human mind. For God the Father could have chosen to allow the earthly mind to have more or less access to the contents of the divine mind, as might be necessary for completion of his ministry on earth.[4]

I am aware of how presumptuous all of this can sound. Who are you, one might ask, to pretend to know these sorts of facts about the Incarnation? My defense is this: I am *not* maintaining that I *know* that these claims about the cognitive features of the Incarnation are true, nor even that I am justified in believing them. But why then, one might wonder, are we doing this? Here it is helpful to remind ourselves about what it is we are doing here. An objector has argued that the Incarnation is incoherent. Above, I have sketched out some of the responses that have been defended by Christian philosophers recently. Some of these accounts seem to be open to theological objections. In response to these I have set out a model which shows us how we might conceive of the Incarnation. I don't claim to know that this model is true. I do claim, however, that (i) it is consistent with our general strategy for dealing with the logical problems the doctrine of the Incarnation allegedly possesses, (ii) it is consistent with the full humanity of Christ and the biblical record, and (iii) we have no good reason to think it is false. I am making no claims to have demonstrably *proven* anything; I maintain only that the reply I've given to the logical incoherence objection is sufficient to blunt the charge as stated. The ball is back in the objector's court.

Section V: The Doctrine of the Trinity

It is not possible to have a deep or even adequate understanding of the Incarnation without having some conception of the doctrine of the Trinity.

4. Thomas V. Morris has defended the "two minds" view of the Incarnation in chapter six of his book, *The Logic of God Incarnate* (Ithaca: Cornell University Press, 1986).

We've seen that the former doctrine asserts that Jesus Christ is identical to God the Son. But who is that? Although this hasn't yet been mentioned, there is a terrific difference between the claims *Jesus Christ is God the Son* and *Jesus Christ is God.* We will see later why the latter is problematic. For now, though, simply note that the former makes a rather more specific kind of claim, a claim about God the Son.

Oversimplifying a bit, we can say for starters that the doctrine of the Trinity is the claim that *God is three persons and yet one*. An initial difficulty with this formulation is that it invites the reading that God is one and yet three *of the same thing.* But that is not the genuine content of the doctrine. Rather, the traditional understanding is that God is three *persons* and one *substance*. Christians maintain that they are monotheists (rather than tri-theists) because they assert a single divine substance. The three persons of the Trinity are God the Father, God the Son, and God the Holy Spirit.

We will have to say more about the content of this doctrine as we discuss the puzzles it generates, but for a second pass we can characterize its content as: *The Godhead is three persons (God the Father, God the Son, and God the Holy Spirit) and yet a single substance.*

It might go without saying that this has been an exceedingly quick and cursory description of a complex and much-debated doctrine. But since this chapter is primarily about the logical issues generated by these doctrines, it has been necessary to keep the discussion brief. We move now to a consideration of the logical difficulties raised by the doctrine of the Trinity.

Section VI: The Incoherence Objection to the Trinity

In many ways, the logical oddity of the doctrine of the Trinity is more readily apparent. Superficially, it looks like the Christian makes the following set of claims about God: *The Father is God, The Son is God, The Holy Spirit is God.* This, by itself, doesn't cause problems. For suppose that a certain person, Susan, is (a) the oldest daughter of Millie, (b) the mother of Calvin, and (c) the wife of Tim. We can then assert the following three things: *The oldest daughter of Millie is Susan, The mother of Calvin is Susan,* and *The wife of Tim is Susan.*

Since it looks like we might apply a similar strategy in the case of the Trinity, one might wonder what the problem is. It will begin to become clear if you think for a minute about what follows from these three claims about Susan (we will call these the "Susan triad"). If the three statements composing the Susan triad are true, then the oldest daughter of Millie is the wife of Tim and the mother of Calvin is the oldest daughter of Millie. (Math enthusiasts can note that the "transitivity of identity" is what allows us to draw these inferences.) The problem with the trinitarian triad is that they represent only a part of what the Christian says about the Godhead. In addition, she insists that the Father and Son are *not identical,* the Son and the Spirit are *not identical,* and that the Father and the Spirit are *not identical.* It appears to be just as if one were to grant that Susan is the mother of Calvin and that Susan is the wife of Tim but then deny that the mother of Calvin is identical to (i.e., is the same person as) the wife of Tim. Inasmuch as that would be contradictory, the critic asserts, so is it contradictory to make the trinitarian claims above but deny the identity of the Father, Son, and Spirit.

Section VII: Responding to the Trinitarian Critic

The logical issues surrounding the Incarnation and those surrounding the Trinity are different enough that the response we've offered to the critic of the Incarnation will not work here.

As we have seen, the problem is that the Christian makes a set of claims which apparently imply that the Father, Son, and Spirit are identical. However, the orthodox understanding of the Trinity denies the identity of the persons while insisting that the three are yet "one God." So the trick is to find a way of explaining the doctrine that keeps the three persons *distinct* while maintaining the *unity* of the Godhead.

The Heretical Extremes: Modalism and Tritheism

A good way to begin this discussion is to get a clear view of just what a fine line it is the Christian theologian must follow if she wants to walk the straight and narrow of trinitarian orthodoxy. This can be seen by considering a couple kinds of explanation of the Trinity that were labeled as heresies by early Church councils. First, consider *modalism.* The modalist explained the Trinity by stressing the underlying unity or oneness of God. The Father, Son, and Spirit, the modalist claims, correspond to different modes or manifestations of the divine. The Incarnate God the Son, on this view, is the same being and person as God the Father. The difference is only in the way that he has manifested himself. This view was condemned as heresy because, while it clearly avoided the charge of polytheism, it failed to do justice to the plurality of persons.

The ditch on the other side of the narrow path of orthodoxy is *tritheism*. A view that stresses the diversity of persons at the expense of the unity of the Godhead will be in danger of polytheism.

Recall that in our initial discussion of doctrines of the Incarnation and Trinity, we made a distinction between the "is" of identity and the "is" of predication. If we now think back to the initial trinitarian triad (i.e., *The Father is God, The Son is God, The Holy Spirit is God*), we can see that we have been treating these claims as *identity* statements. And from this it seems to follow that the Father, the Son, and the Spirit are all the same *person* (something the doctrine of the Trinity forces us to deny). Notice, however, that this troubling consequence follows from the statements *The Son is God* and *The Holy Spirit is God* that *The Son is the Holy Spirit* only if the "is" in these sentences is read as signifying identity. We can easily see that the same bad consequence does not follow if these are "predication" statements, in just the way we can see that *John is human* and *Graham is human* don't together entail that John and Graham are the same person.

So the first point of clarification that the Christian apologist will make is to note that the relevant sentences (i.e., *The Father is God, The Son is God,* and *The Holy Spirit is God*) do not, as one might have first thought, include the "is" of identity but merely the "is" of predication. Another way of stating our trinitarian triad is *The Father is divine, The Son is divine, The Holy Spirit is divine*. This adjustment resolves the logical difficulties for it no more follows from, say, *The Son is God* and *The Father is God* that *The Father is the Son* than it follows from the earlier example that John is Graham.

It would be premature, however, to think that this resolves the problem satisfactorily. Here's the reason: for all we've said so far, the Father, Son, and Spirit are no more one than are any three human beings in virtue of their common humanity. That is to say, if we leave things as we've stated them, we may seem to have fallen prey to the heresy of tritheism since the only sense in which the three are one is that they are each divine, and that is a very thin sense of oneness.

We can now get a sense of the trickiness of this doctrine. For it seems that to the extent that the distinctness of divine persons is stressed, one falls into tritheism. On the other hand, emphasis on the unity of the Godhead threatens to bring with it the heresy of modalism.

Before saying more about how the Trinity might be understood in a way that avoids at least the deepest parts of both ditches, let's make a rather simple, straightforward logical point. Indeed, this rough-and-ready response has been hinted at before, but it is time to make it fully explicit.

One sometimes hears the objection to the Trinity that we've been considering in a far more basic form, to wit:

> Christians say that God is three and yet one. But *nothing* can be both three things and exactly one thing — that is logically incoherent. So the doctrine of the Trinity is logically incoherent.

To this objection, there is a quick and easy solution. When the creeds say that God is three and yet one, they should not be understood as asserting that God is three and one *of the same thing*. That would be contradictory and obviously so. Rather, what is being claimed is that there is an important unity in the Godhead as well as plurality.

Suppose you go into a store to buy some soft drinks for your family. When you return, the kids say, "How many did you get?" You respond, "Six cokes; one six-pack." There is a perfectly clear sense in which what you bought was "six and yet one." Even so, it is clear that if we said that you had bought exactly six and exactly one of the same thing, we'd be saying something foolish and contradictory. What you bought was one *six-pack* and six *cans of soda*.

Fortunately for the sake of orthodoxy, the traditional understanding of the Trinity recognizes the point we are making. As we've seen earlier, the doctrine asserts that there are three *persons* and one *substance,* not that there are three Gods and exactly one God. So it is not open to the simple and common objection of blatant inconsistency.

Still, it cannot be doubted that, as traditionally understood, the creed asserts both a trinity of persons and a fundamental unity, one that makes the charge of tritheism a misunderstanding. So we need some kind of account of divine oneness that allows for a plurality of persons but which provides an underlying unity.

A Trinitarian Model: Plurality in Unity

Here is a way of understanding the Trinity which seems to capture what is essential to the claim of the unity of the Godhead while permitting three distinct persons to dwell therein. It should be kept in mind that I am not offering the following as a model I am convinced is true. I believe, with almost everyone else who has ever thought about the matter, that the doctrine of the Trinity is deeply mysterious. And that seems fully appropriate, since this doctrine concerns the metaphysics of the nature of God and it would be hubris of the highest degree for us to suppose our minds were capable of understanding the divine essence. The point in our offering this model is to indicate that good sense can be made of the notion of God as "three in one." While I have no wish to attempt to *demonstrate* anything about the nature of the Godhead, I do want to defend the *coherence* of the doctrine and one way of doing that is by offering a model according to which it can be understood.

Plurality

Let's begin with the plurality. There are three persons in the Trinity: Father, Son, and Holy Spirit. As three persons, we presume that there are three centers of will and cognition. Each has a distinct function within the Godhead. Being divine, none of the three persons is created; all are eternal. Also, because of his divinity, each person has all the attributes necessary for deity.

But in what sense are the three one? It is not enough that they are one in the same way that three humans are one in virtue of their all being human. Were this all the divine oneness comes to, the charge of tritheism would be legitimate.

In Unity

Many Christians are unaware of the fact that part of the traditional doctrine of the Trinity includes the claim that there are central relations among the members of the Trinity.[5] Some of the traditional ways that have been suggested for seeing the divine Trinity as one are the following. The relationship between the Father and the Son is said to be one of *eternal generation. Eternal* because there is no temporal priority; the Father

5. A helpful introductory discussion of the doctrine of the Trinity (and many other doctrines of interest) can be found in Alister E. McGrath's *Christian Theology: An Introduction*, 2nd ed. (Cambridge, MA: Blackwell Publishing Co., 1997), chapter 8.

did not exist before the Son. Each is coeternal. *Generation* is also a term carefully chosen. Historically, the use of this term was to insist that the Son is the same kind of being (i.e., divine) as the Father, as against those who claimed that the Son or "Logos" (the term of choice for some early theologians) was *created,* which would have implied that he was of a different kind than the Father.

The Holy Spirit is said to *proceed from* the Father and the Son, once again to insist that the Spirit, like the Father and the Son, is eternal and divine.[6]

What is important to note here is that while there are three coeternal divine Persons, these Persons are said to bear *fundamental metaphysical* ties to each other, much closer ties than those held between member of the same species. For example, the idea of the eternal generation of the Son from the Father suggests an atemporal process, or at least an eternal process underlying the being of the Son at every moment. The procession of the Spirit from the Father and Son together has the same implications.

So one fundamental difference is apparently this: the Father, Son, and Spirit are ontologically united. The existence of any of these persons is logically sufficient for the existence of all three. Put another way, the unity of the Trinity is grounded in necessary relations between the three persons. This means that it is simply not possible for one of the three to exist independently from the other two. Such strong relations between members of the Trinity are certainly not found between any created beings. For even though, at least on certain plausible views, the existence of Mary requires the prior existence of Mary's parents (that is, it is essential to Mary that she be born of her parents rather than any two other people), she is nevertheless quite capable of continuing to exist after their deaths.

So one way in which the relation of the persons of the Trinity is tighter than the relation of humans to each other is that the existence of any one divine person is impossible without the existence of the other two. Still, one might think that this amounts only to claiming that the three are in some way mutually dependent, but not that they are in any significant way *one.*

Yet more can be said regarding their unity. And to see this, let's consider an objection to something I've said so far. Traditional Christian theology claims that each of the persons of the Trinity is divine, i.e., each has

6. This is so according to the traditional creeds of Western Christendom. According to the Eastern church, the Spirit proceeds from the Father only.

the properties necessary for being God. But that means that each is omnipotent. Yet, how, it might be asked, could there exist more than one omnipotent being? For to be omnipotent requires, among other things, being at least as powerful as anything else that exists. Suppose, then, that there are two omnipotent beings, A and B, and that A plans to see to it that a certain event, X, comes to pass and B plans to see to it that X not come to pass. Now, either X will come to pass or it won't. If it does, then B, who attempted to prevent X, is not omnipotent. On the other hand, if X doesn't come to pass, then A, who attempted to make sure that X came about, is not omnipotent. So perhaps talk about more than one omnipotent person is logically inconsistent.

Necessarily Harmonious Wills

This difficulty depends upon the "coming apart" of the wills of the two allegedly omnipotent beings. Suppose, however, that these two beings have *necessarily harmonious wills.* To have wills like this requires not only that these beings never in fact have a conflict of will, but that they never *could have a conflict of wills.* This isn't to say that their wills are always necessarily the *same.* To have harmonious wills requires only that there are fundamental areas of agreement of will and no areas of disagreement. So imagine a couple, Steve and Jenny. They both will to have a child. Suppose that Jenny doesn't care much about the style of their child's hair or clothes. But she does care about the layout and organization of the nursery and that the baby be breast-fed for the first four months of her life. Steve, on the other hand, doesn't have any real views on breast-feeding or the nursery but is quite particular about the child's wardrobe and hair (when she gets some, that is). Now, the situation I've described is one in which two people have harmonious wills. For there is overlap (they both wanted to have a child) and there are no areas of disagreement.

Still, Steve's and Jenny's wills are harmonious, but not necessarily so. They can and will have their conflicts. But the suggestion regarding the Trinity is that their wills are necessarily aligned so that there is no chance of disagreement. This isn't to say, though, that their wills are identical, only that there is fundamental agreement and a lack of conflict. Now if this were necessarily so, if it is impossible that disagreement arise, then the argument against more than one omnipotent being that we considered above, is irrelevant, depending as it does on conflict of will.

So the Christian can offer a model of the Trinity according to which there are three persons, each having a will, power, and full-range of cognitive faculties, but which also emphasizes necessary relations between them, of being and of will, in which their unity consists. This model, or ones like it, have been labeled by some "social trinitarianism" as it seems to emphasize the triune nature rather than the unity of the Trinity. It should be noted, however, that the Christian who accepts a model similar to that sketched above should not be taken as insisting that that is *all* the unity of the three persons consists in. Rather, she should be understood as claiming that it is *at least* that. The sort of unity that the social trinitarian model suggests is surely significant, but the three may be related in ways that we've yet to conceive.

Section VIII: Conclusion

I have not been trying to take away the sense of mystery that accompanies these important Christian doctrines. I believe these doctrines to express truths of such a high order that our minds will certainly never capture them this side of eternity and may never clearly see them even when we are no longer looking through a glass darkly. What I have attempted to dispel is not mystery but only the charge of logical inconsistency. So I end with the reminder that my only claim for the models of the Incarnation and the Trinity that I have been sketching here is that they are not logically contradictory and they are in general agreement with the historical understandings of these fundamental doctrines of the church.

11

The Resurrection of the Body and the Life Everlasting

Trenton Merricks

But your dead will live; their bodies will rise. You who dwell in the dust, wake up and shout for joy. Your dew is like the dew of the morning; the earth will give birth to her dead.

Isaiah 26:19

I. Introduction

Those who accept the closing line of the Apostles' Creed believe in "the resurrection of the body and the life everlasting." Similarly, the Nicene Creed closes with "I look for the resurrection of the dead, and the life of the world to come. Amen." The Athanasian Creed tells us that, at Christ's coming, "All men shall rise again with their bodies." Below I will present and discuss some of the central passages in the Bible that deal with the resurrection. The Christian tradition has always affirmed — in addition to the resurrection of Jesus Christ — the resurrection and victory over death of all believers.

There are puzzling philosophical questions associated with this doctrine. Consider, for example, the resurrection of the believer whose body was cremated, and whose ashes were then spread on the four winds. Does God gather all the ashes together and *then* resurrect the body? What if some of the ashes were, after death but before that Great Day, annihilated? And does it even make sense to say that one gets the *same,* the *original,* body back on the Day of Resurrection, while at the same time saying that one's body is *changed* and glorified?

Even if these questions can be answered, another, more fundamental question remains. What, if anything, does the resurrection of the body have to do with eternal life? I think that most Christians (indeed, most people) think of themselves as souls — nonphysical, spiritual entities — that inhabit bodies. Most Christians believe that when their *bodies* are placed in the grave, *they* are not. They are souls, and while their bodies may be buried in the ground at their death, they are off to be with God. Absent from the body, present with the Lord. (In support of this view, one might cite near-death experiences of "leaving one's body behind" as one proceeds down a dark tunnel to a light at the far end.) If all this is correct, then life after death is possible, indeed actually occurs, without a body. Why, then, do the creeds and some scriptures seem to mention our hope for everlasting life and our hope for resurrection in the same breath?

The goal of this chapter is to address these sorts of questions. Of course, this will not show that the doctrines of the resurrection and the life everlasting are *true.* I think that we know this only by way of scripture. But it will help us to *defend* these doctrines against objections rooted in the puzzles we will discuss. And, more importantly, it should help us to have a deeper understanding of what it is we believe when we believe in the resurrection and the life of the world to come.

II. Immortality and Personal Identity over Time

> *It is a serious thing to live in a society of possible gods and goddesses, to remember that the dullest and most uninteresting person you can talk to may one day be a creature which, if you saw it now, you would be strongly tempted to worship, or else a horror and a corruption such as you now meet, if at all, only in nightmare.*
>
> C. S. Lewis, "The Weight of Glory"

Let's begin, not with questions of my (presumably) far-off post-resurrection existence in glory, but with my comparatively recent *past* existence as a little child. When I was one year old, I had a different personality and different beliefs, memories, attitudes, desires, and opinions from those I now have. Not only was I different psychologically, but I was different physically: I was shaped differently, had a different height and weight, had less hair, and so on. Merricks of today is vastly different from Merricks as a one-year-old child. Yet there is, of course, only one person in question. That is why I can truthfully assert such commonplaces as "I was once a one-year-old child." In other words, I am the *same person* as the one-year-old child in question. Yet because of the great differences between the way I am and the way the child was, I am *not the same person* as that child.

Despite initial appearances, there is no contradiction here. There is, instead, an *ambiguity* in the expression "is the same person as." Compare: "There is a bank beside the James River" and "There is not a bank beside the James River." If the word "bank" means riverbank in the first sentence, but financial institution in the second, then these sentences — because "bank" is ambiguous — do not contradict each other.

Sometimes we use the expressions "is the same person as" and "is not the same person as" when we are comparing the way a person is at one time to the way that (same!) person is at another. This is what is going on if one says, for example, "she is not the same person she was before she became famous." This does not mean that one person literally ceased to exist and was replaced by a new (and famous) person. What is normally meant by sentences like "she is not the same person she was before she became famous" is that the person in question used to have certain salient and central qualities or features, and now has very different qualities or features. So perhaps she was friendly and approachable before becoming famous, but now is aloof and distant. And, conversely, when we say "he's just the same person he was in college" we mean that the way he was in college is, in important respects, very much like the way he is now. Because this sort of sameness is a sameness in a person's features or "qualities," it is called "qualitative sameness" or "qualitative identity."

But we do not always use the expressions "is the same person as" and "is not the same person as" in this way. For instance, suppose the prosecuting attorney asks you in court whether the man being tried is the same person that you saw rob the bank. It would not do to think to yourself "well, while robbing the bank he was friendly and approachable, but now he is aloof and distant" and then to answer "no."

The reason this would not do is that the prosecutor is *not* asking you whether the man before you now has undergone any deep and extensive changes; she is *not* asking about qualitative sameness. The prosecutor is asking about another sort of sameness associated with persons, the second sort of sameness associated with the expression "is the same person as." This sort of sameness is called "numerical sameness" or "numerical identity."[1] We presupposed facts of numerical sameness throughout the discussion of qualitative sameness. For example, in the case of the woman who became famous, we assumed that one person — the very same person — can undergo, over a stretch of time, change in qualities, such as a change from being approachable to being aloof.

We can now see that there is no contradiction in saying that, in one way, I am the same person as the one-year-old Merricks, but in another, not. All this means is that while I am numerically identical with that one-year-old — there is just one person in question — the qualities I had then are not the same as the qualities I have now.

Besides being used to refer to numerical and qualitative identity, there are a number of other ways that the expression "personal identity" is used in everyday conversation. For instance, we can imagine a great ballerina saying that if she could no longer dance, she would lose her "identity." Or we might say that an avid athlete's "identity" is all tied up in his ability to play sports. I once told a woman that I was writing an article on personal identity, and she began to explain to me how her husband strayed while trying to "find his identity." And when I made a comment about personal identity on another occasion, I was asked "How do you know that there is any personal identity? Is there really a self?"

So there are many ways in which the expressions 'identity" and "personal identity" are used in everyday English. And more than one of these might be relevant to our future existence in Heaven. One might argue that in Heaven, it matters to me not only that I exist, but that I exist with my "self" intact. (This is something people say — though I admit I'm not sure I understand what they mean by "self" in this context.) But no matter what else I want in Heaven, at least *part* of what I want is that someone there is numerically identical with me.[2] For it cannot be that *I*

1. This sort of sameness or identity is called "numerical" because it is associated with counting. For if the man who stands before you in court is numerically identical with the man who committed the crime, then there is only *one* man in question. If the accused man is not numerically identical with the guilty man, then there are *two* men in question — the accused and the guilty.

2. I think that it is obviously true that part of what one should want when one wants future survival is that someone numerically identical with oneself exists in the future. But this has been denied by Derek Parfit in "Personal Identity," *The Philosophical Review* 80 (1971): 3-27 and *Reasons and Persons* (Oxford: Oxford University Press, 1984), Part III. For my response to Parfit's arguments, see "Endurance, Psychological Continuity, and the Importance of Identity," *Philosophy and Phenomenological Research* (forthcoming).

have my self intact in Heaven if *I* am not there. Again, I cannot exist in Heaven complete with whatever other features matter to me unless, obviously, I exist in Heaven. And it is this last part — the future existence in Heaven of a person numerically identical with me — that I am concerned with here. Whenever I talk about personal identity over time (or, for short, personal identity) in this paper, I am talking about the numerical identity over time of a person.

There is more at stake here than mere terminology. For the point is not that I shall use the expression "personal identity" in a certain way. The point is that there are a number of separate, distinct topics that people sometimes mistakenly lump together, and I want to disentangle them. Progress has been made in our discussion if we can see that claims about qualitative sameness of a person, about numerical identity of a person, and about a person's "identity" being wrapped up in playing football are all *different* claims.

They are all different claims, but at least some of them are interrelated in interesting and important ways. For instance, a central philosophical question about numerical personal identity over time is just how much, and what kind of, qualitative change a person can experience. To see some of the issues involved here, ask yourself whether you think it is possible that *you* could continue to exist but turn into a single speck of dust. Most of us would say "no": you could not exchange all the features or qualities you now have for all the qualities of a speck of dust. So — although numerical sameness is not always threatened by qualitative differences — certain very special or very extreme qualitative differences seem to imply that you would cease to exist.

It seems that we cannot survive just any sort of qualitative change. But what is most interesting here, I think, is not the sort of changes that we *cannot* survive, but the deep and radical changes that we *can* and *do* survive. For instance, you were once a one-year-old child. (Even more strikingly, there is the fact — as I take it — that you were once a fetus.) So the answer to the question "can a person continue to exist through a process of radical and deep psychological and physical change?" is "yes." The proof is that you, yourself, have already done it.

It is part of the Christian hope that we will one day, in Heaven, be perfectly conformed to the image of Christ. We will one day actually be what it is we have been created to be. For all of us, this will involve deep and radical change. If you were able to "peer into the future" and see yourself as you will be millions of years from now, glorified and united with God, you would not, I imagine, recognize yourself. This might cause you to worry about how that person could really be *you*. But you should not worry. As a one-year-old child you would not, presumably, have been able to recognize yourself as you now are. As a one-year-old child, you could not have even *imagined* what it would be like to be the adult you now are. You could not have imagined, for example, many of the things that occupy your thoughts as an adult.

The promise of eternal life in Heaven is really two promises. The first is that we shall enjoy personal identity over time forever — far into the future, for ever and ever, there will always exist a person who is numerically identical with each one of us. In less complicated terminology, the first promise is simply that *we* shall exist for ever and ever. The second is that during our future existence, we shall undergo deep and even unimaginable changes — or, better, deep and even unimaginable improvements. These are the things we hope for when we hope for immortality. And our hopes make sense; they are coherent. For just as you can be numerically identical with someone who was once a one-year-old child, so you can be numerically identical with someone who will one day be ancient beyond imagining and glorious and holy.

III. Resurrection and Bodily Identity over Time

Where be all the splinters of that Bone, which a shot hath shivered and scattered in the Ayre? Where be all the Atoms of that flesh, which a Corrasive hath eat away, or a Consumption hath breath'd, and exhal'd away from our arms, or other Limbs? In what wrinkle, in what furrow, in what bowel of the earth, ly all the graines of the ashes of a body burnt a thousand years since? . . . One humour of our dead body produces worms, and those worms suck and exhaust all other humour, and then all dies, and all dries, and molders into dust, and that dust is blowen into the River, and that puddled water tumbled into the sea, and that ebs and flows in infinite revolutions, and still, still, God knows . . . in what part of the world every graine of every mans dust lies . . . he whispers, he hisses, he beckens for the bodies of his Saints, and in the twinckling of an eye, that body that was scattered over all the elements, is sate down at the right hand of God, in a glorious resurrection.

John Donne, "At the Earl of Bridgewater's House in London at the Marriage of his Daughter"

The topic of personal identity over time is really just one particular instance or example of a more general topic, that of (numerical) identity over time of *any* sort of thing. Since bodily identity over time and personal identity over time are both specific instances of the same overall topic — identity over time — we should not be surprised if some of the observations made in the previous section about personal identity were relevant to questions one might have about bodily identity over time. And they are. For instance, we can now answer directly one worry raised in the introduction: How can it be that I have this very body in the afterlife, if my body is to be glorified and made new? And how can one who is blind, lame, crippled, broken, weak, or hurting have *his* very same body in Heaven, if in Heaven he will be whole and healthy?

The answer here obviously turns on the general issue of numerical versus qualitative identity. There is no contradiction in saying that on Resurrection Day I will have the same body I now have, and, at the same time, saying that my body now is weak and flawed, but at resurrection my body will be perfect and glorified. There is no contradiction because when we say that one will have *the same* body at resurrection, we mean that one's current body is *numerically identical* with one's resurrection body. But when we say that one's resurrection body will *not be the same* as one's current body, but will be glorified, we mean that the way one's body will be at resurrection is *qualitatively different* from the way it is now.

We don't know much about the ways in which our resurrected bodies will differ from our bodies as they now are. And the few details we are given are subject to various interpretations. (There is, for example, notorious disagreement about what it means to say that the resurrected body will be "a spiritual body.") Perhaps all we really know for sure is that the way our bodies will be at resurrection is very different from the way they are now. Perhaps the way your body will be on Resurrection Day differs from the way your body is now as much as (or more than) the way your body is now differs from the way it was when you were a fetus. Perhaps the way your body will be at resurrection differs from the way your body is now as much as a fully mature plant differs from the way it was when it was only a seed.

We don't know the details about how our bodies, at resurrection, will differ from our bodies right now. All we really know is that they will be greatly qualitatively changed (and changed for the better!). Great qualitative change, as we have seen, is consistent with numerical identity. So we know of nothing at all in the promise of glorification that threatens your earthly body's identity with your resurrection body. And that is a good thing. For if *your* body (in other words, a body numerically identical with your body) does not rise glorified on the Day of Resurrection, then, obviously, your body will not be resurrected. Just as *personal* identity over time is crucial to immortality — if you are not numerically identical with a person who exists in Heaven in the distant future, then you do not have immortality — so *bodily* identity is crucial to resurrection.

One might object that our resurrection need *not* include getting the numerically same body back. For one might claim that a person is resurrected just so long as *some glorified body or other* comes into existence on the Day of Resurrection, and is then given to that person. If this claim were right, then on the Day of Resurrection, a person might not get her old body back at all, but rather a numerically distinct one. But there are two reasons that I think this claim is not right.

First, the overwhelming majority of theologians and philosophers in the history of the church have endorsed the claim of numerical identity. Historical debates surrounding the resurrection were over *how* (not whether) a dead earthly body would secure identity with a resurrection body. We'll look more closely at some of the issues in these debates below. But for now I want only to point out that those debates *presuppose* that the very same body that dies (and perishes) will rise again.[3] Theologians and philosophers throughout the history of the church presupposed this because — and this is the second reason I think the resurrected body and the earthly body are one — this seems to be what scripture teaches.

Why do I think scripture seems to teach this? Note that the Lord's resurrected body was numerically identical with his preresurrection body, the body that was crucified on the cross. At least, this seems to be the obvious conclusion to draw from the fact that after his resurrection, Jesus bore the scars of crucifixion. Christ's resurrection was the kind of resurrection we can all hope for; Christ's resurrection was the "firstfruits" of the general resurrection to come (1 Cor. 15:20). So each of us can expect that after his or her body dies, it too — that very body — will be resurrected.

In 1 Corinthians 15, Paul does affirm *qualitative* differences between the way our bodies are now and the way they will be at resurrection. But note also that Paul's way of presenting the qualitative differences implies that there is only one body in question; it implies the numerical

3. For a fascinating study of the history of views on the resurrection, see Caroline Walker Bynum's *The Resurrection of the Body in Western Christianity, 200-1336* (New York: Columbia University Press, 1995).

identity of the earthly body with its resurrection counterpart. Consider vv. 42-44:

> The body that is sown is perishable, it is raised imperishable; it is sown in dishonor, it is raised in glory; it is sown in weakness, it is raised in power; it is sown a natural body, it is raised a spiritual body.

Paul talks of "it" — the one body that is both sown and raised — not of "them," as he would were the earthly body numerically distinct from the resurrected one. It is no coincidence that the word "resurrection" has its roots in a Latin word which literally means to rise *again* — if the body that is resurrected is rising again, it has risen before, and so is not coming into existence for the first time on the Day of Resurrection.

The body you will be given at resurrection is none other than the body you have in this life. This claim seems to be supported by the Bible, and is about as historically uncontroversial as any point of philosophical theology. This claim, as we have seen, is not threatened by the great qualitative changes of glorification. But it is threatened in another way. To begin to see the worry, note that not all dead bodies remain well-preserved from death to resurrection. Indeed, because of decay or cannibals or cremation, some bodies, probably most bodies, actually pass out of existence at some point in time after death. Corpses dissolve into dust and then are no more. So it appears that the doctrine of the resurrection commits us to the claim that after a body has ceased to exist, it can, at a later date — the Day of Resurrection — come back into existence.

Many philosophers balk at the claim that a thing that has ceased to exist can come back into existence at some later date. To see why, imagine the following scenario. A terrible fire sweeps through the Louvre, destroying the *Mona Lisa*. You read about this in the newspaper. A month later, a friend tells you that she has just returned from Paris, adding that she saw the *Mona Lisa* hours before her flight home. You ask "Ah, so it escaped the fire after all?" and your friend responds "No; it was destroyed completely, burned to ashes. And the ashes themselves were even dissolved in water from the fire hoses. But a crack team of curators got the painting back. I had to pay a lot to see it, though, what with all the restoration costs."

You would rightly suspect that your friend was duped. For, so you would reasonably think, once the *Mona Lisa* has been totally destroyed, it cannot possibly be "restored" by any team of curators. You know, although your gullible friend does not, that she saw a mere copy of the

Mona Lisa, not the original. Again, you know that while the painting your friend saw might have been *qualitatively* identical with the *Mona Lisa,* it could not have been *numerically* identical with Da Vinci's masterpiece. And you know this without having ever examined the copy, without having discovered, for example, some telltale flaw. You know your friend saw a copy *simply because you know that the original was destroyed.* For you know that because the original was destroyed, it, the original, is gone for good.

So much seems right, even obviously right. But as it goes with great masterpieces, many philosophers have thought, so it goes with all physical objects, including human bodies. Once they are gone, they are gone for good. And these philosophers have thought that getting the same body back is not merely impossible for curators or other human beings, but is *absolutely impossible,* impossible even for God.[4] This claim seems to undermine the doctrine of resurrection. For, as we have seen, the doctrine of the resurrection implies that a body can cease to exist and then — on the Day of Resurrection — that very same body can come back into existence again.

Whether ceasing to exist and then coming back into existence is absolutely impossible is something philosophers debate. In my opinion, there are no conclusive philosophical arguments one way or the other on this issue. So, if all we have are the tools of philosophy, perhaps we ought to say we have no idea whether a thing can utterly cease to exist and then come back into existence later. But we have more than the tools of philosophy at our disposal. We have divine revelation. And, as we have already seen, given the fact that at least some bodies decay and cease to exist, scripture teaches that a body which has ceased to exist will come back into existence on the Day of Resurrection. And, since what will happen must be possible, scripture implies that it is possible for a thing which has ceased to exist to come back into existence. So we know that this *is* possible. (This is one nice example of how our philosophical views can be informed by scripture.)

But even those Christian philosophers who believe that long-gone bodies *will* come back into existence have puzzled over *how,* exactly, this is supposed to happen. Indeed, it is no exaggeration to say that a historical survey of philosophical discussions of the resurrection would, in large part, be a survey of discussions about how a body that has been destroyed

4. For a defense of the claim that even God cannot do what is absolutely impossible, see the contribution to this volume by Davison.

could possibly be numerically identical with a body that exists long after the destruction.[5] So let's dig a little deeper.

To understand better the issues here, let me ask you to imagine something rather fanciful. Imagine that you build a time machine that can "take you to the future." You push the "start" button. Observers see you and the machine disappear here in 1998. You (and your machine) then reappear in the year 2030. Now there are easier ways to travel to the future. Just sit there for a minute, and you'll move ahead a minute in time. The whole purpose of the time machine, of course, is to allow you to get to the future — in this case, to 2030 — while "skipping" all the times in between.

One way to describe what the time machine does is to say that it allows you to travel to future times, skipping the years in between. But there is another, equally accurate description. We could say that, because of the machine, you cease to exist at 1998 and come back into existence in 2030, even though *you fail to exist at any of the times in between.* The machine — and this is the point of introducing the time machine into our discussion of resurrection — causes a "temporal gap" in your life. This is just what the resurrection seems to cause when it comes to the career of (at least some) human bodies. For the doctrine of the resurrection seems to imply that a body which has decayed or has been cremated or for some other reason has gone out of existence can, on Resurrection Day, come back into existence; in other words, it seems to imply that it is possible that a body "jump ahead" in time.[6]

5. Such discussions go on even today. One contemporary Christian philosopher, Peter van Inwagen, is so sure that a body which has ceased to exist could not come back into existence that he suggests that perhaps corpses do not really decay and cease to exist, but rather are stored (somewhere) for Resurrection Day by God, while clever replicas decay in their place. See his "The Possibility of Resurrection," *International Journal for Philosophy of Religion* 9 (1978): 114-21.

The fact that a corpse can cease to exist has convinced the authors of two contemporary books that deal with the resurrection to deny the numerical identity of the resurrection body with the earthly one. See Bruce Reichenbach *Is Man the Phoenix?* (Grand Rapids: Eerdmans, 1978), 182, and John W. Cooper, *Body, Soul, and Life Everlasting* (Grand Rapids: Eerdmans, 1989), 188ff.

6. The way in which we probably imagine the time machine causing your body to jump ahead in time is a little different from the way in which your body will jump ahead to Resurrection Day. We probably imagine that when someone pushes the "start" button in the time machine, not only the passenger's body ceases to exist, but, in addition, so do all the body's parts. In contrast, when a body ceases to exist at death or decay, some of its parts — atoms, for example — usually remain. (Of course, it is plausible that some of a body's other parts, such as its organs, do cease to exist when the body does.)

Thinking of ceasing to exist and then coming back into existence as "jumping ahead" in time makes it seem more plausible that, possibly, a destroyed object could come back into existence. And the possibility of temporal gaps can be made to seem even more plausible if we consider — not the burning *Mona Lisa* — but a watch that is disassembled, perhaps for cleaning, and then reassembled. It seems that, once disassembled, the watch no longer exists. And it seems that reassembly brings the original watch back into existence. So this seems to be an example of a genuine temporal gap in the watch's career.[7]

The watch example seems to show that temporal gaps in an object's existence are possible. Moreover, it is pretty clear *how* the watch comes back into existence after having ceased to exist. It comes back into existence because all of its original parts are reassembled in just the way that they were before disassembly. One might think that, as it goes with watches, so it goes with human bodies. So one might hold that if a body that has been destroyed is to come back into existence, then all of its parts — such as the atoms — that composed it at death must be gathered back together and reassembled.[8]

This "reassembly of last parts" view was the dominant view of resurrection for a very long time — for all I know, it may *still* be the dominant view. And it seems to have at least one obvious benefit. For while a body may decay and rot and pass out of existence, it could be that the very smallest things that compose that body — such as atoms or electrons or quarks — do not pass out of existence. While my body may not be around in a thousand years, perhaps its smallest parts will. And if those smallest parts still exist, then the "reassembly" view of resurrection can

7. I hedge my comments here with the word "seems," because there are many assumptions underlying the claim that disassembling and reassembling a watch provides a genuine temporal gap in an object's career. I will note just one in order to illustrate why the watch example is controversial — the assumption that, when disassembled, the watch actually ceases to exist. Some philosophers claim that, when disassembled, the watch *still exists* but is spread out all over the jeweler's workbench. (Philosophers would call a watch spread out like that a "scattered object.") Obviously, if the watch continues existing all through the process of disassembly and reassembly, the process of disassembly and reassembly is not an example of a temporal gap in the watch's existence.

8. More carefully, the view here is that one must gather all of a body's parts *of a certain size*. For suppose I die and my body decays. My body presumably had parts such as my liver and my heart. But these organs ceased to exist along with my body, and so cannot be "gathered back" and reassembled. It is the small parts — the atoms, perhaps — with which the friends of reassembly are concerned.

explain how my body can, just like the watch, come back into existence after it has been very efficiently "disassembled" by decay or cremation or being eaten by a tiger.

But there are three problems with the view that resurrection of the body consists in God's reassembling the still-existing parts that composed the body at death. First, it is not obvious that all of the atoms that composed, say, Noah when he died, exist today. Maybe they do. Or maybe the atoms themselves are gone, but all the parts of all those atoms, like electrons or quarks, still exist. But maybe some of them do not. And maybe some of my parts, even some of the smallest ones, will have somehow passed out of existence in a thousand years. If so, then they won't be around for reassembly. And so reassembly of all my still-existing smallest parts cannot secure my resurrection in a thousand years.

The second problem with "resurrection as reassembly" has its roots in the fact that the atoms that compose a body at death can eventually find their way into another body. Cannibalism offers a striking and clear illustration of this problem, and so worries about cannibalism occupied Christian thinkers from very early on. So let's suppose that you are eaten by a cannibal. The cannibal then digests your body, and some of the atoms that composed your body at death then compose the cannibal's body. The cannibal then dies. Resurrection Day comes, and God sets out to reassemble both your body and the cannibal's body from the atoms that composed each body at its last moment. But some of the atoms that composed you at death also composed the cannibal at death. If the shared atoms go to you, then they cannot go to the cannibal; if they go to the cannibal, they cannot go to you. God cannot, therefore, reassemble both your body *and* the body of the cannibal.

So if it is true that a body comes back into existence at resurrection only if all of the atoms that composed it at death are reassembled, it is not possible that both you and the cannibal get resurrected. But it must be possible for you and the cannibal to be resurrected. For, as the scripture passages quoted later in this paper show, *everyone* gets resurrected on Resurrection Day. Our hope in the resurrection is not — contrary to the beliefs of some early enemies of the church — held hostage to what happens to our bodies after we die.[9]

A number of moves have been suggested to make the "reassembly

9. In a second-century persecution, the Romans thought they could extinguish the Christians' hope of resurrection by burning and scattering the bodies of martyrs. See Bynum, *The Resurrection of the Body*, 49.

of last parts" view consistent with the doctrine that every body (and so everybody) will be resurrected. My personal favorite is the claim, first defended by Athenagoras in the second century, that human flesh was simply not digestible.[10] If Athenagoras was right, when the cannibal eats you, the atoms that compose you pass right through. They *never* are parts of the cannibal. So at the Last Day, you are the only one with a claim to those atoms. (After they had passed through a cannibal, would you want them back?) Of course, Athenagoras' solution won't wash; he had the facts wrong; human flesh is digestible.

In addition to the question of just how long atoms survive, and in addition to puzzles about cannibalism — and in general puzzles about the fact that atoms that compose one body at death can in a variety of ways eventually find their way into another person's body — there is a third and more fundamental worry about the reassembly view. To start to see the worry, suppose, again, that you take a watch to be cleaned; when you return later, the jeweler hands you a watch that he *says* is yours, although he adds that he replaced *every single part*. You would rightly insist that the jeweler has got it wrong — he's not returned your old watch with new parts; rather, he's given you a new watch. Considerations such as these lend plausibility to the general claim that a watch cannot continue to exist after every single one of its parts is replaced.[11] Conversely, it seems that just so long as you have all the original parts of the watch, in all their original positions, you have the original watch. A watch's numerical identity over time seems to be tied very closely to the numerical identity of its parts.

But these facts are not true of organisms like human bodies. Human bodies can — and *do* — survive the replacement of all their parts. All, or nearly all, of the atoms that composed me twenty years ago no longer compose me today. (To illustrate this point, only about half of the atoms that composed your liver just *five days ago* are in your liver today.)[12] Moreover, getting all the parts that compose a human body at one time, and reassembling them, does not necessarily bring that very same human

10. Bynum, *The Resurrection of the Body,* 33.

11. But this is controversial. Suppose that you replaced the watch's parts, one by one, over a very long period of time. Then maybe the watch would survive. Philosophical puzzles are lurking close by, since you could then gather all the original parts and reassemble *them* into a watch. Which watch — the one that is the product of the gradual replacement or the one that is made of all the original parts — is the original watch?

12. I ran across this fun fact in van Inwagen's *Material Beings* (Ithaca: Cornell University Press, 1990), 93-94.

body back. To see this, suppose God were to find all the atoms that composed you when you were five years old and reassemble them into a living five-year-old child, and then set that five-year-old child next to you. Would that child have *your body?* Certainly not; you are standing (and so your body is standing) right *next to* the five-year-old's body. We have two bodies here, one numerically distinct from the other.

So we can see that a human body's numerical identity over time is not tied to the numerical identity of its parts in the simple and straightforward way that the numerical identity of an inanimate object like a watch seems to be. This should make us cautious about the reassembly view of resurrection. And we can press this point a bit more. We have seen that the fact that some group or set or collection of atoms composed your body at some time in history — such as on your fifth birthday — does not imply that those atoms, when reassembled, would compose your body. If this is right, then we should worry that the fact that some collection of atoms composes your body at the time in history at which you happen to die might not imply that *those* atoms, when reassembled, would compose *your* body.

Since the parts that compose a human body constantly change throughout life, there seems to be something arbitrary in insisting that the human body at resurrection must be composed of the parts that composed that body *at death.* And reassembling the parts that compose the person at any other particular time during the person's life would be arbitrary in the same way. So the problem here is with resurrection as reassembly in general, not just resurrection as reassembly of *last* parts.

Defenders of the reassembly view of resurrection were aware of this charge and have offered responses (this charge was made as early as the second century by Origen, one of the first to reject explicitly the reassembly view).[13] Athenagoras, for instance, claimed that a human body neither loses nor gains any parts throughout one's life; he thought that one never exhales nor excretes any atoms that ever composed one's body, and that no new atoms are ever added to one's body by eating and drinking.[14] So, Athenagoras could claim, there is nothing arbitrary about focusing on the *last* parts after all, since the parts you have at your last moment of life are the very same parts you had at every moment of life. But this defense won't work since, again, Athenagoras had the facts wrong.

I think the above points suggest that there is good reason to reject the "reassembly of last bits" description of how resurrection occurs. But if it is

13. Bynum, *The Resurrection of the Body,* 64.
14. Bynum, *The Resurrection of the Body,* 69.

not in virtue of reassembly, then *in virtue of what,* one might ask, is the resurrected body numerically identical with the body that has died?[15] There have been other answers to this question. The most well-known, after reassembly, is the ancient rabbinical tradition that just so long as the resurrected body is composed around an indestructible bone from the earthly body's spinal column, the identity of the earthly body with the resurrected one is fixed.[16] But this answer has even more problems than reassembly. For one thing, there is no totally indestructible bone in the spinal column.

Suppose that we have *no* satisfactory account of what makes for the identity of the earthly body with the resurrection one. All that follows is that none of us has any clear idea *how* resurrection will work. That, however, is no threat at all to the doctrine that it *will* work. What *would* be a genuine threat to the doctrine of resurrection would be some sort of proof or argument that temporal gaps in the career of a body are *impossible.* But the fact that we cannot see how resurrection is supposed to go, that we cannot explain what God does to bring an annihilated body back into existence, does not imply that God's doing this is impossible; it implies only that we are ignorant.

Indeed, since the resurrection of a no-longer-existing human body is contrary to the normal way nature proceeds, it would be no surprise if our models of how a physical thing enjoys numerical identity over time in everyday life suggest no plausible account of how a human body that dies and decays could be identical with a body that is resurrected. Resurrection of the body may not be impossible, but it will take a miracle.

IV. Immortality and Resurrection and Persons and Bodies

The LORD God formed the man from the dust of the ground and breathed into his nostrils the breath of life, and the man became a living being.

By the sweat of your brow you will eat your food until you re-

15. My own answer to this question, which I won't develop here because it is both complicated and controversial, is that the resurrection body is identical with the earthly one *just because it is,* and this does not need to be explained by anything else. To better understand why I say this, see my "There Are No Criteria of Identity Over Time," *Noûs* (forthcoming).

16. See Bynum, *The Resurrection of the Body,* 54, and Cooper, *Body, Soul and Life Everlasting,* 188.

turn to the ground, since from it you were taken; for dust you are and to dust you will return.

Genesis 2:7; 3:19

The previous two sections of this paper have dealt with two topics: The life everlasting and the resurrection of the body. As we shall see below, scripture often speaks of these two topics in the same breath, seeming to treat them as two sides of a single coin. A similar point holds of the creeds mentioned at the start of this chapter. This should strike many of us as puzzling. Life after death is one thing, so many of us think, and the resurrection of the body is something else altogether. In this final, more speculative section of this chapter, I shall explain one way of thinking about human persons — I shall call this way of thinking "physicalism" — according to which the resurrection of one's body and one's life after death are, in fact, two ways of describing the very same thing.

We shall see that the fact that physicalism links everlasting life to resurrection in the most direct way possible is a powerful reason to think physicalism is true. I want to concede right from the start, however, that this reason, although powerful, is neither a proof nor a full-scale defense of physicalism.[17] A full defense would consider all the arguments for and against physicalism, taking into account all of physicalism's rivals. But such a project — besides being enormously difficult and involved — would take us too far from the focus of this section, the relation of resurrection to life after death.[18]

17. And this is a topic that Christians can quite reasonably disagree on. There is, of course, a true view. If physicalism is false, then I am wrong in believing it. If physicalism is true, then those who reject it are themselves mistaken. But the true view is not obvious. Although I will use scripture to defend physicalism about human beings, I do not mean to accuse those who disagree with me of being "soft on scripture" or otherwise suspect.

18. That said, two theories of personal identity that I won't discuss in the text, two theories which fail to unite immortality and resurrection in the direct way that physicalism does, are at least worth noting:

Some people think that human beings are souls, but deny that souls are non-physical. Instead, they seem to think of a soul as a very thin and wispy physical thing like a cloud or fog; a soul is — just barely — visible after death and perhaps weighs just a little bit. A soul is like a ghost. For good or for ill, philosophers do not take this position seriously. I mention it only because this view (as opposed to standard dualism) seems to be implicit in the story of the Witch of Endor when the witch says that Samuel's spirit *looks like* an old man wearing a robe (1 Samuel 28:14).

Some philosophers deny that a person is a physical object like an organism and

Although we will not take all of physicalism's rivals into account, we will consider its chief rival, dualism. For comparing and contrasting physicalism to dualism will allow us better to understand physicalism itself. Most Christians — or at least most Christians who have a clear and consistent opinion on the matter — are dualists. (Please read carefully my explanation of how I will use the word "dualism.")[19] Dualists believe in the existence of nonphysical souls. To say that a soul is *nonphysical* means, at least, that a soul does not have standard physical properties such as color or weight or visibility or spatiality. So it is impossible for a soul to weigh an ounce or to be seen. Although a soul lacks physical properties, it has mental properties. This means, among other things, that a soul can be thinking about the weather, a soul can be confused, and a soul can accept or reject the claims of the gospel.

Dualists believe that, in this life, each soul is intimately associated with a body. They might say that in this life a soul "has" a body. Very roughly, a soul's "having" a body amounts to that soul's exercising direct causal control over a body and receiving sensory input directly from that same body. An example of direct causal control: When a soul has the mental property of intending to move a left arm, the left arm of "its" body moves.[20] An example of sensory input: When someone pinches a body, the associated soul feels pain. While dualists think that souls "have" bodies in this life, they don't think that having a body is essential to a soul's existence. For they think that upon death, the soul continues to exist without a body.

---

also deny that a person is a nonphysical object like a soul. This is because they think that a person is no sort of object at all, but rather a series of mental events or thoughts. This view was presupposed by a recent newspaper story I read which claimed that we will one day achieve immortality by storing our thoughts and memories on a computer chip. Just so long as our "thoughts" continue to exist, we continue to exist, for we are just our thoughts. I do not really understand this view.

19. The word "dualism" has been used in many different ways and in many different contexts. I mean by "dualism" exactly the view I explain in the text, and nothing else at all. So, after reading my discussion in the text, it should be obvious that dualism (as I understand it here) has nothing to do with, for example, the doctrine that there are two forces in the universe, one for good, the other for evil. Nor does it imply, to offer a second example, that matter is evil and that having a body is a bad thing.

20. I call this *direct* causal control to distinguish it from *indirect* causal control. *My* soul could have indirect causal control over *your* arm if I could cause your arm to move, but could not do so simply by intending it. I might do so, instead, by moving your arm with my hand. The dualist insists that one's soul exerts *direct* causal control over one's own body; it controls it simply by intending to do so.

And not just the *soul* continues to exist after death without a body, but so does the *person herself.* In fact, dualists think that after death (and before resurrection) a person *just is* a soul. This leads many dualists to conclude that a human person is numerically identical with a soul in *this* life, *before* death. For they reason that since a person can survive the destruction of her body, and since only the person's soul can survive the destruction of her body, the person must be nothing other than a soul. These dualists do not deny, of course, that in this life, the person (who is a soul) is intimately associated with a body. They just don't think that the body is really a part of the person herself. Other dualists agree that a person survives death as only a soul, yet somehow maintain that, in this life, a person is *not* identical with a soul, but rather is identical with a composite of both body and soul. (Just as a person's body is composed of a left half and a right half, but is identical with neither, so the person herself, according to some dualists, is in this life composed of a soul and a body, but identical with neither.)

The above comments should give us a good idea of what the dualist believes, and they also set the stage for an explanation of physicalism. The physicalist rejects dualism. The physicalist, at least the sort of physicalist I have in mind, agrees that something has mental properties; she just thinks that that something is a physical human being rather than a nonphysical soul. The physicalist does not think that the relation of you to your body is one of merely direct causal control and sensory input. Nor does she think that your body is just one part of you and your soul another. Rather, she thinks that there are *no* souls and that you are the *very same thing as* your body. So anything true of the physical human organism that is your body is true of you; anything true of you is true of that organism.[21]

It should be clear that in the debate between the dualist and the physicalist, the word "soul" has a very specific meaning. In less philosophical contexts, the word "soul" often has other meanings. For example, a die-hard Notre Dame football fan might say "My soul is blue and gold." She probably doesn't mean that she is or has a nonphysical, yet colored, object — that would be absurd. Rather, she is probably using the

21. As with "dualism," the word "physicalism" has been used in a variety of ways. In this chapter, it means only and exactly the claim that a human person is identical with the organism that is his or her body. It does *not* mean, in this chapter, that *everything* is physical. The Christian physicalist will insist, for example, that God is nonphysical.

word "soul" only to testify, in a picturesque way, to her commitment to the Fighting Irish. Indeed, in *this* sense of the word "soul," someone who is a physicalist could say — without contradicting his physicalism — that *his* soul is blue and gold.

Along similar lines, the physicalist should have no problem with saying that one should "love God with all of one's heart, all of one's soul, and all of one's strength." She will just insist that "soul" — in this context — does not mean "nonphysical entity with mental properties." To love God with all of one's soul, she might insist, is nothing other than to love God deeply and with great passion and in one's "innermost being." Likewise, the physicalist can be enthusiastic about saving souls, although she will be careful to explain that this means nothing more and nothing less than being enthusiastic about saving people. The physicalist might even grant that she *has* a soul, in contexts where the word "soul" means something like mind or personality.

So when the physicalist denies that she has (or is) a soul, she is denying only the dualist's very specific claim that she has (or is) a nonphysical mental entity. She is not denying that the word "soul" can be used in other contexts and in other ways, and when used in these other ways, she might affirm that she has a soul, that she wants to see souls saved, or that she likes soul food. Because of this, I do not think that we need to worry about an attack on physicalism that does no more than simply point out a Bible verse that has the word "soul" in it; for the physicalist might well agree that in the sense of "soul" at issue there, she *does* have a soul.[22] Indeed, it might be better to say that the physicalist and the dualist agree that people *have souls,* they just disagree about what a person's *soul is like*. Nevertheless, I will follow standard *philosophical* usage in this paper, and use the word "soul" to mean the sort of nonphysical mental entity that the dualist believes in. Given this very special and philosophical usage of the word "soul," it is correct to say that the physicalist does not believe that people have souls.

As we shall see in the verses below, the Bible treats the resurrection as very important. But if dualism were true, it is hard to see why our resurrection would be a big deal. Now the dualist might object that a soul in Heaven without a body is somehow mutilated or incomplete, and so the

22. Along similar lines, the physicalist can claim that human persons are "spiritual" beings, but that this means (for example) that they can have a certain kind of relationship with God. She can also agree that we should worship God in spirit and in truth. And so on.

dualist might therefore insist that resurrection is a blessing. But it is hard to know just how much stress she should put on the value of resurrection, since stress on what we gain in resurrection is, by its very nature, stress on what we lack before resurrection. Preresurrection existence united with God in Heaven is not supposed to be *too* bad; indeed, it is supposed to be *very good.*

And however the dualist might deal with this problem, one thing is certain: The dualist cannot say that resurrection is *necessary* for eternal life. After all, Christian dualists often claim that an advantage of their theory — even *the* advantage of their theory — is that it allows humans to live on after death but before the general resurrection. And, obviously, one cannot maintain both that life after death occurs *before* resurrection and also that life after death *requires* resurrection.

If, on the other hand, we are physical organisms, then our resurrected bodies coming back into existence on that Great Day just is *our* coming back into existence. If we are physical organisms, the resurrection of the body is the whole ball game as far as life after death goes. If we are physical organisms, then our hope for life after death and our hope for resurrection of the body are one and the same thing. If we are physical organisms, death is defeated in, and only in, the resurrection.

With these thoughts in mind, note — along with the passage from Isaiah that opened this paper — the following scriptures:

> At that time Michael, the great prince who protects your people, will arise. There will be a time of distress such as has not happened from the beginning of nations until then. But at that time your people — everyone whose name is found written in the book — will be delivered. Multitudes who sleep in the dust of the earth will awake: some to everlasting life, others to shame and everlasting contempt. (Daniel 12:1-2)

> When you give a luncheon or dinner, do not invite your friends, your brothers or relatives, or your rich neighbors; if you do, they may invite you back and so you will be repaid. But when you give a banquet, invite the poor, the crippled, the lame, the blind, and you will be blessed. Although they cannot repay you, you will be repaid at the resurrection of the righteous. (Matthew 14:12-14)

> I tell you the truth, whoever hears my word and believes him who sent me has eternal life and will not be condemned; he has crossed over from death to life. I tell you the truth, a time is coming and has now

come when the dead will hear the voice of the Son of God and those who hear will live. For as the Father has life in himself, so he has granted the Son to have life in himself. And he has given him authority to judge because he is the Son of Man. Do not be amazed at this, for a time is coming when all who are in their graves will hear his voice and come out — those who have done good will rise to live, and those who have done evil will rise to be condemned. (John 5:24-29)

I believe everything that agrees with the Law and that is written in the Prophets, and I have the same hope in God as these men, that there will be a resurrection of both the righteous and the wicked. (Paul, responding to his accusers at his trial before Felix in Acts 24)

Brothers, we do not want you to be ignorant about those who fall asleep, or to grieve like the rest of men, who have no hope. We believe that Jesus died and rose again and so we believe that God will bring with Jesus those who have fallen asleep in him. According to the Lord's own word, we tell you that we who are still alive will certainly not precede those who have fallen asleep. For the Lord himself will come down from heaven with a loud command, with the voice of the archangel and with the trumpet call of God, and the dead in Christ will rise first. After that, we who are still alive and are left will be caught up together with them in the clouds to meet the Lord in the air. And so we will be with the Lord forever. Therefore encourage each other with these words. (1 Thessalonians 4:13-18)

For if the dead are not raised, then Christ has not been raised either. And if Christ has not been raised, your faith is futile; you are still in your sins. Then those also who have fallen asleep in Christ are lost. If only for this life we have hope in Christ, we are to be pitied more than all men. (1 Corinthians 15:16-19)

If I fought wild beasts in Ephesus for merely human reasons, what have I gained? If the dead are not raised, "Let us eat and drink, for tomorrow we die." (1 Corinthians 15:32)

We will not all sleep, but we will all be changed — in a flash, in the twinkling of an eye, at the last trumpet. For the trumpet will sound, the dead will be raised imperishable, and we will all be changed. For the perishable must clothe itself with the imperishable, and the mortal with immortality. When the perishable has been clothed with the imperishable, and the mortal with immortality, then the saying that is

> written will come true: "Death has been swallowed up in victory." "Where, O death, is your victory? Where O death is your sting?" (1 Corinthians 15:51-55)

If we take the above passages at face value, it is dead *people* that are raised to life; *hope of resurrection* is the believer's *hope of eternal life*. If that is correct, then resurrection is much more than "getting your body back" (as good as that may be) — it is the believer's victory over death. It is the guarantor of a final judgment and entrance into eternal union with God or eternal separation from him. It is what gives us hope in God and keeps us from saying "let us eat and drink, for tomorrow we die." The physicalist will find the picture of resurrection painted in the verses above a very natural one. For he will insist that *life after death* and *resurrection* are, for physical organisms like us, *one and the same thing*.

While the physicalist holds that life after death and resurrection are one, the dualist does not. The dualist does not believe that dead *people* are raised to life; rather, she believes that dead *bodies* are raised to be reunited with already living people (who are, in the intermediate state at least, souls). I think that means that the picture of resurrection painted in the verses above does not sit comfortably with dualism. I do not deny that the dualist can interpret these passages in a way consistent with her view. I claim only that her interpretation of these passages will not be as natural or plausible as that of the physicalist, and so I think these passages support physicalism over dualism.

The physicalist should also take comfort in the fact, noted in the previous section of this paper, that the resurrection body is numerically identical with the body one has in this life. For if a human being is identical with her body, she cannot exist after death unless her body, that is, an object numerically identical with the very organism that was her body in this life, exists after death. So, given physicalism, it is part and parcel of the promise of eternal life that one's "original" body will itself be resurrected. The numerical identity of the earthly body with the resurrection body is just what the physicalist who believes in life after death would expect.

But if dualism were true, one would not expect the resurrection body to be numerically identical with the earthly one. For even granting that a soul without a body is mutilated or incomplete, there is no reason to think that a soul needs the very same body it had before death. The identity of the resurrection body with the body of this life is not inconsistent with dualism, of course. But it does seem to be rather pointless, except for the fact that our original bodies might have some sentimental value to us.[23] Like the centrality of the resurrection to our hope for eternal life, the nature of the resurrection body — insofar as its identity with the earthly body is concerned — fits hand in glove with physicalism but makes little sense given dualism.

If we are identical with our bodies, then we do not exist when our bodies do not exist. Therefore, if physicalism is true, at some point between the death and total decay of one's body, one literally ceases to exist. Ceasing to exist is different from existing and being "asleep," and even different — if this makes any sense at all — from existing and being dead. It may be hard for you to imagine your nonexistence, but there is nothing incoherent here. (After all, you did not exist, e.g., in the year 500 B.C.). It is bad that beings like us, created for eternal life, pass away into nothingness. So I can insist on what I think the scriptures affirm. I can insist that death is a bad thing. Death is an enemy. Death is a curse. Death's doom is sealed, of course; we know at resurrection it will be conquered once and for all. But a doomed enemy is an enemy nevertheless.[24]

It is not clear that the dualist can agree that death is bad. When the Christian dies, according to the dualist, he or she goes immediately to a much better place. Death for the believer, according to the dualist, is nothing other than exchanging the travails of this life for immediate and glorious union with the Father in Heaven. Death, it would seem, is even better than quitting your job and moving to a beachfront villa in Hawaii. I think this is a problem for dualism. For I think the scriptures teach that death is a bad thing, a curse, an enemy; and an enemy defeated in resurrection. If physicalism is true, it is easy to see how bad death is and also how death is defeated in resurrection. But if dualism is true, it is hard to

23. And the whole emphasis on Resurrection Day and the bodies we get then seems to me absolutely pointless if those forms of dualism are true which insist that after death, but before resurrection, we are given "interim" bodies.

24. So if I am right, you will cease to exist when you die and then, on the Day of Resurrection, you will come back into existence. Some dualists might object that this requires a "temporal gap" in a person's life. And they might object that such gaps are impossible. (They might then add that an advantage of their view is that a person is a soul and never goes out of existence, not even between death and resurrection.) But I do not think that this is a very strong objection. For I think that whether one is a dualist, physicalist, or otherwise, one ought to agree that temporal gaps in a human *body's* career are implied by the resurrection. Once that is granted, however, one cannot object to physicalism on the grounds that it endorses temporal gaps. Physicalists and dualists agree that a person's body can "jump ahead in time" to the Day of Resurrection; physicalists just add to this that a person and her body are the same thing.

see how death is an enemy, and harder still to see how it is overcome in resurrection.

Now the dualist might reply that death is separation from your body and that this separation is very bad. And she might add that resurrection is the end of this separation and thus very good. Fair enough. Nevertheless, death is much worse given physicalism than dualism. To see this, imagine what you would say to a mourner at a Christian's funeral if you and the mourner knew for certain that *dualism* were true. You could comfort the mourner by noting that now the deceased is in a better place and with the Lord. She is much happier than she was before death (happier, even, than she would be on the beach in Hawaii . . .). If, on the other hand, you and the mourner knew for certain that *physicalism* were true, you would have only one comfort — the resurrection. You might say "For now, there is little to comfort you. But someday the dead will rise again." Physicalism makes death all the worse and resurrection all the more glorious. This fits very well with scripture's attitudes toward death and resurrection.

Or at least with some of the attitudes expressed in scripture. For scripture also says "To die is gain." Since the dualist can understand death as immediate passage to God, without having to await resurrection, passages of scripture that seem to teach that death is gain are passages, I think, that seem to support dualism over physicalism.

What should the Christian physicalist say about these passages? Perhaps the answer is found in the story of the time machine. If I thought that I were about to take a ride on the time machine and that the very next moment at which I would exist would be the glorious Day of Resurrection, I would be quite excited. So while my dying results in my literal nonexistence, I can nevertheless be comforted at my death in knowing that death's defeat is the very next thing I shall experience. With the fact in mind that to die is to jump ahead in time to the Day of Resurrection, I could say that "to die is gain." And I could think to myself, as I lie on my deathbed, that, so far as things seem to me — and only because of the resurrection of the body — this day I shall be with the Lord in paradise.

I have not addressed even a fraction of the passages of scripture that bear on whether or not one exists between death and resurrection or, more generally, on physicalism and dualism. This is a topic of deep controversy among biblical scholars, and for those who are interested in pursuing it, there is no end of materials to read.[25] As far as biblical interpre-

25. One good place to start is John W. Cooper's *Body, Soul, and Life Everlasting.* Cooper's book is very accessible, presupposing no prior knowledge of theology or philos-

tation goes, my aim in this final, more speculative, section of this chapter is fairly modest. It is to suggest one way — the best way, I think — to make sense of the picture of resurrection that the Bible seems to endorse. That picture involves the numerical identity of the earthly body with the resurrection body, a close connection between our hope for resurrection and our hope for eternal life, and the defeat of a bitter enemy — death — in the resurrection.

You may remain unconvinced. You may remain a stalwart of dualism and dualistic interpretations of scripture. I still think the above discussion ought to convince you of at least one significant thing — that the Christian's belief in life after death does not necessarily and absolutely require dualism. For in the doctrine of the resurrection, we have the resources to make sense of — and have hope for — eternal life even if physicalism is true. Because of this, the believer need not feel threatened when scientists, philosophers, or psychologists pronounce belief in the soul irrational or demonstrably false. Such pronouncements (although sadly common) are unjustified. But it is nice to know that even if, someday, someone proves that physicalism is true, nothing essential to the Christian faith would be undermined.

---

ophy. Cooper defends the claim that scripture teaches some form of dualism. The book is useful not only because of Cooper's own arguments, but because of the many footnotes and references he gives to papers and books defending both sides of the issue.

12

Heaven and Hell

Michael J. Murray

Everyone will die and go to heaven,
And we will all be angels one day,
What you are in this world,
Don't count for nothin',
We are only children,
Just lost long the way.
Yes, we will all be angels,
someday.

Randy Travis

Then he will say to those on his left, 'Depart from me, you who are cursed, into the eternal fire prepared for the devil and his angels. . . ' Then they will go away to eternal punishment, but the righteous to eternal life.

Matthew 25:41, 46

I am deeply indebted to Daniel Howard-Snyder, Trenton Merricks, Eleonore Stump, and William Alston for comments on earlier drafts of this chapter. Thanks as well are due to Steve Butts for helping me avoid certain theological infelicities, and to the many lay readers at Blackhawk Evangelical Free Church who helped me make some obscure parts of the text a little less obscure. Thanks are also due to the remaining authors of this book for their input during our collective discussion of this chapter.

Anyone who has spent much time talking to a non-Christian about the Christian faith has inevitably encountered the topic of hell. For non-Christians, and for many Christians as well, the doctrine of hell seems downright incompatible with the Christian view of God. C. S. Lewis put it this way:

> [The doctrine of hell] is one of the chief grounds on which Christianity is attacked as barbarous and the goodness of God impugned. We are told that it is a detestable doctrine, and I too detest it from the bottom of my heart, and am reminded of the tragedies in human life which have come from believing it. Of the tragedies that come from not believing it we are told less. For these reasons, and these reasons alone, it becomes necessary to discuss hell. The problem is not simply of a God who consigns some of his creatures to final ruin. Christianity, true, as always, to the complexities of the real, presents us with something knottier and more ambiguous; a God so full of mercy that he becomes a man and dies by torture to avert that final ruin from his creatures and who yet, where that heroic remedy fails, seems unwilling, or even unable to arrest the ruin by an act of mere power.[1]

One of my students once explained his way of seeing the problem as follows. For him the Christian worldview made human existence out to be like an episode of the old show Let's Make a Deal. On the show, contestants were selected from the audience and given an opportunity to select blindly one of three curtains, each of which hid a certain prize. The prizes might be desirable (a new car) or undesirable (a goat or a chicken). The host offers the contestants financial incentives to take this or that door, but in the end, the contestants make what is essentially a blind choice, and take the prize they are given. Likewise, on the Christian picture, he explained, fallen human beings stumble around in a world in which they have to make choices, choices which amount to giving allegiance to one religion or another (or no religion at all). For the most part, the choices are made blindly since the evidence one way or the other is either ambiguous, or thin, or just nonexistent. Furthermore, along the way there are incentives or "temptations" to give one's allegiance to one religion or another. Even the Christian thinks that the devil stands ready to lure people away from the "right door." But at the end of the day, everyone blindly stakes their claim one way or the other. On the Christian view, those who select the single "correct" curtain

1. C. S. Lewis, *The Problem of Pain* (Glasgow: William Collins Sons, 1983), 107-8.

are both lucky and rewarded (with eternal bliss). But what about those who choose any other curtain? They are immediately snatched away to live for eternity in a hell where they are burned alive but never die.

This is powerful imagery — imagery which illustrates a number of criticisms that have been raised against the traditional Christian doctrine of hell. Those criticisms can roughly be divided into two groups, those who claim that there is something *unjust* about hell, and those who claim that there is something *unloving* about a God who allows people to go (or sends them!) there. How should the Christian respond to these critical challenges? In recent years, Christian theologians and philosophers have taken up the challenge posed by the doctrine of hell and have sketched a wide variety of solutions to it. Some have defended the traditional notion of hell as the destiny of those without Christ, commencing immediately upon death and judgment and continuing for eternity without ceasing.[2] Others have proposed what appear to be less harsh conceptions of hell, arguing that the duration of hell might be finite, either because one ceases to exist after a certain length of time or because one finally repents and is allowed to join the company of those in heaven.[3] Others have argued that while hell exists, it is empty, because while anyone who would pass through the judgment unrepentant would go there, no one ever remains unrepentant in God's presence.[4]

The most natural reading of the text of Scripture and the words of the Lord is certainly the one reflected in the first interpretation above. As a result, it is the one we should look to defend first. If such a defense turns

2. William Lane Craig, "'No Other Name': A Middle Knowledge Perspective on the Exclusivity of Salvation Through Christ," *Faith and Philosophy* 6 (April 1989): 297-308; Richard Swinburne "A Theodicy of Heaven and Hell," in Alfred J. Freddoso, *The Existence of God* (Notre Dame: Notre Dame University Press, 1983); Eleonore Stump, "Dante's Hell and Aquinas' Moral Theory, and the Love of God," *Canadian Journal of Philosophy* (June 1986): 181-98; George Schlesinger, "The Scope of Human Autonomy," in *Our Knowledge of God*, ed. K. J. Clark (Dordrecht: Kluwer Academic Publishers), 215-23.

3. Jonathan Kvanvig, *The Problem of Hell* (Oxford: Oxford University Press, 1993), see especially chapter 4; Marylin Adams, "Divine Justice, Divine Love, and the Life to Come," *Crux* 13 (1976-77): 12-28; Clark Pinnock, "The Destruction of the Finally Impenitent," *Criswell Theological Review* 4 (1990): 243-59, and "Fire, Then Nothing," *Christianity Today* (March 20, 1987): 40-41; Edward William Fudge, *The Fire That Consumes: The Biblical Case for Conditional Immortality* (Carlisle: Paternoster, 1994).

4. See for an example Thomas Talbott, "Craig on the Possibility of Eternal Damnation," *Religious Studies* 28 (1992): 500ff.

out to be unsustainable, then we might have grounds for falling back to a different position. But until we see that such a view is unsustainable, it seems preferable to follow the dictum I learned in my high school youth group: if the plain sense of the text makes good sense, seek no other sense.

In what follows I would like to show just how a Christian might argue that the plain sense *does* make good sense when it comes to the biblical teaching on hell. In the first part of the chapter I will explain the two central models that have been proposed for understanding the traditional doctrine of hell. I will look at each in turn, discussing some of the problems that have been raised for each. I will show that the first model can successfully answer the objections that are raised against it, but that the second model has a number of explanatory advantages. Still, those advantages are offset by a serious difficulty, a difficulty which might be fixed by combining the two models into a hybrid.

In the second part of the chapter, we can then turn and address the charges that the traditional view of hell renders God unjust or unloving. It is these charges which have led some to jettison the traditional view, in favor of alternatives, most commonly annihilationism (the view that those who are not saved are punished for a time and then cease to exist) and universalism (the view that all are ultimately saved).

Two Models

In what follows I will set out two main theories that have been proposed for making sense of the doctrine of hell. But let me say a brief word for those who think this is an odd exercise. I can imagine someone saying at this point: "I am not sure what you are trying to do here. Scripture teaches that those who die without Christ are judged and assigned to hell for eternity. That is that. So what is it that you are doing when you are proposing 'two theories' on the doctrine of hell?"

This is a fair question. What I am doing here is trying to set aside the worry expressed by C. S. Lewis (and by my student). While it is true that the plain reading of Scripture teaches that those without Christ are judged and assigned to hell for eternity,[5] this fact seems to sit uncomfortably with other things that Christians know. Since we know that Scripture teaches that God wishes that none perish but that all would come to repentance

5. See for example, Matt. 25:41; Luke 16:22ff.; Heb. 10:26, 27; and Jude 7.

(2 Pet. 3:9), and we know that God is all-powerful, one might think that the frustration of God's desire requires some explaining. Why is it that, in light of this desire on God's part, some nevertheless escape the saving power of his love? And there are other troubles. Why is it that the finite amount of wrong that one can do in this life merits punishment that is infinite? And why is it that the traditional view proposes that those who are in hell recognize their bad condition but are unable to repent (or at least, if they do repent, why is it a repentance which is not accepted by God)? It is these questions and others like them that the theories of hell I propose below attempt to answer. Neither model denies the central features of the orthodox theory of hell. Each attempts to explain, instead, how it is that the orthodox conception of hell fits together with the other elements of Christian doctrine with which they seem initially to have an ill fit.

The Penalty Model

With that said, we turn to the two models. The first I will call the "penalty model" while the second I will call the "natural consequence model." We can set out the penalty model as follows:

> According to Scripture "all have sinned and fall short of the glory of God." The result of this sinfulness is that the sinner incurs a penalty, a penalty which Scripture describes as "death." However, the penalty of "death" mentioned in, for example, Romans 6:23 does not refer simply to the physical death all will experience. Instead, "death" refers to spiritual death, a death which involves separation of the person from God for eternity. As a result, each person who sins incurs this penalty. And since each person has only one life to give, each is thereby bound to be separated from God, unless the penalty incurred can be satisfied in some other fashion. To this end, God has established a means of satisfaction or payment of the penalty. God the Father wrought the Incarnation, yielding a person who was fully God and also fully human, yet without fault. And since he was faultless, and so had no penalty of his own to pay, he could, by offering himself in our place, satisfy the penalty on our behalf. As a result, those who are willing to allow the penalty to be paid on their behalf by Christ, must simply accept that gift by repenting of their former ways and placing their faith in Christ's work on the cross and in his victory in resurrection. Failure to do this means eternal separation from God with the attending punishment that this separation brings.

This is a view that many Christians espouse concerning sin, salvation, and eternal human destinies. There are many modifications of it to be found in this or that denomination or sect. But the above represents a rough approximation of the intersection of the beliefs of a very wide range of Christians.

Objections to the Penalty Model

There are a number of objections that have been raised against the penalty model. For example, one might object that there seems to be something downright immoral about punishing a perfectly innocent party to satisfy the penalty incurred by the guilty. And even if the innocent party offered to bear the punishment willingly, it is hard to see why any just person should accept the punishment of (even a willing) innocent person as an appropriate way of satisfying the guilt and penalty of the guilty person, a person who gets away "scot-free." These, however, are objections aimed more at the view of atonement presupposed in the penalty model. As closely related as issues of atonement are to the doctrine of hell, space does not permit discussion of them here.

One might object to the penalty model further by pointing out that there is a grave disproportion between the amount of wrong one can do in this life, and the eternal duration and intensity of the punishment this wrong is claimed to merit. It seems that a necessary principle of fairness or justice is that penalties or punishments must be meted out in a way that is commensurate with the gravity of the offense. But since there is no offense that we finite beings could commit in a finite time that would merit infinite punishment, the punishment proposed by the penalty model is unfair.[6]

How should one respond to this powerful criticism? There are at least two ways one might respond and I will look at each in turn.[7] According to the *first* way, the objector is *right:* no wrongs we do in this life *can* merit infinite punishment. But, the defender continues, this does not mean that those in hell might not be rightly punished for eternity none-

6. There are a number of philosophers who have defended an argument of this sort. A couple of oft-cited examples are Marylin Adams, "Hell and the Justice of God," *Religious Studies* 11 (1979): 433-47; and Thomas Talbott, "Punishment, Forgiveness, and Divine Justice," *Religious Studies* 29 (1993): 151-68.

7. It is worth noting that these two responses are incompatible; one can't adopt both of them.

theless. To see why, consider a criminal who commits a crime, is caught, and is then sentenced to twenty years in prison. While in prison, however, he continues to commit further crimes, and for these further crimes he receives additional sentencing time. The result is that while none of the crimes he commits merits a life sentence, the cumulative sentence for crimes committed before and while in prison is never exhausted. Likewise, one might hold, those who are judged and sentenced to hell might not have a sentence which initially merits an eternal punishment. But their unchecked sinful desires continue to lead them to sin even in hell and so continue to mount penalties which are never satisfied.

The *second* way to respond to this step in the critic's argument is to argue that the critic is mistaken in her belief that the sins we commit in this life *merit only a finite penalty.* If all sin is sin against God, then all sin is of infinite weight since it amounts to a transgression against an infinitely great being. This response, however, rests on two controversial assumptions. First, it assumes that all sins are sins against God, and second, it assumes that the gravity of an offense is in part dependent on the *type of being* offended.[8]

While both of the claims have been criticized, neither seems especially problematic. Since the Christian holds that all moral commands find their source in God,[9] it is reasonable to think that all transgressions are *at least* sins against God. It may be true, of course, that if I bring harm to an innocent person, I have sinned against *that person,* but there is no reason to think that this precludes my having sinned against God *as well.* We think something similar in cases of transgressions of laws of the state. Crimes which I commit against citizens in my community, are certainly crimes against *them,* but it is also perfectly reasonable to see these crimes as crimes "against the Commonwealth of Pennsylvania," at least if you live in my state.[10]

The second assumption might seem slightly more controversial. If the gravity of the crime is increased with the greatness of the person of-

8. This pair of assumptions is pointed out and discussed in detail by Kvanvig, *The Problem of Hell;* see especially chapter 1.

9. Alas this too is a controversial assumption, as Frances Howard-Snyder makes clear in the chapter on Christianity and Ethics (pp. 375-98).

10. We defend the claim that all sins are sins against God in other ways as well. Since, in sinning, we hurt God's children, this can be viewed as an offense against God, just as it would be an offense against both my daughter and me if you took her life. Another defense of this claim can be found in Kvanvig, *The Problem of Hell,* chapter 1.

fended, it seems that slapping Gandhi or Mother Teresa should merit a greater penalty than slapping my next door neighbor.[11] But this hardly seems right and our criminal law certainly takes no account of such differences. It is true that, when put this way, the principle in question seems implausible. But maybe *this* is not the principle that lies behind the penalty model. One might say, for example, that the weight of an offense depends, not on the *greatness of the person* offended, but on the greatness of the *type of being* offended. Thus, bringing injury to a tree, a frog, and a human would merit increasing penalties. Plants, animals, and humans are three quite different kinds of beings. While bringing injury to one *human* may merit the same punishment as bringing the same injury to any other *human,* it may merit a greater penalty than bringing the corresponding injury to a *dog.* In light of this, why is it implausible to think that offenses against God, who is infinitely greater than any human, merit a correspondingly greater penalty?

The trouble with the second assumption might, however, be put a different way. The critic might say that this view seems to have the consequence that all sins are of equal weight, that is, that all sins merit the *very same penalty,* since all are, in the end, sins against God, and thus of infinite weight. But something seems strange, the critic continues, in holding that telling a "little white lie" ("Yes, I think your tie is very nice") and torturing someone to death merit the same penalty. But such a strange consequence is not actually required on this view. One might think that the most minor of sins merits punishment of infinite weight (duration or intensity), and think that more serious sins merit ten times as much. This means, of course, that no one in hell could ever satisfy the penalty merited by their offense. But that is not an objection against the penalty view. To focus on duration, maybe the penalty merited by our sins is so great that it would take punishment of infinite upon infinite duration to satisfy. But there is nothing in this that the advocate of the penalty model must shrink from. In fact, that is exactly what the model asserts.

The Natural Consequence Model

I offer the penalty model above as one of the two main models of hell that have been defended by Christian orthodoxy and criticized by many in re-

11. This is a modified version of the example endorsed by Marylin Adams in her "Hell and the Justice of God," 442.

cent days. And while I think the penalty model is completely defensible, there is another model which may have more explanatory power. This second model, as we will see, has some features that are initially troubling. But all of these, except one, disappear on further investigation. Here, then, is the view in summary form:

> It is clear from the Genesis account of creation that one of the central aims God had in creating human beings was to make creatures in the "divine image." While the passage does not tell us all that this entails, it demonstrates that God was about the business of creating beings that were as much like God as they, finite and created as they were, could be. Many features of the divine nature could be replicated in creatures in characteristically finite ways: the ability to reason, to govern behavior on the basis of moral considerations, and to act freely, for example. This last feature is especially important since, because of it, humans are able to enter into a genuinely loving relationship with God. Without it, those who professed love for God (as the first great command dictates — Matt. 22:37) and who strove to be imitators of him (Eph. 5:1), would simply be robots or parrots, spitting back words of praise and behaving in ways that are simply a matter of preprogramming. Of course, such praise and behavior are not genuine expressions of love. In addition, having the ability to behave freely in these ways allows creatures to come close to exhibiting another divine attribute: self-existence. It is traditionally held that God has the attribute of self-existence (sometimes referred to as "a-seity" by philosophers and theologians [from the Latin phrase "a se" meaning "from oneself"]). Of course, no created thing can be self-existent (by definition!). But God might be able to make creatures who are self-existent at least in *certain respects,* and maybe in the most interesting and valuable respects, the respects which define what sort of person one is, and in particular, with respect to whether or not one will be a God-lover or not. God, wanting us to be creatures made in his image, wants us to be God-lovers. But recognizing that robots or preprogrammed parrots cannot be genuine God-lovers (although they can be preprogrammed to exhibit God-loving behaviors), God also gives us freedom, freedom to be self-made in a certain (very important) respect.
>
> As a result, God situates us, for a time, in this earthly life. And this earthly life is to act as a time of sanctification or, as some have called it, *soul-making:* a time when we have powers to make free choices to be a person of one sort or another. God's aim, of course, is that all will

see that being a God-lover is something to value over all else. But free creatures can, in virtue of their free powers, choose to reject this sort of life. They can instead become lovers of self and haters of God.

Once the course of one's life is complete, and one has, through conscious decision and behavior, become one sort of person or another, what then? For those who have become lovers of God, the natural consequence would be for them to enter into the divine presence to love God and enjoy him forever. But what of the others? What of those who simply have no interest in doing *that?* Why not, one might wonder, just accept them into the divine presence anyway? There are at least two reasons. The first is that doing this would amount to robbing the creature of the very freedom of self-determination that made their lives significant. The point of our earthly lives, on this account, is that we might be able to autonomously become creatures of one or another sort. But if we do not, after all, have that ability (because God will force the same "end" upon all of us), then our dignity is stolen. The second reason is that if those who lived lives in which they rejected God were nonetheless forced into God's presence forever, such a life would be utterly odious to them. It would be like forcing one who hates opera to sit through *Der Ring des Nibelungen* for eternity. This wouldn't be eternal bliss for *them.* It would be an eternal *nightmare.* As a result, the natural consequence for cultivating such a life would be eternal separation from God. And this is what hell is.

As I said, the above is a summary of the natural consequence (NC) view. Any Christian who is thinking carefully will find a number of questions immediately coming to mind. So, we will need to develop the view a bit further in order to show how it integrates the various central features of the orthodox Christian faith. In doing so, I think we will also display its significant explanatory power.

The Earthly Life and the Process of Sanctification

One of the more puzzling features of the Christian doctrine of hell is that hell is taken to be inescapable. The Lord teaches that for those in hell there is a chasm fixed so that those who are there cannot pass over into heaven. Similarly, we know that those who are in heaven remain there forever, eternally without sin. How can it come to pass, one might wonder, that those who can sin or refrain from sin while on earth, suddenly become, as Thomas Aquinas put it, "confirmed in good or evil" thereafter?

The natural consequence view has an answer to this question. One interesting and noteworthy feature of human nature is our ability to make free choices. But a further interesting feature is that we are *habit formers*. That is, our behaviors can influence future behaviors by *disposing us* to desire or think in certain ways. When I was a teenager, I didn't like fine coffee, but by drinking it I came to "acquire a taste" for it. The result is that it is something that I now like and even seek out. My desire for coffee and my thinking about it has changed in virtue of behaviors I engaged in. And we can bring about changes in our dispositions in matters more complex than tastes for food as well. Numerous books on marriage enrichment, for example, prescribe that one of the best ways to preserve or restore romantic feelings for your spouse, is to do special things for them (buying surprise gifts, sending flowers, giving cards without occasion, etc.) As odd as it might be, we are beings for whom thought and desire often *follow* action. And the dispositions that we develop from such behaviors seem to become quite firmly entrenched over time.

Why would we be designed by God in such a way that the actions I perform form habits in me, the Christian might ask? One reason might be this: that were I to have to think through my choices completely every time I made one, it would take me forever to get around in the world. We can get in and out of restaurants in less than a day because we take preferences, formed by past choices, with us to the menu, and these preferences make our decision procedure much quicker. We can easily make selections among alternatives without agonizing over every option. Simply, it makes it possible for us to effectively navigate in the world.

But more than that, this is part of the way in which we can use the freedom that God has given us to *become a certain sort of person*. What does it mean to become a certain sort of person except to become disposed to think and desire and act in certain ways? So, it is essential for becoming a "person of a certain sort" that we have such disposition-forming capacities.

As we cultivate these dispositions, the range of choices open to us in a given circumstance becomes narrower and narrower. As I become more disposed to eat foods of the sort one finds in America, I find foods from distant and exotic cultures to be less palatable, to the point where I might have no desire for them whatsoever. Eating the eyes of fish or squirrel brains, delicacies in some cultures, is simply no longer one of the things I can choose, because there is nothing about the thought of such a thing that is attractive to me. We have a phrase to describe this phenomenon: "becoming set in your ways." The more "set in our ways" we become, the less options we have in choosing. We might then think of those in heaven and hell as those who are *maximally set in their ways.* That is, they are disposed to act as lovers of God or lovers of self *without fail.*[12] The result is that those who are in heaven are no longer able to break the hold of the dispositions which they have acquired and likewise for those in hell.

The Role of Grace

One of the things that looks troubling about the natural consequence view is that it appears to teach straightforward works salvation. And because of this one should be inclined to think, at this point, that this view just cannot be reconciled with passages which claim that "he saved us, not because of things we have done, but because of his mercy. He saved us through the washing of rebirth and renewal by the Holy Spirit, whom he poured out on us generously through Jesus Christ our Savior, so that having been justified by his grace, we might become heirs having hope of eternal life" (Titus 1:9); or "It is by grace you have been saved through faith, and this not from yourselves, it is the gift of God, not as a result of works, so that no one can boast" (Eph. 2:8, 9). There is not a *hint* here that heaven is for those who have, by means of their choices in life, become lovers of God, as the natural consequence view seems to hold.

There is, however, more to the NC story than what was set out above, the NC theorist will maintain. All other things being equal, the aim of our earthly lives is to cultivate God-loving characters so that we can become meaningfully related to God. But such meaning can only be had by allowing people to freely choose to become God-lovers or not. All other things being equal, we do this, on this view, by making choices to engage in God-loving or self-loving types of activity and thereby to make ourselves into one sort of person or another, again, all other things being equal. But all other things *aren't* equal. When it comes to being a self-lover, there is no problem. We are able, all on our own, to become utterly

12. This feature of the natural consequence view is itself somewhat controversial. Some doubt that our habits can be so strong that they actually block our ability to make certain choices. For some defenders of the view that such habits can become this strong see Peter van Inwagen, "When Is the Will Free?" in *Philosophical Perspectives 3: Philosophy of Mind and Action Theory,* ed. James E. Tomberlin (Atascadero, CA: Ridgeview Publishing Company, 1989), see especially 407-8; and Michael Murray and David Dudrick, "Are Coerced Acts Free?" *American Philosophical Quarterly* 32:2 (April 1995): 147-61.

self-absorbed and self-centered lovers of self, and thereby to merit hell as a natural consequence. In other words, we are fully able to bring about *damnation by works.* Orthodox Christian belief has no quarrel with this.

But when it comes to being *God-lovers,* the Bible surely teaches something different. Sin has brought devastation to the world, a devastation which makes it impossible for us to cultivate God-loving habits, and thus a meaningful God-loving character. Not only is the world, as a result, filled with enticements that serve to draw us away from God, but our very souls are contaminated with the love of sin and self. The fallen world we have been placed in puts us in a position where becoming a God-lover by our own efforts is difficult to the point of impossibility. Sin is a crippling and debilitating influence that drags us all farther and farther from God unless its influence is graciously reversed. And thus, grace is necessary in order for us to be transformed into lovers of God.

The NC theorist will insist on all of this as much as the defender of the penalty model. And it is precisely here, on the NC view, that the need for grace becomes obvious. It is only by grace that anyone has the ability, in the first place, to choose to repent and seek reconciliation with God. In turn, it is only by God then granting the grace of reconciliation that the person is given the ability to be free of the power of sin and so to begin the process of becoming a lover of God, a process we call sanctification. So, the NC view includes the claim that divine grace is a *necessary condition* for being able to seek freely reconciliation with God and for being set free from the bondage to sin that prevents us from cultivating God-loving characters (i.e., from becoming sanctified).

Fire and Brimstone

The natural consequence view maintains that those who choose to be self-lovers are thereby separated from God for eternity, forever unable to enjoy the presence of God. While this tells us what the damned *do not* experience, what, according to the natural consequence view, *does* happen to those who are damned? On this view, it seems initially that hell is not so much a place where the damned suffer but rather just a place certain goods are lacking. Yet in Scripture hell is portrayed as more than just a *lack.* We see things like "eternal fire" and "raging fire" leading to "weeping and gnashing of teeth" and "torment."

As a rule, natural consequence theorists hold that talk of "fire" with respect to hell is metaphorical. But, they might argue, we are all obligated to take the talk of fire more or less metaphorically. After all, fire cannot really burn nonphysical souls.[13] In any case, one would do better to understand the fires of hell as a metaphor for an intense and severe sort of suffering. The penalty model thinks of this suffering as a penalty. The natural consequence model instead thinks of the suffering of hell as an agonizing and conscious awareness of loss — an awareness which is the natural consequence for having become a self-lover.

It seems from the Scriptures that those in hell are aware of the fact that they have been judged and sent away from the divine presence as a result of this judgment. And parables such as the rich man and Lazarus, seem to indicate that those in hell are continuously aware of the loss that they suffer from being in hell (Luke 16:19-31). The NC view holds that the loss one feels is the sort of loss felt by someone who recognizes that they are responsible for missing out on the highest in human fulfillment and happiness. Thus, a deep, eternal regret nags at the person who becomes a lover of self.

One is, of course, likely to ask how reasonable it is to think that those in hell can recognize how bad off they are in their state of separation and still never seek reconciliation with God. If they are suffering in such agony, why not repent? The answer can be seen in what was already said earlier: since they are maximally disposed to be self-lovers, i.e., they have become *set in their ways,* they might intellectually recognize how bad off they are in their condition, but still not *desire* to change it. NC theorists often liken this state to the state of an unwilling drug addict. The addict recognizes his ruined condition, and wishes that he no longer wanted to take drugs. But nonetheless, he *does* want to take them and thus continues to do so. Similarly, the one in hell, though recognizing that he would be better off if he loved God, still refuses to do so. And we need not resort to the drastic examples of the unwilling drug addict to illustrate this phenomenon. People who are addicted to smoking, or who simply love foods that are devastating to their health are not situated much differently. They see full well that the behaviors they are engaging in are harmful and destructive for them. They may even wish that they didn't desire to engage in these behaviors. But they nonetheless *do* desire to continue to engage in these behaviors.

13. At least one must think of this fire metaphorically for those who are in hell prior to the general resurrection of the wicked. Talk of the fire as metaphor is not new, of course. It was the view of, among others, Calvin. See *Commentary on a Harmony of the Evangelists,* volume 1, trans. W. Pringle (Grand Rapids: Eerdmans, 1948), 200.

Premature Deaths and Later Life Conversions

Before we complete our treatment of the natural consequence view, it is worth exploring one other issue that NC theorists would have to address, specifically, the fate of those without fully formed characters. A couple of such cases readily come to mind, the most obvious being cases of those who die as children. But in addition, the natural consequence theorist will have to say something about cases of deathbed or merely late-in-life conversions. Since none of these will have an opportunity to cultivate God-loving characters by making free choices in their earthly lives, what, on this view, is their eternal fate? It would seem on this view that such people would not have cultivated characters suited for heaven. And yet parables such as the laborers in the vineyard seem to emphasize that such people receive the same "wage" as those who have participated in the process of sanctification for a longer period of time (Matt. 20:1-16). I will briefly address both types of case, looking at the second one first.

Recall that the natural consequence view holds that there is something intrinsically valuable about being able to engage freely in soul-making (that is, in freely becoming a person of a certain sort). In fact, that is the main purpose for our earthly life. Now what of those who repent and are reconciled to God but who do not have opportunity to develop God-loving characters (that is, what about cases of late-in-life conversions)? It seems that the right thing for the NC theorist to say is that in such cases, God transforms them and provides them with such a character. In doing so, God would then merely provide them with the desire of their hearts.

But one might wonder why then God doesn't do the same for everyone. Why bother to have people work through the process of sanctification at all? If it is possible to be sanctified without it, why not do so in every case? The NC theorist has a response to this objection. The following utterly fictional story will help me to illustrate it:

> In the waning years of his life, the great sculptor Michelangelo became physically debilitated and unable to sculpt. This was intensely frustrating for him because there were other works of art he had envisioned and desperately wanted to create. In fact, he had drawn elaborate sketches for many of the sculptures that he hoped to craft. A student of his suggested that possibly he, the student, might assist the great artist. By using the sketches, the student could create the sculptures that Michelangelo had sketched and thus bring his life's work to

completion. The student worked with diligence and great care and over the course of a few years completed the sculptures. During the final year of his life a number of Michelangelo's works were displayed, among them a few that were produced by the student from the sketches. While Michelangelo took great pride in the works and in the accolades he received from those who viewed them, he could not help but feel a little less pride in the works that were completed by the student. In one sense, no doubt, they were his, yet in another sense, they were not quite.

We might imagine something analogous going on in the case of later life conversions. That is, God provides, to use the language of the parable of the vineyard, the same wage to each of those who have come to believe in Christ. But some were able to complete more of the task than others. And while the wage (or, better, the result) in each case is the same (that is, each is transformed into a lover of God, enjoying him forever) there is a qualitative difference in their ability to enjoy the result. Those who have cultivated a God-loving character through a long process of sanctification enjoy the reward more than those who have not, either because of later life conversion or a failure to cultivate holiness in their daily lives.

But what of the case of children and others who might be unable to make even the initial choice to reconcile themselves to God and seek his face? There are a number of things one might say about such cases. The simplest would be to say that God in his omniscience knows which among them would choose to turn to him if they had lived on and which would not. As a result, God gives to each a character in keeping with the decision that they would have made. Notice that, if one were to take this view, one would have to say, as in the above case, that since these characters are not directly and freely brought about, they will provide experiences that are not quite as intrinsically valuable (for those in heaven, and we might add, that the experiences of those in hell might not be as intrinsically sorrowful).[14]

14. This is only one of the solutions that might be offered at this point, and it too is controversial. Some philosophers do not believe that the sort of knowledge presupposed in this solution is knowledge that God could have. For a discussion of this point see Scott Davison's chapter on divine providence and human freedom (pp. 217-37). Others would argue that even if such knowledge is generally available it is not available here since it assumes that there is a single right answer to the question "what would have happened to P if P had not died as a child?" Some would argue that there simply is no single correct answer to that question and so, this is not something even God could know.

A Problem and a Compromise

Above I have set out the natural consequence model and explored some of the additional explanatory power that this model seems to have. But there is one serious difficulty with the natural consequence model. The philosopher Eleonore Stump, in a context similar to the one we are discussing here, puts the problem this way:

> [On a view such as this] there seems no need, in fact no room, in this process for the atonement. If God can do the work of making a believer righteous in virtue of the believer's assent to God's work, then what is the role of atonement in salvation? Why shouldn't God have done the entire work of justification without the suffering and death of the incarnate Christ? On the other hand, if we can describe the Atonement in such a way as to make it an integral part of salvation, what is its relation to the process of justification by faith? How does the atonement contribute to justification . . . ?[15]

You might think that we have addressed this above when discussing the role of grace on the NC model. But all that is really said there is that the NC model is not a "works salvation" model since it positively *requires the operation of divine grace* in salvation and sanctification. But the problem raised here can be seen by considering this question: how exactly does the story of *Christ's death and resurrection* figure into the grace that we receive according to the NC model? Why, on this model, did God incarnate have to come to earth to *suffer and die?*

It is abundantly clear in Scripture that our sin has caused us to be cut off from God and that Christ's death is the remedy for this. It is also clear in Scripture that the effects of sin which serve to cut us off from God are numerous. But one of those effects is surely that our sins merit punishment. And one of the things that Christ's death achieves for us is the satisfaction of that punishment. Undoubtedly, this is a controversial claim among Christian theologians, but it is one that the teachings of Scripture make it hard to escape. The fact that justification is set out in terms of violation of "law" and resultant "condemnation" which necessitates "justification" and "satisfaction" or "propitiation" surely makes the salvation story look very much like the story proposed in the penalty model. And passages

15. "Aquinas on Atonement," in *Trinity, Incarnation, and Atonement,* ed. Cornelius Plantinga and Ronald Feenstra (Notre Dame: University of Notre Dame Press, 1989), 198.

such as 2 Thessalonians 1:7-9 make it clear that part of what keeps us separated from God is a penalty that sin has brought upon us — a penalty that requires payment: "God is just. . . . He will punish those who do not know God and do not obey the gospel of our Lord Jesus. They will be punished with everlasting destruction and shut out from the presence of the Lord and from the majesty of His power. . . ."

This feature seems to be at the heart of the penalty model while there seems to be no role for it at all in the natural consequence model. One way to solve this problem would be adopt a hybrid model, that is a model which accepts *both* the penalty model *and* the natural consequence model. There is no reason why we could not append to the NC model the claim that in addition to destroying our ability to become God-lovers (God's intended purpose for us) sin also carries a penalty, a penalty which we could not pay on our own. Without the payment being made we cannot receive the grace necessary to cure the disease. So, the atonement made on the cross then is a necessary condition for receiving divine grace, which in turn is necessary for being made fit for spending eternity in God's presence.

On the hybrid view, then, it is true that there is a penalty, a penalty which Christ's death pays on behalf of those who accept it. But it is also true that those who fail to accept it put themselves into a state which leads them naturally to being self-lovers and thus naturally to spend eternity apart from God. Incorporating the natural consequence model brings along answers to questions that do not seem to be available on that model alone, questions, as noted above, such as why those in hell can never be saved.

Unloving/Unjust?

Now that we have had the chance to propose a model for understanding and defending the traditional doctrine of hell, let's turn to look at the objections to the view raised by its critics. As I said at the beginning, the charge of the critics most often amounts to the claim that there is something unloving or unjust or both about the traditional view of hell. Let's look at each of these charges in turn.

The discussions of these charges have been long, complex, and frequently intertwined. One might argue, for example, that a God who admits people to hell is unloving *because* he is unjust. Thus, we cannot completely unhook one charge from the other. We can try to do so for our purposes here by dividing up the objections as follows. We will discuss the four most central charges of this type in turn (all of these are meant to be understood as objections raised against the belief that God allows a hell of the sort described in what I will, from here forward, call the "hybrid model"):

1. God is *unjust* because the punishment received in hell does not fit the crime.
2. God is *unjust* because some who go to hell never had a chance to hear or understand the gospel.
3. God is *unloving* because true love would not allow the beloved to suffer such a fate.
4. God is *unloving* because he would not make the eternal consequences of heaven and hell depend on what we think and choose in earthly lives of this sort.

Charge 1: God is *unjust* because the punishment received in hell does not fit the crime.

Reply to Charge 1: A reply to this charge was already given in detail in the section entitled "Objections to the Penalty Model."

Charge 2: God is unjust because some who go to hell never had a chance to hear or understand the gospel.

Reply to Charge 2:[16] Before presenting what I take to be an adequate response to this charge, it is worthwhile to pause briefly in order to say a few words about a very common response to this charge offered by Christian apologists and theologians. The response can be put like this:

> The trouble with this charge is that it is based on a faulty presupposition. Since it claims that God is unfair in setting things up in the way

16. It is worth mentioning that there are a number of related objections that one can raise here. For example, one might say that God is unfair because he leaves the spreading of the gospel in the hands of lazy, sinful, selfish, and limited human beings, or because he does not make the gospel known by means of celestial fireworks or voices from the heavens. Unfortunately, space does not allow me to address all of the objections (though some of these related objections are treated by John O'Leary-Hawthorn in the chapter on arguments for atheism, pp. 116-34). Instead I will focus on the basic charge as stated.

> that he has, it presupposes that God was somehow *obligated* to set it up so as to give each person the opportunity to be saved. But it is just wrong to think that God *owes us* salvation or even that he owes us a *shot at it*. Since salvation is an utterly unmerited gift, we can think of the situation along the lines of the following analogy. A rich philanthropist visits a homeless shelter. This philanthropist walks around a bit and then picks out three individuals and tells them that he will gladly buy them the house of their choosing. And away they go. Now those who were not picked might be saddened by the fact that they were not among those selected. But it would be sheer folly for any of these to claim that the philanthropist acted *unfairly*. He wasn't obliged to house any of them. He certainly cannot be faulted for not housing *all* of them. Likewise, God owes none of his fallen creatures salvation. And thus he cannot be criticized as somehow unfair for failing to save all of them, or even for failing to offer all of them an equal shot at salvation.

I think that the response offered above is, strictly speaking, correct. The defender of the traditional view here is saying that there is nothing *unfair* or *unjust* about God saving some of his creatures and not others. But while this is right, it does not really undermine the force of the charge. The reason is that even if this scenario does not raise any trouble for God's justice, it does seem to be inconsistent with his *love*. For imagine our philanthropist again, but this time imagine that he has infinite financial resources. In addition, this philanthropist claims to love all the people in the homeless shelter intensely and equally, as a parent loves a child. If this philanthropist goes to the homeless shelter and agrees to buy houses for only three of them, it seems to put the lie to the claim that he loves all of them, much less intensely. And the same lesson seems to apply in Charge 2 above. So, there is an issue here that needs to be addressed: isn't it somehow contrary to God's claim to *love* all of his children that he makes it that some of them never hear?

Solution One

Of course an answer to this first charge might not be hard to find at all. To see why, let's first consider carefully what it is that we find troubling about the fact that some perish never having heard. The trouble, it seems, is that those who don't hear are disadvantaged. They don't believe because they are not given the opportunity. But this claim presupposes that some who never hear *would believe if they did hear.* But why should we think that is true? For all we know, those who never hear are such that were they to hear, they would not believe anyway. If this is right, God has not done anything unjust or unloving in not letting them hear in the first place. He has just allowed to occur what would have happened no matter what.[17]

Someone might object to this solution by claiming that it is obviously false. The fact that people come to believe in Christ when the gospel is proclaimed in areas which were formerly unreached, shows that there are people in unreached areas who would believe if they did hear. Notice, however, that this objection is mistaken. What Solution One denies is this: "that those who *never* hear, wouldn't believe if they did." Stated this way, we can never have evidence that such people would respond if they heard. Why? Because to have such evidence, we would have to notice that some such people *do* respond. But if that were to happen, they would (obviously) be among those who *did hear* and thus not be part of the relevant group (i.e., those who never hear) in the first place!

Solution Two

Solution One is a brief answer to the charge and many will find it unsatisfactory. Still, there aren't any especially good reasons to find it unsatisfactory. In fact, if God is the loving creator Christians claim he is, it makes eminently good sense. But there are other answers that can be developed. Let me gesture at a recipe for constructing another answer, though I won't actually construct it here. Part of what Charge 2 assumes is that those who do not have the gospel preached to them verbally do not have the necessary information to be saved. But the natural question that arises here is: what information *is* necessary exactly? Maybe it turns out that the information necessary for salvation can be discovered in nature, though it might take some efforts to discover it. So, for example, would it be enough if someone who had never believed the gospel nonetheless believed:

1. that God exists
2. that one is sinful

17. One version of this response to Charge 1 is defended in detail by William Lane Craig in his "'No Other Name': A Middle Knowledge Perspective on the Exclusivity of Salvation Through Christ," cited earlier.

3. that sin separates us from God
4. that there must be some means of reconciliation

and as a result of believing 1-4 is moved by an act of will to repent and avail himself or herself of the reconciliation? These are difficult questions I don't intend to try to resolve here. As I said, this is a recipe for responding to Charge 2. How one responds depends on what one thinks the necessary beliefs are. If the necessary beliefs can be gleaned without receiving the verbal witness of the gospel, Charge 2 may be based on an utterly faulty presupposition.

Solution Three

One last solution that some have offered holds that those who did not hear in this life must then be given an opportunity to hear immediately after death but before judgment. There is, of course, no clear scriptural support for such "second chances" though it does not seem to be directly contradicted by any passages either. As a result, this is another response that one might consider to Charge 2.

Charge 3: God is unloving because true love would not allow the beloved to suffer such a fate. If God loved us all he would do whatever is necessary to guarantee that we are all saved.

Reply to Charge 3: Let's call Charge 3, the "universalist charge" since it reflects the sentiments underlying the position of most universalists. The criticism embodied in the universalist charge cuts to the heart of what most people find objectionable in the traditional doctrine of hell. Even those who, like myself, think that the traditional doctrine is true cannot help but struggle at times in thinking that true love for someone is inconsistent with assigning someone to hell forever.

What is it exactly that underlies this sentiment? Why do we all feel the tug of the objection that claims that God's love is inconsistent with the doctrine of hell? A look at the recent literature on the topic indicates at least two motivations. The first I will discuss here, the second below. The first motivation springs from the belief that a loving God would do whatever is necessary to prevent those who are destined for hell from going there. On our hybrid position above we have seen that this would mean doing two things:

1. Canceling the penalty due as a result of sin, and
2. Blocking the natural consequences which result from the life lived by the hell-bound person.

So, the critic who raises Charge 3 should be viewed as saying:

Revised Charge 3: God is unloving because true love would (i) cancel the penalty due as a result of sin and (ii) block the natural consequences which result from the life lived by the hell-bound person.

Is this true? I think there is a lot to be said about (i). But let's leave that aside here since both traditionalist and universalist agree that God, out of his love, has sent his Son to "cancel the penalty of sin."

Must God "Block" the Natural Consequences?

Does love require that God do (ii) as well? Remember that on the hybrid view described above, the purpose of the earthly life is soul-making. That is, while on this earth God gives us meaningful freedom which allows us to become a person of a certain sort. And becoming a person of a certain sort means becoming a person who is resolute either in their love of self or in their love of God. Love of self, as we noted, is something which we can become resolutely settled in if we continue to spurn God's grace in this life. Love of God is something that we can strive for in this life, through the power of grace, and achieve when transformed by God in eternity. What the universalist is asking for, then, is that God reverse the natural consequences of a life of self-love. Thomas Talbott puts it this way:

> If I sink deeply into moral corruption, an omnipotent being may be unable, consistent with my freedom, simply to reconstitute me with a good character, but he surely can, as often as he likes, release me from my *bondage* to a bad character. . . . [A good physician would surely give a drug addict a remedy that would break the power of the addiction if he had one. To do so would be to restore the addict to freedom.] And the same would be true of a God who releases terribly corrupt persons from their bondage to unhealthy desires or from the psychological impossibility of doing what is right; whether such bondage is their own fault or not, a God who releases them from it and restores them to freedom, but neither causes them to act rightly nor pre-

vents them from continuing to act wrongly, would in no way violate their moral freedom.[18]

"Blocking" Natural Consequences Makes Freedom Meaningless

What can the traditionalist who defends the hybrid view say here? The first thing one should say is that if God were to operate in this way he would make our freedom *meaningless.*[19] What do I mean by this? Let me introduce a distinction here that might make the notion clear. We might think of our freedom of action in this life as having two components. When I act freely I first *make a choice among alternatives.* After making the choice, my body is set in motion in certain ways, ways which then have an impact on the world around me. So, if I, as a shortstop, decide to throw the ball to second base, I first make the decision to throw it there, and that in turn leads to my moving my muscles, which in turn leads to the ball moving towards the second baseman. Simple enough. What makes my freedom *real* we might say, is that I really can choose among alternatives. But what makes my freedom *meaningful* is that the choices I make have an impact on what happens in the world, that is, that because of my choosing, my muscles move in a certain way and the ball then flies through the air.

One could have real freedom *without* having meaningful freedom. Some philosophers, in the context of discussing the problem of evil have suggested, in fact, that God should have made the world in just this way. That is, God should have allowed us to make choices, but then should not have allowed those choices to have *real* consequences in the world. So, if I choose to shoot my neighbor, God would give me an illusion that I actually do it (so that I at least believe that my freedom is meaningful) but in fact, my evil choice has no real bad effect on the world (though it would have a bad effect on my character).[20] But while God might have been able to set up the world in this way, to do so would be to make our freedom *meaningless.* For freedom to be meaningful, it is not only true that we have to be able to choose among alternatives. It must also be the case that

18. Thomas Talbott, "Providence, Freedom, and Human Destiny," *Religious Studies,* 26:232.

19. This may be a bit too strong. It might be better simply to claim that operating in this way would render our freedom much less meaningful.

20. For more on this approach to the problem of evil see Daniel Howard-Snyder's chapter on evil, pp. 76-115.

the course of events varies with our choices. If I choose to become a self-lover, but God blocks my choices from having their effect, he has prevented my freedom from being what it was supposed to be, that is, a means by which I can engage in meaningful soul-making. I can engage in soul-making, but God won't let me become the person I choose to become. I can only become the sort of person he wants me to become. But then, of course, it looks like I don't have freedom to engage in soul-making after all.

Some might find nothing objectionable about such a picture in which humans have real but not meaningful freedom. Someone might, as Talbott does, ask us to imagine earthly parents who are watching their child making a choice that will have devastating consequences. The parents might allow the child to make the choice if the choice and its bad consequence will end up helping the child in the long run. In such cases, it may be better to allow them to make the bad choice. But if the bad choice will *only* be harmful (not to mention eternally destructive), no good parent would allow such a choice to be carried out, that is, to have its consequences. So, some might say, we all agree that it is more loving, in such cases, to permit the child to have real but not "meaningful" freedom. But is this really true? It is true that we override the decisions of our young children if the choice will have devastating consequences. I don't allow my child to toddle out into traffic or to drink battery acid. But when our focus shifts to adult children, the picture changes. If my son decides to choose a career, a mate, etc., which I believe (or know) will be destructive for him, I may counsel him in the strongest terms not to do so. But if I were to kidnap him and surgically or chemically alter his brain so that he will not choose those things, I would be meddling in a way that displayed disrespect for his autonomy as a person.[21] To interfere in this way would be to remove the *meaningfulness* of his freedom, and this would be to undermine both his human dignity and the real purpose of the earthly life: autonomous soul-making. Thus, if love requires respect for the freedom and individual autonomy of the person who is loved, the universalist charge is false because love does not require (ii).

It is worth noting here that the universalist may disagree with this way of seeing things, however. Some universalists agree with part of the account just given, but not all of it. These universalists agree that there is

21. Assuming, of course, that he is not suffering from a condition that prevents him from making these decisions on his own (that is, he is free from organic mental illness, etc.).

intrinsic worth in autonomous soul-making. As a result, they would argue, God leaves us free to try to become God-lovers by turning to him, accepting his grace, and struggling forward in the process of sanctification. But if that process fails, that is, if the person fails to turn to God and develop a God-loving character by choice, it is more loving for God to save that person *against their will,* so to speak, than to allow their choices to have their natural consequences, namely, being a self-lover, a God-hater, and thus separated from God for eternity.

Thus, as the universalists see it, it is more loving to interfere with the choices of those who want to be apart from God than it is to respect their freedom and autonomy. But it does seem that on this point it is the traditional view that is more in keeping with our impressions about how genuine love is to be expressed.

The discussion of Charge 3 leads naturally to Charge 4 which, you will recall, was put as follows:

Charge 4: God is unloving because he would not make the eternal consequences of heaven and hell depend on what we think and choose in earthly lives of this sort.

Reply to Charge 4: The charge raised here is one, again, that has been advanced in recent writings by universalists. Their central claim is that God has put us in an environment in which it is too hard for us to see that the point of this life is to become lovers of God. And even if God has provided us with enough evidence to make it clear to us that this is the purpose of this life, he has given us such frail human faculties that he could not reasonably have expected us to be able to succeed in the task. The Yale philosopher and theologian Marilyn Adams puts it this way:

> . . . I draw two conclusions: first, that [a human adult, impaired as we are] is no more competent to be entrusted with its (individual or collective) eternal destiny than a two year old . . . is to be allowed choices that could result in its death or serious physical impairment; and second, that the fact that the choices of such impaired agents come between the divine creator of the environment and their infernal outcome no more reduces divine responsibility for the damnation than two-year old agency reduces the responsibility of the adult caretaker.[22]

22. Marylin Adams, "The Problem of Hell: A Problem of Evil for Christians," in *Reasoned Faith,* ed. Eleonore Stump (Ithaca: Cornell University Press, 1993), 313.

It should be clear that this charge can be easily related to the one discussed above. The universalist might say, "On the hybrid view, to be a lover of God one must first turn to him and accept the grace that pays the penalty for our sin and gives us the power to break the bondage of sin. But to do *that* one must accept that initial grace and turn to God. And as we make choices in our daily lives, choices which might slowly but surely lead us away from God and into self-love, we unwittingly cut ourselves off from being able to will to turn to God in the first place. And, given our impaired condition and circumstances, it is almost impossible to prevent ourselves from cutting ourselves off from God in this way. And if God truly loves us, he would never put us in such a condition."

Thus, we might rephrase Charge 4 as follows:

Revised Charge 4: If God is hanging such great significance on the course of our earthly lives, he is obliged to make it very clear to us just what that significance is, and he is obliged to give us the tools and environment that allow us to meet the challenge. If he doesn't do these things, and then consigns to hell those who fail at the task, he is unloving. And surely he does *not* do these things, since many people do not even believe in an afterlife, never mind believing that the choices made in their daily lives have some connection to this eternal fate.

The claim of the defender of Charge 4, then, is that the task of human existence is not clear, and the tools for the task insufficient. Is this correct? To answer that question we must first answer the question of just how clear the task is supposed to be. One might think initially that it should be so clear that no one can possibly miss it, that is, as clear as modern advertising slogans. If mere human powers can implant these thoughts deeply in our minds, can't God do the same concerning this very central fact?

Can God Make It Clearer?

Some, myself included, have argued that God cannot make things quite that evident.[23] One reason is that if he were to demonstrate to us that there were two courses, one leading to life and one to eternal separation in a forceful and obvious way, God would remove the freedom necessary for

23. We cannot launch into an extended discussion of this issue here. A detailed disussion of this issue can be found in the chapter "Arguments for Atheism," pp. 116-34.

autonomous soul-making by subjecting us to a form of divine coercion.[24] So, if he cannot make the truth as fully evident as *that,* how evident must it be to make it fairly accessible while not coercively overpowering? For all we know, the answer is: just as accessible as it is.

Are We Properly Equipped to Achieve the Aims of This Life?

What about the claim, then, that the tools that God has given us are insufficient for the task? Is it true that our abilities to think about our fate and to make choices about it in this life are so drastically impaired that doing what is required of us is unfairly difficult? The problem with this question is that it is not really clear what it is asking. Assuming that we have adequately addressed the "is the task evident enough?" objection, the only thing it could be asking is whether or not we can choose to be lovers of God once we recognize that that is what we *ought* to do. No doubt doing this is hard. But its difficulty is part of what makes it soul-making. It is having to make the choices in the face of temptations that makes our choices *real* choices among alternatives. So the question is, once we recognize what the task of life is (becoming lovers of God rather than self), are the temptations to be lovers of self so strong that we don't have a fair opportunity to do otherwise? The universalist claims that the temptations are too strong, the traditionalist claims that divine grace overcomes the power of sin and allows us to choose to turn to God. It is by no means clear that the universalist is right on this score, and thus, we might say, there is no compelling reason to give up the traditional position on the basis of Charge 4.

No doubt, the issues raised here are deep and complex. Complete resolution of them would require a great deal more discussion than I can give them here. But the question we have been addressing in this section is whether or not the universalist has any successful objections against the traditionalist. What I have tried to show here is that it is far from clear that he does. As a result, I think we can conclude that we have seen no good

24. See for example my essay "Coercion and the Hiddenness of God," *American Philosophical Quarterly* 30:1 (1993): 27-38, as well as essays by Daniel Howard-Snyder, "The Argument from Divine Hiddenness," *Canadian Journal of Philosophy* 26 (1996): 433-53, and Richard Swinburne, *The Existence of God* (Oxford: Clarendon Press, 1979), 153ff.

reason to think that the plain sense of Scripture does not make good sense, and so no good reason to abandon the traditional doctrine of hell.

A Note on Annihilation and Reincarnation

In recent years there has been a growing number of thinkers who have defended positions on the nature of postmortem existence that are neither universalist nor traditionalist in nature. One of the most commonly discussed views is annihilationism. On the annihilationist picture, those who fail to accept Christ are judged and punished for their sins after death in hell. But the punishment they receive is not of infinite duration. Instead, they are punished for a period of time commensurate with the severity and amount of sin committed in this life and after this time, they simply cease to be. Thus, on this view, it is not true that all human beings are immortal. Those who end up in hell are there to receive the penalty merited by their sin, after which time they no longer exist.[25]

The annihilationist view has some support in Scripture (see, for example, Matt. 7:13; 10:28; Rom. 9:22; Heb. 10:26-27), though it looks as if certain texts (e.g., Matt. 25:46; Rev. 20:10) are nearly impossible to reconcile with annihilationist claims. My aim here, however, is not to address annihilationism from the point of view of Scripture (since this has been done quite adequately in my view in a number of other places),[26] but to speak about the philosophical inadequacies that, to my mind, make the annihilationist view less palatable than the traditional view.

While I think there are a number of difficulties for the annihilationist on philosophical grounds, let me just raise one brief one here. It is this: annihilationism supposes that in eternity, capital punishment is less severe than a "life sentence." And while this may be true, it surely runs counter to the way in which we view these matters in earthly affairs. Why do we think that being imprisoned for life is better than facing lethal injection? I am not sure. But I suspect it is because we think that being taken out of existence is the ultimate penalty: maximal deprivation, the removal of the minimal necessary condition for enjoying any good. But then why do we think differently about these matters when it comes to eternity? It might be because we have a conception of hell as eternal physical torture. I have

25. For examples of defenses of annihilationism, see note 3.

26. See as one example D. A. Carson, *The Gagging of God: Christianity Confronts Pluralism* (Grand Rapids: Zondervan, 1996), chapter 13.

argued above that this way of thinking about hell is mistaken. If that is right, the annihilationist at least owes us an account of why our judgments differ in the cases of earthly punishments and eternal ones.

Some have also criticized the Christian picture by arguing that an all-good God would have employed reincarnation as a way of bringing all to repentance. Wouldn't it be better, they ask, to recycle those who are unrepentant at the end of their life and give them a "fresh start" rather than simply consigning them to hell?! In other words, the reincarnationist argues: "If the Christian God exists he would do things in the most suitable manner. But certainly reincarnating those who fail to accept the gospel is vastly preferable to consigning them to hell for eternity. Thus, the Christian God does not exist." Notice that pointing to scriptural passages that deny the existence of reincarnation does not help when it comes to a critic of this sort. Still, there are serious philosophical problems for the reincarnationist.

First, the reincarnation view assumes that everyone will come around eventually. But how can one be so confident that all would come around after a finite number of earthly lives? How can we be confident that there would be even *one more* person who comes around if given further lives in which to try? There may simply be some who don't want to be a lover of God, and that's it!

But the difficulties with reincarnation run deeper. Above I argued that for this earthly life to have meaning, it must have some connection to one's eternal destiny. And so, one is given the opportunity to decide to become a lover of self, or to seek God's reconciliation in order to become a lover of God. But on the reincarnationist view, the one who works to become a lover of self is not allowed to *be* a lover of self. Instead, one who becomes a thoroughgoing lover of self is recycled back into a new body, a new infancy, and a new life. One difficulty with this picture is that it, like the universalist picture described earlier, seems to rob freedom of its *meaningfulness* (since here again it looks as if my free choices are blocked from having their consequences).

But something more troubling arises when we consider what sort of transformation is supposed to be involved in reincarnation. Presumably it at least involves erasing my dispositions to be a lover of self so that I can "start over again." But one might wonder: if my dispositions to be a person who is a self-lover are utterly erased, is it really true that *I* am starting over in the reincarnated body? Isn't what really happens that the person who has become a self-lover is *destroyed* and a new person comes into existence? In other words, if God takes my soul at death and wipes away all the desires, wishes, hopes, inclinations, habits and so on that make me uniquely *me,* and then reincarnates that soul in a new body, isn't it better to say that *I* no longer exist, but merely the soul which once contained me? If so, it seems that the sort of reincarnation described here as an alternative for the traditional view is not only no better than the traditional view, it may not even be coherent![27]

Conclusion

The testimony of the Lord, the Scriptures, and the tradition of the Christian church speak almost with one voice in favor of the traditional doctrine of hell. Still, all Christians struggle with this seemingly harsh side of the Christian worldview. What I have tried to do here is show that the Christian doctrine of hell has a central place in helping us think about the purpose of the earthly life, the value of human autonomy, and the depth of divine love. Though some have offered powerful arguments that the traditional view of hell proves God to be unloving or unjust, I have shown here that there is no reason to think these arguments are successful. While we have not plumbed all of these issues to their very depths, my hope is that this provides the reader with a grasp of how to understand the doctrine and to defend it against some of the more powerful objections.

27. The issues raised here take us to the heart of the problem of "numerical personal identity" discussed by Trenton Merricks in his chapter on resurrection, pp. 261-86.

13

Religion and Science

W. Christopher Stewart

This essay focuses on the interactions between religion and science as ways of knowing. Few if any developments have impacted the shape of Western civilization more than the rise of science. Modern science emerged from its humble beginnings in the seventeenth century to become one of the dominant forces in Western culture, influencing not merely the way we live, but more importantly for our purposes here, the way we understand the nature of the universe and the place of humanity within the cosmos. It is with respect to the latter in particular that science brushes up against issues that have been widely regarded for centuries as the special domain of religion.

If history has taught us anything at this juncture, it is that the relationships between religion and science are exceedingly complicated, so much so in fact that general claims about science and religion are usually difficult to sustain, and are frequently laced with numerous caveats. As a special case of the relationship between faith and reason, the issues one must grapple with in the attempt to do justice to the interactions between religion and science reach across multiple academic disciplines and are often extremely complicated, both historically and conceptually. Strictly speaking, when we refer to science and religion, whether we intend to

---

I am deeply indebted to the growing number of philosophers, theologians, historians, sociologists, and scientists who have written on the themes addressed in this essay, most often with more eloquence and clarity than I can muster. My thanks extend to all those authors who, reading these pages, recognize their insights.

make a distinction between particular institutions within society (such as the National Science Foundation and the Southern Baptist Church), or more generally between alternative ways of knowing, we must recognize that science and religion per se do not interact; people do. The course and tone of interpersonal interactions always reflect the peculiarities of the social and historical context, including the peculiar and very often complex agendas of the various parties involved. A lot of recent work by historians and sociologists of science has made it pretty clear that these agendas are never merely logical or theoretical, but often involve political, social, and (in the case of individuals) psychological factors, such as greed, envy, or ambition, the effect of which on the scientific enterprise is not always entirely wholesome. Thus there is something slightly artificial about any discussion of science and religion which treats them as abstractions, isolated from the often messy details of history. If we want to make genuine progress on the subject, we must be prepared to take a deep and honest look at the diverse history of the interactions between science and religion.[1]

Before getting down to business, let me add one more introductory point. In order to focus attention on what seem to me to be the most crucial issues (which, as we shall see, have mostly to do with *method*, or what you might call one's general *approach* to reality as distinct from one's actual opinions about reality), I won't say a great deal about the *content* of particular scientific theories, such as the big bang theory of the origin of the universe or the theory of evolution by natural selection, or indeed about specific points of theology, except for the purpose of illustrating more general comments about how scientific attempts to understand the world and our place in it ought to relate to religious or theological claims along the same lines. Furthermore, as the best of the most recent scholarship on the relationship between science and religion makes abundantly clear, the fundamental problem is not to defend religion against science,

1. Given spatial limitations, although the historical allusions in this essay will be honest, or at least as honest as I can make them, they will not be deep. It would indeed be impossible to summarize the great wealth of historical research on science and religion published in the past twenty years or so. The best and most readable books of this sort include: *God and Nature: Historical Essays on the Encounter Between Christianity and Science,* edited by David Lindberg and Ronald Numbers (Berkeley: University of California Press, 1986); *Creation and the History of Science,* by Christopher Kaiser (Grand Rapids: Eerdmans, 1991); and *Science and Religion: Some Historical Perspectives* by John Hedley Brooke (New York: Cambridge University Press, 1991).

or vice versa. In this essay, one of my principal aims is to explain why it seems to me (and many others) that such arguments are unnecessary and even counterproductive.

There are a number of worries that Christians (and religious believers generally) have about science. For many Christians, modern science is threatening because of the fact that opponents of religion frequently take it for granted that the results of science have undermined the intellectual respectability of belief in God. Science, it is argued, renders belief in God somehow superfluous or unnecessary. Even worse, in some cases the results of science seem on the face of it directly to contradict (and thus defeat) the claims of Christianity. Very often, the idea that science somehow defeats Christianity depends upon a general view of the relationship between religion and science according to which the two are locked in mortal conflict — a struggle to the death in which there can be but one survivor. In what follows, I'm going to show what's wrongheaded about the suggestion that science somehow defeats religion. I'm also going to show why "warfare" rhetoric is inappropriate and misleading in connection with general discussions about religion and science. Having "demilitarized" the zone between religion and science by clearing away these misconceptions, I'm going to suggest in the final section some ways Christians can and should move beyond conflict to a more constructive approach to thinking about the relationship between science and religious belief.

Does Science Defeat Religion?

To begin with, then, let's examine the commonly repeated argument that science proves (or at the very least strongly suggests) that there is no God. What exactly is it about science that is supposed to undermine religion in general, and Christianity in particular? As I've already intimated, the answer usually has either to do with the suggestion that science renders belief in God somehow superfluous or unnecessary, or that the results of science directly contradict (and thus defeat) the claims of Christianity.[2] For the moment, let's focus on the former claim: that science renders belief in God superfluous or unnecessary.

2. Along these lines, in the late eighteenth century, the brilliant mathematician and physicist Laplace wrote a book on celestial mechanics widely regarded as the greatest scientific treatise since Newton's *Principia*. The story is told that when asked

Argument 1: Science Defeats Religion Because It Has Successfully "Filled the Gaps"

Most often, people who think that science renders belief in God superfluous have adopted a confused "God-of-the-gaps" conception of theism. According to this view, belief in the existence of God was reasonable in the past because, in the past, the existence of God was used to explain a host of physical phenomena. Science has now shown us, however, that God is not necessary to explain any of these phenomena; purely natural explanations are utterly sufficient. The result is that science has shown us that we no longer need the God-hypothesis, and thus we are obliged to set religion aside.

Though it is often characteristic of critics of religion, this sort of God-of-the-gaps thinking is also sometimes used by religious believers to fence off certain areas as "God's doing," and therefore as beyond the reach of science. Both the critics and believers who employ this sort of thinking seem to believe that the fact that there are some events that science cannot (so far) explain is among the best evidence we have for the existence of God. From this, the critic argues from what science *has* explained to the claim that religious belief is no longer justified, while the religious believer points out that what science *has not* explained shows us, as it were, that we still have room for God.

God-of-the-gaps thinking should be avoided by the serious Christian (and anyone else, for that matter). By attempting to fill the gaps in scientific explanations with religious ones, God-of-the-gaps thinking mistakenly eliminates the possibility that one can say of an event that "God did it" and at the same time offer a physical explanation for how it happened. In short, God-of-the-gaps thinking confuses God's relationship to nature. God does not operate "alongside" the laws of nature as a distinct force. Natural laws are not independent of God. For the Christian theist, God upholds nature in existence, sustaining it (nearly always via natural

---

by the emperor of France (to whom Laplace had given a copy of his book), "Where is God in your system?" (or words to that effect), Laplace replied simply, "I have no need of that hypothesis." What Laplace must have intended is that he had no need of God to explain, for example, the motions of the planets, with respect to which Newton had earlier invoked God's periodically adjusting the orbits of the planets to explain aspects of their motions that he hadn't been able to account for in terms of his physical theory. (It is said that upon hearing of this exchange, Lagrange, another scientific luminary of the late eighteenth century, remarked, "It is a good hypothesis; it explains a lot.")

laws or "regularities") in a providential way. Finally, contrary to God-of-the-gaps thinking, the existence of God is not best regarded as a large-scale hypothesis postulated to explain anything, let alone those things science cannot explain.[3] We arrive at our knowledge of God by way of revelation, both "generally" (through creation) and "specially" (in Jesus Christ, as well as through the Scriptures and the church). The problem with God-of-the-gaps thinking is not that there are no gaps in scientific understanding. There are plenty! But this fact should not be interpreted as evidence for the existence of God. To do so is to make religious belief an easy target as the gaps in scientific understanding narrow with each scientific discovery.

As a result, we can see that this effort to show religious belief superfluous fails. Since it is wrong to think of belief in the existence of God as one among many scientific hypotheses in the first place, the fact that science explains most or all natural phenomena does not count against religious belief.

Argument 2: Science Defeats Religion by Excluding It

A person's worldview is or reflects, as the word suggests, his or her overall view of the world. More precisely, a worldview is a conceptual scheme or system of ideas into which we consciously or unconsciously fit (or attempt to fit) everything we believe, through which we interpret our experience, and from which our actions (with varying degrees of consistency) flow. It's fair to point out that a worldview is more than this. A worldview is a view *for* life as well as a view *of* life. As such, it includes, for example, a person's values and perhaps other elements, not all of which are easy to formulate in precise terms. But a worldview is at the very least a way of looking at things. A worldview is a systematic development and expression of a particular point of view or perspective.

At the heart of any worldview are a number of basic intellectual commitments or presuppositions about human beings and their capacities, the world, and God. These basic assumptions represent a "hard core" of practical and theoretical commitments that we cling to far more tenaciously than other more peripheral beliefs. One's most fundamental

3. This is not to say, of course, that it is inappropriate to talk about the explanatory power of theism as a worldview. Explanatory power is one aspect of intellectual adequacy of a given worldview.

intellectual commitments represent the assumptions we must make, as it were, before we begin to think. They comprise the notions that we bring *to* all of our thinking, and in light of which we evaluate new ideas. As Augustine once said, "We must believe something in order to know anything." So considered, intellectual activity of any sort ordinarily presupposes certain "faith assumptions" about the world.

In the West, there are two worldview traditions that compete for our allegiance. Both have been around a long time and there are no indications that either is going to fade from the scene any time soon. These two worldview traditions are theism and naturalism. (I refer to worldview "traditions" because there is more than one way to express each of these points of view. Theism, for example, includes Islamic perspectives as well as Christian. I also ignore pantheism, not because it is unimportant or not worth considering, but simply because it does not exert much of an attractive force on most Westerners, at least not in comparison to theism and naturalism.)

There's more than one way to sum up theism. For my purposes, and at the risk of gross oversimplification, I shall reduce it to two affirmations: (1) God and the created realm, the *cosmos*, are distinct but also intimately related, and (2) human persons, as products of divine creation, are unique among terrestrial organisms in a way that fundamentally informs the meaning, value, and purpose of human existence. To the theist, humans are not (or at least not merely) products of blind natural forces acting upon material that has (apparently) always existed, but rather a link of sorts between nature and something beyond nature — "midway between brutes and angels," as Pascal so colorfully expresses it. On the other hand, the advocate of naturalism as a worldview regards humans as no different in any significant or qualitative way from the rest of nature. We are merely products of purely natural (that is to say, physical or material) processes. In the famous words of the late Carl Sagan, "The cosmos is all there is or ever was or ever will be." There is no God-creation distinction and relationship because, as a matter of fact, there is no God. More generally, there is no nonnatural, or supernatural, dimension to reality. If "metaphysics" signifies one's beliefs about what does and does not exist, then theism and naturalism can be viewed as competing metaphysical outlooks, or outlooks on reality. To the theist, reality is ultimately personal, whereas to the atheist it is ultimately impersonal. ("Ontology" is a term often used to refer to one's view of *ultimate* reality.)

Christianity, as I've already indicated, is a variety of theism. The specific contours of an individual Christian's worldview depend on a variety of influences in addition to the Bible, such as the particular theological tradition (if any) a person identifies with. Theology (ignoring for the present the distinction between biblical and systematic theology) contributes importantly to our understanding of several fundamental points, including and especially the nature of God (as revealed in the Old Testament and in Christ), God's relationship to creation (including humanity), and God's role in human history. Moreover, contemporary formulations of a Christian worldview will reflect and respond in a variety of ways to contemporary culture and science. Here we confront the question of how exactly science ought to contribute (if at all) to the shape of a Christian view of things. A prior question, however, is whether science renders a religious outlook (Christian or otherwise) absurd, untenable, or irrational. What exactly is the role of science in the choice between competing worldviews?

With the above questions in mind, let's come back once again to the suggestion that science proves (or at the very least strongly suggests) that there is no God, that is, that naturalism is correct and theism is false. Many scientists, including many (maybe most) scientists who are Christians, maintain that the scientific process assumes a kind of *methodological* commitment to naturalism. This methodological commitment is, these scientists insist, distinct from *metaphysical* naturalism, or a commitment to naturalism as an overall metaphysical outlook. Methodological naturalism stipulates that scientific accounts must refer to wholly natural phenomena without reference to immediate or direct contributions by nonnatural or supernatural forces or agents. For instance, a chemist writing up her laboratory report is precluded from appealing to divine intervention in the description of her results (particularly so if the intent is to explain their divergence from what one ought to expect according to prevailing scientific theories). It may be perfectly acceptable to talk about nonnatural or supernatural activity, but such talk does not, strictly speaking, belong to science. To call this methodological naturalism serves to highlight the fact that it is a way of characterizing a particular methodology, nothing more. It does not suggest (or is at least not normally intended to suggest) a larger metaphysical or ontological claim about what sort of activity is or is not possible in the real world.

Some have thought, however, that the naturalism presupposed in scientific inquiry does even more than this. These critics argue that since science is inherently naturalistic, anyone who accepts science and its deliverances must thereby reject "supernaturalism." This line of reasoning is, however, utterly mistaken. As I have shown above, science at most presupposes *methodological naturalism* not *metaphysical naturalism,* and methodological naturalism does not in any way exclude religious belief.

But even if one did (mistakenly) think that methodological naturalism requires a commitment to metaphysical naturalism there is, on the face of it, something logically suspect about the claim that "science proves metaphysical naturalism." More precisely, this argument seems to commit the fallacy logicians call "begging the question" — assuming the very thing one is attempting to prove. If science *presupposes* naturalism for methodological purposes, then there is something singularly uninteresting and downright misleading about the claim that science *proves* that there is no such thing as supernatural agency operative in the universe. The Christian theist's response should be, "Of course it suggests that, it *assumes* it!" Of course, if the critics of even methodological commitments to naturalism within science (whom I have yet to discuss) are correct, then it also does not even follow that science suggests that metaphysical naturalism is correct and theism is false. More will be said about this matter below.

The Conflict Thesis

If we concede that science neither decisively refutes belief in God nor renders religious belief straightforwardly irrational or unsupportable, we are still left with the question of how best to conceive of the relationship between religion and science. In this section, I shall critically examine a widely entertained thesis about the interface between religion and science, according to which science and religion are inherently opposed to one another, so that to embrace one is ultimately to reject the other. A state of war is said to exist between the two, and in the current stage of the conflict science is usually considered to have the upper hand. I shall refer to this view as "The Confict Thesis."

The Conflict Thesis encapsulates what is perhaps the standard view of religion and science, the immediate historical origins of which are associated with the "culture wars" of the latter half of the nineteenth century. Its widespread currency may be traced back to the appearance at the end of the nineteenth century of two books, both written by Americans, both of which depict religion as tyrannical and stifling with respect to science, and both of which (along with the writings of others influenced by them, whether positively or negatively) continued to exert a powerful influence on the terms of the debate for nearly a century.[4] In the last decade or so, the Conflict Thesis has come in for some heavy weather. The Conflict Thesis is nourished for the most part by a false and misleading reading of the history of science, as well as some persistent and widespread conceptual misunderstandings of religion and science as processes of understanding, or ways of knowing. Despite its lingering popularity, historians, philosophers, theologians, and biblical scholars have taken aim at the Conflict Thesis from several angles. I shall boil these criticisms down to two main points: (1) the Conflict Thesis is historically misleading, and (2) some defenses of the Conflict Thesis exaggerate the force or status of scientific claims about the world, especially in comparison to religious or theological claims about the world. In the context of examining the historical record in connection with the first point, we shall see that some advocates of the Conflict Thesis (generally on the side of religion) rely on an approach to the Bible that does not take into full account the complexities of biblical interpretation. It is important to understand what's wrong with the Conflict Thesis in view of the fact that very often the perceived threat to religion from science (or vice versa) stems from its tacit acceptance.

The Conflict Thesis and the History of Science

Let's begin with the point that the Conflict Thesis is historically misleading. The way that the history of science is frequently used by some proponents of the Conflict Thesis (especially those who advocate naturalism as a worldview) completely ignores the historical reliance of science on religion for presupposition, sanction, and in some cases, even motivation. By focusing attention on (and often distorting) cases of opposition by religious extremists to scientific ideas which eventually carried the day, these scholars obscure the positive influence of the Christian tradition on the development of Western science.[5]

4. For those interested, I refer to John William Draper's *History of the Conflict Between Religion and Science* (1874), and Andrew Dickson White's *A History of the Warfare of Science with Theology in Christendom* (1896).

5. Historical critiques of the Conflict Thesis can also be found in, among other places, the books by Christopher Kaiser, John Hedley Brooke, and David Lindberg and Ronald Numbers, mentioned in an earlier footnote, and from which I derive many of the points I make in this section. Another very useful book in this regard is David N. Livingstone's *Darwin's Forgotten Defenders* (Grand Rapids: Eerdmans, 1987).

Contemporary historians have documented a loose set of theologically motivated presuppositions or ideals which served to inspire and regulate scientific inquiry from as early as the second century B.C. Its main tenets are the comprehensibility of the world, the unity of the celestial heavens and earth, and the relative autonomy of nature (that is, the idea that there is a fundamental or "functional" integrity or self-sufficiency in the natural order by virtue of the fact that God has granted it laws of operation). One of the more remarkable features of the tradition inspired by these ideals is not its resistance to new scientific ideas, but rather its ability to assimilate them.

The doctrine of creation early on served as a rationale for the reliance of modern science on experience and controlled experimentation. Late medieval theologians insisted on the radical contingency of the natural world, by which they meant that an omnipotent God is free to create a world structured in whatever way and governed by whatever laws God chooses, there being no necessity governing God's choices in this regard. Accordingly, to discover the actual structure of the world and discern the laws of its governance, it cannot suffice to reason them out prior to any actual experience, as it were, just by thinking about it, as if the world must of necessity exist in accordance with some set of principles discoverable by purely rational means. Instead, we've got to go out and have a look.

In the seventeenth century, belief in the doctrine of creation served to buttress the confidence of natural philosophers (the old word for "scientists," which was not coined until the nineteenth century) in the existence of a dependable order or uniformity behind the flux of nature. The search for order was regarded by the early practitioners of modern science from Copernicus through Galileo, Kepler, and Newton as a worthy and legitimate response to a universe regulated by an intelligent Creator, who had also created the human mind in such a way that it was fitted to the intelligibility of nature. This twofold belief, in the rationality of creation and the suitability of our faculties to understand the created order, together secured the possibility of scientific knowledge and a foundation for the scientist's confidence in the reliability of his most fundamental assumptions. By the end of the eighteenth century, however, secular science simply retained belief in the comprehensibility, unity, and autonomy of the world, while surrendering the original theological moorings which justified them. Thus the confidence of present-day scientists in the rationality of nature and the power of the human intellect to fathom nature's mysteries are, in fact, vestiges of the formative influence of Christianity on the study of the natural world.

So, against the suggestion that the history of interaction between science and religion reveals tyrannical dominance of the former by the latter, recent historical research has revealed a far more sophisticated conception of the relation between science and religion. It is now clear that the development of science can be and has been positively affected by religious ideas, not merely as targets for reaction, but as sources of insight. Theology has been shown to play a variety of such roles within scientific inquiry, from legitimizing the modern scientific enterprise in the early stages of its history, to stimulating lines of inquiry that have led to the development of alternative scientific explanations of natural phenomena.

Galileo, Darwin, and the Bible

In the context of talking about the historically misleading character of the Conflict Thesis, two cases merit particular attention (far more in fact than I have the space or the resources to give them) because they are the focus of so many popular myths, myths which typically serve to reinforce the Conflict Thesis by allegedly presenting us with prominent moral victories in the war of enlightened science with obscurantist religion. These cases involve the seventeenth-century physicist and astronomer Galileo, and the nineteenth-century biologist Charles Darwin.

On closer inspection, the case of Galileo reveals a clash not between science and religion as generally supposed, but between the "world system" associated with Greek science and the new conceptions of nature and the cosmos championed by Galileo. In the centuries before Galileo was brought to trial on the suspicion that he entertained beliefs (such as the idea that the heavens were neither perfect nor unchanging, and that the earth moves in orbit around the sun) held by many (though not all) religious authorities to be inconsistent with the teachings of the church, Christian theology and the interpretation of various texts of scripture had been closely linked to the picture of the cosmos outlined by the Greeks, most notably Aristotle and Ptolemy. Ptolemy's model of the solar system placed the earth rather than the sun at its center. Thus, in undermining Aristotelean and Ptolemaic ideas, Galileo pitted himself in opposition to philosophers and theologians with considerable stake (both intellectual and professional) in the preservation of the traditional picture of the cosmos. In addition, it must be noted that Galileo had the misfortune to become embroiled in a struggle against a religious bureaucracy committed to controlling the boundaries of legitimate opinion through an elaborate mechanism of censorship which was part of the Roman Catholic Church's response to the Reformation (often called the "Counter Reformation"). The issue of who could interpret the Bible was particularly sensitive at this time, and it appeared to some that Galileo was presuming to interpret it himself in light of his own observations of the natural world.

So the idea that "the Galileo affair" is best analyzed as a textbook case of the conflict between religion and science is false and misleading for several reasons. To begin with, the fact is that Galileo remained a devout Catholic until his death, and never repudiated his religious faith. Secondly, Galileo received a great deal of support and encouragement from church leaders, despite the fact that he was interrogated by the Inquisition (the religious tribunal charged with investigating charges of heresy) for allegedly advocating views at odds with the official teachings of the Catholic Church. Thirdly, in Galileo's day, Aristotelean physics and Ptolemaic astronomy, undermined by Galileo's ideas about terrestrial motion and the shape of the solar system, were defended by many scientists and intellectuals outside the church, and for (at that time) very good reasons. After all, from our vantage point on the surface of the earth, the sun does indeed appear to be moving. The earth, on the other hand, feels stationary. If the earth moves around the sun, covering a vast distance in a single year, one would expect everything to be blown off the earth's surface by a powerful wind. Likewise, common sense suggested that a spinning earth would fling off everything that wasn't nailed down. Cannon balls fired straight into the air would be expected to fall to the west of the firing point due to the earth's rotation while the ball is in the air. The problem for Galileo's theory was that none of these expected effects had been observed. Finally, from the point of view of present-day theories about space and time, whether the earth moves around the sun or vice versa depends on where you fix your sense of "rest" and "motion."

Along with the earth, Galileo did nonetheless set in motion developments that would reach a second climax in the context of nineteenth-century biology. The case of Darwin and the Darwinian revolution must be disentangled from the culture wars of the latter half of the nineteenth century, to which I've already alluded, and in which aggressive opponents of religion such as Thomas Huxley (who became known as "Darwin's bulldog") appropriated Darwin's theory of evolution by natural selection as a tool with which to promote a broad social agenda aimed at establishing science as the dominant force within Western culture. In point of fact, the encounter between evangelical theology and evolutionary thought in the latter half of the nineteenth century is marked by considerable diversity, from outright rejection of both Darwin's ideas about natural selection and the broader theory of evolution (which Darwin did not invent) to readiness to appropriate the implications of the new biology, for which appropriation many evangelicals were able to gather sufficient theological resources.[6]

Nevertheless, we cannot ignore the fact that, unlike Galilean mechanics and astronomy, the theory of evolution continues to excite controversy among Christians, and between Christians and the adherents of naturalism. To be more specific, it is the "macroevolutionary paradigm" which has been the focus of most of this controversy. We might define this paradigm as essentially made up of two core claims: (1) that there is an entirely naturalistic explanation of the development of life from a common point of origin (sometimes referred to as "the thesis of common ancestry") and from simple to complex forms (the leading candidate being natural selection acting on random genetic mutation, though the actual explanation could conceivably turn out to be some other mechanism), and (2) that life itself developed from nonliving matter without any special creative activity of God, just by virtue of the laws of physics and chemistry.

Some worry that the theory of evolution by natural selection appears wasteful, indiscriminate, or just plain inefficient, not the sort of world one would expect the God of the Bible to create. Others see a contradiction between Scripture, which seems to assert that God played a direct and immediate role in the creation of life on earth, and evolutionary theory, which seems to suggest (at most) a more indirect causal role for God in the natural process that culminated in human life. Another apparent threat to religion frequently regarded as stemming from evolution, then, is that it does not appear necessary to invoke God to explain human origins (as distinct, say, from the origin of the entire universe). The genealogical continuity from simple to complex life forms is said to leave nothing for God to do, thus making it possible to become, as one famous scientist once remarked, "an intellectually fulfilled atheist."[7]

Maybe so, but as I've already discussed (in the paragraphs on God-of-the-gaps thinking), it is not, strictly speaking, proper to regard divine activity as an *alternative* to a scientific explanation. But even if it is true that the macroevolutionary paradigm does allow one to be an intellectu-

6. In this connection, see Livingstone's *Darwin's Forgotten Defenders.*

7. This remark is from Richard Dawkins, *The Blind Watchmaker* (New York: W. W. Norton, 1986), 6.

ally satisfied atheist (something I am not at all willing to concede), it is not clear that this paradigm would, even if ultimately shown to be correct, count as evidence against belief in Christianity. Christians remain divided on the issue of whether evolution counts for naturalism and against theism, or whether in fact the scientific core of the theory of evolution (as distinct from the attempts to argue for atheism that have sprung up from it) is logically neutral between naturalism and theism. A lot of the most recent debate revolves around the likelihood of the notion of "special creation" — the claim that God created humankind as well as many kinds of plants and animals separately and specially, in such a way that the thesis of common ancestry is false.[8] An adequate summary of just this one aspect of the debate surrounding evolution would require at the very least a separate essay. It is perhaps sufficient in the context of this essay to note that sincere, intelligent, and well-informed Christians disagree on the point. Some argue that the thesis of common ancestry does not appear to be particularly likely from the standpoint of Christian theism, even after you throw in the empirical evidence bearing on the origin of life. Others argue that special creation lacks biblical, theological, and empirical support. These authors often cite various affirmations by prominent Christian theologians (past and present) of the "functional integrity" of the natural world created by God, as well as the developmental cosmology of Augustine (according to which God created the world out of nothing and imbued it with "seed principles" to govern the subsequent generation of the successive orders of complexity that comprise our world, including human life). Whatever the outcome of these debates, it is far from obvious that the theory of evolution (boiled down to its scientific essentials) counts against theism, and thus does not in and of itself pose an obvious or immediate threat to religion.

8. For an extended treatment of these issues, consult the September 1991 issue of *Christian Scholar's Review,* which contains essays by Alvin Plantinga ("When Faith and Reason Clash: Evolution and the Bible"), Howard Van Till ("When Faith and Reason Cooperate"), and Ernan McMullin ("Plantinga's Defense of Special Creation"), along with a reply by Plantinga entitled "Evolution, Neutrality, and Antecedent Probability: A Reply to Van Till and McMullin." The June 1993 issue of *Christian Scholar's Review* contains another essay by Van Till entitled "Is Special Creationism a Heresy?" McMullin has also written a follow-up essay entitled "Evolution and Special Creation," which appeared in the September 1993 issue of *Zygon.* Plantinga's riposte is "Science: Augustinian or Duhemian," contained in the July 1996 issue of *Faith and Philosophy,* the journal of the Society of Christian Philosophers.

Interpreting Scripture and Interpreting Nature

The case of Darwin, like that of Galileo, does nevertheless underscore the inescapable possibility of tensions between the claims of science and those of Christian theology. The key here is to understand how these tensions should be handled. Sometimes, apparent conflicts between science and Christianity involve interpretations of the Bible that do not take into full account the complexities of biblical interpretation. Very often, hostile relations between science and religion are rooted in an apparent contradiction between the deliverances of science and the deliverances of faith, or between the results of our encounter with nature (as guided by scientific method) and the results of our encounter with the Bible (as guided by various principles of interpretation, or "hermeneutics"). This is not the place for a lengthy discussion of the difficulties associated with determining what the Bible teaches, or what God intends to teach us through the Bible. Its importance for us here concerns interpretations of the Bible (notably the early chapters of Genesis) that on the face of it appear to conflict with particular scientific theories (such as the big bang theory of the origin of the universe, or evolutionary theories of the origin of life).

Many have struggled with the issues of biblical interpretation as these bear on issues of cosmology, beginning with Augustine in the fifth century A.D. and continuing to the present day. Some argue that the Scriptures in general should not be taken to have direct cosmological intent or implications. Many conservative biblical scholars maintain that the backdrop or point of departure of the creationist texts in Genesis, for example, is not cosmology or the origin of species but polytheism, the divinization of nature, the eternity of matter, and astrology. One can hold a high view of Scripture and biblical authority (according to which what God teaches us in the Bible is entirely trustworthy) without embracing a strictly literal reading of biblical texts that appear to have cosmological significance. Problems arise when "plain readings" or "face-value interpretations" of the Bible that do not comport with established scientific theories are regarded as self-evident facts or dead certainties. Having said that, I should add that there are some "plain readings" of Scripture that it's difficult to imagine a Christian ever giving up in the face of apparently contradictory evidence, scientific or otherwise, such as the belief (based on Scripture) that dead people sometimes come back to life, or that postmenopausal women or virgins sometimes have babies, or at the very least that such events have occurred in the past.

There is widespread agreement among Christian scholars that we should draw a distinction between our understanding or grasp of the teaching of Scripture with the teaching of Scripture. While the latter might never be mistaken, the former surely sometimes is. And just as we shouldn't believe that our intepretations of Scripture are unfailingly true, nor, for reasons which I have yet to discuss, should we regard the deliverances of science (or any other form of intellectual activity) as unfailingly true. When there is a conflict between science and our grasp of the teaching of Scripture, we should not automatically assume that it is science that is wrong and must yield to our interpretation of Scripture. Nor should we automatically assume that it is our interpretation of Scripture that is at fault. Deciding which of these routes to follow, and to what extent, can be a difficult business. Science can illuminate and shape our interpretation of Scripture; and Scripture (as well as the theology derivative from it) can inform science. What I am suggesting here does not, alas, eliminate the possibility of tension between science and our grasp of Scripture. It does suggest, however, that the tension is often a fruitful one (not unlike tensions between "levels" of explanation within science itself), and calls for a healthy dose of humility with respect to every means of knowledge at our disposal.

The Objectivity and the Certainty of Science

So far (in the last two sections), I've been focusing on the historically misleading character of the Conflict Thesis. In this section, I want to focus on my other major point of criticism of the Conflict Thesis, namely that it very often exaggerates the force or status of scientific claims about the world, especially in comparison to religious or theological claims about the world. The Conflict Thesis is nourished by some popular conceptual misunderstandings of religion and science as processes of understanding, or ways of knowing. A persistent and widely held opinion is that science is, on account of its method, uniquely privileged as a way of knowing. Scientific method is, unlike the process of forming religious beliefs, essentially disinterested and unbiased. Moreover, it is claimed that the results of science achieve a level of certainty of which religion is incapable. Suspicion and resentment of the scientific enterprise among Christians is often fueled in large measure (and often subconsciously) by the persistence of these notions, despite the fact that each has been the target of considerable criticism in recent years. On the flip side, many cases of theoretical opposition to religion among atheists is likewise supported by such misconceptions about the scientific enterprise.

But such strong claims about the privileged status of science (specifically the pure objectivity of science and the certainty of its results) have been utterly rejected by the academic community over the past thirty years or so. My general aim in summarizing some of this research is not to undermine the value of science in coming to an understanding of the natural world or to take away from its evident success along those very lines. Rather, my aim is to debunk the idea that religion is (unlike science) entirely subjective and speculative, whereas science is (unlike religion) all objective and certain. On the contrary, in the words of the scientist and theologian Arthur Peacocke, "the scientific and theological enterprises share alike the tools of groping humanity."[9]

To begin with, one common way to privilege science as a way of knowing is to assert that whereas religion trades in opinions, science gives us facts. Opinions, moreover, are held to be subjective, whereas the facts about which science informs us are objective. Unfortunately, the terms "subjective" and "objective" are frequently used without any clear idea of their meaning. Generally speaking, to say that a topic of conversation (the usual examples being morality or religion) is subjective is to say that there is no distinction between the truth of the matter and what a particular person thinks about it, so that believing something to be so makes it so, at least for that person. (This is, of course, none other than the doctrine of relativism.) If an issue is subjective (such as whether vanilla tastes better than chocolate), then people are free to believe what they like, even if they don't agree. Thus, strictly speaking, it is not possible for a person to be mistaken about subjective issues. Issues such as how many planets there are in the solar system, or the atomic weight of oxygen, on the other hand, are *objective* because a distinction is maintained between what is the case and what you, me, or anyone else believes to be the case. My believing that there are exactly nine planets in the solar system, or that the atomic weight of oxygen is thirty-two, doesn't make it so in either case. What makes these claims true is entirely independent of what I believe or don't believe. What makes these claims true has to do with the way the world actually is, quite independently of what I think about it.

If by "objective" we mean "dependent on a reality which itself is independent of the mind," then science is (for most people anyway) objective. It's "object" is external to the human mind. By contrast, religion is sometimes considered to be subjective in the sense that there isn't any-

9. Arthur Peacocke, *Intimations of Reality* (Notre Dame: University of Notre Dame Press, 1984), 51.

thing "out there" for religious convictions to correspond to, as there is in the case of science. Everyone is free to believe whatever they like because, when it comes to religion, there is no "way the world is" for religious beliefs to correspond to, no right or wrong answers to religious questions. If religious beliefs are about anything, they're about the people who hold them — the "subject" of the beliefs. Thus religious beliefs do not have an "object" in the same sense that scientific beliefs have an object. Suffice it to say that to criticize religious belief by branding it as "subjective" is simply antireligious propaganda. No religious tradition has ever endorsed the claim that science is, whereas religion is not, objective in the sense of pertaining to realities that exist independently of the human mind. The ultimate object of religious beliefs (in a nutshell, God) is as mind-independent a reality as the planet Jupiter.

On the other hand, if by "objective" we mean "neutral" in the sense of entirely free of theoretical presuppositions, then it has become clear (to the academic community anyway) that neither science nor religion is objective. To see why requires some explanation. Scientists don't just have views about the world, they are *led* to those views as a result of a process that involves, among other things, an encounter with the world and a subsequent process of reflection on that encounter, a process of reflection that involves a series of complicated inferences which culminate in a view of what "the facts" are. The twentieth century has witnessed many changes in the way that the academic community thinks about the inferences that constitute the scientific process, which changes have important implications for the nature of scientific knowledge and its place within a person's overall worldview.

For example, it is no longer acceptable to describe the scientist's encounter with the world as an encounter with "the facts" if by "facts" we mean something we grasp without any antecedent theoretical commitments. Scientists don't begin with facts in that sense. Observations of the world play a crucial role at the beginning and end of every scientific investigation. But every individual's perceptions are conditioned by her beliefs in a way that has become known as the "theory-ladenness of observations." People who bring different background beliefs or theoretical frameworks to the same situation see the world differently. Consider, for example, a sunrise. Someone who believes that the earth is the center of the solar system sees the sun rising, whereas someone who believes that the sun is the center of the solar system sees the earth turning toward the sun. Both are correct *from the point of view of their respective background beliefs*, though of course only one (or neither) is correct in the final analysis.

Let's adopt the phrase "naive realism" for the view that human beings have direct, unmediated access to Reality (the way things are). On this view, our grasp of Truth is immediate and human perception is untainted by prior theoretical commitments. Contrast "naive realism" with what is often called "critical realism" (or sometimes "perspectivalism"), according to which there is a Reality independent of the minds of individuals, but we as individuals do not have direct access to it. Our grasp of Reality is mediated. Our perception (and with it our understanding) is mediated by the beliefs we presently hold, that is to say, our present worldview. Human perception thus involves an element of interpretation, which is subject to the constraints of human finitude and human fallenness. There is Truth, but our grasp of it is limited and "fallible," not final. The point here is not to open the floodgates to a view of our encounter with the world that regards the data of experience as so pliable that "anything goes." Critical realism does not commit us to relativism — the view that we have no grip at all on any "Reality" outside the minds of individuals. "Reality" according to the relativist is a "construct" (of society or of individuals). There is no "Truth," there is only "truth." The immediate aim is simply to challenge lingering assumptions about the objectivity of science that are often used to reinforce its alleged superiority to religion.

In the past few decades, intellectuals have not only taken a second look at the notion of objectivity. They have also and for similar reasons reexamined the prospect for certainty with respect to human knowledge generally. To ascribe certainty to science and something less to other ways of knowing is another approach to privileging science and subordinating (if not undercutting completely) religion. According to a conception of science that goes all the way back to Aristotle, science is "demonstrative" in the sense of delivering us "proofs" of what must be so and cannot be otherwise with respect to the natural world. Aristotle believed that the mind had the power of directly grasping the first principles of the natural order (the *arche* of nature), from which explanations of natural phenomena could proceed in an orderly process of deduction (that is, totally secure inferences). Descartes (d. 1650) was perhaps the last natural philosopher to attempt to produce a "demonstrative" science.

The problem with the demonstrative ideal (according to which scientific knowledge is knowledge of what must be so and cannot be otherwise) is that it simply does not reflect what scientists actually do. What science is about (ultimately) is the development of theories that enable us to explain the observational data (those features of the world that scientists directly observe) or the laws inferred from those data, as well as to predict and (in some cases) control the course of nature. The process of generalizing from experience to laws or regularities in nature is known as "(enumerative) induction." It is well established that inductive procedures of the sort painstakingly outlined by Francis Bacon and later by John Stuart Mill and applied by people like Robert Boyle (Boyle's ideal gas law being a textbook case) are not capable of delivering certainty. There is always the possibility that the future course of nature will not resemble the past in every respect. Induction, along with deduction and what I shall refer to in a moment as "abduction," together comprise the various inferences that scientists (along with the rest of us) routinely employ.

One of the problems is that for any given body of observational data, there are always an indefinite number of theories or hypotheses capable of explaining the data. (This is known as the "underdetermination of theory by data.") Consider a simple example. Suppose my favorite mug is missing from my office. There are a number of theories capable of explaining this observation. It could be that I brought it home and forgot about it. It could be that I left it in a classroom. It could be that the janitor stole it. It could be that Scotty beamed it aboard the *U.S.S. Enterprise*. Perhaps none of these hypotheses is correct. The challenge is in deciding which of the alternative explanations provides the most plausible, or best explanation of the facts as known. What has become evident is that this decision is not entirely logical or rule-governed. It requires insight. The correct explanatory hypothesis does not leap off the data in a straightforward way. Scientists (as well as detectives and ordinary people like you and me) have criteria for selecting which of the alternative hypotheses to subject to closer empirical scrutiny (that is, the test of experiment), such as the "fit" with well-established background beliefs, the resources a given hypothesis provides for making novel predictions, the relative simplicity of a hypothesis (and thus the ease of testing it experimentally), and even aesthetic criteria such as beauty or elegance. Clearly, not all of these values are straightforwardly rule-governed values. Some of them, in fact, such as beauty or elegance, seem downright subjective.

That the scientific community successfully arrives at the truth about the natural world by relying on such values suggests a peculiar "fit" between the human mind and the world, which fit is itself remarkable and puzzling, though more so perhaps for the atheist than for the Christian. Because the human mind and senses were, according to the Christian, designed by an intelligent (and benevolent) creator, it is reasonable to assume that when these faculties are functioning properly in an appropriate environment they will lead us (in the end) to the truth about our surroundings. The atheist seems to have a harder task explaining why reliance on such values leads to true beliefs about the world, as distinct from the aim of, say, "fitness" or "survival advantage," neither of which have any *essential* connection to truth. (For example, if believing that the earth is flat significantly enhanced the overall fitness of the human species, the mechanism of evolution might well "select" that belief over other options, making it rather than any of the alternatives the norm for the species.)

To sum up, scientists do not "deduce" theories from data in a straightforward way. The inference to theory is far more complex and "open-ended." The inference to theory has been variously called "abduction," "retroduction," or "inference to the best explanation." Whatever you call it, it is decidedly not a demonstrative inference. The logical "gap" between the data we hope to explain and the explanations (that is, the hypotheses) we come up with is filled by a variety of "values," some of which I mentioned a moment ago, adopted for the purposes of comparing competing hypotheses.[10] By the end of the nineteenth century, it had become clear (notably so in the case of William Whewell and Charles Sanders Peirce) that the entire edifice of science rests on a bed of hypotheses or conjectures. This should not be understood to undermine the legitimacy of science or to justify a dismissive attitude with respect to its results. To criticize a scientific proposal for the simple reason that it is "just a theory" is to misunderstand the nature of science, and indeed human knowledge generally.

The bottom line of the preceding discussion of objectivity and certainty is that we should be what philosophers call "fallibilists" with respect to human knowledge, including science. Fallibilists are humble with respect to their grasp of the way things are. They are not skeptics, nor are

10. It is perhaps worth noting at this point that contemporary critics of science often allege that the "gap" between data and theories is rather filled by a variety of social and psychological factors such as peer pressure, or the desire to win the Nobel Prize or obtain a promotion. These critics maintain that scientific theories are "social constructs" without epistemic significance, that is, they are not "true" in the traditional sense. The various arguments and evidence that scientists adduce to defend their theories are "fifth wheels" with respect to the process whereby theories are "invented" (as opposed to "discovered") to explain the data, which are themselves socially conditioned. Suffice it to say that I do not share this pessimistic assessment of the implications of the "open-endedness" of abductive inference, which assessment readers will recognize as a tacit endorsement of relativism.

they tentative about making knowledge claims. The demise of popular assumptions about the objectivity of human reason coupled with the loss of certainty neither opens the door to relativism nor eliminates forever the possibility of tension between scientific and religious ways of understanding. To say that human perception is "theory-laden" (and with it our grasp of "the facts") or that theories are "underdetermined" by the facts (or data) is not to say that human theorizing is a loose cannon not subject to constraints from the external world. There's a big difference between *perceiving* something and just *imagining* it, or making it up. Moreover, the Christian's belief in an intelligent and benevolent creator responsible for the design of our cognitive resources (the mind and the senses) also helps turn back the "anything goes" response to the collapse of exaggerated modern assumptions about the objectivity and certainty of scientific and every other kind of human knowledge. The end result of a proper and moderate understanding of the force or status of scientific claims about the world, together with a more balanced and accurate reading of the history of science is the "demilitarization" of the zone between religion and science.

The Presuppositions of Science

My primary concern in this essay has been to attack what I have called "The Conflict Thesis" concerning the relationship between religion and science. Before drawing the essay to a close with a few suggestions as to how one might move beyond the Conflict Thesis to a more harmonious perspective on religion and science, I would like to return briefly to the question of the presuppositions of science, though what I have to say here is perhaps more relevant to the practitioner of science than to the layperson. One alleged presupposition of science has been the focus of a great deal of attention very recently, namely, methodological naturalism.[11] At stake is whether or not science is, because of its presuppositions, laden with an inherent bias against religious explanations. My own answer to this question is yes and no (which is perhaps just what you would expect a philosopher to say). There are a number of bad reasons offered

11. Many articles have been written in the past ten years on whether or not methodological naturalism is an essential part of science. It was the focus of a major conference at the University of Texas in February of 1997, which brought together a wide variety of disparate opinions voiced by specialists in a wide range of disciplines.

in support of methodological naturalism. One such bad reason, in my estimation, is *metaphysical* naturalism itself, which certainly seems to entail methodological naturalism.

The best defenses of methodological naturalism connect it with its contribution to achieving science's goal of understanding the natural world. It has been suggested, for instance, that to allow appeals to nonnatural forces or divine agency in scientific explanations would cut off inquiry prematurely, before we've exhausted the full range of possible natural causes. To forswear methodological naturalism thus amounts to a "science stopper."[12] If the aims of science include not simply the goals of understanding or description, but also prediction and (in some cases) the control of natural phenomena, it simply doesn't help much to explain why something happened by saying, in effect, "because God did it." In addition, the reasons for the success of modern science include not only its superior logic (with respect to the Aristotelean science it replaced) but also its social dimension. The history of science is punctuated by the formation and dissolution of consensus. Consensus is indeed the immediate practical aim of scientific inquiry (while the cognitive aim is truth). Science is something we do together, all of us, and thus it should preclude appeals to metaphysical or religious views that are not universally shared. Otherwise, agreement becomes impossible.

Critics of methodological naturalism maintain that despite the above very sensible reasons for the principle, it must be conceded that these reasons do not support the claim that science is religiously neutral. Perhaps so, but is this lack of neutrality benign or malignant? Here it must be said that sincere, intelligent, and well-informed Christians disagree. Those who opt for the former insist that the point of methodological naturalism is not to restrict our study of nature, but simply to define which sorts of study qualify as scientific. Those who opt for the latter assessment wonder whether science must presuppose naturalism in any way, shape, or form. These individuals recommend what has come to be called "theistic" science, that is, science that does not involve a commitment (even a methodological one) to naturalism. It should be stressed that advocates of theistic science do not suggest that research carried out under its auspices be evaluated by criteria other than those currently employed by the vast majority of scientists (minus, of course, the constraint of methodological naturalism). Neither is the point of theistic science to de-

12. This is a phrase coined by Alvin Plantinga, one of the most vocal and forceful of the recent critics of methodological naturalism.

fend or support Christian theology, which does not require such support. The point of theistic science is to produce good scientific theories, not to bolster or promote religion, which would amount to a return to the sort of "God-of-the-gaps" thinking I rejected earlier in this essay.

It would be inappropriate to rule out in advance the possibility that theistic science can achieve greater success relative to what has been achieved by science subject to the constraint of methodological naturalism. In the context of apologetics, the important point (mentioned earlier) is that, properly understood, science's relationship to naturalism is not (or at least not obviously) a threat to religious belief. This is a point agreed to by Christian scholars on both sides of the dispute over methodological naturalism.

Beyond Conflict

One possible but inadequate way to respond to the failure of the Conflict Thesis is to say that all of the apparent conflicts between religion and science rest on a misunderstanding of the differences between them. Despite the evident fact that religion and science have interacted in the past in a variety of ways, properly understood these two ways of knowing are somehow *logically* distinct. According to this view, which I'll refer to as "The Independence Thesis" to highlight the contrast between it and the Conflict Thesis, science and religion each have their own distinctive domain and their own methods, so there is no possibility of conflict (nor, of course, any possibility of fruitful interaction). The Independence Thesis has very little to commend it. It's worth mentioning in passing, however, in order to stress the point that Christians should oppose this view (and others like it) because it fails to do justice to the idea that "all truth is God's truth." At its worst, the Independence Thesis raises the specter of a kind of "two truths" theory of human knowledge — the truths of faith and the truths of reason. Christians should resist the temptation to avoid conflict by insulating our theology from our science, and vice versa. The fact of the matter is that influence between science and religion is both legitimate and mutually enriching. The "streams of relevance and implication," to borrow a phrase from John Hedley Brooke, flow both ways. That tensions arise between them from time to time should not be surprising, any more than the fact that within science tensions persist between rival theories (such as the rivalry between "steady state" and "big bang" theories about the origin of the universe, which seems recently to have been largely resolved, for the present, in favor of the latter). Christian theology has always been subject to reinterpretation (as distinct from denial) in the light of scientific understanding, and science has depended on religion in a variety of ways (as described in my analysis of the Conflict Thesis). Religion has played a constructive role in relation to science as a source of presupposition, sanction, and insight.

A proper understanding of the relationship between religion and science lies somewhere between the Conflict Thesis and the Independence Thesis. What we want is a view according to which the scientific and theological enterprises can be seen as interacting and mutually illuminating approaches to reality. One way to do this is to recognize, with Arthur Peacocke, that there is "a hierarchy of order in the natural world." Theology, Peacocke suggests, "refers to a higher level in the hierarchy of complexity [than science, namely,] the interaction of nature, man, and God. . . ."[13] Complete understanding requires explanations at all levels, rather than the "reduction" (or elimination) of explanations at higher levels to (or in favor of) explanations couched exclusively in terms appropriate to lower levels of complexity.

More simply, perhaps, one could draw a distinction between "how" questions (that is, questions having to do with the underlying mechanisms or causal structures behind natural events — the stuff of science) and "why" questions (such as questions having to do with the ultimate source of the world's existence, its purpose, value, and ultimate meaning, or the relationship between natural and material processes on the one hand and divine governance on the other). The former are clearly questions accessible to modern science. The latter questions, however, seem to outstrip the resources of modern science. Howard Van Till suggests that we regard the former questions ("how" or "when" questions) as matters "internal" to the universe, and the latter questions ("who" or "why" questions) as concerning the relationships between the universe and beings distinct from it, such as God.[14] The point is that scientific explanations are not the only kind of explanations. They are not even necessarily the best kind of explanation for all purposes. I'm not here advocating a disguised version of the Independence Thesis. One should avoid the idea that science and religion are disparate ways of knowing that do not intersect or that pertain to fundamentally incompatible realities, or (worse) different truths.

13. Peacocke, *Intimations of Reality*, 51.
14. Van Till, "When Faith and Reason Cooperate," 40.

As I discussed earlier, the fundamental problem of apologetics is the choice between alternative and competing worldviews. The criteria of adequacy with respect to the choice of a worldview are much broader than any internal to either science or theology, and encompass both what you might call intellectual adequacy on the one hand (a matter of explanatory power and logical consistency), and existential or practical adequacy on the other (a matter of satisfying the needs and aspirations of human persons). I noted in the discussion of the objectivity and certainty of science that the logical "gap" between the data for which we require an explanation and the hypotheses we come up with to explain them is filled by a broad and somewhat open-ended set of criteria for assessing competing hypotheses. As Ernan McMullin suggests, there is no reason to think that in the context of the construction of a larger and more comprehensive worldview, of which natural science is only a part, "consistency with other well-supported beliefs," including theological beliefs, ought not be one of the criteria we employ.[15] (By "well-supported" here he means in terms peculiar to the source domain itself, in this case Christian theology.)

The aim with respect to theology and science is, as McMullin elsewhere urges, "consonance without direct implication."[16] There is little reason to object to a notion of science (or for that matter theology) that locates it, as Howard Van Till explains, "within the framework of an all-encompassing, biblically informed, theistic worldview that does indeed draw from *all* that we know about God, his creation and his revelation."[17] We can, it seems, join the battle for the inclusion of references to the direct and immediate activity of a divine agent in explanations of human experience at a point internal to natural science (as in the debate over methodological naturalism), or at the level of overall worldviews.[18] Within the community of Christian scholars, supporters and critics of methodological naturalism politely disagree with respect to the former. With respect to the latter (that is, the construction of an overall worldview), however, they agree enthusiastically.

When it comes to the relationship between religion and science, the

15. McMullin, "Models of Scientific Inference," *CTNS Bulletin* 8:2 (1988): 11.

16. McMullin, "How Should Cosmology Relate to Theology?" in *The Sciences and Theology in the Twentieth Century*, ed. Arthur Peacocke (Notre Dame: University of Notre Dame Press, 1981), 17.

17. Van Till, "When Faith and Reason Cooperate," 45.

18. See also Robert C. O'Connor, "Science on Trial: Exploring the Rationality of Methodological Naturalism," *Perspectives on Science and the Christian Faith* 49:1 (March 1997): 17.

most basic issues have to do with the nature of human knowledge, or more specifically with the question of how two different kinds of knowledge claims are to be related. As explanation-seeking enterprises, there are significant methodological parallels between these two modes of understanding. But these parallels should not obscure the significant differences that exist between them (perhaps best understood in terms of the "levels" view I described a moment ago). The Conflict Thesis cannot be maintained in the face of the historical record, nor in light of recent criticisms of the various ways some have tried to privilege science as a way of knowing. Nor should we gloss over the scope for fruitful tension between religion and science, any more than we should do so with respect to the tensions between competing research programs within science. My overall aim in this essay has been to show why it seems to me that Christians do not have a readily definable stake in the outcome of science, not by rejecting science or insulating theology from its effects (or vice versa), but rather by construing religion and science as, to borrow one last phrase from John Hedley Brooke, "complex social activities involving different expressions of human concern."[19] There is but one cosmos (notwithstanding the "many-worlds" interpretations of quantum mechanics!), one Creator, and one truth about the cosmos.

19. Brooke, *Science and Religion,* 42.

14

Miracles and Christian Theism

J. A. Cover

I. Introduction

Most Christians read their Bibles in a way that makes "believing in miracles" a pretty natural thing to do. Indeed most would regard belief in miracles to be part and parcel of embracing the Christian faith, echoing St. Paul's judgment that the bodily resurrection of Christ is an unnegotiable part of it (1 Cor. 15:17). If his resurrection is not just one more occurrence in the natural order of things, but instead an occurrence *contra natura* — as our Church Fathers would have described an exception to the stable and lawful order of nature — then so too, presumably, is Christ's revival of Lazarus' corpse after four days in the grave, and his turning water into wine at Cana, and his feeding a multitude in the wilderness from a few loaves and fishes. For most Christians, these and many other events recorded in Scripture are genuine miracles, accepted as such with the same readiness as they accept the biblical record to be an account of God's sovereign omnipotence generally and the divinity of Christ in particular.

There's no news in any of that. If the existence of miracles is what one would expect in a world into which God reaches down to make him-

---

I am very grateful to Michael Murray for working patiently to turn a difficult ancestor of this chapter into something less difficult. If it is still too hard, that is entirely my fault. I'm also indebted to my colleagues Mike Bergmann (a thinking Christian) and Martin Curd (a thinking skeptic) for talking with me at length about miracles.

self known, there seems at first glance little about miracles for the contemporary Christian to fuss over. *Philosophers* are of course free to puzzle over them. But armchair philosophizing aside, what of any consequence arises for the believer in respect to miracles?

Well, Christians aren't alone in the world. While Christians find believing in miracles a pretty natural thing to do, many others will express a good deal more skepticism about miracles. Some have claimed that belief in miracles is *irrational*, or more severely that miracles are *impossible*. And here the believer may well confess to being rather at a loss to explain such an attitude: what exactly is the source of such skeptical doubts about miracles, and what could motivate the claim that "believing in miracles is irrational" or that "miracles are impossible"? No doubt the parties to such doubts and claims as these are not believers. But to many thinking Christians this renders such doubts and claims all the more puzzling. For by their reckoning, miracles look to offer a veritable *argument* for God's existence, or at very least they serve as good evidence for it: miracles (the thinking Christian might say) point to God in just the way that any effect points to its cause.

These are the broader issues of concern to us in this chapter. To get a feel for things, let's consider straight off that last item — the simple idea that since miracles point to God, they serve as good grounds for believing (good evidence) that there is a divine being.

The idea is in a way too simple. Miracles point to God only if *there are* miracles. While the existence of miracles is pretty much what is to be expected by someone believing that ours is a world into which God has reached down to make himself known, the atheist or agnostic — who does not (yet) believe there exists any such God — can scarcely be supposed to share that expectation. So if anything like an "argument from miracles" is legitimately to play a role in Christian evidences (and this is something we have yet to determine), the reasons a believer might offer to the skeptic for judging this or that event to be miraculous oughtn't depend on a *prior commitment* to the existence of God. For such an argument to be successful, it must be possible to determine that something is indeed a miracle without first supposing that God exists. The thinking Christian, then, will know what conditions must be met if one is reasonably to believe that some event is indeed miraculous.[1] But one cannot evaluate the

1. That is to say, the thinking Christian will have paid some attention to the *epistemology* of miracles. "Epistemology" is just the complicated-sounding (but etymologically well-deserved) word that philosophers have long attached to the study of

reasonableness of believing that some event is a miracle unless one knows what a miracle *is* — that is, knows what conditions an event must satisfy if it is to count as miraculous. The thinking Christian, then, will know what a miracle is.[2]

Three points about this little exercise we've just conducted: First, it is clearly an exercise in armchair philosophizing, and just as clearly it is the sort of thing we'd better not set aside. If the Christian faith is a reasonable one, then it will satisfy the objective demands of rational inquiry that believers and nonbelievers of intellectual good will and honesty alike strive to meet. Whatever our beliefs, it's no good defending them with bad arguments. This isn't to claim, of course, that some ivory-tower method of purely *a priori* theorizing (thinking hard with our eyes and ears closed) can settle the issue between believers and unbelievers. Nor is it to insist on what is sometimes called an "evidentialist" apologetics — according to which we are rational in believing some bit of the Christian faith only if we are in possession of some other belief or beliefs serving as evidence for them. Historically, thinking Christians have differed in their views about whether such an evidentialist approach is or isn't the best way to go. But *whatever* stance we might choose to take on the role of miracles in supporting the fundamental beliefs of Christianity, miracles are important not simply because they might help us defend the faith. And that is a second point: miracles have found a central place in Christian thought from St. Augustine down to the present day because they figure crucially in the larger story of God's relation to us, his creatures. The thinking Christian will want to understand that story, and to be able intelligently to express the place of miracles within it. Our little exercise above is a first step in that direction. It takes that step by slowing down long enough to distinguish carefully, as Augustine himself did, two central questions — arguably *the* two central questions — about miracles: (A) What are miracles? (that is the metaphysical question) and (B) On what grounds would one be rationally warranted in believing that there are miracles? (that is the epistemo-

---

knowledge — to the study of what makes a true belief sufficiently warranted or justified (well-earned, you might say) to count as knowledge. Given its currency in apologetic discussions, we might as well have it in our vocabulary.

2. That is to say, the thinking Christian will have paid some attention to the *metaphysics* of miracles. 'Metaphysics' is just a complicated-sounding (and etymologically not-very-well-deserved) title that philosophers have long attached to the study of what there is and the nature of what there is. Given its currency, we might as well have this word in our vocabulary too.

logical question). Here then is the third point about our little exercise above. It sets for us something of an agenda, a pair of questions that must be added to those bothering many thinking Christians about the skeptical view of miracles generally.

We shan't aim for complete answers to all of these questions (alas there are many others) about the nature and evidential value of miracles, in this chapter. But since miracles are a fundamental part of the Christian faith, and since thinking Christians seek to clarify and defend the rationality of its most fundamental commitments, let's see what progress can be made in addressing some of them. Our ultimate goals are to determine to what extent some strong apologetic strategy — some argument from miracles to the existence of God — is workable, and to defend the rationality of believing in miracles. Along the way, we'll be able to address some important subsidiary questions that both believers and unbelievers are led to ask when thinking about miracles.

II. What Is a Miracle? The Standard Conception

It's a fact about language that words often get used in various ways. The deployment of "miracle" in common usage has come to permit such expressions as "her recovery was a miracle" or "it was a miracle that he wasn't seriously injured." Descriptions of this sort typically highlight the remarkable, unexpected nature of the event. Unbelievers and Christians alike admit that in a universe as complex and complicated as ours, there will arise remarkable and unexpected occurrences: those with welcome consequences may invite this loose description of "miracle" without any implication of religious significance or divine intervention. Where for many believers such usage will underscore the providential character of an event, serving perhaps to confirm or strengthen one's faith, the event in question (the astounding recovery or amazing lack of injury) might still be viewed as admitting of some explanation — however complicated, however elusive — in terms of natural causes. Such welcome but remarkable events, no less than an unexpected tragedy or unfortunate freak of nature, will have their place in the divine economy, an economy that God in his wisdom and power has woven into the fabric of nature itself.

So not all providential events are miracles. Let's stick with what would seem to be a clear case. A man of seeming good health suddenly takes seriously ill. Despite the prayers of his sisters, he soon thereafter ceases breathing, his heart stops, and he dies. He is buried in an earthen grave. Four days later, as the body begins to manifest signs of decay, a religious figure of devoted following arrives at the graveside. He weeps, but then declares with a loud voice, "Lazarus, come forth." The man emerges whole and living from the earthen grave.

Supposing (as believers do) that such an event occurs, what sort of special event is this?

On the *standard conception,* an event is a miracle only if it is contrary to the natural order. To say that an event is "contrary to the natural order" is simply to say that it is an exception to the regular order of natural occurrences. Dead people do not, in the natural course of events, come back to life. In the words of David Hume, the eighteenth-century skeptic and outspoken opponent of miracles, "A miracle is a violation of the laws of nature."[3]

If being a violation of at least one law of nature is necessary for an event's being a miracle, it is not enough. An event is a miracle, one is inclined to say, only if it is caused directly by God. That might prove to be a bit too strong, leaving no room for (say) Peter's healing the lame man (Acts 3:1-9) to count as the performance of a miracle. Let's say that an event is a miracle only if it is *caused by God either directly or through some divine agency,* leaving further details aside. (From such details it may well emerge that another condition will prove to be necessary: perhaps an event is a miracle only if it *serves as a sign to rational creatures that God is acting,* or more weakly only if it has some religious significance. To make our task manageable, we won't include this final condition in our working "definition" of a miracle below. No doubt it's very important.)

So we have at least two conditions that must be met in order for an event to count as a miracle, on the standard conception. To state it carefully:

An event *e* is a miracle only if:

3. David Hume, *An Enquiry Concerning Human Understanding,* 3rd ed., edited by L. A. Selby-Bigge and P. H. Nidditch (Oxford: Clarendon Press, 1975), 114. From the same paragraph: "It is no miracle that a man, seemingly in good health, should die on a sudden. . . . But it is a miracle, that a dead man should come to life. . . ." We'll encounter presently Hume's reason for claiming that one should never believe such accounts as the Lazarus story. (What we called an "exception" Hume has called a "violation." Those mean the same thing. Don't think of a violation of a law as something *naughty.* Think of it as an exception.)

(1) *e* violates at least one law of nature, and
(2) *e* is caused by God either directly or through some divine agency.[4]

III. What Does Reasonable Belief in Miracles Require?

Conditions (1) and (2) serve as our working definition of "miracle," on the standard construal. Now it's obvious that defining something — e.g. "dog," "Santa Claus," "water," "extraterrestrial" — doesn't get the thing (or things) into existence. The skeptic doubts that there *are* any miraculous events: she doubts that there are (or have been) any events satisfying our defining conditions (1) and (2). And believers think otherwise. Suppose, then, that the believer is confronted with (or is otherwise considering, perhaps in the form of historical testimony or an eyewitness report) some event that she takes to be a miracle. From our discussion so far, it is pretty clear that she will need to answer two questions concerning that event: (a) Is the event a violation of a law of nature (i.e., is it what we'll call an *anomalous event*)?[5] and (b) Is the event caused by God? That is, with our standard conception of a miraculous event in hand, a miracle will have to meet the *A*nomalous *E*vent condition (AE) and the *D*ivine *C*ause condition (DC). An event *e* is a miracle only if

(AE) *e* is an anomalous event, and
(DC) *e* is caused by God either directly or through some divine agency.

Now in the introduction to this chapter, we encountered two pressing concerns: the concern of many believers to deploy miracles in the role of a positive argument for the existence of God, and the concern of all thinking Christians to better understand the skeptical attitude of unbelievers. Let's set aside for now the most severe skeptical attitude, according to which miracles are impossible. If miracles are to figure in a strong

4. Thus David Hume's "accurate definition" includes both conditions: a miracle is *"a transgression of a law of nature by a particular volition of the Deity, or by the interposition of some invisible agent"* (*An Enquiry,* 115, n. 1). Don't fret over the little *"e"* in our formulation, needed to render the definition perfectly general. It's just a placeholder, to be filled in by any event whatsoever. It functions rather like "something" and "it" in English when we define (say) "dog" by claiming that "Something is a dog if and only if it is a member of the family *canidea*."

5. "Anomalous" literally means non-lawful, from *a-* ("not-") and *nomos* ("law").

Christian apologetic, in the form of an "argument from miracles," then the believer must acknowledge that even if the skeptic grants that miracles are *possible,* there may yet be challenges to believing rationally that miracles are *actual.* Here's a little challenge to the aim of giving an argument from miracles, just to get things started: notice that according to the divine cause condition (DC), there can be no miracles unless God exists. As a result, we can imagine one objecting that "there cannot be miracles which are evidence for God's existence, because accepting a description of an event as a miracle commits a man to accept[ing] the existence of God."[6] Our definition itself looks to beg the question against the unbelieving skeptic about miracles.

But is that right? Surely we can define "miracle" in a way that, should any occur, entails the existence of God, without begging the question in favor of theism generally or Christianity in particular. What is at issue between the believer and unbelieving skeptic, presumably, isn't *whether miracles are good evidence for theism or Christianity,* but *whether there is good evidence for miracles* in the first place. And traditionally, it is precisely (AE) — the existence of what we are calling an anomalous event — that is offered *as evidence for (DC)* — the existence of a divine cause. What the above objection teaches us, then, if it teaches us anything, turns out to be a reminder of something we encountered in our little opening exercise: if the believer aims to deploy a strong apologetic strategy, arguing from miracles to the existence of a divine being, then it must be possible for the skeptic to recognize evidence for, and form a reasonable belief about, the truth of (AE) without requiring prior evidence for the truth of (DC). The strong apologetic strategy requires unbiased — one might say "theistically neutral" — grounds for claiming that some event is anomalous.

So what evidential value *can* the believer fairly expect miracles to contribute in the Christian apologetic? The answer to this question, as we can now see, depends on how the Christian confronts a serious challenge from the skeptic. The challenge is twofold, directed at two distinct tasks in the effort to bring miracles into some strong apologetic service. One task is giving reasons for judging that an anomalous event has occurred; another task is showing that such an anomalous event points to God. So

6. Apparently one needn't imagine this objection: the quoted misgiving is offered on p. 7 of Richard Swinburne's *The Concept of Miracles* (London: SCM Press, 1964), as grounds for taking seriously the claim that such a definition of "miracle" ". . . seems to place a restriction on the use of the term not justified in general by practice."

(AE) figures in the strong project of justifying Christian religious belief in two ways. For given some candidate-event *e*, one confronts two questions: first, Is (AE) indeed true? and second, Does the truth of (AE) establish the truth of (DC)? More carefully:

(I) Are there (theistically neutral) grounds on which to justify the belief that (AE) is true?
(II) Does the truth of (AE) serve as (theistically neutral) evidence for believing that (DC) is true?

The issue before us is whether the believer is well-placed to deploy miracles as evidence for believing in the existence of God. If the strong apologetic undertaking is to be workable, these central questions must each receive the answer "yes."

IV. Three Objections to Miracles

The stage is now properly set for confronting our two concerns — the concern of many believers to deploy miracles in arguing for the existence of God, and the concern of all thinking Christians to better understand the skeptical attitude of unbelievers. There are three basic objections that skeptics might raise in an attempt to explain why we are not (ever) able to answer "yes" to our two central questions above. The first two argue that we can never expect an affirmative answer to the first question. The latter argues that we cannot get an affirmative answer to the second question. In this section, we'll have a look at the objections themselves. The task of sections V and VI is to evaluate the prospects for a Christian apologetic of miracles in light of them.

(1) The Humean Objection

In his famous essay "Of Miracles,"[7] David Hume argued that it is never reasonable to believe that a miraculous violation of law has occurred. His argument begins with a reminder of how we do in fact seem to justify (to fairly *earn,* so to speak) our belief that something counts as a law of nature: observing that two kinds of objects or events repeatedly and regu-

7. The essay comprises Section X of Hume's *An Enquiry,* 109-31.

larly occur together (unsuspended objects and falling, say, or deaths and irreversible decay) counts as very strong evidence that "All Fs are Gs" is a genuine law (of gravity, or of irreversible biological decay).[8] Indeed the constant and repeated co-occurrence of such events amounts to what Hume would call a "proof" of the law. And that seems to be right; for surely we can't discover the laws of nature *a priori,* that is by simply thinking hard with our eyes and ears closed. Rather, we must do so empirically. Observing the uniform and regular behavior of objects and events provides the strongest evidence one could possibly have for judging some generalization of the form "All Fs are Gs" to be a law of nature.

What, then, should the rational person believe if confronted with testimony for an alleged miraculous rising from the dead (say) — an eyewitness report of even the strongest credentials amounting to its own "proof"? Well, we must weigh evidence against evidence, proof against proof. And here the evidence for it being true that all Fs are Gs must inevitably outweigh the evidence for it being true that there is an F that is not a G; for against the testimony of our witness stands the whole host of repeated experiences to the contrary, of regular and constant co-occurrences of Fs and Gs. Since (as Hume puts it) "the wise man always proportions his belief to the evidence," and since the testimonial evidence for a miracle can never outweigh the repeated observational evidence for a law of nature, no evidence will ever allow us rationally to believe a reported violation of law.[9] In short, one is never justified (warranted) in be-

8. Here again, don't fret over the "Fs" and "Gs." They're just placeholders, needed to render the form in which we state a law of nature perfectly general, to be filled in with descriptions of objects or events. "All Fs are Gs" is thus a sort of shorthand for "All metals are conductors," or for "All unsupported bodies are falling bodies," or the like.

9. Hume's argument begins with "a reminder of how we justify our belief that some generalization of the form 'All Fs are Gs' is a law of nature," namely by repeated observation of the regular conjunction of Fs with Gs. Leaving an assessment of Hume's argument for a later section, two points are worth noting here. First, it may be objected that Hume is just wrong about this "reminder" — that in fact scientists don't proceed in this way at all, and that his argument is fundamentally flawed from the outset. The objection is correct this far: while it is agreed on nearly all hands that Hume is right to say that our justification for postulating some candidate L as a law of nature is nondeductive in character, it remains a point of controversy to what extent scientists rely on the form of "enumerative induction" that Hume offers here — as opposed to some alternative "abductive" inference to the best explanation. (The matter is complicated in part by the difficulty of always clearly distinguishing methods of discovery from methods of justification, and by the fact that the formulation of many laws involves idealizations relative to actual data.) But, second, even if we can't rely on Hume

lieving that (AE) is true for some event. The answer to our Question (I) is "no." That is Hume's Objection.

(2) The Wrong Laws Objection

But suppose that we can answer the Humean Objection, so that it's still an open question whether one might reasonably believe that a law of nature has been violated. Suppose that a candidate for such a case is in fact offered, i.e., that we have good grounds for believing some distinctive and unexpected event to have occurred. Shall we claim that the anomalous event condition (AE) is true and that some law is violated? Well, even if we are confronted with such evidence that *e* violates some accepted law of nature, the skeptic will encourage us to see that the most reasonable conclusion to draw — or anyway, an equally good conclusion to draw from the evidence — is *not* that a law of nature is violated, but rather that *what we took to be a law turns out not to be a genuine law of nature after all.* Remember: there is no *a priori* method of determining the correct laws of nature. Since the method of all working scientists is an empirical one, it must remain open to the empirical scientist to recognize evidence against proposed laws when it arises. And just as science itself works in part by rejecting supposed laws when the evidence no longer fits them, so the skeptic will argue that this unexpected event — the supposed miracle — is simply good evidence that *we have not understood the relevant laws of nature correctly.* Indeed, if we had properly latched on to the true laws of nature, then we should no longer judge the actual event *e* as contrary to them. *Nothing that actually happens is contrary to the truth.* So if the man really was dead and really did come to life, then surely there is something about the difficult and complex biology of human organisms we have yet to learn. Of course, were someone (the believer, say) *already* disposed to anticipate supernatural intrusions into the natural order — were one already inclined to see remarkable events like *e* as divine interventions — then they would more readily judge events

---

(who was no philosopher of science) to accurately describe scientists' warrant for proposing the laws they do, he is still very much correct in claiming that we do indeed *possess* the evidence of repeated and regular conjunction of Fs with Gs: and this provides the force of his point that such evidence always outweighs the single-case evidence for it being true that there is an F that is not a G. For more on laws of nature, including Humean and competing accounts, see chapter 7, "Laws of Nature" (pp. 805-901) of Martin Curd and J. A. Cover, *Philosophy of Science: The Central Issues* (New York & London: W. W. Norton and Company, 1998).

of that remarkable sort to be genuinely anomalous violations of law. But the conditions for judging an event as genuinely anomalous must (recall) be unbiased, theistically neutral. So the skeptic is under no obligation whatever to do otherwise than regard an unexpected, heretofore unobserved event precisely as any empirical scientist would: *e* is at best evidence for the need to reconsider our present understanding of the powers in nature and the laws governing them. Once again, we cannot conclude that (AE) is true; again, the answer to our central Question (I) is "no." That is the Wrong Laws Objection.

(3) The Non-Miraculous Anomaly Objection

But suppose that we can adequately address both of these objections, so that the anomalous event condition (AE) *is* acknowledged to be true. That is, suppose we are warranted in believing *e* to be an event that violates a law of nature, and so can answer "yes" to Question (I). From the existence of such an anomalous event, can we infer the existence of a divine cause? Not at all straightaway, we can't. From the truth of (AE) we can infer the truth of (DC) *only if we are sure that every anomalous event must have a divine cause.* But since, for all we know, some events are anomalous precisely because they are radically spontaneous or otherwise uncaused events, there may be anomalous events that are not miracles.[10] Such events would be "non-miraculous anomalies." The skeptical worry here is an important one; for it is not at all clear on what grounds the believer could argue that such non-miraculous anomalies are impossible. An event's lacking a natural cause does not entail its having a supernatural cause. If non-miraculous anomalous events are possible, and if there is no unbiased, theistically neutral reason for saying "it's more likely that *e* has a supernatural cause than that *e* is radically spontaneous (random) or otherwise uncaused," then the evidential value of *e* emerges to be practically nil. A man rose from the dead. So? So it scarcely follows that God did it. We are thus without any good reason for judging the anomalous event to be evidence of the existence and activity of a divine being. (DC) cannot be thereby reckoned true, and the answer to our Question (II) is "no." That is the Non-Miraculous Anomaly Objection.

10. Alternatively, for all we know the event *was* caused — but by Satan or some angel. That is another problem we shan't dwell on, in this chapter: we'll suppose that non-miraculous anomalies are uncaused events. Sort of like flukes of nature.

Here then are three significant challenges to the strong apologetic strategy of offering a positive "argument from miracles" in defense of the Christian faith. In the course of assessing these objections, we shall be able to consider again the nature of miracles (the metaphysical question), and to reevaluate the evidential worth of miracles in justifying Christian religious belief (the epistemological question). Let's begin with the Humean Objection, since it leads us pretty quickly to rethinking the first, metaphysical question — the one about *what miracles are*.

V. The Metaphysical Question: A Response to Hume and a New Conception of Miracles

A. A Response to Hume's Objection

Recall again Hume's Objection. Miracles, if any there be, are violations of at least one law of nature — violations of at least one generalization about the course of events that we've expressed in the form "All Fs are Gs." The evidence we have for any law of nature, consisting in our empirical observation of the repeated and regular occurrence of Fs followed by Gs, amounts to what Hume calls a "proof" of the law. What then of someone's claim that (say) a person rose from the dead? Says Hume, we weigh evidence against evidence, proof against proof. And over against this testimony of our witness that there is some F that is not a G, stands all the weight of repeated experiences to the contrary, of that very evidence of regular and constant concurrence of Fs with Gs which proves our law that all Fs are Gs. Since the evidence of a violation will never be strong enough to outweigh the evidence for the law, and since the rational person is obliged to judge on the side of the greatest evidence, one is never justified in believing that the anomalous event *e* occurred: we are never in a position to assert that (AE) is true.

There are two things to point out about Hume's challenge, two important weaknesses. Let's consider these, approached here in the form of two objections: doing so will lead us readily into a more potent sort of Humean challenge — one providing us with a chance to think more clearly about the nature of miracles and laws.

First, Hume's Objection supposes that the only evidence one might have for a miracle is the testimony of someone's claim to direct observation. But there may be — indeed, typically will be — evidence of another, *indirect* sort; and such indirect evidence may well be strong enough to warrant our supposing the existence of a genuinely anomalous event as its best explanation. Let's consider a simple, more familiar example first. Imagine that a good friend and family man, Jones (as philosophers inevitably call him), is found lying dead on his bedroom floor. Here is a surprising event that we ache to have explained. Suppose someone tells us and the authorities that they saw Jones commit suicide. No detective worth his salt (nor you or I, for that matter) would stop with evidence of that sort, and call it a day. After all, the witness might be lying, or deluded, or have poor eyesight. Rather, the detective will seek out indirect evidence — Jones's own fingerprints on a gun lying nearby, a suicide note on the table, a host of antidepressant drugs in the medicine cabinet, and so on. Where the direct testimony of our witness might prove insufficient, further indirect evidence might prove overwhelming: indeed, the hypothesis that Jones committed suicide might well explain all the other, indirect evidence much better than any alternative hypothesis (murder in a bungled robbery attempt, say).

Now think about the case of a purported (i.e., supposed) miracle. Here too, quite apart from the direct testimony of a witness, there may well be many other such bits of indirect evidence that are best explained by the hypothesis that an anomalous event did indeed occur, and which might well be far stronger than the direct evidence. Thus, in addition to direct testimony for the claim that Christ arose ("I saw him in the garden and he spoke to me!") would be the empty tomb itself and the burial clothes, the despondency of the Christ's followers suddenly giving way to great cheer and a deep faith, and so on. Surely these things need explaining; and it may emerge that such bits of indirect evidence are much better explained by Christ's actual resurrection than by any competing hypothesis, and that such evidence is even stronger than the testimony of our witness. Hume's objection is one about the weight of evidence, and he has said nothing whatsoever about adding the weight of indirect evidence for a genuinely anomalous event.

Second, Hume's Objection appears on reflection to be much too strong. The evidence of past experience for some regularity of nature (all Fs are Gs) will, on his account, always be weightier than new contrary evidence for a violation. But if that were true as a general principle, it would seem to show that it is *never* rational to believe — on the basis of direct testimony or any other evidence — that an event which never occurred before has in fact occurred. But this, surely, is not at all plausible as a general principle. Indeed, were Hume's Objection against miracles taken seriously, it's partner objection — the Wrong Laws Objection — could never even arise: one could *never* have good reasons for saying (as scientists clearly sometimes must) that supposed scientific laws need to be revised on the basis of new, contrary evidence. Hume seems to think that the invariable experience of past occurrences must always win out, and that one could never have good grounds to revise laws in the way scientists actually do. And that, clearly, is much too strong. Hume has vastly overestimated the weight of past experience.

B. A More Potent Humean Objection

Recall from our introduction to this chapter a concern of many thinking Christians to understand the most severe form of skepticism about miracles, namely that they are impossible. One might understand Hume's stance on miracles to express exactly this form of severe skepticism. While this is perhaps not the most charitable way of reading Hume's own claims, an extreme skepticism is at least *beneath the surface* of what he says about miracles and their relation to laws of nature. For on reflection, it looks as if Hume has understood miracles and laws in a way that would render miracles impossible. Miracles, on the standard conception, are violations of at least one law of nature. But laws of nature are simply true statements of the uniform and regular behavior of natural objects and events. Were there no such uniform and regular behavior of the natural objects and events, we should have no grounds for calling those statements *laws* at all. Hence, our grounds for calling them laws are precisely our grounds for denying any event as miraculous.

Here then arises the more severe (we might still reckon it Humean) challenge to miracles: given the standard definition that miracles violate a law of nature, there are no miracles, *because they are impossible*. Let's state this argument more explicitly, as follows:

> We discover genuine laws of nature by discovering the orderly, regular behavior of natural objects, like dead bodies irreversibly decaying, and heavy bodies falling, and so on. It is a law of nature that (say) all metals are conductors of electricity, that all bodies on which no net forces are acting remain at rest or move at uniform velocity in a straight line, and so on. In short, a law of nature is what is called a *true universal generalization,* of the form "All Fs are Gs" or "All so-and-sos do such-and-such." This is the standard account of a law of nature. Hence, anything that is a genuine law of nature has *no exceptions,* no

> counterinstances: if it really *is* a law of nature that all Fs are Gs, then there cannot be an F that is not a G. But a miracle is by definition a violation of a law of nature. Thus: if (i) nothing could be a law of nature unless it is unviolated, and (ii) no event could be a miracle unless it violates a law of nature, then no event could be a miracle. Miracles are impossible.[11]

That's a pretty scary argument. What should the thinking Christian make of it?

C. Miracles as Non-Violations of Law

Given the believer's commitment to miracles, it may be quite natural to respond as follows: "I smell a trick. It's all just a matter of definition, of how miracles are defined in relation to laws. If this really shows that miracles aren't possible, well, alright, so there are no 'miracles.' But it doesn't show that Christ didn't raise Lazarus from the dead, or that he didn't walk on the water, or that he didn't multiply the loaves and fishes. Call them what you want: no abstract philosophical argument like this can show that he couldn't raise Lazarus or walk on water, and that's all I need."

But hold on now: that's *not* all the believer needs. Not, at least, if the believer aims to deploy such remarkable events as these to any apologetic advantage — strong or otherwise — as evidence for the existence of God or the divinity of Christ. Whatever apologetic role we might want miracles to play, this response threatens to cut it off, by conceding that such events have no special status in relation to natural laws. If the believer simply gives up on insisting that miracles have some genuinely *anomalous status* in relation to laws of nature, then it becomes altogether unclear what there is about such events that points to something *outside* the natural order.[12] (Mere *rarity* won't do it.) And if miracles point to

11. Representatives of this line of argument can be found in Nicholas Everitt, "The Impossibility of Miracles," *Religious Studies* 23 (1987): 347-49 and in Alastair McKinnon, "'Miracle' and 'Paradox'," *American Philosophical Quarterly* 4 (1967): 308-14.

12. The point being made here was encountered earlier in Section II, with the words "traditionally, it is precisely (AE) — the existence of what we are calling an anomalous event — that is offered as evidence for (DC) — the existence of a divine cause."

nothing outside the natural order, one can scarcely hope to use them to apologetic advantage. No: the believer needs to recognize in such events something distinctive in their relation to the natural course of law-governed events, something more than the quick response just offered acknowledges.

Let's take the severe skeptical argument seriously, as Christian philosophers universally have. If miracles are actual, as believers claim, then they *are* possible. Given the above argument for their impossibility, then, the available options are pretty clear, aren't they? There are two options, corresponding to the two main premises of the argument above — that (i) nothing could be a law of nature unless it is unviolated, and that (ii) no event could be a miracle unless it violates a law of nature. Since it is an unnegotiable part of the Christian faith that miracles are possible (since actual), the believer must deny one of these two premises. That is, the believer must either claim that laws of nature can be violated, or else claim that miracles are not violations of the laws of nature but are in some other way anomalous.

D. Salvaging the Possibility of Miracles

There is plenty to be learned from thinking about the second of these options — lots of fun metaphysics, if you want to think of it that way (or even if you don't), but more importantly, plenty to help us advance our thinking about the apologetic role of miracles. Let's see what can be said in reply to this severe skeptical argument against the possibility of miracles by taking the second route. Our task is to determine whether we can arrive at a coherent story about miracles that is different from the standard conception of them as violations of laws. Let's do it in two steps.

(i) An Assessment of the Problem

We can best start by asking how we got into this mess. (Let's hear nothing of it being the author's fault. The mess is an old and important one, and we are going to get out of it.) We got into the mess by adopting the standard picture of miracles, as violations of laws of nature. And where did that come from? Well, it came from two fundamental beliefs, shared by many theists and nontheists alike, which motivate the picture we've been working with up till now:

(a) Miracles, if any there be, are fundamentally divine interventions into the causal order of nature; and
(b) The concept of causality is fundamentally a concept of *lawlike regularity* among events.

Those might have seemed innocuous enough. Especially the first: the believer, surely, will be happy enough with (a) — with the idea that miracles are brought about by God in a supernatural way, from outside of nature. The challenge (the mess) confronting believers who also accept (b) is to explain the idea that something could be a law of nature despite having a miraculous violation: and as the above argument suggests, it's far from clear how a law could be a true statement of the form "All Fs are Gs" if there are cases of an F that *isn't* a G. We're trying to avoid that bugaboo. And it is important to see that we can. It is important to see that accepting (a) doesn't in any way *require* one to accept (b).

(ii) Accounting for Miracles Without (b)

On the Humean conception, we are led to think of causality in terms of lawlike regularity, and to think of miracles as *violations* of such laws. Is there some other way of thinking about causality, laws, and miracles that would avoid the challenge confronting us? There is. Consider first the idea of miraculous intervention itself. When we speak of God's miraculous activity in the natural order, we can, surely, understand such divine intervention not simply in terms of laws themselves as descriptions of the (otherwise) regular course of nature, but rather in terms of God's having the power *to bring about occurrences that cannot be caused by the natural forces operative in the created objects* left to themselves. That is to say — now following two Christian philosophers of a bygone age, St. Thomas Aquinas and G. W. Leibniz — that miracles are occurrences which are *beyond the natural power of any created thing to cause or bring about:* the natural forces operative in a human body dead for four days cannot cause that body to rise anew in living health. What God can cause is something the powers operative in the body itself *cannot* cause. And that is a somewhat different picture of causality and laws — a non-Humean picture. How so, exactly? Well, according to the Humean idea (b), causality is fundamentally a concept of lawfulness, and laws are simply descriptions of the regular behavior of objects and events. But on this alternative picture, causality is fundamentally a concept about the causal powers in things; and laws, accordingly, are not mere descriptions of regularities, but instead expressions of what the objects in nature are capable of producing in virtue of the powers they possess.

And so notice, then, how miracles are related to laws on this new, alternative picture. Miracles are not "violations" of the laws of nature at all. The laws of nature, recall, describe what objects in nature are capable of producing in light of the powers that they have. And miracles, recall, are occurrences that are beyond the natural power of any created thing to cause or bring about. Thus, miraculous events — those events not caused by the operation of natural powers in created objects — do nothing to threaten the truth of natural laws about natural causes. The idea of some event rendering a claim of the form "All Fs are Gs" false while that claim remains a law was the difficulty with accepting (b) above, the bugaboo we aimed to avoid. We can now see that believing in events having supernatural causes needn't saddle one with believing that there are *false laws of nature,* laws having exceptions. Miracles are so to speak "gaps" in nature, occurrences having causes about which laws of nature are simply silent. The laws are true, but simply don't speak to events caused by divine intervention. (Laws of nature are, after all, laws *of nature,* not supernature. As our Church Fathers might have expressed it, miracles can be *supra natura* without being *contra natura.*) In short, then, miracles are anomalous — non-nomological, non-lawlike — not because they violate laws of nature, but rather because the laws of nature don't speak to their causes at all.

So much for our rescue of the possibility of miracles. We've secured here a new picture of miracles, a better picture: we've secured it by getting a better picture of laws of nature and the relation of miracles to them. Our new picture, of miracles as anomalous events not violating laws of nature, pulls the teeth from any severe skeptical argument against the very possibility of miracles.

Thus we can, at last, judge the first of our three objections to miracles — the broadly Humean misgiving(s) — to be safely behind us. But what about the Wrong Laws Objection to miracles, and the Non-Miraculous Anomaly Objection? These are still on board. Let's consider them now, in the context of facing head-on our main question yet outstanding: What evidential role can believers fairly expect miracles to play in a Christian apologetic?

VI. The Epistemological Question: Miracles and Evidence

One shouldn't, I think — and now grant me, as you just have, the luxury of speaking in the first person — expect too much.[13] Recall again (from the introduction) that many Christians will confess to being perplexed when confronting someone who is utterly skeptical about miracles. Don't miracles point to God in the way any effect points to its cause? True enough, if miracles are impossible, then there is no hope of engaging such an argumentative strategy. But that severe skepticism is well behind us. Isn't there a positive "argument from miracles" to the existence of God, what we've called a strong apologetic strategy for showing someone that God exists? Thus we ended our introduction with this: "Our ultimate goals are to determine to what extent some strong apologetic strategy — some argument from miracles to the existence of God — is workable, and to defend the rationality of believing in miracles." What I should like to emphasize in these final sections is that those are indeed *two* goals, and that the success of defending a rational belief in miracles is *in no way* dependent upon the success of giving "an argument from miracles to the existence of God." The remaining objections to miracles — the Wrong Laws Objection and the Non-Miraculous Anomaly Objection — provide a good context in which to clarify these points. I shall recommend that while these objections may *have some force* against a strong apologetic of miracles, they have *little or no force* against a more moderate apologetic strategy, and that they *count not at all* against the rationality of believing in miracles. Let's gird up our loins one last time, and confront these objections.

A. Miracles: Possibility vs. Actuality

Miracles are not impossible. There is nothing incoherent about them, as the severe Humean skeptic might have it. But a *coherent* story about the world needn't be a *true* story: wide is the gate to coherence, and narrow the way to truth. Now according to the Wrong Laws Objection, any candidate

13. Most chapters in this volume are written in the first person. I adopt the first person here, in part to indicate that many believers are (I gather) inclined to be rather more optimistic than I about the role of miracles in a Christian apologetic. They won't reckon anything in the remainder of this chapter to be outright false; they'll just read it as being too pessimistic. At least the record is straight: from here on out I'm speaking for myself, as most authors have spoken through their entire chapters.

e for an anomalous event — one which the laws of nature together with prior natural events cannot in any way explain — is at best evidence that we've gotten the laws of nature wrong. And according to the Non-Miraculous Anomaly Objection, even if that remarkable event *is* anomalous and falls outside the scope of the true laws of nature, it points to God only if every anomaly must have a divine cause (or, put another way, only if *non-miraculous* anomalies are impossible). Both of these objections, then, are directed squarely against the truth of the miracle claims of theism generally and Christianity in particular. How strong are these objections?

If the Humean Objection emerges as weak overall, the same cannot quite be said of these remaining objections. Recall again our working "definition" of a miracle: *e* is a miracle only if

(AE) *e* is an anomalous event, and
(DC) *e* is caused by God either directly or through some divine agency.

And recall again our two central questions: given some remarkable event *e*,

(I) Are there (theistically neutral) grounds on which to justify the belief that (AE) is true?
(II) Does the truth of (AE) serve as (theistically neutral) evidence for believing that (DC) is true?

The strong apologetic, aiming to argue from miracles to the existence of God, requires that each of these central questions receive the answer "yes." Confronting this apologetic is the skeptic who claims that, while miracles are possible, they are not actual — that belief in miracles is coherent but not true. Such a skeptic will think about miracles, perhaps, in much the way you and I are likely to think about (for example) UFOs and extraterrestrials. (The analogy isn't perfect, but few analogies are: maybe it'll help.) If someone aimed to offer a sort of "argument" for extraterrestrials — an argument from the reality of UFOs, say — then you and I, as fair-minded skeptics, can grant that such creatures are *possible* while nevertheless persisting in the rational belief that extraterrestrial creatures are *not actual.* Far from shrinking in the face of "evidence from UFOs," we have in place a much larger, overarching view of the world according to which such "evidence" from UFOs is really no evidence at all: however remarkable and curious those lights in the sky may be, we will persist in the belief that there is available some alternative, if perhaps complex, hypothesis that can more plausibly explain that phenomena. Of course if one were already disposed to believe in the existence of extraterrestrials, then one would more quickly judge the remarkable and curious events to involve some object from another planet. But that's scarcely a neutral stance, and the believer in extraterrestrials cannot expect you and I to share beliefs of that sort. Moreover, even if (for whatever reasons) we came to believe that such curious events *did* involve some object from outside our atmosphere, this alone does not show that there are sentient and intelligent creatures visiting us on earth aboard them. It's not at all easy to *show* that there are extraterrestrials.

Now our skeptic about miracles, while granting the *possibility* of genuinely anomalous events, may fairly persist in a view of the physical world according to which they are *not actual.* Among nonbelieving skeptics about miracles, it is very common to have in place a larger, overarching view of the world according to which each event that occurs is caused by prior events, in accordance with the laws of nature. Let's call this prevalent worldview *Naturalism.* And consider then some remarkable and unexpected event *e*. The naturalist, far from shrinking in the face of "evidence from remarkable and unexpected events," will presumably recommend what many see as the hallmark of a proper scientific methodology — expanding and revising our account of nature and the laws governing occurrences within it, in the face of new and contrary observations. Should some remarkable event *e* appear to have no explanation in terms of prior events and causal laws, the naturalist will encourage us to remember that it is in precisely this way that currently formulated *laws of science* are shown not yet properly to capture the genuine *laws of nature*. Putative evidence is always evaluated relative to some prior beliefs or worldview. So whatever "evidence from remarkable events" we might offer for *e* being an event having no cause in prior natural events, the naturalist skeptic will surely regard it as evidence that we have misunderstood the laws of nature. When regarded in this way, such an event *counts not at all* as evidence for the existence of genuine anomalies. Of course, if one were already disposed to believe in divine interventions into the natural causal order, one would more quickly judge *e* to be genuinely anomalous. But that's scarcely a neutral stance, and the believer in miracles can hardly expect the skeptic to share those beliefs. No remarkable event *all by itself* counts as unbiased, theistically neutral evidence for being genuinely anomalous. Thus the Wrong Laws Objection is always available to the skeptic. Given the demand for neutral evidence, the answer to our central question (I) looks to be "no."

Moreover, even if the skeptic were, for whatever reasons, to become convinced that some remarkable event was not caused by prior *natural* events, he might still insist that whatever *is* caused to occur is caused *by prior natural events.* That is, such a skeptic will be prepared to admit two options: either an event is caused or uncaused. If it is caused, its cause is *natural.* If it is uncaused, well then, of course, nothing caused it: the event is a radically spontaneous and inexplicable event. And here again, no such inexplicable event all by itself counts as unbiased, theistically neutral evidence for its having a divine cause. Thus our skeptic can fairly and rationally claim that the anomalous event is not miraculous: the Non-Miraculous Anomaly Objection is always available to the skeptic. So the answer to our central question (II) looks to be "no."

In short, there is no *forcing* one to accept the occurrence of miracles.

But of course, there is no *forcing* anyone to believe *anything.* The real question is what it is most reasonable to believe. While the Wrong Laws and the Non-Miraculous Anomaly objections are always at least *available* as options one might take, they may not always be the most *reasonable,* the most rational options to take. Let's pause briefly to reflect on what might be said against these options being the most reasonable options to take. Doing so will lead us to some final thoughts, in the direction of a more moderate apologetic strategy and the rationality of believing in miracles.

B. The Wrong Laws Objection

How reasonable the Wrong Laws Objection proves to be, in particular cases, will depend upon lots of details. Different cases of supposed anomalies will bring with them different details. Avoiding too many details, let's suppose that we grant the familiar demand for theistically neutral evidence (although soon, I shall urge that we needn't grant it). Even granting this demand, there may be cases of supposed anomalies where our remarkable event *e* turns out — after the most serious and persistent efforts to reformulate our scientific laws — stubbornly to resist any naturalistic causal explanation whatever. In such a case, we might think that the unity of science is better preserved by admitting that *e* is truly an anomaly than by working toward a radical revamping of scientific laws.

Suppose that a small group of unbelieving biologists and forensic scientists, all committed to Naturalism, were confronted with what, by any examination of the relevant facts, seems to be the raising of a man from the dead after four days in the grave. The accepted and successful laws of natural science cannot explain such an occurrence, and no diligent efforts to uncover new laws, or ingenious efforts to revamp existing ones, succeed in explaining the occurrence. Our scientists might persist in their commitment to Naturalism. If so, they can only judge their larger belief-system to be in pretty serious disarray. The truth about biology, whatever it is, must be reckoned quite different from what existing biological science tells us — a strained admission in light of the ability of existing science to explain all relevant biological phenomena *except* the man's rising. Moreover they are yet without any explanation whatsoever about the apparent anomaly. Now remaining in this state of "cognitive vertigo" is, surely, an option. And yet, in light of the evidence, one cannot help but think that our scientists' degree of (well-earned) confidence in the laws of science ought to be *higher* than their confidence in Naturalism.[14] They do of course *believe* that every event must be causally explainable in terms of prior natural events and the laws of nature; but — here is the *key* question — is it reasonable to continue believing this, in the face of an event that seems resistant to explanation by biological laws, given the otherwise great success of these laws?

That question is not easily answered. For our thoroughgoing naturalists, the anomaly has shaken their confidence in the established laws of science, but not their belief that every event has natural cause. (More than once, they will remind us, the history of science has witnessed such upheavals: in all such cases, the community of scientists, far from giving up their Naturalism, retrenched their efforts to work out a more adequate account of the world consistent with it.) Yet to many, it would — all things considered — seem far more reasonable to retain the existing canons of biology, and grant the following inference to the best explanation: the phenomenon is genuinely anomalous, and Naturalism is false.

One can't help but wish for some clearer way of deciding, on purely neutral grounds, when one stance is more reasonable than another. Which of the two stances, prior to any other considerations or details, is *in its own right* objectively more reasonable, or is more likely to be true — the idea of Naturalism, or the idea of events having no natural causes? I

14. Indeed, it is presumably because the general run of natural scientists abhor such cognitive vertigo that, given their commitment to Naturalism, they are keen to deny the historical basis of the biblical testimony to miracles in the first place. The historical reliability of the biblical record is, alas, another question we haven't pursued here: see footnote 15.

confess to thinking that there is no good answer to this question, no "right" answer that anyone who is rational would be obliged to accept.

C. The Non-Miraculous Anomaly Objection

Something similar arises in connection with the Non-Miraculous Anomaly Objection. Here, as with the Wrong Laws Objection, the believer might at least make progress without arriving at anything like a proof; and then, despite the progress, one may still confront residual worries about what is most reasonable to believe. Let's see why.

Suppose it were granted that some remarkable event *e* is genuinely anomalous. Such an anomalous event points to God (i.e., is genuinely miraculous) only if it has a divine cause. But as the Non-Miraculous Anomaly Objection is keen to remind us, we can prove that our anomalous event *e* has a divine cause only if we can give some proof against its having some other cause or indeed *no cause at all.* And this simply cannot be proven. The event could be anomalous precisely because it is a spontaneous, uncaused event. In other words, there is no direct, deductive proof of the divine cause condition (DC) from the anomalous event premise (AE). That's the challenge against being able to answer "yes" to our central question (II).

But perhaps all is not immediately lost here. The objection seems to require that the only available argumentative route to a conclusion — the only way of supporting some claim as reasonable to believe — is a deductive one, in the form of a genuine proof. Surely this is too strong. Even if there is *no deductive route* from (DC) to (AE), it hardly follows that there is *no route whatever* from (DC) to (AE) — no way at all in which an anomaly can serve as rational grounds or good evidence for believing that it has a divine cause. Indeed, much of legal and scientific reasoning takes the form of a (nondeductive) "inference to the best explanation." Long ago, astronomers came to realize that the orbit of Uranus exhibited unexpected deviations from their best calculations of what it should be. The best explanation — the only reasonable explanation, given everything else that was known about the solar system — was that there must exist a gravitational force exerted by some theretofore unknown (and as yet undiscovered) heavenly body, affecting the orbit of Uranus. That reasonable belief led astronomers to search for, and eventually discover, the planet we call Neptune. Or consider a miniature "legal" case — of two hopelessly failing students whose final exam papers are remarkably high-score

'A's. If, on inspection, both exams are exactly alike (even down to the few mistakes), then we can reasonably believe that our students have cheated: given the evidence, that is far and away the best explanation, the best inference to make. Now in both of these cases, as in a vast range of others like them, while we lack anything like a deductive proof, we nevertheless have very strong evidence grounding our inference to what best explains it. It is of course *possible* that (unlike all other planets) there is no gravitational explanation for the orbit of Uranus, or that the failing students suddenly knew the course material remarkably well and by chance inexplicably wrote the same things on their papers. But surely it is far and away more reasonable, given the evidence, to believe here that some other gravitational body exists, and that the students have cheated.

In the same way, while a positive "argument from miracles" may not be available to *prove* the existence of God, it may nevertheless be *more reasonable* to claim that *e* has a divine cause than to claim that *e* is spontaneous, inexplicable, uncaused. The occurrence of some remarkable event that is inexplicable in terms of past events and the laws of nature is perhaps good evidence that it was caused by something outside nature: perhaps the best explanation is that *e* is caused by God. Indeed many people would claim that the idea of an event being altogether *uncaused* (having no causal explanation whatsoever) is simply unreasonable.

That's fair enough. But is it right? How would one show, or plausibly defend, this view that the idea of an uncaused event is unreasonable? Indeed, how would one go about showing or defending even the weaker claim — that uncaused events are less reasonable than divinely caused events? While many of us do in fact find ourselves quite naturally believing this weaker claim, the skeptic might find himself quite naturally believing otherwise: to the skeptic, it seems more reasonable to accept the existence of an uncaused event than to accept the existence of an invisible divine cause. Which view, *in its own right,* all on its own, is objectively more rational, more likely to be true? Once again, I confess to thinking that there is no good answer to this question, no "right" answer that anyone who is rational would be obliged to accept.

Yet perhaps the challenge from Non-Miraculous Anomalies isn't so dim as all that. As before, different cases bring with them different details. Mightn't there be cases presenting us with *evidence,* quite beyond the anomalous event itself, for their having a divine cause? You can have evidence for my causing some occurrence if you see me bring it about. That sort of evidence won't be available in the case of an invisible God. But suppose that you know me and my inner character well — well enough to know that if you call me on the phone and ask that I send you $50, then you will receive the money from me. Should you ask me for money, receiving it is evidence that I sent it. Had you not asked, you almost certainly wouldn't have found an envelope with money taped to your front door: surely the best explanation for the money's appearing on your door is that I put it there. Elijah knew the inner character of the God of Abraham and Isaac well enough: he asked God to consume the bullock and stones and wood and water on Mt. Carmel, and fire came down from a cloudless sky to consume the altar. That, surely, is evidence of God's causing the fire. In this case at least, isn't it more reasonable to suppose that fire from a cloudless sky was caused by God, and less reasonable to suppose it was uncaused?

It sure seems so. The skeptic might, alas, wonder if the Elijah story is even true, and add that he himself has no evidence that any miracle like the one described in the case of Elijah has actually occurred. For better or worse, we have rather fewer examples of candidate miracles, nowadays, earning a spot in the broadcasts of reputable evening newscasts, to present to our skeptic. It *is* worth remembering that a strong apologetic of miracles, aiming to provide the skeptic with an "argument from miracles" to the existence of God, needs an event to offer up for discussion that the skeptic will accept as a candidate.[15] As we've said, there is no forcing one

15. A tall order, perhaps, if we aim to enlist the help of Elijah. I've studiously avoided the question of how one should go about establishing the inspiration and authority of the biblical record and its reliability as a true statement of past events. The second of these won't follow straight from the first: we'd need other premises (on which fair-minded believers have disagreed) about literal reading and inerrancy and more. I have no expertise on such matters, and shan't pronounce on it. I have no expertise on the first issue (of inspiration and authority) either, but will pronounce on it this far: the divine authority of Scripture seems to me not something that one could really establish at all. Some of us came to believe it at our parents' knee. (But then, how'd *they* come to know it?) To accept the authority of Scripture on the authority of my parents will work all right as an explanation of why I *do* believe it, but hardly works as a justification of the belief itself (why I *should* believe it). My own view is that no amount of historical scholarship can establish the inspiration and authority of scripture. We've got historical evidence about the life of President Washington sufficient to underwrite the belief that he owned slaves; but what sort of evidence could there be about God inspiring the Gospel writers (say) or the selection of the Canon that would underwrite belief in those? (Here I commend to the reader the later chapters of Alvin Plantinga's *Warranted Christian Belief* (Oxford University Press, forthcoming), and his discussions there of the Principle of Dwindling Probabilities. My suspicion is that Plantinga is right: our warrant in believing the Bible to be the authoritative Word of God owes to the work of the Holy Spirit. Full stop, pretty much.)

to believe in miracles. But our latest effort has been in the direction of cutting a path that could in principle be followed in arguing from the occurrence of a genuine anomaly to the existence of a divine cause. Whether our skeptic is well enough on board to grant the occurrence of a genuine anomaly will depend on the particular case at issue, and how well the Wrong Laws Objection can be met in that particular case. If, in light of our previous reflections, it can in that case be met, then our latest effort has shown that such a case might also point to a divine cause, even if the route to this conclusion is something weaker than a deductive proof — something rather more like an inference to the best explanation.

VII. Belief in Miracles and a Moderate Apologetic Strategy

So far as I can see, apologetics is about defending the rationality of the Christian faith, not *proving* it. There is probably no convincing proof for Naturalism, but it is not thereby irrational to believe that Naturalism is true. There is probably no argument for theism that every rational person must accept, but theism isn't thereby irrational to believe. Suppose the challenges from Wrong Laws and Non-Miraculous Anomalies cast some doubt on our confidence that questions (I) and (II) can readily be answered affirmatively. This result counts at most against what we have been calling the strong apologetic undertaking, of proving the existence of God by appeal to miracles: it tells not at all against the rationality of believing in miracles, nor against their deployment in a more moderate apologetic strategy. Let me close with some brief reflections on those issues. My purpose is to address the two residual worries most recently nipping our heels — about the difficulty of judging one view to be objectively more reasonable or likely than another, and about the demand for theistically neutral evidence. Neither of these, on reflection, are genuine worries at all.

A. The Rationality of Believing in Miracles

The believer oughtn't shoulder the mistaken idea that the rationality of the Christian faith stands or falls with the success or failure of positive arguments proving the existence of God. Likewise, the Christian would be equally mistaken to suppose that the rationality of believing in miracles stands or falls with the success or failure of an argument showing that some event is indeed anomalous and has a divine cause. Let's think about the first of these, first. If the central apologetic task is one of defending the rationality of the Christian faith, then the thinking Christian is concerned with answering the charge that believing in God is somehow illegitimate — that in light of the evidence, accepting theism is in one way or another irrational, or less than fully rational. But what evidence *is* that, and what exactly makes believing theism in light of it irrational or unreasonable? The skeptic will say that theistic belief is unreasonable because it simply isn't very credible, isn't very likely to be true, given other accepted beliefs. But surely a lot rides on (i) what those other beliefs *are,* and (ii) how likely or reasonable *they* are said to be. Concerning (ii), I've already spilled the beans: few if any "deep" beliefs wear an obvious and objective degree of likelihood or reasonableness marked plainly on their sleeves. (Which is objectively more likely to be true — that time had a beginning, or that there is no beginning to time? Which, all on its own, is objectively more likely to be true — that in our heavenly abode we are souls or spirits, or that we have physical (if incorruptible) bodies? None of these wears an obvious and objective likelihood on its sleeve. None of these, *all on its own,* is objectively more reasonable, more likely.) This brings us straight to (i): What *are* these other beliefs, on the basis of which theism is judged to be not very likely true, not very credible? No doubt theism is not very likely, when judged from the basis of Naturalism. But the believer is scarcely obliged to judge the credibility of theism against the "evidence" of Naturalism. (No doubt the claim "Time had a beginning" is not very likely, when judged from the view that every event must be caused by a temporally earlier event. But one needn't believe that latter causal hypothesis: it isn't all on its own more objectively likely, something that anyone who is rational is obliged to accept.)

Is the believer rational in accepting theism? Well, the reasonableness or likelihood one associates with that belief will depend on the reasonableness or likelihood associated with other of his or her beliefs. Among these beliefs may be — *why not?* — the deliverances of religious experience, and/or the fine-tuning version of the teleological argument (say), and/or an acquired faith via general revelation, and/or the work of the Holy Spirit. If the believer is in possession of no good reason for doubting the deliverances of one or another of these sources of belief, then their likelihood for that person will be sufficiently high to count for them as evidence for believing in theism.

Now return to miracles. The skeptic may insist that belief in miracles is unreasonable simply because it isn't very credible, isn't very likely to be true, given other beliefs about the world. As before, a lot rides on (i) what those "other beliefs about the world" *are*, and (ii) how likely or reasonable *they* are said to be. Concerning (ii), there is no obvious and objective degree of likelihood or reasonableness marked plainly on the sleeves of the naturalist claim that laws of nature have no "gaps," or that nature encounters no outside intervention. The likelihood that there are sometimes genuinely anomalous events, events having no cause in some prior natural event, will for the believer be judged on the basis of other beliefs she has, and the likelihood she attaches to them. Among these other beliefs may be — why not? — the deliverances of religious experience, and/or arguments for the existence of God, and/or an acquired faith via general revelation, and/or the work of the Holy Spirit. If the believer is in possession of good reasons for accepting (no outweighing reasons for rejecting) the deliverances of one or another of these sources of belief, then the likelihood of those beliefs, for that person, may be sufficiently high to count as good grounds for reckoning the belief in genuine anomalies to be very reasonable. Indeed, the contents of these other beliefs may be such as to invite the *expectation* of divine intervention. True enough: if what is counted as good grounds for believing some claim is to be judged on the basis of the likelihood or reasonableness of other, prior beliefs, then an unbeliever — sharing no such beliefs as those deliverances of religious experience and natural theology and faith might provide — may well lack sufficient grounds for believing in miracles. But the believer needn't be in that position. And the believer who isn't in that position, who aims to defend the rationality of believing in miracles, needn't presume the posture of "adopting" it by obliging the familiar demand for "theistically neutral evidence."

B. The Moderate Apologetic

These latest reflections suggest how in broad outlines one might conceive the relevance of miracles to a more attenuated, moderate Christian apologetic. The evidential contribution of miracles, rather than figuring at the front end (the beginning) of an effort to demonstrate the existence of a divine being, will instead figure in the middle of an effort to establish the warrant for other central religious beliefs — the Christian plan of salvation generally, say, or the divinity of Christ in particular. At the front end will be located those of one's beliefs already enjoying sufficiently high likelihood, thanks to the arguments of natural theology or to religious experience or general revelation or the work of the Holy Spirit. Here the believer may have sufficient (and let's call it what it is — *theistic*) evidential grounds not simply for judging miracles to be possible, but to be expected from a Creator having those attributes such beliefs give reason to believe he has. And since Hume's argument against testimony is no longer in place, the believer may safely enlist the evidence of historical testimony as well. The route taken by this moderate apologetic is thus from theistic belief (supplemented by historical testimony or not), to rational belief in miracles, to belief in the authority and truth of claims to which miracles are a confirming witness. The raising of Lazarus, the walking on water, the multiplication of loaves and fishes — all alike serve as confirming evidence that Jesus of Nazareth is who he said he is, namely the divine Son of God.[16]

Many further questions remain, about the stronger positive argument from miracles and the moderate apologetic strategy lately suggested. The purpose of this chapter has been to point the thinking believer in the direction of these questions, to illustrate how philosophical reflection is fruitfully brought to bear in approaching them and their forerunners, and to recommend that, in light of its inherent difficulty, thinking Christians approach an "apologetic from miracles" with a refined mixture of intellectual humility and tenacity. There is no forcing one to believe in miracles. But neither is there any reason to shrink from seeing in events like the resurrection evidence of God's reaching down to make himself known to creatures.

16. And here it is perhaps worth asking why Jesus performed the miracles recorded in the New Testament scriptures. We can pretty safely say that it was in part because he had compassion for people. But did he intend them to play some (let's go ahead and call it) apologetic role? If so, the theistic beliefs of his Jewish audience were already well in place, and the point would be to confirm his status as the divine Son of God. That's the moderate role proposed here. But notice that even in this case, many theists refused to believe, and called him a magician; moreover, recall Christ's impatience with this "evil generation demanding a sign." We oughtn't expect too much from any apologetic of miracles: there's no *forcing* a theist to be a Christian.

15

Christianity and Ethics

Frances Howard-Snyder

Ethics is making a comeback. The success of books like William Bennett's *The Book of Virtues* makes this evident, as do the constant references by politicians to "family values" and anxieties about sexual harassment and discrimination. But what is striking to the average Christian is just how ill-fitting these tendencies are with the seemingly near-universal belief that "ethics is relative." Allan Bloom, in his oft-quoted book, *The Closing of the American Mind,* claims that relativism is the only true value embraced by contemporary American college and university students. While this is undoubtedly an exaggeration, ethical relativism does seem to be enormously popular.

This puts Christians in a difficult position when they discuss ethical issues with those around them, since they are well known (and frequently scorned) for believing that ethical truths are not relative. Many opponents of Christianity hold that this makes us intolerant and even ignorant. As a result, Christians' views on ethics often set them at odds with the unbelieving world, and so it seems appropriate in a chapter with this title, to think a bit about how the Christian should respond to such challenges. That is, to think about what the Christian might say to the person who re-

---

I am indebted to Michael Murray, Mike Murphy, Laura Ekstrom, Daniel Howard-Snyder, and other authors of this volume for helpful criticism in writing this chapter. I did not accept their advice on every point, however. So they are not responsible for any defects which remain.

gards Christianity as unacceptable because of its opposition to relativism. This is the topic of the first part of this chapter.

But we should want to go one step beyond this in our thinking about ethics. It is one thing to show critics that relativism, as an ethical view, faces severe, I would even say fatal, difficulties, and another to explain to critics exactly what sort of alternative the Christian endorses. So, after discussing relativism, we will want to explore a bit just what it is that is distinctively Christian about Christian ethics. Does the Christian ethic consist of just the Two Great Love Commandments that Jesus described as the source and summary of the Law, or is there more than that? If that is all there is, what should we make of the many other commands given throughout the New and Old Testaments? And if that is not all, how do we make the various pieces fit together so that we can know how we ought to act on specific occasions? These are the questions I will ask in parts two and three.

1. Ethical Relativism: Right for Me, Wrong for You?

The Bible contains many moral rules. While some of these may have been intended to apply only to a particular group at a particular time (such as laws about eating pork, etc.) many are clearly intended to apply to everyone everywhere. By contrast, it's common to hear students, politicians, and others voicing the thought that right and wrong vary from society to society and even from individual to individual, and that acts are right or wrong because of the attitudes of the person performing the action or those of her society. Let's formulate ethical relativism explicitly as the view that:

1. An act is right or wrong because the agent's society says it is.[1]

1. "Agent" here refers to the person performing the act whose rightness or wrongness is in question. If you tell a lie, you are the agent of the lie, as opposed to the person you lie to or some third party who observes and judges your action.

The phrase "says it is" is sometimes replaced with something more complicated. For example, the relativist might say that an act is right because the agent's society *requires* it and wrong because the agent's society *condemns* it.

1a. Three Difficulties for Ethical Relativism

Ethical relativism is incompatible with moral progress: not because it implies that mores do not change, but simply because it cannot consistently regard those changes as progress. If the majority of our society approves of slavery at one time and disapproves of it at another time, ethical relativism cannot say that we have shaken off an incorrect moral view and acquired a correct one. It must say, instead, that we have simply gone from having one correct view — that slavery was permissible — to having a different correct view — that slavery is wrong. This also means that moral giants who, in retrospect, we regard as being far ahead of their times — early opponents of slavery, for example, were in fact mistaken, because they were in the minority.

A second difficulty derives from the fact that each of us belongs to more than one group or society, and the majority of one of these groups may have a different view on some issue from that of the majority of another group. Consider, for example, Susan, an American feminist who lives in Saudi Arabia. One group she belongs to holds that it is wrong for a woman to drive a car. Another group she belongs to holds that it is not wrong. So, her action of driving her Ford to the store for coffee on Tuesday morning is both wrong and not wrong. But that's impossible. A *particular* action cannot be both wrong and not wrong. That's as crazy as saying that she is both over 5′ 6″ and not over 5′ 6″, or that the earth is both flat and not flat. A contradiction (a statement and its denial) is always false.

Note a third problem. This view can lead to extreme intolerance. The relativist insists that whether Susan's drive was permissible depends on what the majority of people in her society think. Moreover, they also insist that whether Susan's Christian worship is permissible also depends on what people around her think.

To avoid the second and third difficulties, relativists often shift to individual ethical relativism, according to which:

2. An act is right or wrong because the agent *herself* thinks (or says) it is.

There is no (obvious) danger of contradiction, because Susan's drive is wrong or right depending on what *Susan* thinks about the matter. Moreover, if she is in the minority in her opinion, there is no danger that an oppressive intolerant majority will override her private choice on such a matter.

1b. Difficulties for Individual Ethical Relativism

Perhaps the most serious problem with individual ethical relativism appears when we think about actions which involve radically injuring other people. According to that view, if Timothy McVeigh believes that he does nothing wrong in killing hundreds of innocent people as an act of vengeance against the United States, then he has done nothing wrong. But that's very implausible. Even if we think of actions which are less obviously violations of others' rights, such as adultery or divorce, it seems implausible that only one person's views (the agent's) should count in determining the moral status of the action. Other people were crucially involved. Why do their views on the matter not count in determining whether it was wrong?

Individual ethical relativism faces other difficulties, including one analogous to the complaint against group ethical relativism, that it did not allow for moral progress. Individual ethical relativism appears to imply that *individuals* do not develop morally, because they can never be mistaken. But our experience rebels against this implication. We can all remember — perhaps with a shudder — some horrible moral mistake we made in the past.

1c. Arguments for Ethical Relativism

If both versions of ethical relativism face so many objections, why are they so popular? This is an important question. Perhaps the motivations for ethical relativism are so powerful that we should accept some version of it in spite of its troubling implications. But how powerful are they?

One common motivation is the following. Consider the claim that:

3. *Beliefs* about right and wrong vary from society to society.

This appears to be uncontroversially true (although the amount of disagreement from society to society is often exaggerated).[2] Many people fail to distinguish (3) from a very different claim that:

4. *What really is* right and wrong varies from society to society

2. For a careful discussion of the common content of a variety of different traditions, see C. S. Lewis, *The Abolition of Man.*

and so assume that (4) is just as uncontroversial as (3). But (3) and (4) are not equivalent. To see this, consider someone who accepts (3) and rejects (4) — say, a Jesuit priest who is also an anthropologist who has travelled the world encountering a variety of different cultures. He might acknowledge that people have different beliefs about right and wrong, just as they have different beliefs about chemistry and biology, etc., but insist that what is really right and wrong does not vary, just as the facts about chemistry and biology do not vary. Once the distinction between (3) and (4) is clearly made, one of the motivations for ethical relativism should evaporate.

A second motivation to embrace relativism is a reaction to the intolerance and ethnocentricism of earlier imperialists who travelled to distant lands and attempted to impose Western values in insensitive and even disastrous ways. The idea might be summed up like this: "If you deny ethical relativism, then you must believe that there is one true morality. Of course, you think the one true morality is *your own*. But that is arrogant and intolerant and ethnocentric." But this commitment to tolerance is problematic for relativists. For one thing, if one says that tolerance is always good, one seems to be endorsing a *universal* moral value, one which would not have been popular in many other cultures. At the same time, ethical relativism does not promote tolerance very well. The ethical relativist has to allow that all sorts of terribly intolerant behavior is perfectly morally acceptable. Timothy McVeigh's behavior is judged acceptable and even encouraged by individual ethical relativism, although it is hardly tolerant behavior. Moreover, if the majority decides that all the members of a minority religion who live amongst them ought to be executed, then group ethical relativism endorses the practice.

1d. Relativism and Absolutism

A third motivation for relativism is the thought that the only alternative to relativism is absolutism. If this is correct, and if absolutism turns out to be false, then relativism is true. Absolutism is not an easy notion to define. Suppose we understand it like this: "The actions on the following list are always, absolutely wrong no matter what the circumstances or results: lying, killing, adultery, stealing. . . ." If absolutism says that, then it faces difficulties. Absolutism about, say, lying, is a tough view to defend. In the early chapters of Exodus, the Hebrew midwives lie to Pharaoh in order to save the baby Hebrew boys from death. We are told that God was good to the midwives for their action. Such examples suggest that lying is not always wrong. But note that if absolutism implies that lying is always wrong, then absolutism and relativism are not the only available alternatives. One can say that certain kinds of action are always universally wrong independently of what anyone thinks, but that lying is not one of them.

On the other hand, suppose we define a more sophisticated absolutism as the view that there are *some* kinds of action which are absolutely always wrong no matter what the consequences or circumstances. Now, it may be true that relativism and this view are the only two available.[3] But if they are, this version of absolutism is much more difficult to attack. You cannot attack absolutism per se by pointing out that some lies are permissible, or even that some thefts or killings are permissible.

The various versions of ethical relativism face serious difficulties, and, on reflection, are not well motivated. The fact that it is incompatible with ethical relativism, therefore, should not be considered a liability for Christianity.

2. What Makes Right Acts Right?

2a. Divine Command Theory

But if it is not my opinions or the opinions of my society that make wrong acts wrong and right acts right, what is it? Many Christians will claim that it is God's opinion, or better, God's commandments. This view is the Divine Command Theory (henceforth, DCT). Strictly stated, this view says:

> An act is right because and only because God commands it, and an act is wrong because and only because God forbids it.

Is the Christian committed to this view?

3. Although probably not. The philosopher W. D. Ross appears to reject both, arguing that there are facts about right and wrong that are independent of what anyone thinks about the matter, but that every moral principle of the form, "Never tell a lie," or even "Never tell a lie in order to save the innocent," is subject to exceptions.

2b. Reasons to Accept Divine Command Theory

One commonly offered reason to say yes is that since God creates everything, he must create morality. A related reason is that since God is all-powerful, he must have the power to determine what is right and wrong. Otherwise, the thought goes, his sovereignty would be undermined. This line of thought is not decisive, however. To say that God creates everything must mean that God creates everything *that is created.* He doesn't, for example, create himself. And there is good reason to think that God does not create the truths of logic or mathematics. Perhaps the truths of morality are like the truths of logic or mathematics: true but not created by anyone.

As for the claim that God is all-powerful, this is usually interpreted as meaning that God can do anything possible. It is not to attribute to him the ability to make round squares or a stone so heavy that he cannot lift it, or free creatures who are nevertheless guaranteed to do the right thing always. God cannot make necessary truths false. If moral truths are necessary truths (as there is good reason to believe they are), then they are not *up to* God, in the way they would have to be if he were to create them.

DCT, however, is enormously popular. Perhaps this is because it is hard to see where moral truths or moral rules can come from if not from someone's choice or command; and who is better placed to issue such commands than God?

2c. Difficulties for Divine Command Theory

Attractive as the theory is, it faces serious difficulties. If it is correct, then, if God had commanded us to murder and torture, these things would have been right. But, it seems, murder and torture would be wrong no matter who commanded them.[4] The DCTist has two lines of response here. She can bite the bullet, insisting that, if God were to command murder, murder would indeed be right. Perhaps the story of Abraham and Isaac suggests that this is the truly faithful attitude. A different line of response is to insist that it is *impossible* that God command us to murder or torture other human beings; and hence, that it is foolish to wonder about whether murder or torture would be right in that impossible situation.

4. Notice, incidentally, that this difficulty is very much like a difficulty we raised for ethical relativism: if the majority of Muslims approved of assassinating Rushdie, then ER would imply it was right. But it obviously would not be right.

This last suggestion seems plausible, but it raises the question for the DCTist of *why* God would never command us to murder or torture. Why, indeed, does God command the things he does command? This question is part of an old dilemma: does

(a) God forbid murder because it is wrong or otherwise a bad thing; or
(b) is it wrong because God forbids it?[5]

The implication is that we are faced with two choices: either God forbids murder and so on as a rational response to the badness or wrongness of murder; or he chooses the rules arbitrarily. If (a), that is, if his choice is a rational response to some bad aspect of the behavior, then it is that feature which really explains the wrongness of the behavior, not his forbidding it. On the other hand, if (b), that is, if there is nothing to guide God's choice, then his choice must be arbitrary, but if it is arbitrary, then it is not clear why his forbidding it makes it wrong. Why do we have a moral obligation to obey the arbitrary commands of God? The answer cannot be: that we trust that God's will is for our own and others' good. That answer presupposes that there is such a thing as our good which God is aiming at and which guides his choice.

2d. Responses to the Dilemma

A different answer is often suggested: because he can annihilate us if we refuse. Let's focus on that fact by itself. Suppose a powerful dictator — say, Caligula — threatens to kill you if you don't worship him. It might be prudent to obey, but presumably it would not be *wrong* to refuse. So, it cannot be simply the fact that God is all-powerful that obliges us to obey him.

Well, the DCTist says, perhaps it's not simply God's power, but God's great *knowledge* that creates an obligation to obey his arbitrary commands. But again this seems inadequate. Imagine that the powerful dictator is also all-knowing — an extreme version of Hannibal the Cannibal, perhaps. There still seems no moral obligation to obey him.

"But," you say impatiently, "Caligula and Hannibal are moral monsters. Of course there's no vice in disobeying them. But God is different.

5. This dilemma is known as Euthyphro's Dilemma. It derives from a question Plato's character Socrates raises for Euthyphro in a dialogue of that name.

God is perfectly good. He would not abuse his power or his knowledge. That is why we should obey him." In response, one might wonder what you mean when you say that God is perfectly good. If God's will is the source of all morality, right and wrong, good and bad, then to say that God is perfectly good is simply to say that God approves of his own character and behavior. But that quality — self-satisfaction, even when combined with great power and knowledge — does not make it obligatory to obey the commands of the dictator.[6]

How about the fact that God is our creator? Doesn't this give us an obligation to obey him? We might distinguish two different ideas here. First is the suggestion that if one creates something, then one has the right to determine its purpose. So, if God created us, then his purposes in creating us determine what our good is, and what we ought to do. Second is the suggestion that we are indebted to God for a great deal, including our creation and our continued existence; and this indebtedness obliges us to do what he wants.

The first suggestion — that mere creation gives the creator the right to determine what the creature ought to do — seems implausible. Imagine that you create a human being (by procreation, or by cloning or whatever). You don't thereby have the right to decide how she ought to behave. A human being has desires and feelings and rights, and this sets definite limits on what you may do to her, and what you may morally require of her. Having created a sentient, reasoning, autonomous being, your wanting to torture or enslave or destroy her does not give you the right to

6. Advocates of *Modified* Divine Command Theory object at this point. Robert Adams, for example, makes a distinction between what should be said about rightness and what should be said about goodness by the DCTist. Why not say that rightness is defined in terms of God's will? If something is right, it is because God commanded it, the suggestion goes, but goodness and badness and other evaluative notions are not defined in terms of God's will. To say that God is perfectly good, Robert Adams suggests, is (a) to express our approval, delight, etc., in God and (b) to say that God has certain specific characteristics, such as kindness, a forgiving and loving nature, etc. That is, it is to say more than simply that God has whatever features he chooses to have, or approves of having. We must add to this picture either that God cannot cease to be perfectly good, in this sense, or that if he did cease to be perfectly good, his commands would not create obligations for us. Adams says: x is "right" means "x is commanded by a loving God." This means that if God had not existed or had not forbidden gratuitous cruelty, such cruelty would not have been wrong. It would still be bad, presumably, but it would not be wrong. See Adams, "A Modified Divine Command Theory of Ethical Wrongness," in *The Virtue of Faith* (New York: Oxford University Press, 1987), 9-24.

do so; and it certainly does not give her the obligation to submit. Romans 9:21 compares God to a potter who has the right to do as he pleases with his pots. But what is true of the potter is arguably not true of the shepherd. A pot has no feelings, no desires, no needs, no capacity for pain. Imagine a very clever shepherd who creates his own sheep (call her "Dolly"!) out of nothing. Now, one might argue that this shepherd has the *right* to do what he likes with Dolly — including torturing her to death. This may be true, but it is consistent with that to say that some ways of treating her are *better* than others. (Someone can be acting within his rights and yet acting less well than he could possibly act.) God is more frequently compared to a good shepherd — who knows what is good for his sheep and who does it — than he is to a potter who arbitrarily decides the fate of his pots.

The point about gratitude is more plausible. We do sometimes acquire obligations to do things for people — even to satisfy their arbitrary whims — when we owe them a great debt of gratitude. I owe my parents a lot. If they wanted purple ribbons tied around all the trees in their garden — I might well acquire an obligation to do so. In the same way, undoubtedly, our debt of gratitude to God for our creation, and our continued existence, oblige us to obey even arbitrary whims of God's. For example, if God decides that he would prefer us not to eat the fruit of a certain tree, or to work on a certain day, or wear certain clothes or cut our hair in certain ways, as a conventional sign of our devotion to him, then we certainly acquire obligations to obey. In addition, it may be that our great debt of gratitude to Christ may make behavior obligatory which would otherwise have been supererogatory (that is, good, but beyond the call of duty).

But notice something important. This account of why I ought to obey my parents' whims presupposes a prior obligation: to repay debts of gratitude. It is only because of an already existing obligation that my parents' goodness to me creates a new obligation. This means that gratitude can explain some but not all of my moral obligations.

DCT theory faces some serious difficulties, which I have tried to spell out. These difficulties may not be insurmountable, however. This appears to be one of those issues on which serious thinking Christians can disagree.

2e. Why the Truth or Falsity of Divine Command Theory Makes No Practical Difference

The debate between DCT and competing views is over what makes moral truths true, not about which claims are moral truths. We may agree on what the moral truths *are* while disagreeing over why they are true. Moreover, serious Christians on both sides of this debate agree that God is all-knowing and perfectly good. As such, even if he does not create all of morality, if we can be sure that he commands something, then we can be sure it is right. It may be difficult or impossible for us to determine what is right or wrong without listening to God's word. It makes sense, therefore, for a Christian to rely on God as a source of moral knowledge, whether or not DCT is true. Exactly how one is to do that — by reading the Bible, attending to the tradition of the Church, praying, listening to one's conscience, using one's reason, obeying religious authorities — is a different question, which I shall not attempt to resolve here. I would like to stress, however, that the question of whether DCT is true need make no *practical* difference to a Christian as she attempts to live a righteous and holy life.

3. What We Ought to Do

3a. The Great Commandments

Whether they accept DCT or not, Christians have common sources for their moral knowledge and can claim that that knowledge is distinctive and right. We know that murder, adultery, theft, torture are all wrong, and that keeping your promises, paying your taxes, honoring your parents, feeding your children are all clearly right, at least in most cases. Ethicists often attempt to find a single unifying principle from which all our obligations can be derived. For example, utilitarians argue that we ought to do whatever will produce the most happiness overall; others say that we ought to act in such a way that we would be willing to see everyone act. What is the point of this attempt to find unity? Should a Christian join the attempt? The Bible contains a variety of moral rules. Why try to unify them?

One reason is that if we had a unified "master" principle from which all more particular rules were derived, then it might help us resolve any apparent conflicts between them: for example, the apparent conflict between the commandment prohibiting lying and the divine approval of the lie told by the Hebrew midwives. Second, it might help us to understand them. The commandment to keep the Sabbath holy is not crystal clear. Jesus illuminates it in Mark. His illumination stems from a deep understanding of the underlying point of the law rather than a legalistic knowledge of its surface details. Thirdly, the Bible says nothing explicit about many matters which concern us today, such as the ethics of e-mail correspondence or of artificial insemination. If there were a single principle from which all other rules were derived, it would help fill in the gaps.

Christianity offers a distinctive unifying principle. Jesus said:

> 'You shall love the Lord your God with all your heart, with all your soul, and with all your mind.' This is the first and great commandment;
> And the second is like it: 'You shall love your neighbor as yourself.'
> On these two commandments hang all the Law and the Prophets. (Matthew 22:37-40)[7]

As a simplifying assumption let us understand this as saying that the first commandment summarizes our moral obligations to God; and the second, our obligations to our fellow human beings; and that, in cases of conflict, the first is to take precedence. As a sort of case study, I shall focus on the second commandment and try to see whether it is an adequate foundation for morals when it comes to our dealings with our fellow human beings.

3b. Love and Emotion

The second great commandment instructs us to love our neighbors as ourselves. But "love" is ambiguous. What sort of love ought we to have for our neighbors? It is sometimes argued that love, as an affection, cannot be commanded.[8] Since we have little or no control over our emotions, the claim goes, the most this commandment can be requiring is loving behavior.

7. Jesus was quoting the Old Testament for each of the two commandments: Deuteronomy 6:4 and Leviticus 19:18, respectively. (Here and throughout, I use the *New King James Version*.)

8. Immanuel Kant raises this objection to the idea of "pathological love." *The Fundamental Principles of the Metaphysics of Morals,* trans. Thomas Abbot (Indianapolis: The Bobbs-Merrill Company, 1949), 17.

But this cannot be right. Consider 1 Corinthians 13:3: "And though I bestow all my goods to feed the poor, and though I give my body to be burned, but have not love, it profits me nothing." Acting in a loving manner is not equivalent to loving. One can perform all the correct outward behavior and still fall dramatically short. The Gospels confront us with a repeated emphasis that inner states are at least as important as outward behavior. The Sermon on the Mount contains the clearest examples of this:

> You have heard it was said to those of old, 'You shall not murder,' and whoever murders will be in danger of the judgment.
>
> But I say to you that whoever is angry with his brother without a cause shall be in danger of the judgment. . . .
>
> [W]hoever looks at a woman to lust for her has already committed adultery with her in his heart. (Matthew 5:21-22, and 28)

If the love that is commanded is some sort of inner state, an emotion or set of desires, which emotion or set of desires is it? Undoubtedly, at least a significant part of it is *benevolence* — the desire for the well-being of others. But is there anything else? How do we tell? The first piece of evidence is the word which is translated as "love." This is *agape* in the Greek and *ahebh* in the Hebrew. Apparently the Hebrew word did not have the distinctive "charity as opposed to eros" connotations which we associate with Christian love, as it was the word used to describe romantic love. Moreover, before its use in the New Testament, the Greek word *agape* appears not to have had a very precise meaning either.[9] The color we now associate with it was absorbed from its new surroundings. Let us turn to these.

One aspect of its context is what else we are told about love in the New Testament. The second great commandment is like the first. It is fair to assume that the love we owe our neighbor is of the same kind as the love we owe God. Our love for God ought to include an appreciation of him and a desire for union with him, in addition to a desire that his will be done. If our love for our neighbor is to be like the love we owe God, this suggests that the love we have for our neighbors should involve the same elements. Indeed, it makes sense that our love for other people should not be simply benevolence or sheer concern for their well-being, but should also involve

9. For points about both the Hebrew and the Greek term, see the entry under "Love" by John Burnaby in *A Dictionary of Christian Ethics*, ed. John Macquarrie (Philadelphia: The Westminster Press, 1967), 197.

desires to be related to them, and an appreciation of what is valuable in them, and enjoyment of them. For if one's attitude towards others were solely that of benevolence, it would seem that one wouldn't want anything they have to offer. Sheer benevolence looks like a kind of arrogance, an attitude of independence and inequality vis-à-vis our neighbors.

This suggests that the love advocated in the second commandment might well include some self-concerned elements — such as appreciation of the good others might have to offer us, and the desire for a relationship with them. (Of course, there are important disanalogies between God and our neighbor, and hence, between the love we owe God and the love we owe our neighbor. For example, worship is no part of the ideal love of another human being.)

The love advocated in the New Testament is unconditional love, love one ought to have for every human being, no matter how much he hurts you, no matter how evil he is. The story of the Good Samaritan makes it clear that this love is owed to every human being, even if all you know about him is that he is human and hurt.[10] The expression itself, "Love your neighbor *as yourself*," gives a further reason for thinking this love should be unconditional.

The guideline here seems to be the *typical* way people love themselves, rather than the particular way each of us loves himself or herself. Sometimes our self-love is destructive or obsessive or otherwise unhealthy. I do not believe that Christ is suggesting that those who love themselves in that way should love others in the same way. What are the salient features of *typical self-love?* Primarily, presumably, its *intensity.* But note also that, while our love for others tends to be greater the greater their attractiveness, goodness, and so on, our love for ourselves does not tend to vary in this way. We are (typically) as much concerned with our own well-being whether or not we judge ourselves to be satisfactory. Our *approval* of ourselves may well vary. But our *self-concern* does not vary in intensity although it might have a different focus. If I judge that I fall short of some standard, this grieves me. If I judge that I excel in some respect, this pleases me. But the grief and the pleasure are equally expressions of my self-concern. They are two sides of a single desire: for my own well-being and success. The strength of my concern is not contingent on how close I come to some standard. This makes the love *unconditional.* If this aspect of typical self-love is part of the blueprint for love of our neighbor, then that love should be similarly unconditional.

10. Or perhaps to *any* human being you encounter.

In spite of the fact that our self-love is unconditional in this way, we feel for ourselves a warmth beyond merely disinterested benevolence. I would guess that most of us can remember being a naughty child, indulging in tantrums or destructive behavior, but desperately wanting, at that moment, to be loved in spite of our naughtiness, perhaps because of some wonderful potential hidden in us that a wise parent or teacher should be able to discern.[11] This tender, unconditional love seemed to us most desirable and most appropriate from this perspective. It is more difficult to see it as desirable and appropriate from the perspective of the one who is called on to give it. But perhaps if we remember the perspective of the one who wants to be loved in spite of everything, we will make better sense of it. I would venture to suggest that the reference to "ourselves" is an invitation to take up this perspective.

A distinctive feature of our self-love is that we regard ourselves as considerably *more malleable* than we regard others. Behavior which we would sum up and react to in others with such thoughts as "What a spoilt child!" or "He's always so badly behaved! Let's not invite him again" would be regarded in ourselves as a temporary aberration: "I was like that yesterday. But maybe I'll be different tomorrow." Because we regard our own future as open to change and development, we regard ourselves as possibly wonderful, and hope that others will see that in us. If we see others in the same way — instead of regarding them as two-dimensional types in a drama in which we are the heroes or heroines — perhaps we will find them easier to love.

Jesus' injunctions to forgive can be seen as part of this idea:

> For if you forgive men their trespasses, your heavenly Father will also forgive you. But if you do not forgive men their trespasses, neither will your Father forgive your trespasses. (Matthew 6:14-15)

> And why do you look at the speck in your brother's eye, but do not consider the plank in your own eye? (Matthew 7:3)

Such sayings tell us to see ourselves as we see others, and to see others as we see ourselves, recognizing the imperfections in ourselves that we are so eager to discover in them, and projecting onto them the malleableness and forgivableness that we perceive in ourselves.[12]

11. If you can't remember it, maybe you can remember thinking about doing it, or perhaps simply imaginatively identifying with a son or daughter in this state.

12. Reinhold Niebuhr, "Love as Forgiveness," in *An Interpretation of Christian*

So the nature of biblically commanded love has an affective component with many facets. The love we are commanded to have for our neighbor includes benevolence as well as a desire to be related to the beloved, which is intense and unconditional.

3c. Love and Action

The commandments require love, rather than simply loving behavior, but it would be a mistake to infer from this that emotion is enough. Consider Lewis Carroll's Walrus, who addresses some oysters as he greedily devours them:

> "I weep for you," the Walrus said: "I deeply sympathize."
> With sobs and tears he sorted out
> Those of the largest size,
> Holding his pocket handkerchief
> Before his streaming eyes.

Presumably we are not supposed to take the Walrus at his word. He claims to *feel* something — in this case, sympathy — for the oysters, and yet he is not truly sympathic because he is not *acting* sympathetically. Sympathy is not simply a sensation.[13] It cannot be detached from action. Neither is love simply a sensation. It is both a way of seeing and a set of desires. You cannot truly see someone as lovable and truly desire her well-being without taking steps to promote that well-being. The same is true of faith, as James tells us: "Faith without works is dead." And Jesus, although constantly emphasizing the importance of inner states like love, mercy, etc., repeatedly stresses that a tree is known by its fruit. One doesn't count as having the right inner states unless these issue in the right sort of behavior. Of course, this point needs to be qualified slightly. If you are mistaken about what someone's well-being consists in — e.g., you mistake the rat poison for heart medication — or if you're genuinely unable to do

---

Ethics (San Francisco: Harper & Row Publishers, 1935), notes that it is one of the advantages of an impossibly difficult morality that it forces us to recognize our own imperfection, our similarity to other people in this regard, and also our common dependence on God.

13. For more discussion of this example and its general point, see Robert C. Roberts, "What's Wrong with Wicked Feelings," *American Philosophical Quarterly* (1991).

anything to help — you're paralyzed, for example — then your failure to help does not amount to a failure of love. Moreover, you might fail to promote the well-being of one person because doing so would require harming another person (including, perhaps, yourself) to a much greater degree. But, barring such circumstances, love leads to loving behavior. Jesus makes this clear in the story of the Good Samaritan, which tells us, not only who, but how, to love.[14]

To tell someone to love his neighbor is, among other things, to tell him to care about his neighbor's welfare, and to give that neighbor's welfare a fairly significant place in his system of priorities. The commandment implies, then, behavior which results, or can reasonably be expected to result, in improvements in the welfare of others. This has clear implications for many moral choices we face. For example, it seems to imply that we should support agencies which promote famine relief; that we should support governmental and church agencies which successfully fight illiteracy and drug abuse, and other social ills; and that we should be ready to help those around us to satisfy basic needs.

3d. On These Hang All the Law and the Prophets: A Complete Morality?

In Romans 13:8-10, Paul writes:

> "Owe no one anything except to love one another, for he who loves another has fulfilled the law.
>
> For the commandments, 'You shall not commit adultery,' 'You shall not steal,' 'You shall not bear false witness,' 'You shall not covet' and if there is any other commandment, are all summed up in this saying namely, 'You shall love your neighbor as yourself.'
>
> Love does no harm to neighbor; therefore love is the fulfillment of the law."

All the law and the prophets hang on the commandment to love. If you truly love, you cannot do all the things which are otherwise prohibited. That makes sense. If you really love someone, you cannot knife him in the street and take his wallet; if you really love your husband, you cannot cheat on him; if you really love someone, you cannot falsely accuse him of a crime; if you really love someone, you cannot desire possessions in a

14. Luke 10:30-35.

way that would disrupt your relationship with him; you cannot backbite about her; you cannot quarrel without wanting to make up. If you really love someone, you will, as Jesus and Paul urge us again and again, feed her when she is hungry, forgive her when she's wronged you, visit her in prison, gently correct her when she goes astray, strive to teach her the gospel.

Paul suggests that the law of love might be used to resolve moral dilemmas:

> I know and am convinced by the Lord Jesus that there is nothing unclean of itself; but to him who considers it unclean it is unclean.
>
> Yet if your brother is grieved because of your food, you are no longer walking in love. Do not destroy with your food the one for whom Christ died. (Romans 14:14)

In other words, it's not the food that matters, it's the salvation of your neighbor's soul. Don't be so concerned about the rules that you forget the point of the rules.

You and I do not anguish over whether to eat meat that has been sacrificed to idols. But here's a modern analogy: many Christians do anguish about alcohol. I think Paul would be sympathetic to the following thoughts on the matter. Suppose you enjoy the occasional glass of Chardonnay on your back porch. You know you are in no danger of alcoholism or drunk driving. But you have a friend who is a recovering alcoholic. It would be unloving for you to bring out your bottle in this friend's presence, since it would constitute a painful, and perhaps dangerous, temptation for him.

On the other hand, you have another friend, an atheist who has acquired the impression that Christians are fun-hating, rule-bound prigs. If you refuse to drink a glass of champagne at his wedding, you may well confirm his mistaken idea about Christians, and increase the obstacles to his returning to the faith. The loving action, in this case, may well be to raise your glass and then drain it.

There are difficulties, however, in using the law of love as a guide to action. Firstly, moral dilemmas often take the form of not knowing what is good or best for someone. Even if we love him perfectly, it is not always easy to see what will be best for him. Imagine that someone you love is close to death, in great pain, and is pleading to be helped to end his life. Loving him (more) will not help settle whether it would be better to do what he wants or not. Similarly, love does not decide the question of when to tell the painful truth and when to lie or keep silent; when to let someone (say, an adolescent) make important and dangerous decisions for himself and when to protect him from himself.

Common sense and a loving respect suggest certain procedures for trying to determine someone's interests. For example, ask him what he wants, put oneself imaginatively in his shoes, consult others, including those generally regarded as wise; pray, read the Bible. But it is clear that questions may still arise. Mistakes are still possible.

A further difficulty for the claim that the commandment provides a complete guide to how to treat others is that even if it did give us an account of what our neighbor's interest consisted in, it would not always explain how to resolve conflicts between the interests of the neighbor on our left and the interests of the neighbor on our right. John Rawls raises this objection:

> The difficulty is that the love of several persons is thrown into confusion once the claims of these persons conflict. . . . It is quite pointless to say that one is to judge the situation as benevolence dictates. This assumes that we are wrongly swayed by self-concern. Our problem lies elsewhere. Benevolence is at sea as long as its many loves are in opposition in the persons of its many objects.[15]

If the commandment has any answer to the question of how to decide between competing claims of different people, it will have to say something of the form: "Use principle P, because to do so is to decide the issue in the most loving way." Deciding the issue in the most loving way must mean, in part: in the way which expresses that you love the people involved more than some other way would, but also: in the way which expresses the fact that your love for them is most *equal.* (An argument for the view that you ought to love them equally is: to love your neighbor as yourself entails that you love the neighbor on your left as yourself and love your neighbor on your right as yourself. Hence, love your neighbor on your left as you love your neighbor on your right.)[16]

15. John Rawls, *A Theory of Justice* (Cambridge, MA: Harvard University Press, 1971), 190.

16. Is this a good argument? It has a fortunate upshot — that it favors evenhandedness, equality, justice, which seem crucial to morality. But is it genuinely intended by the commandment? Is there really anything wrong with loving one's friends and family more than one loves strangers? Isn't there something dangerously calculating about a concern with whether I love this person exactly as much as I love that person?

One way of telling whether the principle you use is loving (equally loving) is to see whether you could use it in explaining your behavior to the person who lost out in the conflict.[17] Could you convince him that you loved him in spite of the fact that you treated him as you did? This is a "loving" criterion in that it tells the agent to try to reconcile her behavior to the person she has harmed or neglected. If she can do this, she can convince him that she loves him in spite of her decision, and can retain his trust, both of which are important to maintaining a relationship with him, which is one of the goals of love.

But which procedure will be most easy to justify to the beloved? Several different procedures suggest themselves, but they lead in different directions. For example, there is maximization: try to distribute goods and harms in such a way that goods are maximized and harms minimized. This is not entirely satisfactory from the point of view of love, however. To take an extreme example from the philosophical literature: suppose it were possible to procure some great good distributed over a large number of people by torturing one person to death. If maximization of good were our only goal, then we would have to sanction the victimization, but, intuitively, this is not the most "loving" option. A more mundane difficulty would be this. Suppose we have to decide on a regular basis how to distribute some good. Who gets the single ticket to the movie each week? Let's suppose Jane would enjoy it slightly more than Tom. That's a reason to give it to her this week. But what if it would give her more pleasure next week also, and the week after? Should we give it to Jane every week without giving Tom any compensating benefit? This would almost certainly seem (and be?) unfair to Tom, in spite of the fact that it is the strategy which would maximize good. Or what if the ticket was originally given to Tom, but Jane would nevertheless enjoy it more? Forcibly taking it from Tom might again maximize enjoyment, but nevertheless, be objectionably unfair. A second suggestion is egalitarianism. This comes in a couple of different varieties: divide up whatever goods and harms you have equally amongst the potential beneficiaries; or divide up whatever goods and harms you have in such a way that the results are most nearly equal. These strategies seem loving in some cases, but downright silly in others, and sometimes quite clearly unjust. (Think of a case where the good to be distributed is medication that will work effectively only if it is all taken by one person. Or suppose again that

17. J. L. A. Garcia makes a suggestion along these lines in "Love and Absolutes in Christian Ethics," in *Christianity and the Problems of Philosophy,* ed. Thomas Flint (Notre Dame: Notre Dame Press, 1990), 162-99.

the tickets belong to Tom, and that he has worked hard to earn the money to buy them.)

Well, perhaps there is no algorithm. Perhaps there are different considerations one has to bear in mind in resolving such conflicts, and one has to use one's judgment in each case. The different considerations include not only each person's interest, but also a concern to respect rights ("It was his ticket!") and a concern to minimize serious suffering, to promote important interests, to promote equality, etc. The commandment might also suggest going beyond a mere weighing of the two or more sets of interests against each other. In cases of conflict between two people, it would require that the agent attempt some sort of reconciliation between them, to get them to share her dilemma and help her to resolve it, perhaps by voluntarily giving up one of their claims.

This, however, is not going to help in every case. They might not be willing to give up their claims. Or they might both be willing to give up their claims if and only if justice required it. It appears, therefore, that loving (even if we could succeed in loving perfectly) would not enable us to answer many important questions — about what this particular person's interests consisted in nor about how to choose between two people's conflicting interests.

The law of love is, at best, an incomplete aid in resolving moral dilemmas. To admit this is not to deny that all the law and the prophets hang on the law of love. In other words, behavior is *made right* in virtue of being motivated by love and wrong by being motivated by hatred or some other desire which requires indifference to the welfare of others. If one truly loved God with one's whole heart and mind and soul, and truly loved one's neighbor as oneself, one would do no wrong. This is not to say that one would make no mistakes. One could be mistaken about someone's interest or about how to resolve a conflict. But, nevertheless, one would not be morally at fault. I believe that this is the sense in which these two commandments constitute the whole of morality.

To explore the implications of this suggestion, let us consider an important objection to it. Firstly, it may seem to let the wrong sort of people off the hook. What about the genuinely misguided Nazi? Or the Pharisee who is perfectly confident that he is obeying God's law down to the last jot and tittle, including, presumably, the commandments to love God and his neighbor? Or the religious fanatic who believes that his children's good consists in remaining illiterate and untouched by medical science?

In response, let me stress first that you don't get off the hook unless you love. If your genuinely misguided error leads you to believe that certain groups of people don't deserve to live, then you fail to love. The claim is not that *any* genuine error is acceptable. So, presumably, someone who is committed to annihilating all members of races he regards as inferior will not be off the hook. Second, if you fail to make the right sorts of efforts to find out what the interests of others consists in, or if you deliberately, at some level, choose to avoid hearing about avoidable suffering, or if you deceive yourself into thinking that certain vicious or self-serving behavior is in the interests of others, you have failed to love. So, if the portrait of the Pharisees we get in the Gospels is anything to go on, they are not off the hook either.

An important implication of this is that someone could be mistaken about whether he loves (at all, or in the right way) and hence, be mistaken about his own moral status. But this seems obviously correct. Remember the walrus, who was so dramatically deceived about his own lack of compassion. If you realize that love is more than just a feeling, then it is easy to see how one can be mistaken about whether one loves. The third case is more difficult. It seems to me that the parent in the case described might satisfy the Commandment with respect to his children in spite of being misguided about their welfare and in spite of doing them great harm. But, then, again, he might not. It seems unlikely that one could really make the right sorts of efforts to find out what was good for someone and be so far wrong.

It may be objected that if a mistaken judgment were just as morally acceptable as an accurate judgment, then there would be no point in trying to make the correct judgment — say, about the neighbor's best interest. But obviously there is a point in doing so.

This objection misunderstands how love works. If you really love, your primary concern is not with your own moral purity. Recall the film, *Lorenzo's Oil*. In the story, a boy suddenly falls ill with a terribly debilitating and fatal disease. His parents do everything they can to discover a cure for his disease, and, in fact, succeed. These are exemplary parents. They are also very lucky, however, in finding a cure that had escaped far better-educated doctors and scientists. If the parents had made the same sorts of efforts on behalf of the boy, but without success, they would have been no less exemplary and no less loving. But that would hardly have been a consolation to them. Their passionate love for their son meant that they were obsessed with doing what was best for him and had no interest in their own moral status. The difference between a correct and a mistaken judgment about how to treat him made all the difference in the world to them. If they had failed, they would have been distraught. So, the point of trying to determine what is in someone's interest, etc. remains, and should be paramount, in spite of the fact that getting it right is not essential to doing right.[18]

The Bible contains a great deal of moral instruction other than the two great commandments. What attitude does our morally ideal agent take towards these rules? I am not suggesting that the agent is free to ignore these. Remember she is attempting to promote the welfare of others and resolve conflicts between them. Presumably she believes in God and trusts God as omniscient and perfectly good. As such, it makes sense for her to pay attention to God's rules. If she deliberately or negligently ignores them she is irresponsible in the way that a doctor who ignored the best medical knowledge of the day would be irresponsible. But what if the Bible was silent or ambiguous on some point, or what if it was unambiguous but through no fault of her own, she interpreted it incorrectly. In any of these cases, an honest mistake seems possible. If she genuinely loves, then her mistake does not count against her.

In case this all seems too easy, let me emphasize that no one (or almost no one) has ever succeeded in obeying the two commandments. For those of us in this position (that is, almost all of us) perhaps the rest of the law has a different status. Perhaps only supersaints get to the point where everything is permissible but some things are unhelpful. For the rest of us, it seems, many things are definitely impermissible.

4. Conclusion

In this chapter, I have discussed several of the implications of Christianity for ethics, and have argued that these implications are ethically attractive. First, Christianity conflicts with the enormously popular ethical view that

18. Incidentally, this suggests something important about the morally ideal state of mind. It is not principally concerned with doing the right thing. This is somewhat paradoxical, I admit. "What must I do to be perfect?" "Don't think about being perfect! Think about what other people need!" But it is a familiar paradox. Certain desirable states cannot be pursued directly, e.g., how do you follow an order to be spontaneous, or unselfconscious? If you try to be spontaneous, you fail. More interestingly, it is often suggested that a too assiduous attempt to make oneself happy will fail, because true happiness is to be found in caring about something other than oneself. "He who seeks to gain his life will lose it," perhaps expresses this idea. I am suggesting that perhaps morality is like that. If one focuses too much of one's attention on doing the right thing, one will be doing the wrong thing.

the rightness or wrongness of my behavior depends solely on what I or my society believe about the matter. On close inspection, however, this view, ethical relativism, is seen to be seriously flawed, and the fact that Christianity denies it is a mark in its favor rather than an embarrassment. Second, I investigated the claim that if Christianity is true, morality depends on the will of God. In response, I argued that a Christian is not committed to this claim, and that the claim creates difficulties. Finally, I analyzed in some detail what it meant to love one's neighbor as oneself. I also explored the claim that this commandment together with the commandment to love God with one's whole heart and mind and soul and strength, constitute, in some sense, a complete morality.

16

The Authority of Scripture

Douglas Blount

Shaphan the secretary informed the king, "The priest Hilkiah has given me a book." Shaphan then read it aloud to the king.

When the king heard the words of the book of the law, he tore his clothes. Then the king commanded the priest Hilkiah, Ahikam son of Shaphan, Achbor son of Micaiah, Shaphan the secretary, and the king's servant Asaiah, saying, "Go, inquire of the Lord *for me, for the people, and for all Judah, concerning the words of this book that has been found; for great is the wrath of the* Lord *that is kindled against us, because our ancestors did not obey the words of this book, to do according to all that is written concerning us."*

2 Kings 22:10-13, NRSV

So deep was King Josiah's respect for Scripture that, on hearing Shaphan read the books of the law, he rent his clothes in sorrow. Or, at least, so the passage quoted above seems to indicate. Now consider the situation of someone who reads this passage and on the basis of it believes that, on hearing Shaphan read the books of the law, Josiah did indeed tear his

In addition to the contributors to this volume, I'm grateful to John Adair, D. Jeffrey Bingham, Todd Cathey, George L. Klein, and Glenn Kreider for help with various versions of this chapter.

clothes. Is it reasonable for one to believe that Josiah tore his clothes *simply because Scripture affirms that he did?* Is it reasonable *in general* to believe something on the grounds that Scripture affirms it? In what follows, I attempt to show that it *is* reasonable to believe something simply because the Bible says it's so. In short, I attempt to show that, in believing solely on the basis of Scripture that, say, Josiah tore his clothes, one is *not* being irrational.

Knowledge and Rationality

Before taking up the task of showing this, however, we need to begin with a few prefatory remarks about just what it means to be rational or irrational in believing some claim on the grounds that some source (in this case the Bible) says that the claim is true. First, as those familiar with contemporary theories of knowledge know, many different accounts of knowledge and rationality have been put forward.[1] And, while there isn't room here to discuss this vast multitude of accounts, I want at least to provide a sketch of the conceptions of knowledge and rationality at work in what follows.[2] Put roughly, the notion of *rationality* employed below goes as follows: if it is true that a) the means by which one arrives at a particular belief are quite likely to lead to truth, *and* b) one has no convincing reason for giving up that belief, then it is reasonable for one to hold that belief; otherwise, it is not. But what does it mean to say that "the means by which one arrives at a belief to be *quite likely to lead to truth*"? Well, not surprisingly, it means that the beliefs brought about by them are quite likely to be true. So, for instance, suppose that Lucy believes that Ricky is at the club because it seems to her that she sees him there. She enters the club, seems to herself to see him there, and comes to believe that he is at the club. Now, assuming that beliefs which Lucy forms in this way normally turn out to be true, the means by which she comes to believe that Ricky is at the club are quite likely to lead to truth. Thus, assuming that

1. For a good introduction to contemporary theories of knowledge, see John Pollock's *Contemporary Theories of Knowledge* (Totowa, NJ: Rowman & Littlefield, 1986).

2. The sketches of knowledge and rationality which I give have been heavily influenced by William Alston's *Epistemic Justification: Essays in the Theory of Knowledge* (Ithaca: Cornell University Press, 1989) as well as by C. Stephen Evans's discussion of that work in *The Historical Christ and the Jesus of Faith: The Incarnational Narrative as History* (New York: Oxford University Press, 1996).

she has no convincing reason to *disbelieve* that he is at the club, it is reasonable for her to believe that he is there.

Contrast this with Ethel's situation: she believes that Fred is in the room not because she sees him there (as Lucy sees Ricky at the club) but rather because her crystal ball tells her that he is there. In this case, the means of arriving at belief which Ethel employs surely *aren't* quite likely to lead to truth: beliefs formed at the behest of a crystal ball *aren't* likely to be true. Hence, even if Fred *is* in the room, it isn't reasonable for Ethel to believe that he is there solely on the basis of what her crystal ball seems to her to say. These two examples combined thus illustrate the principle of rationality set out above, namely, that if a) the means by which one comes to believe some claim are quite likely to lead to truth and b) one has no convincing reason for ceasing to believe the claim, it is reasonable for one to believe the claim. Otherwise, it's not.

Now let us again consider Lucy's situation. Suppose that she comes to believe that Ricky is at the club in the way mentioned above: she enters the club, seems to herself to see him there, comes to believe that he is at the club, and has no convincing reason for ceasing to believe this. In such a case, I have suggested, her belief is reasonable. Suppose further that, as Lucy believes, Ricky is in fact at the club. In this case, the following are true:

(i) Ricky is at the club,
(ii) Lucy believes that he is at the club, and
(iii) it's reasonable for her to believe that he is at the club.

Here I think that we have a case of *knowledge:* Lucy doesn't *merely believe* that Ricky is at the club, she *knows* that he is there. In short, one who reasonably believes something which is in fact true knows that thing. This then provides us with a principle of *knowledge* to add to the principle of rationality we have been discussing above. The *knowledge principle* is this: if (a) one reasonably believes some claim, *and* (b) the claim is *true,* then one *knows* that which is claimed.

The Doctrine of Inerrancy

My second prefatory remark concerns the *doctrine of inerrancy.* For those unfamiliar with this doctrine, the standard statement of it goes as follows: the term "*inerrant* signifies the quality of being free from all falsehood or mistake and so safeguards the truth that Holy Scripture is entirely true and trustworthy in all its assertions."[3] In short, then, to say that Scripture is inerrant amounts to saying that it makes no false affirmations, assertions, or claims. Whatever it affirms, asserts, or claims is true. And, of course, the doctrine of inerrancy is that doctrine according to which Scripture is inerrant.

Notice that affirming this doctrine does *not* amount to affirming a *flat-footed literalism* which ignores the subtleties of genre and language implicit in the biblical texts.[4] Scripture contains such diverse types of literature as apocalyptic literature, epistolary literature, historical narrative, poetry, and wisdom literature. In affirming the doctrine of inerrancy, one need not — indeed, one *ought* not — give up one's sensitivity to the subtle nuances of these diverse literary genres. Nor need one ignore the complexities of human language arising from the biblical authors' use of figures of speech, hyperbole, metaphor, and the like. So, while John 15:1 records Jesus' claim to be "the true vine," no inerrantist concludes that he needs to be staked down, watered regularly, and prevented from getting too much sunlight! Or, to use a less extreme example, inerrantists need not take

> They heard the sound of the LORD God walking in the garden at the time of the evening breeze . . .

to imply that God *literally* has a physical body with which he *literally, physically* walked in the garden.[5] And, since other passages of Scripture seem plainly to teach that — at least prior to the Incarnation — God has no body,[6] it's fortunate for them that they need not take it in this way. So,

3. Those interested in reading the statement from which this quotation is taken — entitled "The Chicago Statement on Biblical Inerrancy" — in its entirety can find it in *Inerrancy,* ed. Norman L. Geisler (Grand Rapids: Zondervan Publishing House, 1980), 493-502.

4. The remarks of this paragraph are motivated in part by charges either that inerrantists cannot square their view with what one actually finds in the Bible or else that they can do so only by engaging in intellectual gymnastics of one sort or another. See, for instance, Clark Pinnock's claims in "Three Views of the Bible in Contemporary Theology," in *Biblical Authority,* ed. Jack Rogers (Waco, TX: Word Books, 1977), 67: "One of the most serious difficulties the theory of errorlessness faces is the Bible itself. To defend it in a way that does not evade the phenomena of the text requires incredible dexterity and ingenuity."

5. The excerpt is from Genesis 3:8, NRSV.

6. I have in mind here such passages as John 4:24, according to which Jesus said, "God is spirit, and those who worship him must worship in spirit and truth" (NRSV).

while some believe that the meaning of biblical passages verily leaps off its pages at the reader, one who affirms the doctrine of inerrancy need not hold such a view. Indeed, like other reflective readers of the Bible, inerrantists can acknowledge that certain biblical passages frustrate their attempts to interpret them. So also among inerrantists there will be various interpretations of various passages. For, while they agree that everything Scripture affirms, asserts, or claims is true, they very well might — and in fact often do — disagree about what certain passages of Scripture actually affirm, assert, or claim. So then one ought not confuse commitment to the doctrine of inerrancy with commitment to a particular set of *interpretations* of the Bible.

Now, if it's reasonable for one to believe that Scripture is inerrant, it's reasonable for one to believe that, say, Josiah tore his clothes simply on the grounds that Scripture says he did so. Indeed, if it's reasonable for one to believe the doctrine of inerrancy, it's reasonable *in general* for one to believe something solely on the basis of Scripture asserting it. So, in what follows, I attempt to show it to be reasonable for one to believe the doctrine of inerrancy. If this attempt succeeds, it follows that it is also reasonable for one to believe something simply because the Bible says it's so.

Inerrancy and Authority

Of course, even if one doesn't believe Scripture to be inerrant, it might *nonetheless* be reasonable for one to believe something simply because Scripture affirms it. Now, given what I know about my *physical senses,* it would be *un*reasonable for me to believe them to be inerrant. After all, they've deceived me in the past. For instance, I've seen people who appeared from a distance to be acquaintances, only to find out on closer inspection that they were not. But from this it certainly doesn't follow that it's *never* reasonable for me to believe what these senses seem to tell me simply because they seem to do so.[7] Or, to use another example, consider the testimony which I receive from, say, Billy Graham. I need not think that Graham is inerrant in order for it to be reasonable for me to believe what he says simply because he says it. Of course, in a particular situation, I might have reason to doubt my physical senses (or Graham). If so, then in that situation it might not be reasonable for me to believe them (or

7. I owe this illustration to Michael Murray.

him).[8] But, in the absence of reasons for believing that these senses are in fact deceiving me (or that Graham is in fact speaking falsely), it seems reasonable for me to believe what they say (or he says) simply on the grounds that they say (or he says) it. So, even if one doesn't believe that a source of belief is inerrant, it nonetheless might be reasonable for one to believe what it says simply because it says it.

Now some inerrantists have claimed that denying the doctrine of inerrancy is tantamount to denying *biblical authority.*[9] But, in the same way that I can treat my physical senses as authoritative without believing them to be inerrant, it seems that one could treat Scripture as authoritative without believing it to be inerrant. Indeed, one who doesn't affirm the doctrine of inerrancy might nonetheless practice a sort of *methodological inerrancy.* For, while she believes that Scripture might contain errors, she nonetheless might in fact accept whatever Scripture says *simply on the grounds that Scripture says it.* And, assuming both that this means of arriving at belief is quite likely to lead to truth and that she has no overriding reason for giving up beliefs arrived at in this way, it's reasonable for her to proceed in this way even though she doesn't affirm the doctrine of inerrancy. So then accepting biblical inerrancy is *not* a prerequisite for reasonably believing what Scripture says on the grounds that Scripture says it. Still, since one who reasonably believes the doctrine of inerrancy thereby reasonably believes what Scripture says on the grounds that Scripture says it, I attempt, in what follows, to show that one *can* reasonably believe that doctrine.

Dear Christians . . .

Third, in attempting to show this, I address my remarks to Christians. For, with respect to the relationship between believing the doctrine of inerrancy and faith in Christ, at least two possibilities present themselves. First, one might become convinced that Scripture is inerrant and, on this

8. Here we must be careful. For, in such a situation, it might still be reasonable to believe what my senses tell me. For it might be that I have compelling reasons to doubt that my reasons for doubting them are good ones.

9. For instance, Paul Feinberg states: "To divorce inerrancy and authority is impossible. I have never been able to understand how one can be justified in claiming *absolute* authority for the Scriptures and at the same time deny their inerrancy. This seems to be the height of epistemological nonsense and confusion." This quotation is from Paul D. Feinberg, "The Meaning of Inerrancy," in *Inerrancy,* 285.

basis, come to have faith in Christ. Second, one might come to have faith in Christ and then come to believe that Scripture is inerrant. Now, while it's *possible* that one come *first* to believe the doctrine of inerrancy and *then* to faith in Christ, I doubt that many people actually do so. Rather, I suspect that in most cases belief that Scripture is inerrant *results from* — rather than brings about — faith in Christ. Now I don't mean this to imply that believing Scripture to be inerrant is an inevitable consequence of faith in Christ and that those who don't believe this aren't really Christians. Many Christians don't believe that Scripture is inerrant. And, of course, this makes them *no less Christian* than those who do believe it to be inerrant. My point here is simply that most of those who believe Scripture to be inerrant come to believe this *after* — rather than before — they come to faith in Christ. So, while attempts to persuade those who lack faith in Christ that it's reasonable to believe the doctrine of inerrancy aren't likely to have much apologetic value, I think that attempts to persuade Christians of this *are* likely to meet with success. Thus, what follows is intended primarily for those *within* — rather than those without — the church.[10]

Scripture as Divine Revelation

Since I intend these remarks for Christians, I don't intend to include in them a defense of Scripture's claim to have been divinely revealed. That Scripture is a divine revelation seems to me to be an *axiom* of the Christian faith. Still, those interested in such a defense will find in Richard Swinburne's *Revelation* a good starting point.[11] In that work, Swinburne points out that — insofar as we have reasons to believe that there exists a God who lacks nothing by way of goodness or power, that he has created us as people capable of making moral decisions, and that by making poor moral decisions we have brought ourselves to a state of wretchedness — we have reasons to expect that God would reveal himself to

10. However, this does not mean that those outside the church — those who lack faith in Christ — will find nothing of value in what follows. For, if the project attempted below succeeds, they may at the very least gain from it a better understanding of how Christianity looks from the "inside" by seeing how Christians themselves can establish to their own satisfaction — though perhaps not to the satisfaction of their critics — the reasonableness of their commitment to the truth of scripture.

11. See Richard Swinburne, *Revelation: From Metaphor to Analogy* (New York: Oxford University Press, 1992), especially 69-97.

us. And, moreover, Scripture itself claims to be a revelation from God.[12]

But, of course, other religious texts — such as the Koran and the *Book of Mormon* — also claim to be divinely revealed. So, for instance, of itself the Koran states,

> This Qur-án is not such
> As can be produced
> By other than God;
> On the contrary it is
> A confirmation of (revelations)
> That went before it,
> And a fuller explanation
> Of the Book — wherein
> There is no doubt —
> From the Lord of the Worlds.[13]

It also states that

> The revelation
> Of the Book
> Is from God
> The Exalted in Power,
> Full of Wisdom.[14]

Moreover, the *Book of Mormon* contains the following passage:

> And now, my beloved brethren, and also Jew, and ye ends of the earth, hearken unto these words and believe in Christ; and if ye believe not in these words believe in Christ. And if ye shall believe in Christ ye will believe in these words, for they are the words of Christ, and he hath given them unto me; and they teach all men that they should do good.
>
> And if they are not the words of Christ, judge ye — for Christ will show unto you, with power and great glory, that they are his words, at the last day; and you and I shall stand face to face before his bar; and

12. Cf. 2 Timothy 3:16-17; 2 Peter 1:20-21.

13. Sura X.37. The text is from Abdullah Yusuf Ali's two-volume translation, *The Meaning of the Glorious Qur'an* (Cairo and Beirut: Dar Al-Kitab Al-Masri and Dar Al-Kitab Allubnani, 1934).

14. Sura XLV.2. See also Sura III. 1-7, Sura VI. 19-20, Sura XVII. 105, and Sura XXVII. 6.

ye shall know that I have been commanded of him to write these things, notwithstanding my weakness.[15]

And, while the Koran and the *Book of Mormon* serve as good illustrations of religious texts which claim to be revelations from God, one could cite any of a number of other such texts which also make this claim. Clearly, then, the Bible is not alone in *claiming* to be a divine revelation.

So how do we decide whether to believe Scripture's claim to have been divinely revealed rather than the claims put forward by these other texts? Well, according to Swinburne, there are two tests which can help us decide whether to accept something's claim to be a revelation from God. First, there is the *test of content*. In short, according to this test, the contents of divine revelation ought to be the kinds of things we'd expect God to reveal. So, for instance, a revelation from God ought to speak to our deepest needs. Second, there is the *test of miracle*. This test concerns whether an alleged revelation contains claims which only God could know at the time of their disclosure but which later are shown to be true. Now Scripture seems to me to measure up to these tests quite well. Still, since Christians take it as axiomatic that the Bible has been divinely revealed, I won't pursue the point here.

The Possibility of an Inerrant Book

In what follows, I take for granted the *possibility* that Scripture is inerrant. That there be a book (or collection of books) which makes no false affirmations, assertions, or claims *seems* possible. And, moreover, that a *divinely revealed* book (or collection of books) make no false affirmations, assertions, or claims certainly seems possible. After all, God is both omnipotent and omniscient; if he were unable to reveal himself via an inerrant book (or collection of books), it would be rather surprising! So, as a revelation from God, it surely *seems* that the Bible *could* be inerrant.

No doubt some will think that I move too quickly here. For, of course, appearances can deceive. And appearances about what is and isn't possible are *especially* apt to do so. Here an example might be instructive: Initially, it seems possible that God could have created the world so

15. 2 Nephi 33:10-11. The text is from *Book of Mormon: Another Testament of Jesus Christ* (Salt Lake City: The Church of Jesus Christ of Latter-day Saints, 1981). See also 2 Nephi 27:6-23 as well as 2 Nephi 29:1-14.

that it contains moral goodness but no moral evil — that is, that he could have created moral agents who never did evil. Indeed, to a great extent, the fact that this *does* seem possible underlies the problem of evil. Yet, despite this appearance, many philosophers have concluded that this *isn't* possible. In doing so, they have been motivated in large part by consideration of what would be *required* in order for there to be morally responsible agents. For, on the most plausible accounts of moral responsibility, being *morally responsible* requires being *free*.[16] So, in order to have created the world so that it contain moral goodness, God would have had to create *free creatures*. But, as Alvin Plantinga has pointed out,[17] God cannot prevent *genuinely free creatures* from doing what they would freely choose to do *without thereby taking away their freedom*. Thus, if every genuinely free creature would have freely chosen to do evil, it follows that God *couldn't* have created the world so that it contained moral goodness but no moral evil.

Now this is instructive *not merely* because it shows that something which initially seems possible might turn out to be impossible *but also* because it shows us *why* it might not be possible that Scripture is inerrant. For, however precisely we understand the *inspiration* of Scripture, we have good reason to think that God allowed its human authors to express themselves freely when writing it.[18] After all, when one reads Paul's letters, one encounters a *markedly different style* than one encounters in, say, John's letters. And, of course, the differences in style between, say, the historical narratives of the New Testament and, say, those of the Old Testament are obvious. So, when one reads various books of the Bible, one can't help but be impressed by the diversity of styles within them.

But how shall we explain this diversity if not by appealing to the *free-*

16. Sadly, I don't have room here to defend the claim that accounts of moral goodness and responsibility which take freedom to be necessary for moral agency are more plausible than their competitors. Defenses of this claim can be found, however, in other chapters in this book. The reader should consult the chapters on "God, Evil, and Suffering," "Divine Providence and Human Freedom," and "Heaven and Hell" in particular.

17. See his *God, Freedom, and Evil* (Grand Rapids: Eerdmans, 1974).

18. In discussing what he takes to be "the central line of evangelical thought on the truthfulness of the Scriptures," D. A. Carson states: "God in His sovereignty so superintended *the freely composed* human writings we call the Scriptures that the result was nothing less than God's words and, therefore, entirely truthful," emphasis added. The quotation is from his "Recent Developments in the Doctrine of Scripture" in *Hermeneutics, Authority, and Canon*, ed. D. A. Carson and John D. Woodbridge (Grand Rapids: Baker Book House, 1995), 45.

dom of the human authors? So then we have good reason to think that those authors acted freely in writing Scripture. But this fact might seem to raise a problem for the inerrantist, a problem that cannot be easily explained or defused. I say this to caution the reader that the argument of this and the next two paragraphs is a difficult one and thus requires some sustained concentration. The problem, then, is this: the line of reasoning given above for thinking that it might be impossible for God to have created the world so that it contained moral goodness but no moral evil, *might also be taken to show* that it was impossible for him to bring about the writing of Scripture so that it contained the true claims he wanted it to contain but no false ones.[19] Well, I think we must admit that, *if* no human author would have freely written a text containing what God wanted Scripture to contain without inserting false claims into it, it would *not* then be possible for God to have used human authors to freely write an inerrant text containing what he wanted Scripture to contain.

From these considerations, however, it *doesn't* follow that *believing it's possible for God to have created the world so that it contain moral goodness but no moral evil* is on a par with *believing it's possible for God to have brought about the writing of Scripture so that it contain the true claims he wanted it to contain but no false ones.* For, of course, there is this significant difference between moral evil in the world and errors in Scripture: We have *undeniably clear examples* of moral evil in the world, but we *don't* have such examples of errors in Scripture.[20] Now, given this fact, it is reasonable to hold that we have much better reason to distrust our sense that God could have created the world so that it contained moral goodness but no moral evil, than we have to distrust our sense he could have brought about the writing of Scripture so that it contained the true claims he wanted it to contain but no false ones. In fact, as far as I can see, the *only* reasons which the above argument gives us for denying inerrancy are: that *we can be mistaken about what is possible* and that, *this would give us some way of explaining why Scripture must contain some errors* (if it turns out that it must). But these are *hardly* convincing reasons for thinking that, with regard to whether it's possible that Scripture be inerrant, appearances are *in fact* deceiving us! Nor do they give us any reasons for thinking that *in fact* no human author would have freely written a text

19. For an example of the line of reasoning given above being used in this way, see Randall Basinger and David Basinger, "Inerrancy, Dictation, and the Free Will Defense," *The Evangelical Quarterly* 55 (1983): 177-80.

20. More on this below.

containing what God wanted Scripture to contain without inserting false claims into it!

Of course, these remarks amount to little more than an attempt to undercut a reason which might be given for thinking that it is not even possible that Scripture be inerrant. They obviously *don't* amount to an argument for the possibility that it really is inerrant. Still, I shall take for granted in what follows that it *is* possible that Scripture be inerrant. Even so, that Scripture is *possibly* inerrant doesn't mean that it's *actually* inerrant. Nor does it mean that one who believes it to be inerrant is *reasonable* to do so.[21] And, since I think that one *can* reasonably believe the doctrine of inerrancy, I now turn to the task of showing that one can.[22]

The First Case of Belief: There Is a Tree in Front of Me

Let us begin this task by considering a typical belief: I seem to see a tree in front of me and, as I have this *visual experience,* I find myself believing that there is a tree in front of me. Is it reasonable for me to believe this? Well, recall that, in order for a belief to be reasonable, it must be the case both that I have no convincing reason for giving it up and that the means by which I arrived at it are quite likely to lead to truth (in the sense that beliefs brought about by them are quite likely to be true). Now I would have a convincing reason for giving up the belief that there is a tree in front of me if, say, I came to reasonably believe that I was at my local computer store testing virtual reality glasses.[23] For, in such a case, I would have reason to doubt that my visual experience of "seeming to see a tree in front of me" indicates that there actually is a tree in front of me. But, since in this case I have no reason not to take my experience at face value, I have no reason for giving up my belief that there is a tree in front of me.

21. After all, it's possible that, as I write this, Michael Jordan is eating ice cream. But, since I have no reason for believing him to be doing so, it would be quite unreasonable for me to believe that he is in fact now eating ice cream. Thus, even if it's possible that something be true, it nonetheless might be unreasonable to believe it to be true.

22. In so doing, I employ a strategy similar to, and inspired by, one used by C. Stephen Evans in his excellent work on the historicity of the biblical accounts of Jesus' life, *The Historical Christ and the Jesus of Faith.*

23. Of course, if at the time at which I began to have the visual experience I *already* believed myself to be testing virtual reality glasses, this probably would have *prevented* me from coming to believe that there is a tree in front of me in the first place.

So, if the means by which I arrived at this belief are quite likely to lead to truth, it's reasonable for me to hold it. But are they? Well, *ordinarily* when I take my visual experiences at face value and believe what they seem to tell me, what I believe turns out to be *true*. So, it would seem, the means by which I came to believe that there is a tree in front of me *are* quite likely to lead to truth. And, in that case, it's reasonable for me to believe that there is a tree in front of me. Moreover, if there actually *is* a tree in front of me, then I don't *merely believe* but rather *know* that there is a tree in front of me.

The Second Case of Belief: Josiah Tore His Clothes

Let's consider another belief: I'm reading 2 Kings 22 and, as I read this passage, find myself believing that, on hearing Shaphan read the books of the law, Josiah tore his clothes. Is it reasonable for me to believe this? Well, let's assume that I have no convincing reason to give up this belief. So, for instance, I don't have good reason to believe that the passage is the invention of politically motivated priests concerned to insert a pro-Judahite passage into the otherwise sordid history of Judah's kings. Now, in the absence of good reasons to abandon my belief that Josiah tore his clothes, whether it's reasonable for me to hold this belief depends on whether the means by which I have come to hold it are quite likely to lead to truth (that is, on whether beliefs brought about by those means are quite likely to be true). Are they? Clearly, how we answer this question hinges on how exactly we think that I came to hold it.

How *have* I come to believe that Josiah tore his clothes? Well, obviously enough, I've come to believe this by way of reading 2 Kings 22. But, on the Christian account of things, this isn't the whole story. For, on that account, a believer who reads 2 Kings 22 — or any other biblical passage — can expect assistance from the Holy Spirit in doing so. Of the Holy Spirit, Jesus says to his disciples,

> When the Spirit of truth comes, he will guide you into all the truth; for he will not speak on his own, but will speak whatever he hears, and he will declare to you the things that are to come. He will glorify me, because he will take what is mine and declare it to you.[24]

24. John 16:13-14, NRSV. See also 1 Corinthians 2:10-12.

Within the early church, this passage was taken to mean that the Holy Spirit bears witness to Christians of the truth.[25] And, as C. Stephen Evans points out,[26] that the Holy Spirit makes known to Christians the truth of biblical passages finds explicit statement in some of the later creeds.[27] So, on the Christian view of things, I seem to have good reasons for thinking that the Holy Spirit has guided my reading of 2 Kings 22.[28]

Now, assuming that the Holy Spirit has *in fact* guided this reading, the means by which I've come to believe that Josiah tore his clothes *include* the Spirit's having guided me to do so. And, of course, it's hard to imagine a more reliable means of coming to believe something than the guidance of the Holy Spirit! Thus, assuming that the Holy Spirit has guided my reading of 2 Kings 22, the means by which I've come to believe that Josiah tore his clothes are quite likely to lead to truth, and I have no convincing reason for ceasing to believe that he did so. And, in this case, it's reasonable for me to believe that Josiah tore his clothes. Moreover, if Josiah did *in fact* tear his clothes, then I don't *merely believe* but rather *know* that he did so.

25. For instance, Irenaeus (circa A.D. 180) describes the Holy Spirit as One "who furnishes us with a knowledge of the truth," and Tertullian (circa A.D. 200) speaks of being instructed by the Holy Spirit, "the Leader into all truth." See Philip Schaff, ed., *The Creeds of Christendom, Volume II: The Greek and Latin Creeds,* reprint of the 6th edition (Grand Rapids: Baker Book House, 1990), 16-17.

26. In *The Historical Christ and the Jesus of Faith,* 260-62.

27. So, for instance, the Belgic Confession (1561) gives as the main reason for accepting the truthfulness of passages of Scripture the fact that "the Holy Ghost witnesseth in our hearts that they are from God" and the Westminster Confession of Faith (1647) says of Scripture that "our full persuasion and assurance of the infallible truth, and divine authority thereof, is from the inward work of the Holy Spirit, bearing witness by and with the Word in our hearts." See Article V of the Belgic Confession and Article V of the Westminster Confession of Faith in Philip Schaff, ed., *The Creeds of Christendom, Volume III: The Evangelical Protestant Creeds,* reprint of 6th edition (Grand Rapids: Baker Book House, 1990), 386-87, 602-3.

28. Of course, one can easily imagine situations in which I'd have reason to doubt that my reading of a biblical passage had been guided by the Holy Spirit. Suppose, for instance, that I read a certain passage (say, Genesis 3:8) in a thoroughly unorthodox way (say, as suggesting that, prior to the Incarnation, God had legs and feet). In such a case, my reason for believing this reading to result from the guidance of the Holy Spirit is undermined by my belief that it is inconsistent with the way in which Christians have traditionally read the passage.

The Third Case of Belief: Scripture Is Inerrant

Let's consider yet another belief: on coming to faith in Christ, Charity diligently studies the Bible, faithfully attends her church's worship services, and regularly fellowships with other believers. Over time, as she immerses herself in such activities, her confidence in the trustworthiness of Scripture grows. As she studies the Bible, she finds herself amazed at the insights which she gains from it, at the accuracy with which it portrays the human condition, at how it addresses her own deepest desires and needs, and at the sense of peace which comes as she seeks to live in accordance with its claims. During worship services, she finds herself affirming with an ever-growing confidence the historic doctrines of the faith and singing hymns of praise to God with an ever-deepening sense of ownership. And, as she spends time with other Christians, she discovers that, rather than being unique, her experiences seem to be repeated many times over in the lives of other believers.

Now suppose that, in the course of these events, Charity comes to believe that the Bible is inerrant. Is her belief reasonable? For the moment, let's assume that she has no convincing reason for giving up this belief.[29] In such a case, whether her belief in the inerrancy of Scripture turns out to be reasonable depends on how she came to have it. How *has* she come to have it? Well, it seems plausible to see Charity's belief as the product of her experiences with the Bible together with her involvement in the life of her church. And, as mentioned above, the Christian account of things gives us good reasons to think that the Holy Spirit works both within the lives of individual believers as well as within the church to bring them to truth. So, on that account of things, we have good reasons to believe that the Holy Spirit has worked through both her reading of Scripture and her church activities to bring her to believe that the Bible is inerrant. And so, *just as* I have good reasons to think that my reading of 2 Kings 22 has been guided by the Holy Spirit, we have good reasons to see Charity's belief in the inerrancy of Scripture as the result of the Spirit's work both within the church in general and in her in particular. Thus, assuming that the Holy Spirit has in fact worked to bring Charity to believe Scripture to be inerrant, the means by which she has come to believe this turn out to be quite likely to lead to truth. And, in this case, it also turns out to be reasonable for her to believe that the Bible is inerrant.

29. In the next section, I discuss some reasons which one might seem to have for ceasing to believe that Scripture is inerrant.

Moreover, if the Bible actually is inerrant, Charity not only believes but rather *knows* that it is.

Incompatible Beliefs and the Holy Spirit's Guidance

But don't Christians sometimes arrive at *incompatible* beliefs? And don't they sometimes claim that in doing so they have been led by the Holy Spirit? So, for instance, haven't some Christians concluded from such passages as 1 John 2:2 that *Jesus' death atoned for every person's sins* while others have concluded that *his death atoned only for the sins of Christians?* And, in coming to these conclusions, haven't both groups believed themselves to have been led by the Holy Spirit? Shouldn't cases such as this make us dubious about appeals to the Holy Spirit? After all, if one person claims that the Holy Spirit has led her to believe that Jesus' death atoned for everyone's sins and another claims that the Spirit has led her to believe his death atoned only for Christians' sins, doesn't it follow that *at least* one of them is wrong? How can we tell which — if either — of them is correct? Determining when the Holy Spirit is — or isn't — at work isn't always an easy matter! But doesn't this undermine the reasonableness of Charity's belief that Scripture is inerrant?

No. For, while it might be difficult for Charity — or anyone else — to tell whether her belief that the Bible is inerrant results from the Holy Spirit's guidance, what makes her belief reasonable (in the absence of convincing reasons for giving it up) is *not* that *she can tell* it resulted from the Spirit's work but rather that *it actually did* result from the Spirit's work. Here it's important to recognize the difference between the Holy Spirit's work in one's life and one's awareness of that work.[30] What makes one's belief reasonable (in the absence of convincing reasons for giving it up) is that the means by which one comes to have it *actually are* quite likely to lead one to truth. And, of course, it's possible that the means by

30. Discussing beliefs brought about in believers by the Holy Spirit, C. Stephen Evans puts this point well: "In any case, the process whereby the Holy Spirit forms such a belief must not be identified with *how it appears to the believer.* The process must not be identified with an experience, particularly not with an experience that is being construed as evidence. Christians certainly believe it is possible to experience the work of the Holy Spirit, and they regard such an experience as a valuable and precious one. However, the work of the Holy Spirit cannot be regarded as identical with someone's experience of that work, and it is the work of the Spirit that counts." See *The Historical Christ and the Jesus of Faith*, 268-69.

which I come to believe something are quite likely to lead me to truth *even though I'm unaware of them.* So, even if Charity *can't tell* that her belief has resulted from the work of the Holy Spirit, it might nonetheless have *in fact* resulted from the Spirit's work. And, in such a case, her belief is reasonable. Or so it is as long as she has no convincing reason to give it up.

What Would Convince Us That Scripture *Isn't* Inerrant?

So far I have suggested that, in the absence of convincing reasons to cease believing that Scripture is inerrant, it might be reasonable for one to believe it to be so. For, I have suggested, the Christian account of things gives believers good reasons to think that the Holy Spirit works both within their lives and within the church to bring them to truth. Given this, it seems plausible (at least from a Christian point of view) to regard beliefs which Christians come to have as they immerse themselves within the life of the Christian community as the product of the Holy Spirit's work both within them individually and within the church corporately. And, if these beliefs *do in fact result* from the Holy Spirit's work, those in whom the Spirit has brought them about *are in fact reasonable* to hold them. So it seems plausible to regard as reasonable one's belief that the Bible is inerrant when that belief seems to have arisen out of one's experiences within the Christian community. Or, at least, so it does in the absence of convincing reasons not to hold it.

But aren't there such reasons? Aren't there convincing reasons to believe that Scripture *isn't* inerrant? Well, clearly, we would have a convincing reason to believe that the Bible errs if we found *either* contradictions *or* clear factual errors in it. In light of this, then, let's turn our attention to contradictions and clear factual errors.

Scripture and Contradictions

Perhaps the most commonly cited reason for thinking that the Bible errs (and thus that it isn't inerrant) is that it appears to *contradict* itself. So, for instance, a friend of mine once announced to me that he had given up believing the Bible to be inerrant because he had found a contradiction in it. Surprised by this, I asked him to show me this contradiction. He referred me to two passages of Scripture, one of which (Luke 11:23) seems to indicate that Jesus said those who are not for him are against him and the other of which (Mark 9:40) seems to indicate that Jesus said those who are not against him are for him. Clearly, my friend argued, these texts indicate that Jesus contradicted himself. But, assuming that Jesus wouldn't contradict himself, it follows from this that *these texts aren't both true.* Of course, if they aren't both true, then *at least* one of them is false. And, in that case, Scripture is *not* inerrant.

Now at least two things are worth noting here. First, the Bible's being inerrant *does* entail its being *logically consistent.* Or, to put the point differently, it's not possible *both* that Scripture be inerrant *and* that it make logically inconsistent claims. And, moreover, this fact underlies my friend's reason for ceasing to believe the Bible to be inerrant. For, of course, his reason amounts to pointing to an alleged inconsistency in Scripture and concluding from it that Scripture is not inerrant. And, insofar as it rests on the fact that the Bible can be inerrant only if it makes no inconsistent claims, my friend's reasoning appears to be well-founded. Where he goes astray, however, is in thinking that he has found two scriptural claims which are in fact inconsistent. I shall return to this point in a moment.

Second, it also seems worth noting that whether one thinks one has found inconsistencies in Scripture depends (at least in part) on the *assumptions* with which one has approached it. To see this, consider the passages mentioned above, Luke 11:23 and Mark 9:40, which go as follows.

> Whoever is not with me is against me, and whoever does not gather with me scatters. (Luke 11:23, NRSV)
>
> Whoever is not against us is for us. (Mark 9:40, NRSV)

Let's assume that my friend has read these passages correctly. On this assumption, Luke 11:23 indicates that Jesus said *those who aren't for him are against him* and Mark 9:40 indicates that Jesus said *those who aren't against him are for him.* What led my friend to conclude that these passages are at odds with one another? Well, as I understood him, he took Luke 11:23 to be saying that those who take a *neutral* position with respect to Jesus are in fact against him and Mark 9:40 to be saying that those who take such a position are in fact for him. So, he concluded, Scripture indicates that those who are neutral with respect to Jesus are *both* against him *and* for him. And, in such a case, Scripture contradicts itself.[31]

31. Actually, things aren't quite as clear-cut as this. For, even if Scripture indicates that those who are neutral with respect to Jesus are both against him and for him,

Scripture and Assumptions

Of course, *neither* Luke 11 *nor* Mark 9 explicitly mention those who are neutral with respect to Jesus. So, while these passages mention only two positions which one might take with respect to Jesus (i.e., being for him and being against him), my friend *assumed* that there is a third such position (i.e., being neutral). But, as far as I can see, the point of these passages seems to be that *there is no neutral position* with respect to Jesus, that one is *either* for him *or* against him. So then my friend's reading of these passages was driven by an *assumption* with which he had approached them. And, ironically, the assumption with which he had approached them is itself *inconsistent with the point which they seem to be intended to make*. Obviously, one who approaches Scripture with assumptions which are inconsistent with it is *very* likely to find things to be amiss. But, of course, this *hardly* suffices to show anything so momentous as that the Bible errs! Here the error lies not with Scripture but with the one who reads it through a veil of assumptions which are themselves contrary to it.

Now I intend these remarks neither to cast aspersions on my friend nor to suggest that we ought to approach Scripture without any assumptions. The assumption that one can be neutral with respect to Jesus seems pretty plausible on the face of it. In fact, if it *weren't* plausible, there would have been little need for Luke and Mark to record what Jesus said about the matter. So, however unfortunate it might have been, my friend's approaching Scripture as he did is certainly understandable. Moreover, I don't think it possible to approach Scripture — or, for that matter, any other book (or collection of books) — without any assumptions whatsoever. To think otherwise seems to me *exceedingly* naïve. Still, it matters a great deal *which* assumptions one approaches Scripture with. If one approaches Scripture convinced that, say, miracles are impossible, one will have no difficulty finding what one takes to be false claims in it. But, to the extent that one has reason to regard the Bible as inerrant, to that extent one has reason to read it as such.

So, while those who assume that, say, miracles aren't possible are likely to conclude from certain passages of Scripture that it errs, those for

---

it doesn't follow that Scripture contradicts itself unless being both against and for someone isn't possible. But, as far as I can see, this *is* possible. So, for instance, George Patton might have been against the Soviet Marshal Georgi Zhukov *insofar as* he anticipated that the Soviet Union would be the principal opponent of the U.S. in the postwar era and at the same time for Zhukov *insofar as* the two men faced a common enemy in Nazi Germany.

whom it's reasonable to believe the Bible to be inerrant are likely to conclude from such passages that miracles *are* possible. And, of course, this point can be made more generally. For, while cases of the Bible's saying *such-and-such is true* will lead those who believe that such-and-such *isn't* true to conclude that the Bible errs, they will lead those who believe that the Bible doesn't err to conclude that such-and-such *is* true. Moreover, those for whom it's *reasonable* to believe the Bible to be inerrant will be *right* to make such conclusions. Here a comparison might prove helpful: if it's reasonable for me to believe you to be a *thoroughly* reliable witness, then it's reasonable for me to reject *almost* anything which conflicts with your testimony; so also, if it's reasonable for us to believe that Scripture is inerrant (and thus *thoroughly* reliable), it's reasonable for us to reject *almost* any statement which conflicts with what it asserts.

Of course, in testifying you might make statements which are inconsistent *either* with other statements you have made *or* with statements which I have reasons for believing which outweigh my reasons for believing you to be a thoroughly reliable witness. And, if you were to make such statements, I would have a convincing reason to give up believing that you are a thoroughly reliable witness. Likewise, if Scripture were to make statements which are inconsistent either (a) with other statements it makes or (b) with claims which we have reasons for believing which *outweigh* our reasons for believing Scripture to be inerrant, we would have a convincing reason to give up believing it to be inerrant. Thus, we aren't justified in rejecting *any statement whatsoever* which conflicts with Scripture anymore than we are justified in rejecting *any statement whatsoever* which conflicts with your testimony. Our credulity *must* have limits!

Scripture and Contradictions Revisited

Now, since one might think that the passages from Luke and Mark discussed above can be dealt with too easily for them to count as good examples of apparently contradictory passages, let's turn our attention to another pair of passages which seem to be contradictory, Exodus 24:9-11 and Exodus 33:17-20. The first of these goes as follows.

> Then Moses and Aaron, Nadab, and Abihu, and seventy of the elders of Israel went up, and they saw the God of Israel. Under his feet there was something like a pavement of sapphire stone, like the very heaven

> for clearness. God did not lay his hand on the chief men of the people of Israel; also they beheld God, and they ate and drank.
>
> Exodus 24:9-11, NRSV

And, a few chapters later, we find:

> The LORD said to Moses, "I will do the very thing that you have asked; for you have found favor in my sight, and I know you by name." Moses said, "Show me your glory, I pray." And he said, "I will make all my goodness pass before you, and will proclaim before you the name, 'The LORD'; and I will be gracious to whom I will be gracious, and will show mercy on whom I will show mercy. But," he said, "you cannot see my face; for no one shall see me and live."
>
> Exodus 33:17-20, NRSV

On the assumption that God doesn't speak falsely (and, hence, that Exodus 33:20 *isn't* to be understood as stating that he spoke falsely to Moses),[32] these passages *seem* to make inconsistent claims. For, while the first passage indicates (*both* in verse 10 *and* in verse 11) that *Moses and his entourage saw God without dying,* the second passage indicates (in verse 20) that *no one can see God without dying.* So, on the face of it, these passages appear to contradict one another.

Still, it would be ill-advised to conclude that these passages do *in fact* contradict one another. For the statement that Moses and those with him saw God without dying contradicts the statement that no one can see God without dying *only if* both claims mean the same thing by "see." But, since "see" can mean a variety of things, it's plausible to suppose that the sense of "see" employed in the first statement *isn't* the sense of "see" employed in the second statement. Here again an example might be useful: If I were to say to you, "I'd like you to see my basset hound," while handing you a photograph of a basset hound, you wouldn't take me to be implying that, in seeing the photograph, you're *literally* seeing my basset hound. Rather you'd take me to be inviting you to look at a *visible representation* of her. And, of course, you'd be *right* so to take me! But why should we not take Exodus 24:9-11 in just this way? Why not understand it as indicating

32. Obviously, if one assumes that God can speak falsely, it would follow that Exodus 33:20 does *not* contradict Exodus 24:9-11. For, assuming that God *could* speak falsely, it also could be true *both* that Moses and his entourage saw God without dying *and* that God (falsely) told Moses that no one can see him without dying.

not that Moses and his entourage *literally* saw God himself but rather that they saw a *visible representation* of God?

No doubt this reading of Exodus 24:9-11 will strike some as slippery, tricky, or intellectually dishonest in some way. But, as careful attention to other passages of Scripture reveals, such a reading actually turns out to be quite plausible. For, interestingly enough, the language of Exodus 24:9-11 closely resembles language used in other texts to describe visions of God.[33] And, in this case, it's plausible to regard the language of Exodus 24:9-11 as also describing such a vision. But, if Exodus 24:9-11 claims not that Moses and those with him literally saw God but rather that they saw a vision of God, it doesn't contradict Exodus 33:17-20.

Scripture and Clear Factual Errors

Now, if Scripture contradicts itself, it isn't inerrant. So, if one has a convincing reason to think that Scripture does in fact contradict itself, one also has a convincing reason to believe that it *isn't* inerrant. But, of course, contradictions aren't the only things which might lead us to believe that Scripture errs. For, if one has reasons for believing that a statement made by Scripture is false and these reasons outweigh one's reasons for believing it be inerrant, one *cannot* reasonably believe it to be inerrant. So, for instance, if one has a convincing reason for rejecting what one takes to be the *clear moral teaching* of Scripture, one also has a convincing reason for believing that Scripture errs. Indeed, those who reasonably believe that Scripture condones capital punishment (or condemns homosexual activity) but who nonetheless regard its practice as morally indefensible (or morally permissible) find themselves in just this situation *provided that their reasons for so regarding it are convincing.*

But, of course, the proviso is important here. That Scripture makes claims which *seem* to us implausible isn't *by itself* an impressive reason for not thinking it to be inerrant. For, of course, intellectual honesty *demands* from us a certain humility. Only the most arrogant among us think themselves incapable of error! And, given this fact, we should *not* be surprised that an inerrant book (or collection of books) makes claims which seem to us implausible.[34] After all, since considerations of humility give us reason to expect some of our beliefs about, say, morality to be false, it would

33. See, for instance, Daniel 7 and Revelation 4.

34. I owe this point to Thomas Morris.

hardly be surprising if some of the moral claims made by an inerrant book (or collection of books) seemed to us to be false. Indeed, it would be surprising if all its claims seemed to us to be true! Thus, the mere *appearance* of error in Scripture does little to undermine belief in its inerrancy. Rather, in order for such belief to be undermined, one's reasons for thinking that it errs *must be convincing*. And, as mentioned above, they must be *more* convincing than one's reasons for believing it to be inerrant.

Still, a clear example of an error in Scripture would undermine whatever reasons we have for believing it to be inerrant. But, even so, cases in which Scripture clearly errs turn out to be rather hard to find. In fact, I know of no such cases. Nor do I know of any cases in which Scripture contradicts itself. And, as long as we have no convincing reason for ceasing to believe the Bible to be inerrant, it will be reasonable for those of us who reasonably believe it to be inerrant to assume it to be so when reading it. So also, as long as it's reasonable for us to treat the Bible as inerrant, it's reasonable for us to believe that Josiah tore his clothes simply because the Bible says that he did.

Background Beliefs

Now it doesn't follow from this that those who think that Scripture errs are thereby being unreasonable. For, of course, those who *don't* believe the Bible to be inerrant are likely to have a rather different set of *background beliefs* than those who do. Perhaps an example will help here. Suppose that I'm driving on an interstate near Dallas. Suppose further that, as I'm driving along at 65 mph, I notice in my rearview mirror a tiny speck of a car. Although it's far behind me, I notice this car because it's moving *incredibly* fast, weaving in and out of traffic. Cars on either side of it must swerve off the road to avoid being hit by it. It seems to be gaining on me as if I were standing still. Not wanting to be hit by it (or by some other car attempting to get out of its way), I take the next exit and watch as this car flies by me on the interstate. But, as it passes me, I realize that — much to my surprise — the blur driving the car is none other than my own father!

In such a situation, what would I conclude? Would I conclude that my father is a reckless maniac, unconcerned about the effects which his actions have on others? I don't think so. For, since I know my father and believe that he would not drive in such a manner without a compelling reason to do so, I probably would conclude that he had a compelling reason for driving in such a manner. And, given what I *know* about my father, this seems *eminently* reasonable. But notice that other drivers don't bring to the situation the same set of background beliefs which I bring. And, given what other beliefs *they* have, it *might* be that the most reasonable conclusion for them to make is that my father *is* a reckless maniac, unconcerned about how his actions affect others. So then what it's reasonable for one to believe depends (at least in part) on what other beliefs one has.[35] Thus, given the other beliefs which *they* have, it *might* be that those who believe that Scripture errs are rational to do so. Still, like those who conclude that my father is a reckless maniac, they are nonetheless mistaken.

Conclusion

While belief in the authority of Scripture is universally endorsed within the church, belief in inerrancy is not. In fact, belief in inerrancy is, in some quarters, regarded as a hallmark of intellectual naiveté. I cannot, in the conclusion, explain the complicated reasons why belief in inerrancy has fallen into disfavor in these quarters, but I can say that I think these reasons are in the end mistaken. While this chapter does not provide a thoroughly exhaustive defense of the reasonableness of believing in inerrancy, it takes us some way toward not only giving reasons in its favor, but toward undermining the suspect arguments which have been offered against it.

35. I assume that one's background beliefs usually play a role in one's coming to have other beliefs.

Contributors

Douglas Blount, Southwestern Baptist Theological Seminary

Robin Collins, Messiah College

J. A. Cover, Purdue University

William C. Davis, Covenant College (GA)

Scott A. Davison, Morehead State University

Daniel Howard-Snyder, Seattle Pacific University

Frances Howard-Snyder, Western Washington University

Trenton Merricks, Virginia Commonwealth University

Caleb Miller, Messiah College

Michael J. Murray, Franklin and Marshall College

Timothy O'Connor, Indiana University

John O'Leary-Hawthorn, Syracuse University

Thomas D. Senor, University of Arkansas

W. Christopher Stewart, Houghton College

Index